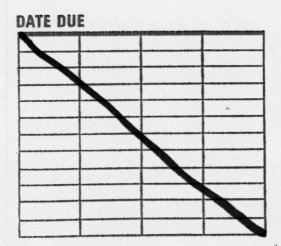

Felix Frankfurter:
Scholar on the Bench

FELIX FRANKFURTER

Scholar on the Bench

HELEN SHIRLEY THOMAS

The Johns Hopkins Press: Baltimore

Distributed in Great Britain by Oxford University Press, London

Printed in the United States of America by Vail-Ballou Press, Binghamton, N.Y.

Library of Congress Catalog Card Number 60-11571

This book has been brought to publication with the assistance of a grant from The Ford Foundation.

*To the memory of
my mother and father*

Preface

The Conference Room of the Supreme Court is largely shrouded in mystery. There are few facts that the outsider knows about proceedings of the Court when it meets to deliberate matters pending before it. It is known that the junior member of the group is the last to express an opinion on the merits of a case but the first to vote on its disposition. It is also known that he acts as messenger for the rest of his brethren, retrieving volumes from the shelves lining the walls of the Conference Room or going to the door and requesting other necessary materials. How he came to these duties is, however, unknown and a matter of conjecture.

Among other topics that interest and stimulate the imagination are the reasons for placement of justices in particular chairs around the conference table. This, once again, is in the realm of speculation. The place occupied by Associate Justice Felix Frankfurter has been dubbed the "Scholar's Seat." His two immediate predecessors in that position were Benjamin Nathan Cardozo, whom

Frankfurter replaced on the Court, and Oliver Wendell Holmes, Jr. Both had gained recognition for their perceptive contributions to American legal literature before their appointment to the Supreme Court. Both were commentators upon and participants in constitutional development.

Outwardly it seems fitting that Felix Frankfurter, Harvard academician and self-proclaimed student of Holmes, should have been chosen by President Franklin D. Roosevelt to carry on the Holmes-Cardozo tradition. As a law school professor, he had published voluminously in lay and professional journals. While the range of his topics was wide, his most persistent interest centered in the Supreme Court and the role of that body in democratic theory. Having struggled in his writings with the formulation of a legal philosophy, he was now given an opportunity to apply theory to concrete situations as a member of the august tribunal that had so long intrigued him.

Justice Frankfurter certainly differs from his predecessors in that he willingly—nay, desirously—assumes the intellectual heritage devised by other men. Unlike Holmes and Cardozo he enjoys donning the mantle spun by other hands. Whereas they were anxious to stand in no man's shadow and to be entirely creative in their own right, his creativity often stems from embroidering on themes originated by others. Of the triumvirate holding the Scholar's Seat in the twentieth century, Felix Frankfurter's traits as a lawyer are perhaps most distinctive. His reveling in the give and take of oral battle and his assumption of the adversary's role, both on paper and in verbal exchanges, mark him as a man of intense interests. Therefore, because he is very committed on so many topics, Justice Frankfurter's objectivity has frequently been questioned, although certainly not his learning in the law and in many other subjects. It may well be that he is primarily interested in scholarship and that he contributes most towards its development through such an interest. He is, however, the present possessor of the scholar's title and must, consequently, be assessed in that light.

Felix Frankfurter has now completed twenty-one years of service on the Supreme Court. During this period he has evoked quite diverse reactions about the quality of his performance. Professor

Fred Rodell of the Yale Law School finds him an "outstanding disappointment." Granting that Frankfurter was the "technical successor to the magnificent Holmes and the great Cardozo," Rodell nevertheless feels that "he stands out as the New Deal Court's most controversial and unhappy figure, its most tragically wasted brilliant mind." [1] Very different is the appraisal of Judge Learned Hand: ". . . I regard him . . . as the most important single figure in our whole judicial system. . . . It would be impossible for me to think of any other judge whose continuance in his duties I welcome more unreservedly." [2] Few other members of the Court have been subjected to such a spectrum of comments. As an individual greatly admired and equally resented, Justice Frankfurter has come in for ridicule and adulatory praise from both eccentric and highly capable students of the Court. For someone extremely interested in establishing his own place and that of his compatriots in Supreme Court history, such differing interpretations should prove more than unsettling.

A minor purpose of the ensuing discussion will be to investigate the causes for such divergent views. But in order to accomplish this end, it is necessary first to perform the basic task of providing an account of Justice Frankfurter's judicial performance and philosophy. By following his written statements on policy from the time when he first came to national prominence until just before his elevation to the Supreme Court in 1939, one can discern a distinct pattern of constitutional interpretation. Premises from which he reasons in many cases of today are premises that have been characteristically his since the first decade of this century. Much that is found in his present opinions can be found in earlier and slightly different formulations contained in law review articles or in his several books.

Many men and movements have influenced Justice Frankfurter's intellectual development. Where feasible, these influences will be identified and discussed. Since he has provided analysts with a library of materials, ranging from pieces for *The Nation* and the *New Republic* to works on varying aspects of Supreme Court

[1] Fred Rodell, *Nine Men* (New York: Random House, 1955), p. 269.
[2] Quoted in Anthony Lewis, "An Appreciation of Justice Frankfurter," *New York Times,* November 10, 1957.

history and personnel, the task of covering his academic period is made easier. As for his tenure on the bench, he has written, as of the end of the 1958 Term, two hundred and forty opinions or judgments for the Court. In addition he has produced over two hundred and fifty dissents and over one hundred and fifty concurrences. Once again the analyst is faced with an abundance of information.

In discussing this material, emphasis will be placed on isolating techniques of legal interpretation, techniques that Felix Frankfurter advocated as an academician and that he has subsequently utilized on the Supreme Court. Stated somewhat differently, a determination will be made of the criteria that recommend themselves to him in ruling on constitutionality or unconstitutionality, legality or illegality. These techniques and concepts are horizontal rather than vertical in character. That is to say, once having been identified, they can with equal ease be applied to cases involving taxation, commerce, civil rights, or any other of the typical controversies to reach the Supreme Court. The concepts run across all categories and are not contained within any one of them. The four major headings under which these techniques will be discussed are designated: Symbolism and Social Unity; The Uses of History; The Constitution as an Instrument of Power; and, Decentralization and Dispersal of Control.

Justice Frankfurter's concepts are uniquely his. His motivations are not those of any of the other justices. The particular set of circumstances that drew his interest to certain topics rather than others, the personal camaraderie felt with certain individuals rather than with others, the attainment of distinction at one time rather than at another, all these factors lead inevitably to a distinctive judicial philosophy. Within this philosophy there has been a high degree of consistency between early and later statement of principle. This is not to say that he has always been consistent in applying his concepts to specific situations, and it is not the purpose of this work either to prove or to disprove consistency in application. Therefore, while not particularly concerned with demonstrating his "perfection" or "imperfection," this analysis does depend heavily on showing his intellectual debts, his own intellectual development, and the culmination of these factors in his Supreme Court opinions.

Justice Frankfurter has claimed that "every man who writes, in large measure writes his autobiography." [3] Although a short biographical section will open this study, introducing the men and movements with which he has been identified, it is indeed true that most of the important insights into his personality will be found in his own writings. In his last published article before taking the Scholar's Seat on the Supreme Court, Felix Frankfurter discussed the characteristics of Benjamin Cardozo as jurist.

> . . . the main path to his view on public law leads from his character. His conception of the Constitution cannot be severed from his conception of a judge's function in applying it. His views of the judge's function derive from his conviction on philosophic issues which implicate the workings of the judicial mind. Such issues in turn involve a man's notion of his relation to the universe. These are abstractions. . . . But the clarity with which a specific controversy is seen in the context of the larger intellectual issues beneath the formal surface of litigation, and the courage with which such analysis infuses decision and opinion, are the ultimate determinants of American public law.[4]

It is no coincidence that this description of Justice Cardozo could with equal validity be applied to his successor, the man who penned the words.

Before further outlining Justice Frankfurter's intellectual debts, I wish to indicate some of my own. The word "some" is necessary, for an author can never fully repay all those persons who have aided the development of a work such as this. Carl Brent Swisher of The Johns Hopkins University gave unstintingly of his time and energy to help in the refinement of ideas here incorporated. His contribution cannot be adequately defined nor adequately acknowledged. Francis E. Rourke of the same institution made many invaluable suggestions for clarification of concepts and

[3] Felix Frankfurter, "Mr. Justice Brandeis," *Harvard Law Review,* LV (December, 1941), 181.

[4] Felix Frankfurter, "Mr. Justice Cardozo and Public Law," *Harvard Law Review,* LII (January, 1939), 440–41.

delineation of materials within divisions. To Samuel J. Konefsky goes my gratitude for freely and sympathetically imparting his vast knowledge about the Court. For moral, and morale, support I am indebted to my pastor, L. Ralph Tabor. Finally, I wish to thank the Social Science Research Council, whose financial award partially made possible completion of this project.

Helen Shirley Thomas

Baltimore
January, 1960

Table of Contents

ONE
From Ivory Tower
to Marble Halls

Justice Felix Frankfurter has undergone a range and intensity of experiences such as have come to few men. Born in Europe, educated in Austria and the United States, inheritor of rich familial and cultural traditions stemming back for centuries, Frankfurter began life with a set of environmental and educational conditions far different from those that usually surround future justices of the United States Supreme Court. Harvard Law School, where first he performed as a student and later as a professor, made a tremendous impression upon his development through both its traditions and its personnel. Active participator in many causes, Felix Frankfurter came in contact with influential individuals in and out of government, not the least of whom was Franklin Delano Roosevelt, who was to help shape the future of the Harvard Professor and whose programs were to be partially shaped by him. This initial section will relate in broad terms how these things came to pass.

I
The Making of a Scholar

When Leopold Frankfurter left Vienna in 1893 to visit the United States and the Chicago World's Fair, his family remained behind. This family consisted of his wife, Emma Winter Frankfurter, plus four sons and two daughters. Once the decision to settle in the United States was made, separation was not long endured. It was but a few months until Leopold was able to save the money necessary to bring his family to join him. In early 1894 the group disembarked from the *Marsala,* and the family was once again a complete unit. What was then left behind in Europe were not immediate personal ties but a whole traditional system of living and a common heritage. Members of the Frankfurter family had been rabbis for over three centuries. Leopold had studied for the rabbinate but had given up his studies in the last year to marry and go into business.

Being a rabbi in the Jewish communities of Europe indicated not only high intellectual attainment but also a temperament suited to making judicious decisions. These traits were inherited by the third Frankfurter son. Felix, born in Vienna on November 15, 1882, gained his early education in Austrian schools. This early formative training on the continent with its emphasis on precision of statement and deductive reasoning left its mark. German was his first tongue, Hungarian his second. When he landed in New York, he did not understand English. Leopold, now getting established as a retail fur merchant on New York's East Side, entered his children in P.S. 25, and it was from this school that Felix first gained some knowledge of the language and customs of his adopted country. When success was attained in later years, the mature Felix Frankfurter did not forget the contributions of the public school system to his development. Maintenance of a viable public school system to transmit the values of American life has been one of his enduring interests.

It is not an exaggeration to say that his attainments in school were quite exceptional. Arriving in this country at the age of twelve, he was unable to communicate with his classmates. By the time he had reached nineteen, he had completed the public schools and had graduated with a B.A. degree, third in his class, from the City College of New York. In the interim he had also gained mastery of the language, a mastery that became fuller and more polished in the years ahead.

While the drive to continue directly from the City College of New York to law school was strong, the Frankfurter family doctor advised against such a course. Feeling that the young man was physically depleted, he directed at least a year's neglect of books and studying. Frankfurter occupied his time during this period as a clerk in the New York City Tenement House Department, a position he gained by passing a civil service examination. His clerkship with the city commission, although not intellectually stimulating, was financially beneficial. Following the course that his mother years before had established in connection with after-school odd jobs, he saved his earnings. Thus he was ready when the opportunity came in 1903 to make his own way to Cambridge, Massachusetts, and the Harvard Law School. To bolster his income while there, he tutored fellow students.

I

It is impossible to measure accurately the influence of Harvard upon Felix Frankfurter. His contacts there as a student with leading teachers and members of the legal profession, his own willing absorption of that mood called "the Harvard atmosphere," and his continued and deep interest in Harvard as an educational institution can be described. But the correct weight that should be assigned to each or any of these factors in evaluating the influence of the School upon the man and his intellectual development is difficult, if not impossible, to estimate. Of one thing we can be sure. Harvard has influenced Felix Frankfurter in many ways, and Felix Frankfurter over the years has influenced Harvard.

When the eager young man arrived in Cambridge in the fall of 1903, the faculty of the Law School included James Barr Ames, Eugene Wambaugh, Joseph Henry Beale, and Samuel Williston. These were the men who initiated his driving, powerful intellect into the intricacies of the law. Each stood as a recognized authority in his own field. Each transmitted to a greater or lesser degree his love and veneration for the legal precepts of the Anglo-American system of jurisprudence.

While one distinguished name does not appear in the Harvard Law School Catalog for 1903–1904, the omission should not be given too much weight. It is true that James Bradley Thayer had died in February, 1902, over a year before the young man from New York arrived at the School. The magnetic influence of Thayer was still so pervasive, however, that it dominated Harvard even after his death. It was Thayer who had broken with the Langdellian system of pure case method instruction and had infused into legal teaching a new life and vitality. As a teacher of constitutional law, Thayer advocated a limited role for the judiciary in trying to solve the problems of an evolving modern society. Positive legislative action was the alternative which he proposed. Almost forty years after his graduation from the Law School, Felix Frankfurter still regretted the lost opportunity of working directly with Thayer: "That James Bradley Thayer was no more when my class entered the School has been a life-long bereavement for at least one member of that class." [1] Still the loss was not total. He absorbed much of the Thayer position and made it his own.

Harvard's Law School had long had an enviable reputation based on the quality of its faculty. Students were drawn to Harvard not alone by the faculty and physical facilities but above all by what the School was trying to accomplish through these two resources. James Barr Ames, in an address before the Association of American Law Schools in 1907, outlined his conception of the School's role.

> The object held up by us at Cambridge is the power of legal reasoning, and we think we can best get that by putting before the students the best models that can be found in the history of English and American law, because we believe that men who are trained, after examining the opinions of the greatest judges that the English Common Law system has produced, are in a better position to know what legal reasoning is and are more likely to possess the power of solving legal problems than they would be by taking up the study of the law of any particular state. . . . That is to say, our School aims above all things to be a national school and not a local school. [2]

These were the main tenets of the creed that the Law School faculty tried to impart to its students in the early 1900's.

Ames apparently was an extremely effective teacher. He avoided easy subject matter and delved deep into the meaning of the law. His students were given a broad perspective on their profession. Such a man found a ready student in young Frankfurter. Ames' faith in the power of legal reasoning, his insistence that all sources of legal precedent should be covered, and his partiality for a national and international rather than a parochial view of the law have all assumed some place in the mature Frankfurter's philosophy. Thus, for example, many years after

---

[1] Felix Frankfurter, "Joseph H. Beale," *Harvard Law Review*, LVI (March, 1943), 701.

[2] Quoted in Charles Warren, *A History of the Harvard Law School* (New York: Lewis Publishing Co., 1908), II, 419.

the Law School experience concluded, we find the now Justice Frankfurter citing extensively from Australian, Canadian, and British law reports.

Ames' influence on his students was almost entirely beneficial. His creed did, however, contain some contradictions. Frankfurter has called attention to the fact that he was concerned "with seeking and promoting the ethical foundations of law." [3] Ames was deeply sensitive to the moral ends that law should serve, yet he was equally insistent that for a conscientious jurist, any choice in action was a logical impossibility. This ambivalence has not been entirely surmounted by Felix Frankfurter. As discussion of his approach in cases involving due process will show, he too is concerned "with seeking and promoting the ethical foundation of law." On the other hand, many of his statements concerning the theory of constitutional and statutory interpretation lead one to believe that for a conscientious justice, any choice of action is impossible.

Felix Frankfurter graduated from Harvard with an LL.B. degree in 1906. His diploma was awarded with highest honors. The teachings of Thayer and Ames, Wambaugh and Beale were now his. The major direction of his intellectual development was at least marked out. Felix Frankfurter came away with more than a diploma in his hand. He bore a letter from Dean Ames recommending him to the New York law firm of Hornblower, Byrne, Miller, and Potter. The young graduate obtained a position there, but, as circumstances would have it, his association was short-lived.

II

Almost coincidentally with Frankfurter's departure from Harvard, Henry L. Stimson was appointed United States Attorney for the Southern District of New York. Charged by Theodore Roosevelt with carrying on an active trust-busting campaign, Stimson was in need of vigorous young assistants. After com-

[3] Quoted in Alexander Bickel, "Justice Frankfurter at Seventy-Five," *New Republic*, CXXXVIII (November 18, 1957), 8.

municating with Dean Ames, Stimson approached Frankfurter
and soon had the young man attached to his staff. They remained
together in the District Attorney's office until 1910. During this
time cases were instigated and carried successfully to completion
against the New York Central and the American Sugar Refining
Company. Charles W. Morse and Edward H. Harriman found
their activities curtailed by the group of young men working
under Mr. Stimson's direction. Felix Frankfurter carried his share
of the work. In the sugar fraud cases, he alone took the government's case to the Court of Appeals and gained a ruling in his
favor.

Frankfurter has said that this initial work with Stimson gave
him "a high and fastidious regard for the administration of criminal justice." [4] His concern with the administration of criminal
justice in later years attests how well the lesson was learned.
Henry L. Stimson gave Frankfurter something more than this,
however. He gave him a feel for the importance of the public
service and the public servant. Stimson described his first feelings
about becoming United States Attorney as having "gotten out
of the dark places where I had been wandering all my life." He
was now "out where I could see the stars and get my bearings
once more." [5] It is significant that since the time when Felix
Frankfurter joined Stimson's staff he has never returned completely to private practice. His life has been devoted to public
service either in government or in teaching.

President William Howard Taft called Stimson to Washington
in 1911 to be his Secretary of War. Frankfurter went along to
serve as Law Officer in the Bureau of Insular Affairs. For three
years he worked in that capacity, arguing a small number of cases
affecting our colonial possessions before the Supreme Court. The
cases that he argued were of immediate importance but not of
long-range significance. What was of long-range significance were
the contacts that he was making.

Frankfurter, during his days in the United States Attorney's
Office, had become imbued with Theodore Roosevelt's trust-

[4] Quoted in *Current Biography* (1941), p. 305.
[5] Henry L. Stimson and McGeorge Bundy, *On Active Service in Peace and War*
(New York: Harper & Brothers, 1947), p. 17.

busting program. The Progressive spirit rested heavily upon him. The liberalism with which he identified himself was the liberalism of the 1912 era. This identification, by his own admission, has continued over the years. It has, however, caused a good deal of misunderstanding of the man and his positions by persons who give to the chameleonic word "liberalism" a meaning that it did not hold for the T.R. Progressives. Frankfurter was early influenced by Herbert Croly's *The Promise of American Life*.[6] This book was almost the Bible of young persons with a social conscience during the Bull Moose days. His association with Croly was more extensive in the years ahead when both had an interest in the *New Republic*. At that time the younger man no doubt continued to absorb many ideas, but it is perhaps not too much to suggest that many of Frankfurter's beliefs of today can still be gleaned from the pages of Croly's work. His Progressivism was thus partially defined.

During the summer of 1912, Frankfurter considered how best to help Roosevelt run for the presidency. Together with such acquaintances as Paul A. Ewert of the Justice Department, he approached T.R. as to the best course to follow. Roosevelt advised that "the men who come with me should be men who have little or nothing to lose . . . ."[7] He thought that Ewert and Frankfurter could contribute more to the community in their present positions and that the time was not ripe for their open affiliation with him. When, however, Roosevelt in August, 1912, gathered his followers at Chicago, discovered himself at Armageddon, and embarked on his battle for the Lord, he found a ready supporter in Felix Frankfurter.

Beyond expending his energies for Roosevelt, Frankfurter devoted himself to making and cementing other acquaintances. His relations with the Boston lawyer, Louis D. Brandeis, grew closer during this period. In 1913 Frankfurter wrote to Norman Hapgood that, for the Progressives, Brandeis

[6] Herbert Croly, *The Promise of American Life* (New York: The Macmillan Co., 1919). For Frankfurter's own statement of this influence, see his "Herbert Croly and American Political Opinion," *New Republic*, LXIII (July 16, 1930), 247–50.

[7] Roosevelt to Ewert, July 5, 1912. *The Letters of Theodore Roosevelt* (Cambridge, Mass.: Harvard University Press, 1954), VII, 572.

has been one of the most commanding leaders in the regenerating movement in our political and social life. . . . To a unique degree, he has pointed out for us definite directions for the realization of those aspirations. . . . His intellectual powers are undisputed— they have been so effective only because they are charged by a burning moral fibre, by an aggressive sense of service.[8]

When in 1914 Brandeis decided that the Money Trust should be curbed, the National Bureau of Public Utilities Research was organized to help in the endeavor. Not surprisingly, Felix Frankfurter's name appeared as one member of the Board of Trustees.

While drawn to the active crusading zeal of Brandeis, Frankfurter was also intrigued and charmed by the work of Supreme Court Justice Oliver Wendell Holmes. Holmes represented the Progressives' hopes on the Court. His treatment of social and economic issues stood in stark contrast to the emotionalism rampant in much Progressive literature. Though often reasoning from totally different premises from those that Brandeis, for example, would have chosen, he often arrived at the same end result. Holmes, then, was an important person to know, and Frankfurter added the Justice to his list of friends. Companionship and communication between the two increased over the next several decades. It was Frankfurter who introduced one of his young friends by the name of Harold J. Laski to the Justice and thus indirectly initiated the well-known series of Holmes-Laski letters. His relationship to Holmes matured to such a point that, after his appointment to the Harvard Law School faculty, he annually provided the Justice with a law clerk, a practice that he also followed for Brandeis after the latter's elevation to the Supreme Court.

This is not the place to discuss in detail the dual but at the same time often contradictory influence of Holmes and Brandeis upon Felix Frankfurter. Nor are circumstances ripe at this point to attempt a critique or evaluation of these influences. Several general observations are, however, in order here. Apparently Frankfurter thinks of himself as the heir of both Holmes and Brandeis. Of all the justices on the Supreme Court during his

[8] Frankfurter to Hapgood, February 12, 1913. Quoted in Alpheus T. Mason, *Brandeis: A Free Man's Life* (New York: The Viking Press, Inc., 1946), p. 390.

tenure, he certainly has had the most extensive personal relations with them. He was accepted by both as an extremely able practitioner and teacher. Brandeis at one time called him "the most useful lawyer in the United States," [9] while Holmes professed amazement at "the number of [his] swift penetrating contacts with such a variety of subjects." [10] Frankfurter may be mistaken in his assumption that intellectually he can combine the attributes of both Holmes and Brandeis; he is not mistaken in his assumption that both men had a high regard for his abilities and, particularly, for his ability to understand their respective positions.

III

Felix Frankfurter returned to Harvard in 1914 by accepting an appointment to the faculty of the Law School. When he returned to Cambridge after an eight-year absence, he found some of his former teachers still active. There were, in addition, many new faces. Ezra Ripley Thayer had assumed the role of both Dean of the Law School and Dane Professor. Roscoe Pound, Edward Henry Warren, and Joseph D. Brannan had also been added to the staff since Frankfurter's departure.

His return to the academic fold did not go unnoticed. In an editorial entitled "Introducing Law to Life," *Outlook* magazine commented on the switch from government employ to the new teaching career. "The Harvard Law School—whose preeminence is unquestionable—is a leader in rendering the law modern. One of the signs of its leadership is the recent appointment of Felix Frankfurter as Professor of Law, charged with the duty of dealing with this relationship between law and modern social and industrial conditions." [11] From the courses listed under Frankfurter's name in the catalog it appears that he immediately set out "Intro-

---

[9] Quoted in Laski to Holmes, December 16, 1928. *The Holmes-Laski Letters* (Cambridge, Mass.: Harvard University Press, 1953), II, 1121.

[10] Holmes to Laski, December 12, 1928. *Ibid.*, p. 1118.

[11] "Introducing Law to Life," *Outlook*, CVII (May, 1914), 55. Cf. "Young Teacher of Live Law," *Independent*, LXXXI (March 22, 1915), 419.

ducing Law to Life." Over the years he taught subjects ranging from Contracts in Restraint of Trade to Jurisdiction and Procedure of the Federal Courts. Many of his courses were not listed on the schedule when Frankfurter himself was a student. He, therefore, played an important part in revolutionizing the curriculum so that it could deal more easily with the myriad problems of modern society.

In 1921 Felix Frankfurter was named to fill the newly created Byrne Professorship of Administrative Law. As fate would have it, this chair was named in honor of one of the members of the New York law firm that Frankfurter left to join the staff of Henry L. Stimson. Frankfurter remained Byrne Professor until his appointment to the Supreme Court in 1939, with the exception of two short periods when he was on leave of absence. From 1917 to 1919 he was engaged in work for the government growing out of World War I. In 1933–1934 he was George Eastman Visiting Professor at Oxford University.

Professor Frankfurter occupied for over twenty years a modest office on the third floor of Langdell Hall. His conception of the role of the teacher was, however, far from modest. Scarcely a year after his appointment to the Harvard faculty, he delivered an address before the American Bar Association setting forth in some detail his views on the subject.

> It is not enough that young men should come from our schools equipped to become skillful practitioners, armed with precedent and ready in argument. We fail in our important office if they do not feel that society has breathed into the law the breath of life and made it a living, serving soul. We must show them the law as an instrument and not an end of organized humanity. We make of them clever pleaders but not lawyers if they fail to catch the glorious vision of the law, not as a harsh Procrustean bed into which all persons and all societies must inexorably be fitted, but as a vital agency for human betterment.[12]

This is a very early articulation of one of Felix Frankfurter's major premises. Lawyers, and one may add jurists, have a great

[12] Felix Frankfurter, "The Law and the Law Schools," *American Bar Association Journal,* i (October, 1915), 539.

responsibility for eliminating any conflict between law and the society that it serves. Society has a right to demand of the law not abject subservience but at least willing service.

Frankfurter's area of specialization at Harvard was administrative law. He had been an active participant in government and knew the importance of recognizing newly emerging areas of government concern. Teaching administrative law merely added to his appreciation of the complexities of organized community living and to his comprehension that expertise in handling administration was needed to some extent. Even while teaching, however, he did not give unqualified endorsement to all administrative actions or supposed panaceas. The textbook on this subject that he did in collaboration with J. Forrester Davison adopted a vertical, rather than a horizontal, approach.[13] He was concerned, that is, with examining judicial review, etc., of administrative action as it affected one agency. This approach allowed him to be selective in his approval of agency action. It withdrew the temptation of giving blanket approval to judicial review, in the abstract, as it applied to all government agencies.

In the catalog, Frankfurter was listed as Byrne Professor. Outside its pages, he was interested in the Supreme Court and all its doings. Described as being "fascinated by, and idolatrous of, that uniquely U.S. institution, the Supreme Court," [14] he gained a reputation as an authority on the Court, its history and personnel. When the opportunity arose he taught Supreme Court history "with all the precision and loving care that a Sunday School teacher might lavish on the Bible." [15] His way of teaching was perhaps different from that employed by any of his colleagues. He disliked formal lecturing and avoided it wherever possible. Frankfurter much preferred the Socratic technique and was a master at its use. Small discussion or seminar groups were his choice as a forum for intellectual stimulation. Students described his course as the Case-of-the-Month Class. There they were pre-

[13] Felix Frankfurter and J. Forrester Davison, *Cases and Other Materials on Administrative Law* (New York: Commerce Clearing House, Inc., 1932).

[14] Rodell, *Nine Men* (New York: Random House, 1955), p. 270.

[15] Fred Rodell, "Felix Frankfurter—Conservative," *Harpers*, CLXXXIII (October, 1941), 454.

sented with extended accounts of all facets of any particular case, from the personal idiosyncrasies of the judge hearing it to minute technical irregularities appearing in the lower court's record.

He did not demand silent acquiescence in all his statements. Students who seemed to him wrong in their conclusions were often recommended for a job if they were competent and capable of defending their views. At one time a student remarked to Frankfurter: "I know how to get on with you—disagree with you."[16] The Socratic method as adapted and refined by Frankfurter was meant for use with only the best students. Men who could not hold their own in sharp interchange, men who were slow in grasping a point under discussion, men who could not cope with the subtlety of Frankfurter's logic, were often ill at ease and critical of the instructor. For those capable of keeping up with the little professor, instruction was a joy. The very best students were often invited to the Frankfurter home on Battle Street in Cambridge of a Sunday evening to continue discussions started in the classroom. For those selected few, Frankfurter's guidance went beyond the classroom and into their personal lives.

In order to assure that the quality of his students was up to his standards, he had the following notice concerning his classes inserted in the catalog: "Open only to students of high standing with the consent of the instructor." This notice was unique, since he alone, of all the faculty, followed this practice. He, no doubt, showed a good deal of impatience toward mediocre students and made no pretense at hiding his irritation at their inability to follow his depth excursions into complex legal materials. He was to show the same sort of irritation years later when, as a member of the Supreme Court, he baited counsel whom he thought unready or unknowledgeable in their presentation of cases. For Frankfurter, "every really good course in law is a course in jurisprudence,"[17] and that meant treating each and every aspect of

[16] As told in R. L. Duffus, "Felix Frankfurter: The Man Behind the Legend," *New York Times*, January 15, 1939.

[17] Frankfurter, "Joseph H. Beale," *loc. cit.*

a case in its philosophic as well as in its legal setting. Again, there are parallels between the academician and the jurist. His Supreme Court opinions are heavily loaded with erudite references and with discussion of issues in a philosophic tone—too much so, indeed, for many persons.

Although Frankfurter, among current justices, probably represents the dovetailing of legal and philosophic materials to the greatest degree, he does not stand alone in the attempt to integrate law with other areas of knowledge. Both the growth of sociological jurisprudence and the school of legal realism as represented by Jerome Frank indicate wide-spread interest in modernizing legal concepts. Mention of sociological jurisprudence necessarily brings to mind the name of Roscoe Pound, one of the foremost exponents of that approach in the United States. Pound was a member of the Harvard faculty when Frankfurter returned in 1914. Since both men had broad interests, they were drawn toward one another, and each profited from the intellectual stimulation the other was able to provide. Working together, they produced a study in 1922 entitled *Criminal Justice in Cleveland*. More important than such formalized co-operation was the informal interchange that came through personal contact. Frankfurter came to an understanding of the "social engineering" theories advocated by Pound. Much of this understanding is reflected in his treatment of issues that come before the Supreme Court. It should be pointed out here, however, that, whether in teaching or in work on the Court, he has never accepted all of Pound's conclusions and therefore he should not be assigned as belonging completely to the sociological school.

IV

Frankfurter in his teaching, while utilizing sociological and historical approaches, mainly relied on what might be termed a "personalized" focus. Proud of his friendship with Justice Holmes and feeling that Holmes exemplified the best of legal thinking and writing, Frankfurter often treated his classes to

an analysis of his mentor's position in certain cases. Contact between Frankfurter and Holmes was strengthened when the former, on a leave of absence from Harvard, went to live and work
in Washington during World War I. Originally an assistant to
Secretary of War Newton D. Baker, he soon transferred his
energies to the Department of Labor, acting as a special assistant
to its Secretary, William B. Wilson. With Wilson as Chairman,
Frankfurter acted as counsel to the President's Mediation Board.
In his role as Board Counsel he was called upon to investigate
two very touchy subjects, the trial of Tom Mooney and the Bisbee
Deportations.

Mooney had been prosecuted and convicted for his alleged
part in the fatal bombing that took place on July 22, 1916, during
San Francisco's Preparedness Day Parade. Some question as to
the fairness of the trial arose and Frankfurter was dispatched
to make a report on the matter since Mooney was a well-known
labor leader and his treatment as a representative of labor's
interest had national overtones. The Bisbee Deportation occurred
on July 12, 1917. It concerned forced mass movement by a vigi-
lante type mob of striking copper miners from Colorado to Ari-
zona. The overseas impression caused by such mob action held
the United States up to ridicule from her Allies and, in order
to prevent such happenings in the future, Frankfurter undertook
an investigation of the forces behind the dispute.

While exciting in and of themselves, these events had longer-
term meaning for the career of the investigator because of the
publicized reaction of Theodore Roosevelt. Frankfurter had
recommended reassessment of the Mooney conviction and strict
accounting from those involved in the Bisbee demonstration.
Concerning the former recommendation, Roosevelt wrote to
Frankfurter that "you have taken, and are taking, on behalf of
the Administration an attitude which seems to me to be fundamentally that of Trotsky and the other Bolsheviki leaders in Rus-
sia; an attitude which may be fraught with mischief to this country." [18] As for the Bisbee Deportations, he was even more
enraged, fulminating that the counsel's report was "as thoroughly

[18] Roosevelt to Frankfurter, December 19, 1917. *The Letters of Theodore Roose-*
velt, VIII, 1262.

misleading a document as could be written on the subject." [19]
These charges became of some importance in the hearings on
the nomination of Frankfurter to the Supreme Court. The hearings and the materials introduced therein conclusively demonstrate that Roosevelt emotionalized the situation through personal connections with some of the principals and that Frankfurter's recommendations were sound, given the facts with which
he had to work. Nevertheless, the charges kept cropping up, and
it was difficult to refute them completely.

Frankfurter's most important post during the war period and
the one which he held at its completion was as Chairman of the
War Labor Policies Board. He had advocated the creation of
such an agency for many months in the hope that centralized
control over man-power policy would alleviate duplication and
waste, thus speeding up the war effort. One of the members of
the Board was a young Assistant Secretary of the Navy, Franklin D. Roosevelt. Frankfurter spent most of his time between
1917 and 1919 in Washington, but he did make at least two war
missions abroad, one to Great Britain and the other to the Middle
East. Although he was not of the orthodox persuasion with which
his family had been identified, he represented the Zionist cause
at the Paris Peace Conference of 1919 terminating World War I
and was consulted by President Wilson and Colonel House on
matters affecting that organization.

Even the war years and all the strenuous activity connected
thereto could not stop Felix Frankfurter from following his
favorite hobby, that of ever enlarging his circle of acquaintances.
Justice Holmes, half-jokingly, called his bachelor quarters in
Washington The House of Truth because of the number of frank
and earnest discussions carried on there concerning good gov-
ernment and how to attain it. When Frankfurter returned to
Harvard and his teaching duties, he did not return alone. In
December, 1919, he married Marian A. Denman of Longmeadow,
Massachusetts, the daughter of a Congregational minister. In-
terestingly enough, the marriage ceremony was performed by
Judge Benjamin Cardozo of the New York Court of Appeals.

[19] *Ibid.*, p. 1263.

V

On resuming life at Harvard, Frankfurter plunged once again into innumerable activities. Even before World War I he had gained some reputation as a champion of labor and labor causes. Between 1916 and 1922 he argued or filed briefs in several important cases involving hours of labor or minimum wages before the Supreme Court, most notably Bunting v. Oregon, Oregon Minimum Wage Cases, and Adkins v. Children's Hospital.[20] Utilizing the techniques worked out by Brandeis before his elevation to the Supreme Court, Frankfurter amassed volumes of factual material to present to the justices along with his oral argument. Hard work and research proved rewarding as he had a good record in carrying his cases to successful completion. A contemporary description of his demeanor in arguing before the Court is of some interest today. The spectator of forty years ago would have seen

> that august tribunal intently listening to the plea of a small, dark, smooth-faced lawyer, mostly head, eyes, and glasses, who looked as if he might have stepped out of the sophomore classroom of a neighborhood college. As a matter of fact, he had just stepped out of a classroom, for he was Professor Felix Frankfurter of the Harvard Law School, and his mode of address indicated that he had merely exchanged one group of pupils for another. He lectured the Court quietly, but with a due sense of its indebtedness to him for setting it right where it had been wrong, and giving it positive opinions where uncertainty had been clouding its mental vision. He was becomingly tolerant when the gray-haired learners asked questions which seemed to him unnecessary, and gentle when he had to correct a mistaken assumption.[21]

One may wonder whether today Justice Frankfurter does not compare the performance of lawyers appearing before him with his own and find the former lacking in poise and persuasiveness.

[20] 243 U.S. 426 (1917); 243 U.S. 629 (1917); and 261 U.S. 525 (1923), respectively.
[21] Tattler, "Sketch," *The Nation*, CIV (March 15, 1917), 320.

Not all Frankfurter's appearances were before the Supreme Court. In May, 1920, at the request of the presiding judge, he filed a brief and argued *amicus curiae* before the Federal Court in Boston the question whether habeas corpus was available to aliens awaiting deportation by the Department of Justice. His affirmative position was accepted by Judge George W. Anderson, who had this to say in his opinion regarding Frankfurter and Zechariah Chafee, Jr., who had argued with Frankfurter.

> I desire to express my appreciation of their unselfish and highly professional endeavors to assist in the proper determination of a cause involving, directly, the fundamental rights of a large number of aliens but poorly equipped with means or knowledge to protect their rights, and, indirectly, questions of far-reaching and general importance to all, whether citizens or aliens.[22]

There were probably several reasons for Frankfurter's involvement in this case. Primarily, however, he was annoyed at the cavalier way in which Attorney-General Palmer was conducting his notorious Red Raids in disregard of many procedural guarantees of the Constitution covering both aliens and citizens. Frankfurter, along with Chafee, Ernst Freund, Roscoe Pound, and others, had already signed a protest against Palmer's tactics. Even in 1920, procedural regularity was one of his main concerns.

Felix Frankfurter first gained prominence in many parts of the country for his role in the Sacco-Vanzetti proceedings. Sacco and Vanzetti had been convicted of murder growing out of the robbery of a Braintree, Massachusetts, factory. There was some feeling that they had been prosecuted because of their radical, alien background and the Palmer-induced anti-Red hysteria of he time, not because they had definitely been identified as ipants in the robbery. While he did not come into contact he case until after the original death sentence had been nced, the Harvard scholar soon made the conflict his own th a 1927 article in the *Atlantic Monthly* [23] questioning many aspects of the trial. Frankfurter was concerned, not with the

---

[22] Colyer *et al.* v. Skeffington, 265 Fed. 17, 48 (1920).

[23] Felix Frankfurter, "The Case of Sacco and Vanzetti," *The Atlantic Monthly,* cxxxix (March, 1927), 409–32. This article was later expanded into a book under the same title (Boston: Little, Brown & Co., 1927).

"liberalness" of the cause—he made a point of never meeting the defendants—but with the procedural irregularities that he felt they suffered at the hands of presiding Judge Webster Thayer. Later misunderstanding of the votes of Justice Frankfurter, supposedly showing him at variance with his "liberal" brethren, often stems from an original misunderstanding about the motives that impelled Frankfurter to intervene in such causes as those swirling about the accused pair.

Whatever the motivation, standing up for the rights of such a fish-monger or shoe-cobbler was not an easy thing to do in Boston. The "better" people were solidly behind Thayer. Harvard Law School was hard pressed to rid itself of the radical professor on the threat of having donations from prominent alum discontinued. Not always sure of administration support, Fra furter replied, when asked about his possible resignation, "Why should I resign? Let Lowell resign." [24] President Lowell of Harvard did, however reluctantly, stand behind his obstreperous law professor. After the furor of the Sacco-Vanzetti case had died down, and perhaps piqued by Frankfurter's statement, Lowell wrote to Roscoe Pound, now Dean of the Law School and a constant supporter of his colleague's actions, that he thought "one Frankfurter to the Pound should be enough." [25] Even such a friend as Justice Holmes had some qualms about the situation that he passed on to Laski. He wrote that Frankfurter was "so good in his chosen business that I think he helps the world more in that way than he does by becoming a knight errant or a martyr —though I don't undervalue or fail to revere his self sacrifice in his excursions and alarums." [26]

Over the years at Harvard Frankfurter continued to have hi "excursions and alarums," though none perhaps as well know the Sacco-Vanzetti affair. Other cases in which he arg gave legal advice included the famous Scopes trial, in the right to teach evolution in the public schools of T H. L. Mencken's arrest in Boston as the aftermath

---

[24] Quoted in *Current Biography*, p. 306.
[25] Quoted in Matthew Josephson, "Jurist," *New Yorker*, xvi (Decen   , 1940), 24.
[26] Holmes to Laski, November 23, 1927. *Holmes-Laski Letters*, ii, 999.

pression of a particular copy of the *American Mercury,* and the 1926 case of the silk strikers in Passaic, New Jersey.

He was also busy outside the courtroom. As one of the founders of the American Civil Liberties Union, as a legal adviser to the National Association for the Advancement of Colored People, as one of the original stockholders and prime contributor to the *New Republic,* and as a member of the board of Survey Associates, publishers of *Survey Graphic,* Frankfurter used up much time that many of his friends thought should be devoted to more scholarly pursuits. Laski early complained that he needed some kind of settling influence. "He wastes the time that ought to be given to the permanent work that is in him in writing fine letters to antiquated New York lawyers with doubts about the Constitution. I wish he were a little more concentrated . . . ." [27] But Frankfurter's letter-writing activities have not decreased; they have multiplied many times over. And if he has become more concentrated, it has only been a change in degree and not in kind. His work on the Supreme Court now, of course, provides the focal point for his activities, but his interests remain wide and varied. Even added years could not diminish his gregariousness, his love of people, and, above all, his enjoyment of stimulating conversation.

Felix Frankfurter did not formally leave Harvard until 1939. His teaching continued up until a few days before he took his place on the Supreme Court. With the advent of the New Deal, however, the direction of his life was bound to change. The decade of the 1930's provided challenges to government previously undreamed of. Frankfurter once more stepped boldly out of the academic fold into the world of hectic activity. He brought to his tasks a richly varied experience as teacher, scholar, and pleader of many causes. The conclusions drawn so many years before in The House of Truth about good government and how to attain it were now to be put to the test.

[27] Laski to Holmes, November 7, 1916. *Ibid.,* i, 35.

II *New Deal and National Prominence*

When Franklin Delano Roosevelt took the oath of office on cold and dread March 4, 1933, the nation waited expectantly for the announcement of his program. It did not have long to wait. The excitement of the first One Hundred Days has been thoroughly chronicled and is now a matter of history as, indeed, is the New Deal itself. What is of interest to this work is the behind-the-scenes role played by Felix Frankfurter in helping to guide the direction that the New Deal would take, his position on controversial issues during the New Deal period, and finally, his elevation to the Supreme Court as one of Roosevelt's New Deal justices.

For his efforts on behalf of the Roosevelt program, Frankfurter was labeled the Iago of the Administration, whose sinister influence pervaded all of the government. Hugh Johnson called him "the most influential single individual in the United States." More good-naturedly he was described as "Jiminey Cricket to President Roosevelt's Pinocchio." Supposedly carrying the latch-key to the

White House in his pocket, Frankfurter was concededly a welcome and frequent guest there. However, the extent and type of influence exerted upon Roosevelt during these visits remains to be seen.

I

Frankfurter and Roosevelt had first met in New York when both were young practicing attorneys. They came in contact again during World War I through joint work on the War Labor Policies Board. In 1928 Frankfurter conferred with Governor-Elect Roosevelt on reform of New York's judicial system. Although little was accomplished along this line, Frankfurter's career as adviser to the rising political figure had started. After F.D.R.'s nomination for the presidency in 1932, his contacts with the Harvard professor increased. Frankfurter was one of the persons invited to Albany to discuss campaign strategy from a program standpoint. Roosevelt once commented: "Felix has more ideas per minute than any man of my acquaintance. He has a brilliant mind but it clicks so fast it makes my head fairly spin. I find him tremendously interesting and stimulating." [1] This admiration led to requests for opinions and advice on any number of topics.

Frankfurter did more than give Roosevelt advice. He worked actively for his election. The National Progressive League was formed in September, 1932, to give what aid it could. George Norris was Chairman, Fred C. Howe was Secretary, and Frankfurter, Harold Ickes, Donald Richberg, and Henry Wallace were on the national committee. These were many of the same men with whom Frankfurter had been associated in the 1912 campaign for T.R. His allegiance was to F.D.R., the man, rather than to F.D.R., candidate of the Democratic party. His history in politics was inconstant if judged by party labels. Support had gone to no one group. T.R., Wilson, the elder La Follette, Al Smith,

---

[1] Quoted in Arthur M. Schlesinger, Jr., *The Crisis of the Old Order* (Boston: Houghton Mifflin Co., 1957), p. 419.

and F.D.R.,[2] representatives of various political factions, gained his backing because of the Progressive type of programs for which they stood. His political history was constant, therefore, if judged by adherence to principle and policy. This is not to suggest that such factors as personal empathy were totally lacking. F.D.R.'s dynamism was an important quality. As Frankfurter himself has written, "In Roosevelt, optimism was not an anodyne, it was an energy . . . ."[3] Above all, what the nation needed in those dark days of the early 1930's was optimism and energy.

The advice that Frankfurter did tender Roosevelt was heavily colored by the former's association with Louis D. Brandeis. Frankfurter consulted with Brandeis over recommendations he was going to make for certain administrative positions. More important, however, was the fact that, in his consultations with F.D.R., he reflected many of Brandeis' basic positions concerning the relation of government to business. One of the fundamental tenets of the Progressive creed was trust-busting, an insertion of the Jeffersonian theory of small economic holdings into T.R.'s New Nationalism and Wilson's New Freedom. Brandeis' dislike and fear of the Curse of Bigness represented a vital strand in Progressive thought and fit in quite naturally with Frankfurter's own predispositions. It followed, therefore, that the Harvard professor, in the course of his conversations with Roosevelt, should advocate a program aimed at dispersing economic concentration, whether in private business or in government.

Due to his weekly trips from Cambridge to Washington, Frankfurter was often thought of as a member of F.D.R.'s famous Brain Trust. It is certainly true that he knew such Brain Trusters as Raymond Moley and Rexford Tugwell. Because of this acquaintance his name was many times linked to theirs. All things considered, however, it appears that this identification is mistaken. Doubtless he concurred on many occasions in recommendations

[2] See the following articles by Frankfurter: "Why I Shall Vote for La Follette," *New Republic*, XL (October 22, 1924), 199–201; "Why I Am for Smith," *New Republic*, LVI (October 31, 1928), 292–95; "Why I Am for Governor Roosevelt," Campaign Speech, November 5, 1932, printed in Archibald MacLeish and E. F. Prichard, Jr. (eds.), *Law and Politics* (New York: Harcourt, Brace & Co., 1939), pp. 329–33.

[3] Felix Frankfurter, "Franklin Delano Roosevelt," *Harvard Alumni Bulletin*, XLVII (April 28, 1945), 449.

emanating from the Brain Trust group. But on just as many occasions he dissented, proposing instead some facet of the Progressive program that he championed. One of his most important functions for the administration was as go-between or emissary drawing together the "old" Progressives with the "new" liberals. Primarily, therefore, he played a different role vis-à-vis F.D.R. than did other members of the High Command.

By the very nature of this counseling and mediational work, Frankfurter initially stayed off-stage. He had several opportunities to change this pattern and accept public office. Even before his relationship with Roosevelt became so pronounced, he preferred to remain in his capacity as teacher and private citizen. In June, 1932, Governor Ely's offer of nomination to the Massachusetts Supreme Judicial Court was turned down with the following explanation:

> The grave problems already upon us and those looming on the horizon require as never before a courageous and learned bar. And from such a bar alone can come an enlightened judiciary. The future direction of bar and bench will be determined by the quality of our law schools.
>
> Moreover, the fabric of the law, particularly our public law, we have been told repeatedly by the most far-sighted in the profession, must be designed chiefly by the law schools.
>
> This work must go forward, and I cannot bring myself to believe that I should prematurely abandon my share in it, however great and honorable the opportunity you offer me.[4]

While many of the nation's liberal weeklies felt downcast by his refusal of Governor Ely's offer, Frankfurter's explanation seemed valid enough to most. They realized that while "Brandeis and Holmes impressed their philosophy upon a generation of lawyers through their opinions from the Supreme Bench Frankfurter, on the other hand, is exerting his influence upon the men just before they cross the threshold into the profession." [5] In later

[4] "Letter Declining Appointment to Mass. Supreme Court," *School and Society*, xxxvi (July, 1932), 110.

[5] "Declines Position on Supreme Court of Massachusetts," *The Nation*, cxxxv (July, 1932), 67. Cf. "Nomination to the Supreme Judicial Court of Massachusetts," *New Republic*, lxxi (July 6, 1932), 191.

years the suggestion was made that Frankfurter did not want to
get lost in an "old-fogey" court and ruin his chance for eventual
nomination to the Supreme Court. Whichever explanation is correct, he did refuse the offer and was thus available when Roosevelt needed him.

Early in 1933 he demurred to the Chief Executive's suggestion
that he become an "official" adviser by taking over the duties of
Solicitor General. Some find the reason for his refusal in the fact
that he had already accepted the George Eastman Professorship
at Oxford for the ensuing year. Pointing to Frankfurter's well-
known Anglophilism, they intimate that nothing, not even responsible government service, could stop him from seeking the
self-satisfaction that would come from carrying on his personal
campaign to unite the Anglo-American world. While probably
there is a good deal of truth in such an explanation, other factors
should not be discounted. By remaining free-lance he was able
to take a continuing part in activities from which he would have
been precluded if in government employ. He served on a committee trying to obtain Tom Mooney's release from prison, a prison
sentence that his report during World War I indicated he thought
should never have been pronounced. Frankfurter, as had become
usual, was called upon on many instances to lend his support to
liberal causes. For example, David Levinson asked him to join
in the defense of radicals accused by the Nazis of starting the
Reichstag fire.[6] While this particular invitation was declined, it
is indicative of the breadth of his interests and reputation. Once
again it should be pointed out that because of the nature of the
causes that he joined Frankfurter's radicalism tended to be over-
emphasized in some quarters. To use a term current today, it was
"radicalism by association" rather than by proof.

II

If the Harvard professor's long-range contribution to the legal
profession came through his teaching, his long-range contribution to the New Deal came through his placement of young men

[6] *New York Times*, June 27, 1933.

in various government posts. Known as America's "most famous legal employment service," [7] and as the keeper of "a sort of racing stable for liberal lawyers," [8] he had been channeling young men into government service for years. The administrations of Coolidge, Harding, and Hoover had all utilized his advice in locating prospective employees. While the New Deal did not, therefore, initiate the innundation of Washington by Frankfurter's "Happy Hot Dogs," as his students and former students were known, it did provide unusual circumstances for the operation of his "employment service."

The proliferation of alphabetical agencies, with their ever-expanding need for skilled personnel, provided the forum through which many of Frankfurter's theories could be put to the test. In 1930 he wrote a book entitled *The Public and Its Government*,[9] in which one of the basic premises was that government should be thought of as a wise man's study. In the same year his article in the *Atlantic Monthly*,[10] took the ground that, while the expert should never be on top, he should always be on tap. Frankfurter sent his young men to Washington for the expertise they could display. And while there must have been a good deal of ego satisfaction in such a practice, the main point remains, nevertheless, that most of the Harvard products did make good and did add to the vitality of the New Deal program. Not overlooking the valid criticism that can be leveled at government and many bureaucratic characteristics, it seems fair to say that in theory and largely in practice the desire to have trained young people given a taste of government service before many of them filtered back into private employ was vindicated on the record. Certainly a good deal of the New Deal program could not have been accomplished without them.

While Frankfurter's much-publicized art of filling offices gained

[7] "Biography," *Fortune*, XIII (January, 1936), 90. Cf. Felix Frankfurter, "Young Men Go to Washington," *Fortune*, XIII (January, 1936), 61ff.

[8] John Franklin Carter, *The New Dealers* (New York: Simon and Schuster, Inc., 1934), p. 317.

[9] Felix Frankfurter, *The Public and Its Government* (New Haven: Yale University Press, 1930).

[10] Felix Frankfurter, "Democracy and the Expert," *Atlantic Monthly*, CXLVI (November, 1930), 649–60.

him the most space in newspapers, his function in helping to draft
New Deal legislation remains relatively unknown. Approximately
a month before F.D.R. took the oath of office, Frankfurter in an
address before Survey Associates outlined some considerations
that he thought important.

> Ways must be found and they must be found through govern-
> mental lead to prevent the terrible psychology of idleness and hope-
> lessness from setting upon the unemployed. The millions of our
> unemployed fellow citizens have shown an extraordinary patient
> temper. The only way to justify it, and, indeed, the only way to
> maintain it, is to make definite progress toward re-employment.[11]

When the time came to draft measures designed to lift the country by its economic boot-straps, Frankfurter was quite sure that
the federal government would have to assume a major part of the
lifting process. Since his views on this subject were often and
vigorously pronounced, some feared that the depression would
be used as an excuse for collectivism. It is apparent that they
missed the real point for wanting government action. Action was
desired, not to undermine the competitive system, but to save it.
Reared in the tradition of small, viable economic units, Frankfurter did not forget his heritage so quickly. A good many of
the early New Deal statutes, such as the National Recovery Act
and the Agricultural Adjustment Act, left him unconvinced as
to their workability or wisdom. He advised caution in drafting
of legislation and statement of principle. If this advice had been
heeded, perhaps the New Deal would have been able to avoid
some of the friction that later developed between it and the Supreme Court.

The National Recovery Act serves as a good example. Not over-
enthusiastic about the program or the program's director, General
Hugh S. Johnson, and more than slightly apprehensive over the
constitutionality of the code arrangement, Frankfurter warned
against trying to get a ruling on N.R.A. too quickly. When asked
early in 1934 why a case on this issue should not be rushed to
the Supreme Court, he replied, "Why are you so anxious for a

[11] *New York Times,* February 2, 1933.

decision until you are sure of getting the right one?" [12] If judged on the basis of allowing an act thought unconstitutional to remain in operation as long as possible without adequate challenge, this position is not praiseworthy. If judged on the basis of making the best of a bad bargain and allowing the nation to reap as much benefit as possible from an act that, because of its inherent weaknesses, would soon enough fall, the position while still not completely unassailable is at least more understandable. Characteristically, this was a pragmatic approach, an approach that Frankfurter has subsequently used as a Supreme Court justice.

General Johnson placed much of the blame for the failure of N.R.A. on the Harvard professor. Arthur Krock, writing in the *New York Times* a few weeks after the Supreme Court had unanimously held the act unconstitutional, took much the same stance: "Unless high NRA officials, past and present, in a position to know the facts are completely misinformed, Professor Frankfurter was responsible for postponing the legal test of NRA for nearly two years, with the disastrous results familiar to everyone." [13] While Krock attributed to Frankfurter a change in the President's political situation "from favorable to distinctly perilous," F.D.R. apparently did not find the Harvard professor's counsel of caution disadvantageous, for it was Frankfurter who was called to the White House immediately after the decision to discuss the future of N.R.A. and the means whereby some type of code program could be made acceptable to the Supreme Court. Mr. Krock's own paper editorialized several months later that if Frankfurter "has given F.D.R. any worse advice than the President received from General Johnson, he has so far covered it up rather cleverly. After all, a live Frankfurter is better than a dead Blue Eagle." [14] Parenthetically, it may be noted that with the passage of time, many of the N.R.A. reforms themselves eventually were repudiated by elements within the liberal camp.

Whether because of his familiarity with so many members of

[12] Quoted in Alpheus T. Mason, "The Supreme Court: Instrument of Power or Revealed Truth?" *Boston University Law Review*, xxxiii (June, 1953), 299.

[13] *New York Times*, July 26, 1935.

[14] *New York Times*, November 10, 1935.

the Court or because of his own extensive knowledge of constitutional law and history, the Harvard professor had a "feel" for many of the dominant issues underlying the New Deal and a comprehension of the limits beyond which it was unsafe to go in trying to remedy the economic imbalance of the country. On March 22, 1933, just a few weeks after Roosevelt's inauguration, Frankfurter warned New York legislators against attempting to broaden the scope of certain bills. "Any attempt to broaden the scope of minimum wage legislation *at present* so as to include men can emanate only from sources hostile to the policy of minimum wage legislation for women or from sources unfamiliar with *technical legal problems involved in translating such a policy into effective legislation.*" [15] Even though the legislators followed his advice, this attempt to establish minimum wages for women was unsuccessful, as the Supreme Court held the legislation unconstitutional.[16] Unhappily in this instance Frankfurter misappraised the situation and thought that limited regulation would be accepted. The purpose behind the use of this situational example is to suggest that Frankfurter was usually attuned to the areas of possible advancement and was not apt to be trapped by all-encompassing panaceas. This trait has shown up in a slightly different form in his Supreme Court opinions when he has refused to acquiesce in absolute, immediate solutions for any problem.

While Frankfurter sat in on meetings devoted to settlement of controversy in the coal industry and gave some advice concerning the drafting of labor legislation, New Deal measures with which he is most readily identified and which clearly carry his imprint are the Securities Act of 1933 and the Public Utilities Holding Company Act of 1935. Joined by Benjamin Cohen and James M. Landis in drafting the New Deal measures, Frankfurter incorporated into his recommended legislation much of the philosophy that a few years earlier had been incorporated in his writings. Both acts had a typically Progressive flavor. The Securities Act was meant to promote free and fair competition on the stock exchange by requiring the registration of any security sold

[15] *New York Times,* March 23, 1933. Emphasis added.
[16] Moorehead v. New York *ex rel.* Tipaldo, 298 U.S. 587 (1936).

in interstate commerce. The Public Utilities Holding Company Act aimed at dispersal of control in the utilities field by requiring that any company having an interest in another show definitely and beyond doubt that the public was better served by such an arrangement. Ultimately, the Securities and Exchange Commission was given supervision over the companies. The utilities did not accept such regulation willingly. Frankfurter estimated that $10 million was used in the fight against passage of the Act.[17] If this amount is nearly accurate, it indicates the fear of the holding companies of a tightly drawn measure that, unlike N.R.A., effectively set out to combat and control the evils at which it was directed. Judicial approval of various sections of these acts followed as a matter of course over the years.

Perhaps of all F.D.R.'s many publicized actions none gained more notoriety than his Court-Packing plan announced in February, 1937. Here, if anywhere, it was thought that Frankfurter's sentiments would be made known. Contrary to expectation, he remained strangely silent. Comments on his thoughts on the plan must, therefore, be highly speculative, guided alone by statements that he had made previously about the size of the Court and its composition. Loyal to the Supreme Court as an institution and loyal to the President as the best man to guide the destiny of the country in the perilous days of the 1930's, Frankfurter no doubt felt torn between the two adversaries. Caught on the horns of this dilemma, he suffered in silence. It is, however, known that he did not want the Constitution or the Court brought into the 1936 campaign.

In 1923 he had written that "multiplying judges by no means multiplies justice."[18] In 1935 he was even more explicit: "There is no magic in the number nine, but . . . experience is conclusive that to enlarge the size of the Supreme Court would be self-defeating."[19] From these sentiments one may gather that the student of the Court was not too happy over the proposals

---

[17] Harold Ickes, *The Secret Diary Of* . . . (New York: Simon and Schuster, Inc., 1953), I, 403.

[18] Felix Frankfurter, "Enforcement of Prohibition," *New Republic*, xxxiii (January, 1923), 150.

[19] Quoted in *Current Biography*, (1941), p. 307.

of F.D.R. Frankfurter thought that the solution to the problem did not lie in increasing judges but was to be found instead in the character of the men placed on the Supreme Court.

While he did not feel free to make these views known through newspapers, he did convey his feelings about the general situation through private correspondence and personal contacts. Frankfurter was early concerned about the growing disparity between Court decisions and the public temper. He did not think that this disparity could be lessened by tinkering with constitutional machinery. Writing to Justice Harlan Fiske Stone, he indicated that for him, "we ought not to make inroads upon our constitutional structure but ought to be zealously alert in the choice of those whom we entrust with the administration of our laws or our lawmaking." [20] Stone apparently agreed with much of what his correspondent had to say, for in a note to him dated May 28, 1937, Stone confessed that he did not believe in appointing men simply because they would probably vote in a certain way. All that Stone would require of an appointee was that he "have integrity, intelligence, and sound legal knowledge, and that he have some appreciation of the world in which we live." Penciled in as an afterthought was the message, "How I wish it would be you." [21]

III

Justice Stone was addressing his remarks to the particular vacancy caused by Justice Willis Van Devanter's retirement in 1937. For this vacancy President Roosevelt nominated Senator Hugo L. Black. When Justice George Sutherland retired the following year, Solicitor General Stanley Reed was named as his successor. Stone's suggestion that Frankfurter would be a proper person to fill a Supreme Court seat recommended itself to many persons, however. When the first two vacancies on the Court occurred the academician was often discussed as a possible choice. Indeed,

[20] Alpheus T. Mason, *Harlan Fiske Stone* (New York: The Viking Press, Inc., 1956), p. 354.

[21] Stone to Frankfurter, May 28, 1937. Quoted in *ibid.*, pp. 462–63.

on innumerable occasions since 1932, Frankfurter's name had been mentioned in this connection. Justice Benjamin N. Cardozo's death in July, 1938, presented Roosevelt with his third opportunity to name a new justice. Once again Frankfurter stood prominent on the list of those under consideration.

The opening statement of note in the concerted campaign on behalf of the Frankfurter candidacy was made by Senator George Norris, long-time friend and acknowledged leader of the old Progressive forces.[22] Other supporters soon made themselves known. Newton Baker came out strongly for his former assistant in World War I, as did Senator Sherman Minton. By the middle of September the Gallup Poll had the following information to report. After canvassing members of the American Bar Association on their choice of a successor to Cardozo, Frankfurter's name was mentioned five times oftener than any other. This was a surprising show of strength, for there were other strong candidates in the field, including Judge Learned Hand, John W. Davis, and Senator Walter George. The Gallup organization also reported that there was no correlation between the choice of Frankfurter and support of the New Deal. Only 38% of those polled indicated that they belonged to the pro-Roosevelt forces, while 62% indicated from mild to extreme anti-Roosevelt feelings.[23] Thus it appears that Frankfurter gained support in spite of the fact that he was identified with F.D.R., not because of such an identification.

One of the factors weighing against the selection of the Harvard professor was a geographical consideration. The Court was already heavily overrepresented with members from east of the Mississippi and especially from the northeastern section of the country. To Roosevelt this was a vital consideration, both politically and for the good of the Court. Norris from Nebraska helped to dispel some of these doubts. Other voices, both Democrat and Republican, from the mid-West were soon heard in support. William Allen White wrote to F.D.R. that "President Hoover indicated that a seven dollar night letter that I sent him a day or two before Cardozo was named had weighed somewhat in the

[22] *New York Times*, August 9, 1938.
[23] *New York Times*, September 23, 1938.

balance. If I could have one word to say to you now it would be to urge the appointment of Felix Frankfurter to succeed Cardozo." [24] Justice Stone appears to have put the quietus on F.D.R.'s geographical doubts. He told him that he could get "a very good man from every judicial circuit in the country, and thus constitute a Supreme Court of character and ability. But you could not get a distinguished Court that way because you cannot find a distinguished judge or lawyer in every circuit." [25] Since Stone wanted the Court on which he sat to be distinguished, he recommended Frankfurter for the Cardozo vacancy.

Interest in having Frankfurter on the Court spread beyond the boundaries of this country. Chief Justice H. V. Evatt of the High Court of Australia sent Solicitor General Robert Jackson a memorandum on the matter and urged Jackson (who needed no urging) to support the Cambridge candidate. Evatt advised that:

> What the Court and the Country need is that the new appointee vice Cardozo will have sufficient power of leadership, of persuasion, of imagination, and of learning to restore unity, if not cause union, among the loose group of progressives on the Court. The appointee must have a social outlook which is in accordance with the general aims and ideals of the Supreme Executive of the Nation. He should have a very close knowledge of the Court's history and practice. He should have, if possible, the general confidence of the legal profession and the law schools, so that confirmation by the Senate will be certain.[26]

While Evatt was joined by many in thinking that Frankfurter possessed all the qualifications requisite to appointment, a few contrary opinions were expressed. General Hugh Johnson was most outspoken in his opposition during this preliminary period when the candidates were sparring for position.

Two themes run through the discussion of Frankfurter's appointment. The first was that even if he did not succeed Cardozo, when Brandeis resigned, his Harvard friend was sure to take his

[24] William Allen White to F.D.R., no date. Franklin D. Roosevelt, *His Personal Letters* (New York: Duell, Sloan & Pearce, Inc., 1950), II, 818.

[25] Quoted in Mason, *Harlan Fiske Stone*, p. 482.

[26] H. V. Evatt to Robert Jackson, November 11, 1938. Quoted in Eugene Gerhardt, *America's Advocate* (Indianapolis: The Bobbs-Merrill Co., 1958), p. 157.

place. There was peril in this approach, however, for no one was sure exactly when Brandeis planned to leave the bench. Harold Ickes, in arguing this point with F.D.R., told him that he was not convinced of Brandeis' intention to retire and "that it would be a terrible thing if, relying upon such an event, Frankfurter should fail of appointment." Ickes then went on to tell the President that if he appointed Frankfurter, "his ability and learning are such that he will dominate the Supreme Court for fifteen or twenty years to come. The result will be that, probably after you are dead, it will still be your Supreme Court." [27] Harold Laski approached Brandeis directly in an effort to convince him that he ought to resign in time for Frankfurter to be appointed by F.D.R.[28] Irrespective of his personal involvement, Brandeis seemed to entertain some doubts as to whether Frankfurter should go onto the Supreme Court. These doubts were based, not on Frankfurter's capabilities, but on the question of whether he could not do more for the legal profession and the country elsewhere. In 1932 the older man had written, "The year has been for Felix . . . one of happy usefulness, with an ever widening appreciation of his rare qualities. His students are becoming teachers. Given another 20 years of such activity, and he will have profoundly affected American life." [29] Frankfurter's own letter to Governor Ely, quoted earlier, emphasized how important he thought the teaching profession was to the law. This letter now came back to be used as an argument against his appointment to the Court.

The second theme that colors discussion of Frankfurter's elevation centers on the need for the individual best able to hold his own with Chief Justice Charles Evans Hughes. The President was impressed with the necessity of naming someone for the vacancy who could match wits with the formidable Chief Justice in the Conference Room and who could thus prevent the venerable and much-respected Hughes from carrying the Court by the mere force of his personality. Jackson wrote the President that

[27] Ickes, *The Secret Diary Of* . . . , ɪɪ, 539–40.

[28] *Ibid.*, ɪɪ, 424.

[29] Quoted in Alexander Bickel, "Justice Frankfurter at Seventy-Five," *New Republic*, cxxxvɪɪɪ (November 18, 1957), 8.

"what is urgently needed at this time is someone who can interpret [the Constitution] with scholarship and with sufficient assurance to face Chief Justice Hughes in conference and hold his
own in discussion. . . . My urgent request, Mr. President, is that
you leave me at the bar of the Supreme Court and give me Felix
as the new Judge." [30]

Bombarded with this type of advice from July to December,
Roosevelt began to show signs of annoyance whenever the Frankfurter nomination was mentioned. He finally decided, however,
that such recommendations were sound and sent to the Senate
on January 5, 1939, the name of Felix Frankfurter for Associate
Justice of the United States Supreme Court. Public reaction was
generally favorable and therefore it came somewhat as a surprise
when the Senate took the most unusual step at that time of an-
nouncing that it would hold hearings on the "fitness" of the nomi-
nee.[31] These hearings were held in Washington on January 11
and 12, 1939. While at first declining to appear before the subcommittee of the Committee on the Judiciary and sending Dean
Acheson to represent him, Frankfurter relented and put in a
personal appearance on the second day.

The hearings did not bring to light any information of significance. Witnesses testifying against the nomination ranged from
Elizabeth Dilling, authoress of sensational exposés, who accused
Frankfurter of master-minding the entire Communist conspiracy
in the United States, to a disgruntled Spanish-American War vet-
eran who thought that Frankfurter should have used his influence
to increase bonuses. One of the lighter moments of the proceedings came when Collis Reed, National Director of Constitutional
Crusaders of America and that organization's sole member, asked,
"Why not an American from Revolution times instead of a Jew
from Austria just naturalized?" Senator Norris' caustic explanation
was that "an American from Revolution times would be too
old." [32]

The serious charges against Frankfurter were basically three.

[30] Gerhardt, *America's Advocate*, pp. 165–66.

[31] U.S. Congress. Senate. Committee on the Judiciary. "Hearings on the Nomination of Felix Frankfurter," 76th Cong., 1st Sess., January 11 and 12, 1939.

[32] *Ibid.*, p. 6.

His association with the American Civil Liberties Union and his work on behalf of Mooney and Sacco and Vanzetti led to the first accusation, that he was an extreme radical, if not a Communist. In the second place, his Jewish background was brought up and discussed. Finally, the fact that he was not a natural-born citizen and that he had derivatively gained citizenship only through his father's naturalization counted heavily with some people. The subcommittee really gave much attention only to the first point. When asked by Senator Pat McCarran whether he believed in the doctrines of Karl Marx or whether he subscribed whole-heartedly to the positions taken in some of Harold Laski's books, Frankfurter replied: "Senator, I do not believe you have ever taken an oath to support the Constitution of the United States with fewer reservations than I have or would now, nor do I believe you are more attached to the theories and practices of Americanism than I am. I rest my answer on that statement." [33] At the end of this statement, the audience at the hearings broke into applause that lasted for more than two minutes. [34]

Felix Frankfurter's appointment was confirmed without a dissenting vote on January 17 and it was on January 30, 1939, that he took his oath to "administer justice without respect to person," thus assuming the Scholar's Seat on the Supreme Court. The crowd at the swearing-in ceremonies was so large that extra chairs had to be moved into the aisles of the Court chamber. Attorney General Frank Murphy and Solicitor General Jackson were among the notables present as were Secretaries Hopkins and Ickes. Such personal friends as Tom Corcoran and Ben Cohen, Dean Acheson and Marguerite LeHand were also there. Professor Joseph Beale, an instructor of the class in which Justice Frankfurter entered Harvard and an intimate friend over the years, summed up the feelings of most people present: "At Harvard we are very enthusiastic over the remarkable record our prize scholar has already made and are confident that he will be one of the outstanding members of the Supreme Court." [35]

[33] *Ibid.,* p. 126.
[34] *New York Times,* January 13, 1939.
[35] *Baltimore Sun,* January 31, 1939.

IV

The Scholar's Seat was once again filled, but what kind of man was the new occupant? Felix Frankfurter was now fifty-six years old. Capping his five-foot-five-inch stocky frame was a finely rounded face, intense and quizzical of expression, reflecting, much as an actor's, any change in mood. Peering through his pince-nez glasses, which stood out sparkling and prominent from his graying head, Frankfurter gave an appearance of tenseness and unbounded energy. "A rapid, sensitive . . . personality, generous in temperament, irrepressible in speech, given to gusts of enthusiasm or outrage . . . ," thus has been described the new member of the Court.[36] Taking his place on Chief Justice Hughes' extreme left, the former teacher appeared dwarfed by some of his brethren. Physically this was so, for one could barely see his head at times behind the large wooden bench. When visible, Frankfurter was usually busy scanning the courtroom, writing off notes, or talking to his immediate neighbor. Intellectually, no member of the Court dwarfed him.

At the time when he assumed his place, Frankfurter thought of himself as a symbol and thought his position on the Court would mean much to the Progressive cause.[37] Certainly all the liberal papers were highly pleased with his new responsibilities, the *New Republic* feeling "surely no American of this generation has been more completely in the great tradition of American jurisprudence than this professor at Harvard Law School." [38] Behind all the superficial agreement as to what "liberal" meant and how a "liberal" judge would vote, there lay vast areas for misunderstanding and recrimination. Even while the Frankfurter nomination was pending, one or two writers were perceptive enough to catch this danger and comment upon it. Louis Stark in the *New York Times* of January 8, 1939, warned that

[36] Arthur Schlesinger, Jr., "The Supreme Court: 1947," *Fortune*, xxxv (January, 1947), 76.

[37] Ickes, *The Secret Diary Of . . .* , ii, 563.

[38] "Justice Frankfurter," *New Republic*, xcvii (January 18, 1939), 298.

Frankfurter's "method of approach to economic problems has always been empirical, and it is assumed that on the bench he will continue to ask for facts and proof rather than assumptions. In short, he may at times disappoint those liberal friends whose zeal for a 'cause' overruns their logic." [39]

The *Baltimore Sun* informed its readers that Frankfurter was not just another New Dealer nor was he merely a satellite of F.D.R. "Philosophically, his path parallels that of the New Deal in numerous respects. . . . Dr. Frankfurter's philosophy is his own philosophy and could well differ, and does differ, from the amorphous doctrines of the President in several respects." [40] Felix Frankfurter, in other words, was completely a New Deal justice only by appointment and not by approach. It was written of him in 1934: "Liberal that he is, he will not change old lamps for new merely because they are new. On the other hand, he does not object to trimming the old." [41] This perhaps in essence is the difference between Frankfurter and some of the other Roosevelt appointees. His philosophy precludes adoption of wholesale changes in the law. Depending upon empirically proven need for change, he has at times appeared to hold back when some of his brethren wished to rush in "where angels fear to tread."

When the Harvard professor went on the bench, everyone expected that he would follow, wherever possible, the leads that his idols Holmes and Brandeis had provided during their tenure. In fact it was charged that intellectually he was their captive and would be unable to act independently. In recent years exactly the opposite charge has been made, namely, that he does not follow the spirit of Holmes and Brandeis often enough. What cannot be denied is the fact that Frankfurter did, and does, often rely on one of the two men for authority. Surely the heroes that anyone picks tell a good deal about the person himself. If Frankfurter thinks of himself as the heir of Holmes and Brandeis, the mere identification has meaning regardless of its validity.

[39] *New York Times*, January 8, 1939.
[40] *Baltimore Sun*, January 6, 1939.
[41] S. J. Woolf, "A Friend of the Brain Trust Speaks Up," *New York Times*, September 30, 1934.

As Frankfurter wrote in 1931, "for all of us, truth is born when we discover it. But intellectual genealogy is important. The history of ideas is essential to culture; thereby we are saved from being intellectually *nouveaux riches*." [42] While disagreement there may be over the question of how much Frankfurter has absorbed from Holmes and Brandeis, it can be agreed that he has absorbed some things. If his intellectual genealogy is to be complete, however, other names such as James Bradley Thayer, Roscoe Pound, Benjamin N. Cardozo, Thorstein Veblein, Charles A. Beard, Herbert Croly, William James, and James Dewey must be included.

Frankfurter's activities as adviser to the President were, of course, curtailed after he took his place on the Supreme Court. On rare occasions, however, Roosevelt still called upon him for aid. A continuing function was as reviewer of F.D.R.'s speeches. Samuel Rosenman, one of the President's chief writers, found Frankfurter helpful. "Frequently, while a speech was in the discussion stage, [I] would drive out to his house in Georgetown to exchange ideas about what it should contain. Our sessions often lasted until the early hours of the morning, and they were always fruitful." [43] It is no wonder that Rosenman and others would turn to Frankfurter for such assistance. The Justice had a penchant for striking phrases, and he was quick to pick up such phrases when used by others. When Jean Monnet visited this country in 1940 on a diplomatic mission, Frankfurter met and engaged him in conversation. Hearing a particularly apt expression, he asked that F.D.R. be allowed to introduce it to the public. The expression was "arsenal of democracy," and it became the archstone for one of Roosevelt's most important speeches concerning the role that the United States was to play in World War II. [44]

The decade of the 1930's was a full one. In its final year Frankfurter gained the position that he probably desired more than any other, that of Associate Justice of the United States Supreme

[42] Felix Frankfurter, "The Early Writings of O. W. Holmes, Jr.," *Harvard Law Review*, xliv (March, 1931), 720.

[43] Samuel Rosenman, *Working With Roosevelt* (New York: Harper & Brothers, 1952), p. 207.

[44] *Ibid.*, pp. 260–61.

Court. His whole background had really been a preparation for this office. It is fitting to close this biographical section with a quotation from the Justice himself. While he was writing of Benjamin N. Cardozo, the sentiments expressed apply equally to Justice Felix Frankfurter: "If surprise there was in anything that he wrote as a Justice, it was not want of disclosure by him as to the way he looked at questions that would come before him." [45]

[45] Felix Frankfurter, "Mr. Justice Cardozo and Public Law," *Harvard Law Review,* LII (January, 1939), 441.

TWO

Symbolism and Social Unity

Justice Frankfurter is interested in the many symbols that allow transmission of values from one individual to another, from one generation to another. For him, symbolism does not stand as a concept by itself. He uses it as a tool to inculcate understanding of a deeper and more fundamental truth—that some type of social unity or social cohesion is necessary in even the most heterogeneous society if democracy is to work. Symbols are the cement that binds society together.

Although Frankfurter has been heavily criticized for his opinions in the flag salute cases, his statements there regarding the importance of symbols in creating and refining social values have remained his credo. While the flag is the obvious symbol in these cases, there is a second but not so obvious one, and that is public education. Schools have dual roles: They are symbols and the transmitters of symbols. In analyzing Justice Frankfurter's hierarchy of values, therefore, the radiation of the flag salute cases into other litigation dealing with education, in the broad sense, must be surveyed.

Frankfurter tends to recognize various sub-societies within society as a whole. Although the terms "labor," "business," and "government" are not completely satisfactory designations, since the breakdown of interests is more complex than these terms suggest, they do indicate the three major loci of power on the economic front. In the area of personal rights, the number of conflicting groups can reach almost to infinity, for the basis of disagreement is often one of a religious, racial, or nationality nature. In trying to alleviate conflicts, it is part of the judicial function to make compromise and adjustment workable principles. In undertaking this task, courts play a symbolic role. These are the themes with which this section will deal.

III

"We Live by Symbols"

On May 10, 1940, German Panzer divisions crossed the borders of the Low Countries, and the Battle of Flanders began. The next three weeks saw the Netherlands and Belgium fall and, in the critical period between May 24 and June 4, the heroic evacuation of British troops from Dunkirk undertaken. On June 3, 1940, the day before the Dunkirk mission was completed, the Supreme Court of the United States handed down a decision that so agitated Justice Harlan Fiske Stone that he departed from recent practice and, in a voice filled with emotion, read his entire dissenting opinion.

I

The issue, in legal terms, that so disturbed Stone was whether public school authorities in Pennsylvania could require children to participate in flag salute ceremonies as a requisite to staying in school. Two children of the Gobitis family, members of Jehovah's Witnesses, one of whose major tenets is that strict adherence should be given the Biblical command not to bow down before any graven image, refused to salute the flag and were expelled. The real question was whether the Pennsylvania requirement interfered with the freedom of religion guarantees of the Constitution. The Court held in a unanimous opinion, except for Stone's defection, that it did not. In nonlegal terms, the Court had to determine whether a school board's belief that symbolic values of national unity could be transmitted through patriotic exercises was so unreasonable and far-fetched as to be unconstitutional.

The opinion of the Court was written by Associate Justice Felix Frankfurter. Relatively new on the Court, Frankfurter had already received assignments in several important cases from Chief Justice Hughes. There was no doubting that in the case now presented to the Court tough issues had to be disposed. On at least three previous occasions the tribunal, through *per curiam* opinions, had refused to review similar state action on the ground that no federal question was involved. Indeed, the last such refusal came only a little over a year before the Gobitis case was argued. In the interim, however, the changing complexion of the world scene inevitably drew attention from members of the Court. Justice Frankfurter in a speech in Boston before the Ford Hall Forum delivered in September, 1939, had argued that the United States could not be neutral regarding the actions of Hitler.[1] His Anglophilism plus his contacts all over the European scene made him extremely sensitive to this threat to western civilization in general and to members of the Jewish race in particular.

The Justice's total personal involvement with the tragic happenings on the Continent cannot be discounted in dealing with the Gobitis decision, but neither can it be made the entire basis for evaluation. After all, he carried seven other strong-willed individuals with him. Even if the times were hectic, it need not be supposed that an overwhelming majority of the Supreme

[1] *New York Times*, September 22, 1939.

Court were stampeded into taking a stand on the flag salute issue solely from fright. Other factors had to be present. Personal involvement may stem from time-place settings, but it does not create them. The fiction of "judicial notice" was evolved to validate the use of extralegal factors in arriving at judicial decisions. Today we hear of the U.S.S.C. operating under the shadow of the U.S.S.R. In 1940, the shadow of the swastika was just as ominous.

On several occasions in the past, though none under the pressure that surrounded the Gobitis case, the Court had been called upon to rule on the status of public schools and on the methods that states employed in their schools to facilitate social cohesion. In one such instance it unanimously struck down an Oregon law making attendance at public school mandatory for all children between the ages of eight and sixteen.[2] If allowed, this statute would automatically have terminated all sectarian and private institutions. In another such instance, a Nebraska enactment declaring that only English could be taught in both private and public schools through the eighth grade was disallowed,[3] but this time there were two dissenters. The strange duo of Justices Holmes and Sutherland thought that, although unwise, the legislation was a "reasonable" way in which the state could foster unity and a common sentiment within its borders. Language was one of the symbols through which values could be transmitted. The difference for Holmes seemed to be that, while the state could not limit education to the public schools, it could require all schools and the students therein to abide by generalized regulations. This distinction was not lost on Justice Frankfurter when he came to write in the Gobitis case.

Shortly after the assignment of the opinion, Justice Stone must have indicated his intention to dissent from the line of reasoning being pursued by the Court. In a letter of extraordinary frankness and tact, Justice Frankfurter wrote to Stone telling him that his doubts had resulted in serious reconsideration of his own

[2] Pierce v. Society of Sisters, 268 U.S. 510 (1925). For Frankfurter's comment on this case, see *New York Times*, June 5, 1925.

[3] Meyers v. Nebraska, 262 U.S. 390 (1923). Cf. Bartels v. Iowa, 262 U.S. 403 (1923).

position but that he remained convinced of the rectitude of the majority stand. In laying out his thoughts, Frankfurter clarified certain points that later appeared in slightly different form in the published opinion. He began by reminding Stone that much of his mature life had been directed against "foolish and harsh manifestations of coercion and for the amplest expression of dissident views . . . ." [4] He explained that, in his view, it was not the Court's function to keep too tight a rein on the organs of popular government. Although he thought it "foolish and perhaps worse, for school authorities to believe . . . that to allow exemption to some of the children goes far towards disrupting the whole patriotic exercise . . . ," he did not think it fantastic. Given the time and circumstances, Justice Frankfurter could not see how the Court could gainsay a school board's desire to have flag salute exercises and to have all children in the public schools participate. It was not just a question of the particular school board's authority; it involved a question of legislative power in general.

Justice Frankfurter cited personal talks with Holmes to the effect that jurists had a duty to take into account external factors when these factors had some real bearing on the disposition of a case. Though not directly stated, the implication was that the Court at the present time had an equal responsibility to face the facts of life. The heritage and purposes of our country might soon be under direct attack and the Court best full well realize it. The crux of Frankfurter's position was, however, that the Court should not be relied upon to safeguard democracy. Only the people themselves through legislatures, school boards, etc. could provide for their own salvation. As he said in the opinion proper, "When all the effective means for inducing political changes are left free from interference, education in the abandonment of foolish legislation is itself a training in liberty." [5]

The last paragraph of the letter was devoted to a recital of what the opinion was not.

[4] Frankfurter to Stone, May 27, 1940. Quoted in Alpheus T. Mason, *Security Through Freedom* (Ithaca: Cornell University Press, 1955), p. 218. A reproduction of the entire letter is given in the Mason work, pp. 217–20. In the following discussion, unless otherwise noted, all quotations are taken from that letter.

[5] Minersville School District v. Gobitis, 310 U.S. 586, 600 (1940).

It is not a case where conformity is exacted for something that you and I regard as foolish—namely, a gesture of respect for the symbol of our national being . . . above all, it is not a case where the slightest restriction is involved against the fullest opportunity to disavow—either on the part of the children or their parents—the meaning that ordinary people attach to the gesture of respect.[6]

The degree of compulsion that the flag salute exerted was as minimal as it could possibly be. Jehovah's Witnesses had opportunity to disavow the act through channels of affirmative free expression. Justice Frankfurter's communication did not persuade Justice Stone, but it did, for future years, make parts of the opinion more intelligible. He was convinced that the decision approved very little and that it left the Court free to work out further refinements. It is to the opinion, therefore, that we must now turn.

The first issue to be met was, of course, that of interference with freedom of religion. The First Amendment and the Fourteenth, through its inclusion of some of the same subject matter as the First, were designed to alleviate centuries of strife over the erection of particular dogmas as exclusive and all-comprehending faiths. Established state religions were prohibited, and every sect guaranteed tolerance in religious matters. "But," protested Justice Frankfurter, "to affirm that the freedom to follow conscience has itself no limits in the life of a society would deny that very plurality of principles which, as a matter of history, underlie protection of religious toleration."[7] The United States is a pluralist society and, as such, finds it difficult enough to compromise all groups within her borders. The flag is the one leading symbol for all her people. It would require far more conclusive showing that interference, if interference there was, with the Jehovah's Witnesses' religious freedom was not justified. "Freedom" is not an absolute. Other values must also be weighed. Therefore, in the conflict of principles, Justice Frankfurter came

[6] For a discussion of the flag as a normative value symbol, see Theodore M. Greene, "The Symbolic Vehicles of Our Cultural Values," in Lyman Bryson (ed.), *Symbols and Society* (New York: Conference on Science, Philosophy and Religion, 1955), pp. 232–33.

[7] Minersville School District v. Gobitis, 310 U.S. 586, 594 (1940).

down on the side of legislative judgment that symbolic importance attached to the flag as the transmitter of social unity.

Because the Gobitis children felt unable to conform with the general regulation of saluting the flag, they had two alternatives. First, they could continue in their refusal, thus being technically labeled as delinquents and subjecting their parents to certain penalties. Second, they could attend private schools that might be more sympathetic to their plight and thus avoid penalties. The financial hardship of private school education for many persons cannot be denied. Often overlooked, however, is the fact that public schools mean common schools, common in the sense that regulations pertaining thereto relate to Negroes and whites equally, to Jews, Roman Catholics, Methodists, and Jehovah's Witnesses undifferentiated.

Those sections of the opinion that deal with the flag salute as an objective means for transmitting national values and with the role of the public school are extremely important for an understanding of Justice Frankfurter's philosophy. The central fact, according to him, is that

> the ultimate foundation of a free society is the binding tie of cohesive sentiment. Such a sentiment is fostered by all those agencies of the mind and spirit which may serve to gather up the traditions of a people, transmit them from generation to generation, and thereby create that continuity of a treasured life which constitutes a civilization. "We live by symbols." [8]

A product of public schools and a city college, he knew through his own experience how much these "agencies of the mind" had helped an immigrant boy adjust to a new pattern of living. In instilling the cohesive sentiment that directs a nation's destiny, schools have to utilize various techniques. The flag salute was one of these and as such was legitimate for Jehovah's Witnesses as well as anybody else. The religious freedom issue dealt with in the opinion was preliminary, if not peripheral, to this central point.

Justice Stone's dissent was strong, vigorous, and telling. His espousal of a philosophy that would give the widest scope to

[8] *Ibid.*, p. 596.

freedom for individual or sectarian idiosyncrasies merits admiration. As is true with most cases that come before the Supreme Court, there is much to be said in favor of both sides. An adverse ruling for one side does not mean that it is totally wrong, only that the law cannot separate the wheat from the chaff. Justice Stone directed his attention almost entirely to the proposition that legislative judgment as reflected in the school board's ruling was not in this instance acceptable. Religious freedom precluded any interference. While Frankfurter thought it was not the Court's function to overthrow legislative judgment or to rush to the aid of a minority group that was supposedly adversely affected by such a judgment, Stone held a different opinion on the function of the tribunal in our system of government. For him the Court was obligated to offer protection in such instances as those now under consideration. For him, too, national security appeared best served by allowing the widest play for individual idiosyncrasies.[9] He, therefore, dealt with the freedom of religion contention as the core of the litigation; Frankfurter dealt with it in order to pass on to what he thought were the more important points, legislative integrity and social unity. At times both men talked by one another and never did face each other's major premises. Disagreement on the imponderables of the case did not lessen personal admiration. In a note to Stone about the time of the Gobitis decision, Justice Frankfurter wrote that "though we read the scales differently in weighing these 'imponderables,' I cannot but feel confident that our scales are the same. In any event . . . we care not differently for the only things that give dignity to man—the things of the spirit."[10]

Both men agreed that constitutional government does mean limitations on power. For Justice Frankfurter it means something more than this, however. It means respect for common laws applicable to all without discrimination and at least some active identification with those symbols that transmit faith in what is commonly called the democratic code. While there are cer-

[9] See Alpheus T. Mason and Richard H. Leach, *In Quest of Freedom* (Englewood Cliffs, N.J.: Prentice-Hall, Inc., 1959), pp. 533–41.

[10] Frankfurter to Stone, handwritten note, undated. Quoted in Mason, *Security Through Freedom*, p. 135.

tainly dangers inherent in any restriction upon the minority by the majority, some restrictions have to be placed at times to keep constitutional government going at all, however much we may dislike the fact. We are so concerned with protecting the minority from the majority that at times we fail to realize that there is a reverse side to this proposition, namely, that minority action can have a deleterious effect upon prevalent values. Who then becomes the protector of the majority?

II

The story of how public recantation by certain members of the Gobitis majority made possible reconsideration of the issues there presented has often been told. In West Virginia State Board of Education v. Barnette [11] the Court reversed itself within the short space of three years and held that participation in patriotic exercises could not be exacted from Jehovah's Witnesses, for their religious freedom would be infringed thereby. The majority opinion was written by a new appointee to the Court, Justice Robert Jackson, who had not participated in the Gobitis case. Although the Court's opinion necessarily dealt with freedom of religion as guaranteed by the First and Fourteenth Amendments, Justice Jackson felt warranted in dealing at some length with the symbolism contention that had come up in the first litigation. Contrary to the dissenting opinion of Justice Stone, Jackson met Frankfurter on his own ground and concluded with the thought that "A person gets from a symbol the meaning he puts into it, and what is one man's comfort and inspiration is another's jest and scorn." [12]

Justice Frankfurter's answer to Jackson was framed to meet the objections raised.

We are told that symbolism is a dramatic but primitive way of communicating ideas. Symbolism is inescapable. Even the most sophisticated live by symbols. But it is not for this Court to make

[11] 319 U.S. 624 (1943).
[12] *Ibid.*, p. 633.

psychological judgments as to the effectiveness of a particular symbol in inculcating concededly indispensable feelings, particularly if the state happens to see fit to utilize the symbol that represents our heritage and our hopes. And surely only flippancy could be responsible for the suggestion that constitutional validity of a requirement to salute our flag implies equal validity of a requirement to salute a dictator. The significance of a symbol lies in what it represents. To reject the swastika does not imply rejection of the Cross. And so it bears repetition to say that it mocks reason and denies our whole history to find in the allowance of a requirement to salute our flag on fitting occasions the seeds of sanction for obeisance to a leader.[13]

This is Justice Frankfurter's basic position. It is now necessary to go back and examine some of the external circumstances surrounding the case.

Arguments before the Court were held on March 11, 1943, and the decision was handed down on June 14. The importance of the Barnette decision for all members of the Court made them hesitant to undertake rapid composition and it certainly exaggerated Justice Frankfurter's tendency to weigh carefully all factors before putting any thoughts down on paper. Adverse reaction to and misunderstanding of his Gobitis decision made precision of statement here even more crucial. For this reason, his initial statement of position is of more than passing interest. This opening sentence of his Barnette opinion has probably been quoted as often as any taken from recent Court writings: "One who belongs to the most vilified and persecuted minority in history is not likely to be insensible to the freedoms guaranteed by our Constitution."[14]

Justice Frankfurter was convinced that the opening was appropriate to the issues under consideration. He apparently felt under a compulsion to answer attacks from various quarters about the relation between his Jewish background and his position in the Gobitis case, a position that supposedly allowed religious or minority persecution.[15] Perhaps partially clarifying Justice

[13] *Ibid.*, p. 662.

[14] *Ibid.*, p. 646.

[15] See Hollis Barber, "Religious Liberty v. Police Power," *American Political Science Review*, XLI (April, 1947), pp. 226–47; Edward Corwin, "The Supreme

Frankfurter's reference to his background and perhaps partially elaborating on his reference to a "vilified and persecuted minority," the Justice the year after the Barnette decision was rendered, in a memoriam to Chaim Weizmann, appraised his own Jewish heritage.

> . . . neither full devotion to the country of one's allegiance nor the esteem of the Gentile world call for truculence or timidity from a Jew. If only he be secure in the citadel of self-respect a Jew will walk erect, with humility as becomes every human and with fortifying but quiet pride as becomes every inheritor of a great past.[16]

Like Jehovah's Witnesses, the Jews were a minority group. For both, however, conforming with generalized regulations could not be turned into religious persecution. Speaking from the vantage point of his own background, Justice Frankfurter knew that minorities, as minorities, did not have to take umbrage at social regulations. Some of them at least had enough self-assurance to blend with the majority on many points.

Since judges in their official capacity were "neither Jew nor Gentile, neither Catholic nor agnostic," and since all of them had "equal attachment to the Constitution" and were "equally bound by . . . judicial obligations," [17] the only way to distinguish the approaches that were being taken was to examine them as parts of the jurist's larger philosophy. Jurists were not to be influenced *merely* by the pressures of the day, but they could not be oblivious to the realities of modern existence. It was correct for the popularly elected branches of government to reflect as adequately as possible changing public temper. But, in Mr. Dooley's idiom, when "th' Supreme Court follows th' illiction returns," it is really forsaking its primary tasks. The longer-range view given members of the judiciary through their per-

---

Court as National School Board," *Law and Contemporary Problems,* xiv (Winter, 1949), 3–18; Charles Nixon, "Freedom v. Unity," *Political Science Quarterly,* lxviii (March, 1953), 70–88.

[16] Felix Frankfurter, "Chaim Weizmann," in Philip Elman (ed.), *Of Law and Men* (New York: Harcourt, Brace & Co., 1956), p. 353.

[17] West Virginia State Board of Education v. Barnette, 319 U.S. 624, 646–47 (1943).

manent appointments should infuse a sense of responsibility for respecting the continuing values of our civilization. One of these values is legislative competence and another is adherence to the symbolic traditions of our nation as captured in the flag, national anthem, and other normative transmitters of deeper feeling. These two considerations coalesced in Justice Frankfurter's opinion.

His Barnette opinion has been variously described as: "the manifesto of the latitudinarian attitude toward the constitution;" [18] "a remarkable personal testimonial," which indicated deep emotional involvement; [19] "a great democratic document." [20] Commentators, both favorable and unfavorable, seem to agree that Justice Frankfurter's basic vision of producing a united nation was noble. His insistence that the Court alone could not provide leadership in tolerance was also acceptable. Where disagreement came was over the question of how far symbols could project underlying community values without at the same time disrupting unique patterns of behavior of certain groups. As was true after the Gobitis decision, prominent individuals divided over the answer. From retirement, former Chief Justice Hughes broke a self-imposed rule of not commenting on current cases and wrote to Frankfurter congratulating him on his stand. He thought that although Jackson had written a strong opinion for the majority, Frankfurter's dissenting opinion was quite powerful and represented the line of reasoning that would have been pursued by Cardozo, Brandeis, and Holmes. In short, the Court had gone astray and the dissenters had all the better of the argument.[21]

Admittedly, the flag is an esoteric symbol. Justice Jackson was probably right in saying that one gets out of a symbol what one puts into it. For Justice Frankfurter the legislatures requiring a

[18] Charles Curtis, *Lions Under the Throne* (Boston: Houghton Mifflin Co., 1947), p. 318.

[19] Alpheus T. Mason, *The Supreme Court from Taft to Warren* (Baton Rouge: Louisiana State University Press, 1958), p. 143.

[20] Arthur Schlesinger, Jr., "The Supreme Court: 1947," *Fortune,* xxxv (January, 1947), 206.

[21] Hughes to Frankfurter, June 17, 1943. Quoted in Merlo J. Pusey, *Charles Evans Hughes* (New York: The Macmillan Co., 1951), ii, 729.

flag salute had something definite in mind when they turned
to this medium for expressing inexpressible thoughts. The year
after the Barnette decision was rendered, he delivered a speech
"On Being an American" in which the following poem was
quoted:

> I am not the flag, not at all. I am its shadow.
> I am whatever you make me nothing more. . . .
> I swing before your eyes as a bright gleam of color, a symbol of
> yourself, the pictured suggestion of that big thing which makes
> this nation. My stars and my stripes are your dreams and your
> labor. They are bright with cheer, brilliant with courage, firm with
> faith, because you have made them so out of your hearts. For
> you are the makers of the flag and it is well that you glory in
> the making.[22]

Justice Frankfurter's quotation of this poem and the sentiments
expressed therein do more to explain his position in the Gobitis
and Barnette cases than any further analysis could do. As with
symbols that may capture the essence of a thought without
articulating it, so poetry may more truly express deep feelings,
which sound self-conscious in prose.

In an evaluation of the two flag salute cases two distinct questions arise. Initially the determination must be made whether
symbolism as such should have a role to play in constitutional
interpretation. Today, as a result of much of our cultural heritage,
to take a speculative approach to problems is often looked at
slightly askance. Even in analyses of the work of the Supreme
Court itself, statistical verification of trends and voting patterns
has taken the spotlight from the more inexact theoretical perspective. We are in a period when "exact" truth is sought at all
costs. Thus the tendency to make rights absolute and constitutional terms fully defined. At such times symbols are considered
mere make-believes, which distort the truth. Much of the aversion to Justice Frankfurter's mention of symbols stems from this
present insistence on reason and reason alone as being an adequate guide for constitutional interpretation.

---

[22] Poem by Franklin K. Lane, quoted in Felix Frankfurter, "On Being An American," *Survey Graphic*, xxxiii (June, 1944), 310. Cf. Felix Frankfurter, "Immigrant
in the United States," *Survey Graphic*, xxviii (February, 1939), 148.

But there is something to be said for the other side. Many years ago Judge Joseph C. Hutcheson suggested that pure rationalism had to be supplemented by "the judgment intuitive," [23] if the law was to be responsive to societal needs. Likewise, legislative feeling that many of the traditional values of our society cannot be encompassed within strictly rational limits but may be captured more fully by symbols also shows an awareness that many avenues are open to the approach of social problems. One is inclined to believe, therefore, that although legal reasoning must be based largely on positive grounds other areas of human perception cannot be totally discounted in arriving at final decisions. They cannot be made to take the place of logical inductive reasoning, but neither can they be pushed to the side as mystical remnants of the past no longer valid for contemporary thinking.

If one were to agree that constitutional interpretation has some room for symbolic representation, a second question still remains to be answered. Was the use made by Justice Frankfurter of this concept warranted in the Gobitis and Barnette cases? Was there any correlation between paying respect to the flag as symbol and the external governmental creed that it purportedly represented? Surely the answer would have to be yes, that there is a definite relationship in the minds of most people between paying respect to the flag and respect for the principles of government that make our social unity possible. Critics of Justice Frankfurter are correct in their insistence that national unity, freedom, and security may be independent of the flag: "To forget this fact is to risk falling into dangerous formalism; it is to confuse the symbol with the thing symbolized; the shadow with the reality; flag saluting with patriotism . . . ." [24] It would indeed turn reality into shadow to suggest that patriotism could *only* be induced through a salute or the recital of a creed. But this is not the main point of contention in the flag salute cases. There was no suggestion that the Jehovah's Witnesses who refused to participate were necessarily unpatriotic. The position taken was that paying

[23] Joseph C. Hutcheson, "The Judgment Intuitive," *Cornell Law Quarterly*, xiv (April, 1929), 274–88.

[24] Francis H. Heller, "A Turning Point for Religious Freedom," *Virginia Law Review*, xxix (January, 1943), 451.

respect to the flag as a symbol was *one* way in which social co-hesion and national feeling could be prompted. It was the legis-lative judgment that generalized regulations employing sym-bolic techniques should be valid for everyone in the public schools. It was with this judgment that Justice Frankfurter agreed. As he pithily explained it: "To deny the power to em-ploy educational symbols is to say that the state's educational system may not stimulate imagination because this may lead to unwise stimulation." [25] The flag as symbol may be anathema to Jehovah's Witnesses, but there are doubtless countless other symbols used in the schools to transmit knowledge that if pressed to extremes could be said to impinge upon some religious doc-trine. To forbid the use of any generalized controversial symbol would be to hamper seriously the educational process.

Group interests bulk large in the Justice's philosophy. This orientation tends to make him sensitive to "social engineering" and a good deal of sociological thinking. Alfred North White-head has said that "the successful adaptation of old symbols to changes of social structure is the final mark of wisdom in socio-logical statemanship." [26] At the time when the flag salute de-cisions were handed down, the social structure of the United States was undergoing profound change. The external pressures of a world in chaos joined with the internal turmoil of a nation mobilizing to fight for its very existence meant at least that some steadying influences were needed. Much of sociological jurisprudence is an attempt to reconcile social control through the ethical customs and moral sense of the community with so-cial control through law. The school boards of Pennsylvania and West Virginia were attempting this reconciliation by reflecting community values in the regulations that they promulgated. All social relations are possible only because some principles and precepts are postulated. The principles that the school boards fol-lowed were of a symbolic nature as captured in the flag salute.

For someone who thinks in terms of group pressures and the importance of public education, the picture of a group of peo-

[25] West Virginia State Board of Education v. Barnette, 319 U.S. 624, 662 (1943).
[26] Alfred North Whitehead, *Symbolism, Its Meaning and Effect* (New York: The Macmillan Co., 1927), p. 61.

ple forcing their way into the public schools on their own terms was inhospitably received. Beyond the encouragement that would thus be given for groups to use pressure tactics in seeking their own way, perhaps to the disadvantage of the public interest, the good order and welfare of the other children in the classroom were also at stake when exemptions were made. Justice Frankfurter intimated that the Supreme Court also had responsibility for the Ninety and Nine who were not Jehovah's Witnesses. Thus in weighing social interests, the fact that one group is numerically superior does not mean that it necessarily is the oppressor.

Many years ago before it was fashionable to attribute so much importance to individual jurist's idiosyncrasies, Thomas Reed Powell noted that constitutional interpretation, especially that part of it which dealt with state police powers, was "to a very large extent the task of weighing competing practical considerations and forming a practical judgment." [27] Normally the decision must rest on the question, not whether there was any deprivation of liberty or property, but whether the deprivation was reasonable or arbitrary. In the flag salute cases this was exactly the type of practical judgment Justice Frankfurter was trying to make. Given the purposes for which the school board's orders were issued and given the fact that symbols could transmit social values, his findings that no unreasonable interference with the religious freedom of the Jehovah's Witnesses came through saluting the flag followed logically.

III

The symbols that attract Justice Frankfurter are national in character. By this is meant that they have an appeal to an overwhelming portion of the population, and the appeal is not made on the basis of social, economic, or religious factors. For those within labor unions or chambers of commerce, these organizations may have real symbolic meaning, but the meaning is largely intelligible only to the membership, and that membership is itself

[27] Thomas Reed Powell, "The Logic and Rhetoric of Constitutional Law," *Journal of Philosophy, Psychology and Scientific Method,* xv (1918), 654.

limited by very definite narrow economic or social interests. It
is in attempting to overcome the radiations of this narrowness
that social unity is attained and attained more easily by the invocation of truly national aspirations. Although labor unions
might be national in the sense that their membership spans the
country, they are not national in the sense in which public education is a really country-wide concern, even though its particular manifestations are controlled by local authorities.

While national awareness of the symbolic difference between
a flag as a unifying element and a labor union or a chamber of
commerce is easily discernible, Justice Frankfurter apparently
believes that in the realm of primary and secondary education,
the symbolic difference for the nation between public schools
and the same two types of economic organizations is just as
pronounced. On the level of higher education in colleges and
universities the symbol becomes that of "academic freedom." It
is a national preoccupation for him that the institutions that are
producing our future leaders—leaders of all segments and sections of our people—should be able to proceed with their role
as producers of men and women capable of dealing with the
intricacies of social unity. In the flag salute cases our attention
was, of course, primarily centered on the national banner. Secondarily, however, the role of the public school and education
in general had to be touched upon. This latter focus becomes
central in other cases.

In one such instance Justice Frankfurter joined in the dissenting opinion against the Court's holding that New Jersey's statute
providing for the reimbursement out of public funds to parents
for transportation expenses incurred in sending their children to
private or sectarian schools did not constitute an "establishment
of religion." [28] Since he did not write in this case, it is very difficult to appraise his exact reaction, except to say that his vote
indicated at least apprehension over the mixing of public and
private school educational matters. In McCollum v. Board of
Education [29] Justice Frankfurter set forth at length the con-

[28] Everson v. Board of Education, 330 U.S. 1 (1947).

[29] 333 U.S. 203 (1948). For a discussion of the Everson & McCollum cases, see
Loren Berth, "The Wall of Separation and the Supreme Court," *Minnesota Law
Review*, xxxviii (February, 1954), 215–27.

siderations that seemed to him especially pertinent for understanding the public school system. The majority held that an Illinois statute providing for a released-time program for religious instruction, in which the physical and personnel facilities of the public schools were utilized, violated the constitutional prohibition against establishment of religion.

Justice Frankfurter's concurring statement is primarily a recital of his belief in the characteristics of the public school. He described it as being "at once the symbol of our democracy and the most pervasive means for promoting our common destiny." [30] In the flag salute cases Justice Frankfurter's main concern seemed to be that sects should not be able forcibly to infuse their divisiveness into the public school system. In the McCollum case almost the reverse preoccupation became apparent in that the Justice seemed to fear the public schools' voluntarily opening themselves to sectarian differences through their liaison with various religious groups.

> Designed to serve as perhaps the most powerful agency for promoting cohesion among a heterogeneous democratic people, the public school must keep scrupulously free from entanglement in the strife of sects. The preservation of the community from divisive conflicts, of Government from irreconcilable pressures by religious groups, of religion from censorship and coercion however subtly exercised, requires strict confinement of the State to instruction other than religious . . . . [31]

The public school thus joins the flag as "a symbol of our secular unity." Although this companionship could have been foretold from the Gobitis and Barnette decisions, it did not come about without doing violence to some other views expressed therein.

In a commentary on the McCollum decision published soon after its appearance John Courtney Murray found that "Justice Frankfurter is still saying, with Holmes, 'We live by symbols.' Only now the life-giving symbol is not Holmes' flag but Horace Mann's public school." [32] Father Murray was concerned lest the

[30] McCollum v. Board of Education, 333 U.S. 203, 231 (1948).
[31] *Ibid.*, pp. 216–17.
[32] John Courtney Murray, "Law or Prepossessions," *Law and Contemporary Problems,* xiv (Winter, 1949), 37.

symbolism of democratic unity be confined to the public schools, leaving the private schools as rather an anachronism on the American scene. For this reason he denied that Frankfurter's operative concepts of symbolism and group pressure were really valid criteria for the McCollum decision. While one can appreciate Father Murray's concern that private and sectarian schools should occupy a place in the American educational pattern, he seems partially to have misunderstood Justice Frankfurter's motivations.

The Justice has a good deal of pluralist theory interwoven in his philosophy. For this reason it would be impossible for him to deny that various groups within society should have their own facilities for expressing cultural differences. Verily, this pluralist tradition would demand that variations be encouraged so that the social fabric would be strengthened. On the other hand, there are certain composites that represent a fusing of group interests. The public school is one of these and, as such, has itself a different role. Father Murray would have to look long and hard in the McCollum opinion to find any intimation that private or sectarian schools should not be allowed a free existence. He would not have to look very hard to find commitment to the view that society is best served by forbidding the public schools to take over or to aid in the performance of functions properly and constitutionally located elsewhere. To a very large degree the symbolism of democratic unity as found in the public schools is possible because we are a pluralist, heterogeneous nation. To work under these conditions and to make it possible for private or sectarian schools to flourish for those who so desire, the public schools must remain as symbols produced by a system of government where all elements can fuse regardless of race, creed, or nationality.

A more telling and valid criticism of Justice Frankfurter's opinion in the McCollum case stems from his change of position on the question of legislative freedom. In the earlier cases much was made of the fact that local school boards should be allowed a good deal of discretion in working out their programs. In both of the establishment of religion cases, however, he stood on the side of those who would strike down local school plans. Thus two of the premises of the flag salute cases—respect for federalism and judicial self-restraint—seem to have been overlooked or pushed aside. This same thing happened in Zorach v. Clauson [33] in which the Court upheld a New York statute that permitted a released-time program on the ground that no use of public school facilities proper—either physical or personnel—was made. Justice Frankfurter dissented from the holding, once again reiterating many of the points that he had made in the McCollum opinion but also once again voting against a local program.

One further caveat should be entered regarding his comparative performance in the flag salute and released-time cases. In the Barnette case he had written that "The Constitution does not give us greater veto power . . . when dealing with grade school regulations than with college regulations that offend conscience." [34] It would thus appear that differences in age or advancement in training could have no effect on whether the flag salute would be a useful symbolic tool. However, in the McCollum case specific allowance was made for the fact that relatively young children were involved: "The law of imitation operates, and nonconformity is not an outstanding characteristic of children. The obvious result is an obvious pressure upon children to attend." [35] Beyond confusion over the question of whether there is any difference in the rationale for treatment of grade and high school pupils, in contradistinction to more advanced students, one may ask why, if there is an obvious pressure upon children to attend religious instruction, the same pressure would not have evidenced itself with regard to Jehovah's Witnesses and flag-saluting and with the same supposed deleterious effect?

Before leaving the restricted area of the symbolic relation between religious freedom and public education, a typical parallel with other cases concerning religious freedoms may be noted. In Saia v. New York [36] the Court was asked to decide whether a municipal ordinance that prohibited the use of sound devices on the public streets except with the permission of the chief of police was so arbitrary as to constitute an abridgment of freedom of

[33] 343 U.S. 306 (1952).

[34] West Virginia State Board of Education v. Barnette, 319 U.S. 624, 648 (1943).

[35] McCollum v. State Board of Education, 333 U.S. 203, 217 (1948).

[36] 334 U.S. 558 (1948). Cf. Edward Cramer, "The Saia and Kovacs Cases," *Cornell Law Quarterly*, xxxiv (Summer, 1949), 626–32.

speech and, in the particular case, freedom of religion, since the equipment was being used for a religious lecture. The majority held that such an abridgment had taken place. Justice Frankfurter dissented. His insistence that religious discussion cannot be foisted upon the general public fits in with his positions in the Gobitis and Barnette cases that minority groups cannot force their way into public schools on their own terms. It also conforms with his position in the McCollum case that pressures for religious instruction cannot be allowed to disrupt community patterns or to threaten the national symbolic value of public education for all, irrespective of race, religion, or nationality.

IV

In the period after World War II a plethora of acts appeared on the statute books having as their purpose the protection of internal security through loyalty oaths and other such means to elicit information about membership in or association with subversive organizations. The teaching profession because of its sensitive role in being able to transmit values and ideals to young people was often covered by such requirements. Inquiring into a teacher's associations often meant inquiring into the philosophies that he held and the types of approaches he would take in teaching. The issue of academic freedom was thus raised as were questions about the aims of education in presenting controversial materials to student groups. Added to this one set of problems were others dealing with the gradual diminution and final disappearance of the doctrine of "separate but equal" from constitutional law in general and from educational matters in particular. Justice Frankfurter, as a staunch supporter of public schools and as a sincere believer in education as the prime means whereby advancements in civilization can be made, spoke out on many of these matters. It was necessary for him to do so, for his view of the national symbolic value of education, as represented by both public schools and academic freedom, was not second to his treatment of patriotic exercises as unifying elements for a heterogeneous people.

In a series of cases dealing with the right of states to foreclose the teaching profession to persons who were identified in some manner with a subversive organization, Justice Frankfurter voted consistently for the individual's right to teach.[37] These votes were predicated on both jurisdictional and procedural grounds, largely leaving in abeyance the substantive issue as to whether knowledgeably holding and advocating subversive doctrine would disqualify a person as an instructor of youth. This very real issue only came to the fore in Sweezy v. New Hampshire,[38] which contains the most important discussion on academic freedom to be found in recent Court history. Under authorization from the state legislature the Attorney General of the state undertook to question Paul Sweezy about the contents of a lecture delivered at the University of New Hampshire and about his connections with the Progressive Party of America. In the light of the record the Supreme Court held that both types of inquiries violated due process of law. Chief Justice Warren delivered the opinion of the Court and made an impassioned plea for academic freedom. "To impose any strait jacket upon the intellectual leaders in our colleges and universities," he wrote, would be to "imperil the future of our Nation." [39]

Justice Frankfurter many years previously in a commencement address at Radcliffe College had told his audience that "our colleges and universities are the distinctive product of what we cherish as western civilization. They shelter and bring to fruit the purposes which must be . . . the ideals and the pursuits of the whole world if civilization is to maintain itself." [40] He has been a frequent speaker at university events, and the theme that he often pursues is the urgency of maintaining the university as the cradle of free inquiry and the symbol of civilized progress. In the Sweezy case he concurred in the result reached by the Court, although he was unable to agree that this could be based on questioning the scope of the authorizing statute, since this was a state

[37] Adler v. Board of Education, 342 U.S. 485 (1952); Wieman v. Updegraff, 344 U.S. 183 (1952); Slochower v. Board of Education, 350 U.S. 551 (1956).

[38] 354 U.S. 234 (1957).

[39] *Ibid.*, p. 250.

[40] Felix Frankfurter, "The Worth of Our Past," *Vital Speeches,* vii (July 15, 1941), 601.

question and had been decided differently by the state courts. In any event, lecturer Sweezy had been subjected to a violation of academic and political freedom. This was enough to void the proceedings. On this issue he was fully in accord with the Court, and his concurring opinion was also an eloquent defense of university autonomy.

> For society's good—if understanding be an essential need of society—inquiries into . . . problems, speculations about them, stimulation in others of reflection upon them, must be left as unfettered as possible. Political power must abstain from intrusion into this activity of freedom, pursued in the interest of wise government and the people's well-being, except for reasons that are exigent and obviously compelling.[41]

A free society is dependent upon free universities, and this means the exclusion of intervention in the academic affairs of a university. Justice Frankfurter's philosophy of a free education, in the sense of education unhampered by political or religious influences, was most fully articulated in the Sweezy decision. The role of the universities and the independence of teachers form an integral part of this philosophy of symbols uniting a free people. As we shall see, he has strongly rejected the doctrine of preferred freedoms. In the area of education, in the college or university at least, the Justice deviates from this rejection and enshrines politically uncontrolled instruction in the sphere of a "preferred freedom." This deviation is not complete, however, as he has recently agreed that because a person is a teacher does not relieve him of answering questions directly pertinent to an investigation that has been duly authorized and carefully delimited.[42]

In the area of desegregation all the cases leading up to the epic Brown v. Board of Education decision [43] were unanimous, with the Chief Justice delivering the opinion. Justice Frankfurter remained silent in the majority when the Court struck down attempts to provide for segregation in law schools [44] and state uni-

[41] Sweezy v. New Hampshire, 354 U.S. 234, 261–62 (1957).
[42] Barenblatt v. United States, 360 U.S. 109 (1959).
[43] 347 U.S. 483 (1954).
[44] Sipuel v. University of Oklahoma, 332 U.S. 631 (1948) and Sweatt v. Painter, 339 U.S. 629 (1950).

versities.[45] It was not until the hearings on the Little Rock, Arkansas, school situation in September, 1958, that he broke silence and wrote the first concurring opinion to come from any of the justices in these cases. This was not the only precedent-breaking feature. In the unanimous opinion that was handed down, refusing further delay in integration, the Court followed a procedure unknown in its history by listing in order of seniority all justices of the Court and indicating their adherence to the policy adopted, both individually and collectively.[46] Justice Frankfurter's action was not as laudatory as the Court's, for his opinion did little to add to our fund of knowledge on the subject. He did not even disagree with the reasoning of his brethren. What he had to say, however, increases somewhat our understanding of his own personal position.

Looking back to the released time cases, Professor Louis Jaffe explained Frankfurter's position in the following manner: "His fear is not of authority but of the breakdown of authority, of the letting loose upon society of the dread war of each against each. . . . a mature judge is one who has outgrown fear of authority, who knows its value and can in good conscience wield it." [47] The explanation for Justice Frankfurter's opinion in the Little Rock case is to be found in Jaffe's analysis. In his search for social unity the Justice is anxious to emphasize the dire results that might ensue from disrespect of the law. When this disrespect is conjoined with disruption of educational processes, processes that are themselves symbolic of the wider, deeper unity in our social polity, the Justice cannot restrain himself. Force must be authorized to meet force. Fundamentally, "violent resistance to law cannot be made a legal reason for its suspension without loosening the fabric of our society." [48]

From the time of the Gobitis and Barnette cases the themes of social cohesion and symbolism have resounded in Justice Frankfurter's opinions. The flag as symbol was one of the early manifestations of his belief that the perduring values of a civilization

[45] McLaurin v. Oklahoma State Regents, 335 U.S. 637 (1950).

[46] Cooper v. Aaron, 358 U.S. 1 (1958).

[47] Louis Jaffe, "The Judicial World of Mr. Justice Frankfurter," *Harvard Law Review,* LXII (January, 1949), 410.

[48] Cooper v. Aaron, 358 U.S. 20, 22 (1958).

can be transmitted in many ways. Through public schools and universities the accommodations that are necessary to preserve basic understanding in a diverse nation can be worked out. But this accommodation will be possible only as long as these institutions are unhampered by religious or political control and are staffed by teachers unafraid to speak their thoughts. Even as to desegregation, "experience attests that such local habits and feelings will yield, gradually though this be, to law and education." [49] It is here that the Court can give some leadership in seeing that group pressures and group interests are compromised so that in the end we will attain a common consensus and a common understanding of our problems.

[49] *Ibid.*, p. 25.

IV

Group Conflict in Modern Society

A good deal of interest in this century has centered on the individual, his rights and responsibilities in modern society. Paralleling this interest, but perhaps not quite so pronounced until recent years, has been the attempt to evaluate the role of groups within a community. The great proliferation of organized group action in the economic field—labor unions, chambers of commerce, retailing associations—and in the noneconomic fields—National Association for the Advancement of Colored People, Polish Alliance—indicates that in many instances the individual in a complex technological age is only able to express himself through an identification with others of like needs and desires. The individual is protected by the group and restrained by it. Groups, then, become the real loci of power within society and in their clashes lies much of the explanation for the tensions of our time, tensions that may become articulate in litigation. It is in the working out of adjustments that the majoritarian elements in Justice Frankfurter's philosophy become evident. Instead of the traditional emphasis on the individual as the basic unit of representation, culminating in a coalescence of wills that can be majoritarian, he utilizes a social, in the sense of nonindividualist, approach. Groups as organic entities become the basic unit for representation. Majoritarianism results, but it is majoritarianism of a different type.

Just as individual rights were created largely to foster social interest in general security, so group rights are the modern counterpart of efforts to maintain social cohesion. Often underemphasized or completely overlooked is the fact that in both instances, rights entail duties. Justice Frankfurter would probably choose as a guiding thought Justice Brandeis' declaration that "All rights are derived from the purposes of the society in which they exist; above all rights rises duty to the community." [1] It is easy for governing bodies representative of economic or political interests to forget the fact that society as a whole must be given some consideration. If these interests are symbols, they are symbols only to a restricted group. It is also easy for minority groups, simply because they are minorities, to insist upon freedom of action, which could prove disruptive in the larger context of community living. Certainly dissent and efforts to persuade others to join their cause must be allowed minorities, but not to the point where the majority is foreclosed from ruling in a peaceful, nondiscriminating manner. The group nature of modern society and the conflicts to which it has given rise exaggerate the need for a feeling of responsibility on the part of each and every individual as citizen and as a member of numerous organized and unorganized bodies. It also means that the state or national government, and particularly the judiciary, must make sure that arbitrary power, whether lodged in groups or in the government itself, does not check freedom.

I

Group conflicts are often most forcefully demonstrated in the area of civil rights. Here "societal self-restraint" must be exercised

[1] Duplex Printing Press Co. v. Deering et al., 254 U.S. 443, 488 (1921).

if the miscellaneous crowd that makes up the nation is to be turned into a smoothly running community. Since one of the most vociferous minorities demanding privileges and protection has been the Jehovah's Witnesses, it is in cases involving this group that Supreme Court discussion of group freedom in the context of societal living has come. It is also in these cases that the Court has had to differentiate group rights from group license.

Beginning in the late 1930's the Supreme Court repeatedly had to determine whether Jehovah's Witnesses could be made to comply with generalized regulations enacted by states and municipalities in furtherance of community policies, mostly in the realm of health and general welfare. Many of these regulations required a license before certain activities could be undertaken—selling magazines through street-corner or house-to-house soliciting, holding public meetings or making speeches in public parks, using amplifying devices. The position of Justice Frankfurter throughout this period was that when religious activities spread into the public domain they lost their immunity and had to meet the obligations that the community created for all and sundry. The public is often called upon to provide extra services in the form of police protection, street cleaning, etc. To require the payment of a license fee or the obtaining of a permit had nothing at all to do with interference with religious matters. It is merely stipulating that each segment of society pay its own way or that it abide by conditions thought necessary for the general welfare. Justice Frankfurter has not questioned tax immunity for religious or philanthropic organizations on the use of their own buildings and resources, although even here sanitary and health standards must be met, pleas of religious freedom to the contrary notwithstanding. What he has really objected to in the licensing and permit cases has been placing one group in a preferred position vis-à-vis society as a whole. In sum, "the constitutional protection of religious freedom terminated disabilities, it did not create new privileges. . . . Its essence is freedom from conformity to religious dogma, not freedom from conformity to law because of religious dogma." [2]

While religious minorities cannot shirk their responsibilities, neither can the community that shelters them act in such an arbi-

[2] West Virginia State Board of Education v. Barnette, 319 U.S. 624, 653 (1943).

trary manner as to make compliance with regulations impossible. Thus Justice Frankfurter joined in striking down a conviction of a Witness who had attempted to get a permit so that a meeting could be held in a public park but who had been refused by municipal authorities in exercise of a power derived, not from a statute or ordinance, but from a local practice containing no standards.[3] The meeting was held anyway, but since no disorder, threats or violence, or riot became evident, the conviction was invalid. Where, however, a city council under authority from a valid enactment wrongfully refused to grant the license requested, a conviction for holding the meeting in disregard of this refusal has been upheld, with Justice Frankfurter concurring.[4] In other like cases he has voted that an administrative official cannot simply refuse a permit without stating the reasons, and that a refusal based on past conduct in ridiculing and denouncing other religious beliefs was insufficient reason.[5]

In their proselytizing activities, Jehovah's Witnesses have encountered other general ordinances that have seemed to them obstacles in spreading their message. One such ordinance made it unlawful for anyone distributing literature to ring a doorbell or otherwise summon the residents to the door for the purpose of receiving such literature. On the surface this might seem arbitrary—as a matter of fact it did to a majority of the Supreme Court [6]—until it is understood that the ordinance was passed by a town, many of whose residents were engaged in war work, often on the night shift, whose needed hours of rest were thus being disturbed. The problem then resolved itself into weighing the social interests—not, let it be emphasized, the religious ones —of the workers and the Witnesses. The town came down on the side of the workers, but the Court did not, bringing the dissenting comment from Justice Frankfurter that "the Due Process Clause of the Fourteenth Amendment did not abrogate the power of the states to recognize that homes are sanctuaries from intrusions upon privacy and of opportunities for leading

[3] Niemotko v. Maryland, 340 U.S. 268 (1951).
[4] Poulos v. New Hampshire, 345 U.S. 395 (1953).
[5] Kunz v. New York, 340 U.S. 290 (1951).
[6] Martin v. Struthers, 319 U.S. 141 (1943).

lives of health and safety." [7] His aversion to intrusions upon privacy was manifested at the end of the last chapter. There, not only could a person be assaulted in his own home, but also in the depths of his personality through the "oral aggression" of messages being blurted out through loud-speakers. No escape was possible. Justice Frankfurter voted, therefore, for restraint of these devices so that reasonable use could be made of their potentialities without entirely disrupting the peace and quiet of the rest of the community.

Concededly, because of their activities, the Witnesses have engendered antipathy from many sources. Their violent and vituperative attacks on other denominations, especially the Roman Catholic Church, have done little to endear them to vast portions of the population. Irrespective of whether Witnesses show enough good sense to restrain themselves, the Court has on more than one occasion protected their right to speak and their access to communities in which to speak. Justice Frankfurter concurred in striking down a state regulation that would have permitted the managers of a company town to warn the Witnesses away. While title to property was regulated by state law, state law could not "control issues of civil liberties which arise primarily because a company town is a town as well as a congerie of property relations." [8] Communities as well as groups have responsibilities.

To say merely that Justice Frankfurter weighs social interests in cases of the nature we have been discussing is to say very little. What seems to be the distinguishing factor is the degree to which groups are willing to work within the bounds of community behavior patterns that have evolved solely for the purpose of making community life possible at all. Order and discipline, while uncongenial to many spirits, are necessary ingredients in any social arrangement. Certain sacrifices are required of all participants. When the incidence of order and discipline do not fall upon a particular group based only on the nature of the group itself, then exemptions from general standards are hard to justify. Thus in a slightly different field, al-

[7] *Ibid.*, p. 153.
[8] Marsh v. Alabama, 326 U.S. 501 (1946).

though governed by the same considerations, Justice Frankfurter has held that no constitutional rights were violated by requiring labor organizers to conform with state regulations that
they register, along with other solicitors, before beginning their
campaigns for members.[9] On some occasions statutes may be
designed to remedy the specific evil flowing from a specific disregard of community welfare—ringing doorbells and awakening
workers. On the other hand, when it appears that statutes or
ordinances are being designed in a vengeful manner primarily
to halt activities of minorities *qua* minorities, these enactments
must fall.

II

In addition to those instances when definite group demands
must be judged against equally clear social considerations, there
are other circumstances when the community must act to protect
itself against disruptive forces that cannot be identified with
any particular group but that are, nevertheless, very real. Publication of literature harmful to public morals, exhibitions of
lewd or obscene movies, speeches that lead to riot or disorder,
and, last, but not least, defamation of one portion of the population by another. Those agencies of modern life such as the
press, radio, and television that devote their energies to dissemi-
nating ideas and ideals should at least feel some responsibility
for the quality of their performance. They should attempt to
add to community welfare, not dissipate it. The circumstances of
modern living, where group tensions are apt to be high, call for
dispelling prejudice rather than arousing it. At times, therefore,
states and communities might have to act to protect their over-all
interests from irresponsible forces.

In the massive cities, where the rise in juvenile delinquency
and crimes of violence have been phenomenal, city authorities
are warranted in prohibiting the publication of criminal news
that centers attention on lust and bloodshed. They could reasona-

[9] See Thomas v. Collins, 323 U.S. 516 (1945) and Hill v. Florida, 325 U.S. 538
(1945).

bly think, based on psychological and sociological studies, that this was one means whereby crimes might be curtailed. Not all criminal news need be prohibited. Obviously, an exercise of judgment must be made, but this is the task of the local authorities based on their own experience. "Unlike the abstract stuff of mathematics, or the quantitatively ascertainable elements of much natural science, legislation is greatly concerned with the multiform psychological complexities of individual and social conduct. Accordingly, the demands upon legislation, and its responses, are variable and multiform." [10] Thus, in other places and under other compulsions, city or state attempts to curtail publications on the basis that their sale might be detrimental to juveniles, but not to adults, would not be acceptable.[11] As with magazines or newspapers, the compact nature of modern communities must be taken into consideration before any final decision can be made regarding the suitability of particular films for particular locales. Heterogeneous New York city might have to be governed differently from rural Iowa.[12]

Beginning with Chaplinsky v. New Hampshire [13] the Court has handled a series of cases in which it has had to determine the range of decency within which speech must operate if it is to be allowed. Speech leading to a breach of the peace could not be lightly suffered by any community. Its interests were as immediate in preventing such an occurrence as were the supposed interests of a person to say anything he wished. This point was emphasized by Justice Frankfurter, dissenting from the Court's holding in Terminiello v. Chicago.[14] Terminiello, a defrocked priest, so inflamed a crowd surrounding the auditorium in which he was speaking that rocks were hurled, windows broken, and general mayhem prevented only by police action. Justice Douglas for the Court held, however, that the statute under which Terminiello was convicted, while aimed primarily at rioting, breach of the peace, or conduct tending to breach of the peace,

[10] Winters v. New York, 333 U.S. 507, 524–25 (1948).

[11] See Butler v. Michigan, 352 U.S. 380 (1957) and Kingsley Books v. Brown, 354 U.S. 436 (1957).

[12] See Burstyn v. Wilson, 343 U.S. 495 (1952).

[13] 315 U.S. 568 (1942).

[14] 337 U.S. 1 (1949).

could not be used against a speech stirring people to anger, inviting public dispute, or bringing about a condition of unrest. To this Justice Frankfurter took exception, thinking the line very thin from the community's point of view between rioting, a condition of unrest, and what occurred on the streets of Chicago.

Very similar in some respects, although different in outcome, was the case of Feiner v. New York.[15] Feiner, a University of Syracuse student, was haranguing a mixed crowd of Negroes and whites from a street corner, urging colored people vigorously to assert their rights. Traffic congestion and murmurs of unrest from the crowd prompted the police to request that Feiner terminate his performance. When he refused to do so, the police arrested him, and his subsequent conviction was upheld by the Supreme Court, Justice Frankfurter concurring. On the same day on which this decision was handed down—indeed, Justice Frankfurter's opinion covered both cases—the Court also gave some direction to New York city officials as to the breadth of lenience that should be allowed speakers on its public streets and parks. Once again one of the decisive points for Justice Frankfurter was the degree to which community welfare would be affected. "We must be mindful," he wrote, "of the enormous difficulties confronting those charged with the task of enabling the polyglot millions in the City of New York to live in peace and tolerance. Street preaching in Columbus Circle is done in a milieu quite different from preaching on a New England village green." [16] Because the milieu is different and because peace and tolerance are fundamentally necessary in a community with the unique characteristics of New York, the malign as well as benign effects of speeches must be considered.

The case of Beauharnais v. Illinois [17] occupies an unequaled position in American jurisprudence since it represents the first occasion on which the Supreme Court accepted a theory of group

[15] 340 U.S. 315 (1951). For a discussion of this case in particular see Lenamyra Saulson, "Municipal Control of Public Streets," *Michigan Law Review*, XLIX (June, 1951), 1185–99, and the problem in general, Elliott Richardson, "Freedom of Expression and the Function of Courts," *Harvard Law Review*, LXV (November, 1951), 1–54.

[16] Niemotko v. Maryland, 340 U.S. 268, 284 (1951).

[17] 343 U.S. 250 (1952).

libel. Publication of a scurrilous flier depicting all members of the Negro race as rapists, dope addicts, and degenerates initiated the proceedings. Heretofore, the common law of criminal libel had provided no redress against actions of this sort. The opinion of the Court in the Beauharnais case was written by Justice Frankfurter. His acceptance of a state's ability to punish libel of a group points up his acceptance of groups as important entities. While incorporated bodies such as business firms had been able to protect themselves somewhat in the past, unincorporated groups had been very much at the mercy of fate. This was especially true of groups whose binding tie was race, religion, or nationality.

It is not surprising to find Justice Frankfurter taking the lead in initiating protection for these groups against the type of persecution they were suffering. Having spent a good part of his boyhood on New York's lower East Side, he knew the hardships that can accrue to a person because of his heritage. His work with the Zionist organization made him realize the difficulty of integrating diverse groups, and from this work he understood intimately the harm that invective wrought. After World War I on a trip to the Near East to study for Zionist purposes the hostility between Syria and Palestine, he saw the breakdown of amiable relations after a hopeful start caused by misunderstanding and fear.[18] Early in his career, 1916 to be exact, he spoke out for the need for compassion and tolerance.

> When regard is had to the complexities of modern society and the necessary specialization and narrowness of individual experience, the need for tolerance and objectivity in realizing, and then respecting, the validity of the experience and beliefs of others, becomes one of the most dynamic factors in the actual disposition of concrete cases.[19]

As no individual is totally perfect or imperfect, so no group is either totally right or totally wrong. Being a heterogeneous nation, we will display a variety of beliefs and creeds, races, and

---

[18] See *New York Times*, March 4, 1919.
[19] Felix Frankfurter, "The Constitutional Opinions of Mr. Justice Holmes," *Harvard Law Review*, xxix (April, 1916), 686.

nationalities, all entitled to mutual respect not only for themselves but also for the good of the country.

Therefore Justice Frankfurter in the Beauharnais case held for the majority that "if an utterance directed at an individual may be the object of communal sanctions, we cannot deny to a State power to punish the same utterance directed at a defined group, unless we can say that this is a wilful and purposeless restriction unrelated to the peace and well-being of the State." [20] He thought that the Court could say no such thing, although he admitted that there might be other objections to the course being pursued by Illinois, namely that obstinate social issues would not be easily resolved by any legislative reform. No solution for group conflict was going to be perfect. Illinois was making an attempt to lessen the probability of tension through use of group libel laws. It was not for the Court to gainsay this advance, however limited it proved.

Justice Black would have none of this. He thought that the majority opinion degraded First Amendment freedoms to a "rational basis" level. He struck out at Frankfurter's reliance on the noted Chaplinsky precedent, saying that "New Hampshire had a state law making it an offense to direct insulting words at an *individual* on a public street. . . . Whether the words used in their context here are 'fighting' words in the same sense is doubtful, but whether so or not they are not addressed to or about *individuals*." [21] Justice Black's own emphasis on individuals should be contrasted with Justice Frankfurter's concern over groups as the important elements in controversies of this nature. Only Black out of the dissenters in this case refused the idea that states might have power to punish for group libel. This tendency to deal solely with individuals, and to individualize justice, stands in marked contrast to the position of Justice Frankfurter. It will stand out in even starker terms when we consider the approaches of the two men to certiorari policy.

Writing almost a decade before the Illinois statute was brought to the Supreme Court, David Riesman startlingly foreshadowed many of the considerations which were to weigh so heavily with Justice Frankfurter. He concluded that "defamatory attacks on

[20] Beauharnais v. Illinois, 343 U.S. 250, 258 (1952).
[21] *Ibid.*, pp. 272–73.

groups are attacks both on the pluralistic forces which make up a democratic society and derivatively on the individual members whose own status derives from their group affiliations." [22] Riesman went on to warn, however, that if stratification was to be avoided and a dynamic social life retained, groups must be subjected to criticism by other groups and by their own members. Justice Frankfurter's acceptance of a theory of group libel did not mean rejection of this latter point. In old-fashioned terms, he was only agreeing that criticism of one group by another had to be kept within the bounds of decency. Group defamation spreads beyond the immediate group. In our scheme of values, the individual gains status and honor to a large degree based on his associations. Therefore at times it is only by guaranteeing adequate protection to groups that individual reputations may be preserved. The isolated individual feeling helpless in his isolation seeks refuge and strength in group association. To strike at the group of which he is a member in an irresponsible way is to strike at the foundation of much modern society.

In treating of group conflict in the area commonly known as that of civil rights, we have seen Justice Frankfurter urging responsibility on the part of groups toward society and toward one another. When this responsibility is not forthcoming voluntarily, the community may have to act, demanding adherence to generalized regulations or intervening to prevent the break-down of the social order. The pluralist position, which is the basis for Justice Frankfurter's acceptance of groups as organic entities within society, usually stops with recognition of these sub-societies within society as a whole. He carries the position further and asks that the independence attributed to both groups and communities be made the foundation for a greater social unity.

III

In the economic realm we are brought face-to-face with easily identifiable and quite powerful aggregates in the form of

[22] David Riesman, "Democracy and Defamation," *Columbia Law Review,* XLII (November, 1942), 731. Cf. "Group Libel Laws: Abortive Efforts to Combat Hate Propaganda," *Yale Law Journal,* LXI (February, 1952), 252–64.

unions, corporations, management associations, etc. In dealing with giant interests of this nature, two drawbacks immediately present themselves; it is more difficult to protect the individual, however derivatively, and it is more difficult to distinguish between special interests and public interests. The collective demands of a union or corporation made in a collective capacity are often impossible to resist, even though in a wider context society as a whole suffers. Quite perceptively, Thomas A. Cowan has differentiated social interests, those made for the good of the community, from social security interests, those which lay claims against the community for some particular part thereof.[23] It is the social security type of interest that predominates in the economic field, and it is this type that has gained the greatest attention from Justice Frankfurter. Community as represented by government, although this time usually the national government, has to step in through administrative agencies and the courts to prevent undue centralization of power in any of the "private" governments in the economic field, be they those of the teamsters, utilities, railroads, or any other agency that could cause economic imbalance.

Professor Frankfurter before his appointment to the Supreme Court was a noted authority on labor problems and on the labor injunction in particular. He had gained practical experience in this field as chairman of the War Labor Policies Board during World War I. Author of many articles touching the use of the labor injunction, he made his greatest scholarly contribution to the subject by collaborating with Nathan Greene on a volume under that title.[24] When he went on the Court, people recalled his writings and also the fact that he had been identified with some of the New Deal legislation bolstering the legal position of labor. For these reasons he was expected to be wholly pro-labor in orientation. However, those who now profess surprise and chagrin that Frankfurter does not follow the plan of the prophecies—or the prophesiers—were really not too familiar with

[23] Thomas A. Cowan, "The Impact of Social Security on the Philosophy of Law," *Rutgers Law Review,* xi (Summer, 1957), 688–703. Cf. by the same author, "Group Interests," *Virginia Law Review,* xliv (April, 1958), 331–46.

[24] Felix Frankfurter and Nathan Greene, *The Labor Injunction* (New York: The Macmillan Co., 1930).

his writings or with the positions that he had taken on labor questions in the past.

The Labor Injunction itself, although of necessity dealing with detrimental effects of peremptory court orders upon the labor movement, was not designed as a pro-labor tract. The central theme of the book was an examination and criticism of the abuse of judicial power as this became evident in the ways in which courts were using injunctions. Professor Frankfurter was concerned peripherally with labor problems, primarily with those of the judiciary. In writing about the famous Coronado Coal Case of the early 1920's,[25] he said that "complete immunity for all conduct is too dangerous immunity to confer upon any group."[26] The United Mine Workers, after a particularly long and nasty dispute with the owners, were resisting attempts to make them amendable to suit under the Sherman Act. Professor Frankfurter thought the majority of the Court, including Justice Brandeis, an avowed friend of labor, quite right in holding the unions responsible for their actions: "If the union can be brought into court as an entity to pay a printer's bill, by the same procedure the union can be hailed into court to respond to a claim for damages unlawfully caused by it in the course of a strike."[27] The Supreme Court was being realistic in holding that unions, like any other association, could be sued and could sue. Unions *qua* unions, just as religious minorities *qua* religious minorities, could not expect special treatment at the hands of the law.

In emphasizing that Justice Frankfurter was not radically pro-labor in New Deal terms, let it not be intimated that he was anti-labor either. It is simply that since he became a member of the Court his opinions dealing with labor questions do not form any identifiable unit if judged merely on the basis of how often he voted to sustain or negate union claims. His votes have been more or less predicated on his understanding of unions as one type of economic collectivity having rights and duties. Early in his career he emphasized that unions had a very important part

[25] United Mine Workers v. Coronado Coal Co., 259 U.S. 344 (1922).

[26] Felix Frankfurter, "The Coronado Case," *New Republic*, xxxi (July, 1922), 330.

[27] *Ibid.* For a very recent statement of these same views, see International Union, UAA & AIG v. Russell, 356 U.S. 634 (1958).

to play in American life, but they were only a part and not the whole. In 1920 he wrote that "these are not the days of Hans Sachs, the village cobbler and artist, man and meister-singer. We are confronted with mass production and mass producers; the individual, in his industrial relations, but a cog in the great collectivity." [28] Such a collectivity had to find representatives, and it was natural that labor unions should appear to fill such a need. He was even willing to agree that "recognition of the social utility and, indeed, of the necessity of trade unions implies acceptance of the economic and social pressure that can come from united action." [29] This having been said, there still remained the troublesome problem of when and how far such pressure should be exerted. The form of concerted action that he preferred for our system was collective bargaining, not strikes.

IV

Justice Frankfurter has been brutally frank about the nature of unions and unionism as he conceives them.

A union is no more than a medium through which individuals are able to act together; union power was begotten of individual helplessness. But the power can come into being only when, and continue to exist only so long as, individual aims are seen to be shared in common with the other members of the group. There is a natural emphasis, however, on what is shared and a resulting tendency to subordinate the inconsistent interests and impulses of individuals. From this, it is an easy transition to thinking of the union as an entity having rights and purposes of its own.[30]

Justice Frankfurter does not make this transition. Unions do have rights and purposes but only as these are granted by the community in recognition of the fact that in our day and age individual economic man can normally be protected only through

[28] Felix Frankfurter, "Law and Order," *Yale Review*, IV, n.s. (January, 1920), 230.
[29] Felix Frankfurter, "Labor Injunctions and Federal Legislation," *Harvard Law Review*, XLII (April, 1929), 771.
[30] American Federation of Labor v. American Sash and Door Co., 335 U.S. 538, 545 (1949).

the group with which he identifies himself. Labor's long hard-won struggle to gain recognition for itself has been aided immeasurably by the changing climate of public opinion as reflected in legislation. But it is important to remember, however, that such legislation is "to a marked degree, the result of conflict and compromise between strong contending forces and deeply held views on the role of organized labor in the free economic life of the Nation and the appropriate balance to be struck between the uncontrolled power of management and labor to further their respective interests." [31] It is in interpreting such legislation that Justice Frankfurter often displays his deepest insights into the nature of group action.

Thus in United States v. United Mine Workers [32] he agreed with the Court that the restrictions on the issuance of injunctions in labor disputes found in the Clayton and Norris-LaGuardia Acts did not apply to the United States government as an employer. The case grew out of John L. Lewis' conviction for criminal contempt for refusing to be bound by a court order postponing unilateral union termination of an agreement with the Federal Coal Mines Administrator. That the government as protector of the national interest supposedly could not deal with such circumstances seemed utterly incredible to Justice Frankfurter.

> In our country law is not a body of technicalities in the keeping of specialists or in the service of any special interest. There can be no free society without law administered through an independent judiciary. If one man can be allowed to determine for himself what is law, every man can. That means first chaos, then tyranny. Legal process is an essential part of the democratic process. For legal process is subject to democratic control by defined, orderly ways which themselves are part of law. In a democracy, power implies responsibility. The greater the power that defies the law the less tolerant can this Court be of defiance. [33]

Although this paragraph was written over a decade ago it could be applied as is to the actions of Governor Faubus of Arkansas. The same considerations that made Justice Frankfurter speak

---

[31] Local 1976, U.B.C. & J. v. National Labor Relations Board, 357 U.S. 93, 99–100 (1958).

[32] 330 U.S. 258 (1947). Cf. United States v. Petrillo, 332 U.S. 1 (1947).

[33] United States v. United Mine Workers, 330 U.S. 258, 312 (1947).

out against the anarchical implications of the Little Rock situation made him speak out many years ago against allowing any man or union to gain a strangle hold on even a limited portion of our economic life. Whether the individual is John L. Lewis or Jimmy Hoffa, union power is exerted and union responsibility accrues through their actions. Therefore, Frankfurter has held unions liable for the deeds of their officers or agents under the Norris-LaGuardia Act.

On a diversified number of issues Justice Frankfurter has first voted for and then against labor depending upon the type of restriction involved and its importance to the community. He has held that union officials must take the loyalty oath prescribed by the Taft-Hartley Act before federal support for collective bargaining rights would be forthcoming.[34] With the majority he held that the Taft-Hartley prohibition against union contributions to political campaigns was not violated by publication of an article in a dues-supported magazine urging backing for a particular candidate.[35] On the other hand, he wrote the opinion of the Court upholding conviction of a union for using its funds to buy television time in order to influence an election.[36]

Although any division between the nature of unionism as a group activity and the methods of unionism possible because it does involve a group is arbitrary, it has seemed best to distinguish the two for analytical purposes. In the picketing cases there is conjoined not only the group aspects of an economic activity but also civil rights aspects under the First Amendment's guarantee of free speech. Since the New Deal all members of the Court have been willing to admit that picketing is a right that warrants protection under either the First or through the due process clause of the Fourteenth Amendment.[37] With this position Justice Frankfurter is wholly in accord. But as with any other right there are duties, and freedom can be turned into license. Therefore, depending upon the circumstances, some restrictions may

[34] American Communications Association v. Douds, 339 U.S. 382 (1950).
[35] United States v. CIO, 335 U.S. 106 (1948).
[36] United States v. International Union, 352 U.S. 567 (1957).
[37] See Thornhill v. Alabama, 310 U.S. 88 (1940). Cf. Joseph Tanenhaus, "Picketing-Free Speech: The Growth of the New Law of Picketing from 1940 to 1952," *Cornell Law Quarterly*, xxxviii (Fall, 1952), 1–50.

have to be placed by the community upon labor's right to picket, just as Jehovah's Witnesses were obliged to conform to standard social regulations.

In Milk Wagon Drivers v. Meadowmoor Dairies [38] Justice Frankfurter took this view very forcefully. A bitter labor dispute in which violence played an important part preceded a recommendation by an Illinois court-appointed master that all picketing, and not merely acts of violence, be enjoined. Frankfurter agreed that the whole situation was so enmeshed in violence that the community's right to protect itself outweighed the union's right to picket. Beyond the mere fact that the Court, if it struck down the Illinois order, would be substituting its beliefs for those of the state court, lay the distinction between rational modes of communication and those based on fear.

> It must never be forgotten . . . that the Bill of Rights was the child of the Enlightenment. Back of the guaranty of free speech lay faith in the power of an appeal to reason by all the peaceful means for gaining access to the mind. . . . But utterance in a context of violence can lose its significance as an appeal to reason and become part of an instrument of force.[39]

Over the caustic dissent of Justice Black, Frankfurter held that even so powerful an aggregate as a union, championing what was inherently a worthy cause, could not appeal to tactics that might prove harmful to the community.

To seal the point that Justice Frankfurter was interested in protecting the general population from violence in the Meadowmoor case, all one has to do is to look at the very next case involving picketing in which he wrote an opinion. In this case he held that even though no immediate employer-employee dispute was evident, a state could not forbid resort to peaceful picketing that had as its aim the unionization of a business employing nonmembers of the union.[40] When, however, it appears that the community must be considered on the basis of the consequences to which economic conflict may lead, Justice Frankfurter will immediately begin to re-evaluate union rights.

[38] 312 U.S. 287 (1941).
[39] *Ibid.*, p. 293.
[40] American Federation of Labor v. Swing, 312 U.S. 321 (1941).

The effects of such a re-evaluation can be seen in Carpenters and Joiners Union v. Ritters Cafe.[41] As said by the Justice in a later case, "the constitutional boundary line between the competing interests of society involved in the use of picketing cannot be established by general provisions."[42] Consequently, a pragmatic approach must be utilized. Since a state may protect itself against economic conflict, it may require that picketing be limited to industrially related disputes. Thus in Ritters Cafe he held for the Court that a state may, consistently with constitutional rights, forbid picketing of the place of business of one who has entered into a contract for the nonunion construction of a building over a mile away, a building having nothing at all to do with the business. Commenting that "the economic contest between employer and employee has never concerned merely the immediate disputants," he then went on to say that "the clash of such conflicting interests inevitably implicates the well-being of the community. Society has therefore been compelled to throw its weight into the contest."[43] Society as it becomes articulate through legislation can require competing elements to show some consideration for the greater good. Amelioration of potential conflict is a legitimate legislative aim.

The Taft-Hartley Act outlawed closed shops. Following this lead, several state legislatures attempted to curtail the growth of union shops. In a deservedly notable opinion in American Federation of Labor v. American Sash and Door Company[44] Justice Frankfurter concurred in the Court's holding that unions were not denied equal protection of the laws by state statutes or constitutional amendments providing that no person be denied an opportunity to obtain or retain employment based on union membership. He thought that "if concern for the individual justifies incorporating in the Constitution itself devices to curb public authority, a legislative judgment that his protection requires the regulation of the private power of unions cannot be dismissed as insupportable."[45] The legislature had a perfect right to decide against the union shop. Professor Frankfurter learned from early

[41] 315 U.S. 722 (1942).
[42] Hughes v. Superior Court of California, 339 U.S. 460, 466 (1950).
[43] Carpenters & Joiners Union v. Ritters Cafe, 315 U.S. 722, 724 (1942).
[44] 335 U.S. 538 (1949).
[45] *Ibid.*, p. 545.

anti-labor decisions that the Court should acknowledge its incompetence and allow legislative determination of union rights. This earned him the reputation of a liberal on labor matters. It is somewhat ironic that when the lesson was put into practice in this case, it exposed him to criticism as a conservative. The very same thing has continued to happen with later cases.[46]

While Justice Frankfurter's labor opinions do not form any identifiable unit because they fit into the wider pattern of his concern with groups and group conflict, it is also true that his picketing opinions cannot be subsumed under discussion of free speech and assembly, for they too reflect vaster considerations as to the nature of community well-being. For him, picketing is not so fundamental a means of communication or so deeply rooted in our system of values that it cannot be limited. Especially is this so when explicit legislative statement defines a policy of limitation. In analyzing group interests, those of labor must be recognized and given the fullest support commensurable with social welfare. But unions as a group can only expect treatment as a part, albeit a very important part, of society. Other associations must have their day.

V

In Justice Frankfurter's philosophy, the economic rights and responsibilities of unions are closely paralleled by those of business, more specifically of corporations in all their various guises. From the time when he took on Cardozo's mantle, he followed somewhat the pattern of his New Deal compatriots on the bench in that he too required of corporations, especially those in the utility field, a good deal of perception and public feeling in their dealings. His requirements stemmed, however, from a more general philosophic view, which recognized economic and property rights as necessary ingredients in the total pattern of human rights and which insisted that corporations have their place in the sun as valid, but responsible, representatives of a good portion of the population.

Before he took his place on the Court he agreed that there

[46] See, for example, International Brotherhood v. Vogt, 354 U.S. 284 (1957).

was "truth behind the familiar contrast between rights of property and rights of man." But he added the very important statement that

> certainly in some of its aspects property is a function of personality, and conversely the free range of the human spirit becomes shrivelled and constrained under economic dependence. Especially in a civilization like ours where the economic interdependence of society is so pervasive, a sharp division between property rights and human rights largely falsifies reality.[47]

He has therefore been equally careful in affording protection to economic rights as he has been in giving Court sanction to civil liberties, whether these be those of Jehovah's Witnesses in religious freedom cases or those of unions in picketing controversies. Likewise, he has required of the recipients of economic rights, be they individuals or corporations, the degree of co-operation for social good that he exacted from religious minorities or laboring groups.

In the fifth case in which he wrote an opinion the Justice warned his brethren that "the only relevant function of law in dealing with the intersection of government and enterprise is to secure observance of those procedural safeguards in the exercise of legislative powers which are the historic foundations of due process." [48] Legislation in general is only the product of compromise between conflicting interests of society. To have the Court intrude into this domain by consciously throwing its influence behind one or another of the combatants would probably upset the delicate equipoise upon which democracy, both political and economic, depends. Many years ago he thought that the Court should constantly keep in mind the elementary facts of modern existence—technology, large-scale industry, progressive urbanization, accentuation of groups and group interests. Only by doing so could the law avoid the pitfall of disassociating legal problems from the general texture of society. "The tasks of government have meaning only as they are set in the perspective of the forces outside government. Modern society is substantially reflected in

---

[47] Felix Frankfurter, *Mr. Justice Holmes* (Cambridge, Mass.: Harvard University Press, 1938), p. 50.

[48] Driscoll v. Edison Light and Power Co., 307 U.S. 104, 122 (1939).

legislation." [49] In giving corporations their due in accord with legislative desires, the Court would merely be bowing before an indisputable fact—that corporations have an indispensable role in the American scene as now constituted.

Although most economic rights and even more corporation rights are based on private arrangements, these arrangements cannot be abstracted from their public context. Even impairment of contract does not preclude a state from assuming that the conditions of the general welfare are implied parts of every contract. According to the Justice, "A more candid statement is to recognize . . . that the . . . police power is an exercise of the sovereign right of the government to protect . . . the general welfare of the people and is paramount to any right under contracts between individuals." [50] Although Frankfurter does think that federal court calendars become unnecessarily loaded through assumption of diversity jurisdiction, there is another reason for his belief that cases based on diversity of citizenship should not be placed under federal auspices. A good deal of diversity litigation entails corporations of one kind or another. To remove these from the reaches of state judicial power means to some extent leaving the state wholly dependent for protection of its economic well-being upon exterior, federal sources.

On the national level, although the government is not as intimately concerned with the contract stage of business organization or with the effects upon the economy of withdrawing local judicial supervisions from corporations, legislative attempts to regulate the concentration of power have been given concerted support by him. Utilizing all the tools that Congresses over the years have provided, he has consistently held corporations strictly to account for their actions. Whether the basis for decision has been the Sherman or Clayton Acts or the Interstate Commerce, Securities and Exchange, Federal Communications Acts, he has insisted that business organizations can and should be made to realize that the rights of the community have to be respected.

[49] Frankfurter, *The Public and Its Government* (New Haven: Yale University Press, 1930), p. 24. For a statement of very much these same views, although given a quarter of a century later, see Morey v. Doud, 354 U.S. 457, 472 (1957).

[50] East New York Savings Bank v. Hahn, 326 U.S. 230, 232 (1945).

Cut-throat competition does little to enhance societal composure. Corporations of course have a right, and even a duty to their stockholders, to advance their interests—but only to the point where no harm will be done the public.

> That there is a national policy favoring competition cannot be maintained today, without careful qualification. . . . Certainly, even in those areas of economic activity where the play of private forces has been subjected only to the negative prohibitions of the Sherman Law, this Court has not held that competition is an absolute.[51]

If corporations themselves do not show some discretion, as well as discrimination in the policies they pursue, the government must step into the picture.

On a number of topics, then, Justice Frankfurter has upheld state and national action. Proration orders limiting the production of oil wells, losses incurred through changes in various tariff acts, and administrative determinations that the public interest would best be served by curtailing the duplication of radio facilities [52] have all been approved on the basis that business organizations may have to suffer some pecuniary disability in the interest of larger community concerns. While agreeing that "the freedom of enterprise protected by the Sherman Law necessarily has different aspects in relation to the press than in the case of ordinary commercial pursuits," [53] Justice Frankfurter has differed from some other members of the Court in that he would require from all organs of communication in their business relations the type of responsibility that is demanded of other profit-seeking firms under the Sherman Act and other anti-trust legislation. Claims of freedom of the press do not justify complete autonomy. And so

---

[51] Federal Communications Commission v. Radio Corporation of America, 346 U.S. 86, 91–92 (1953).

[52] See Railroad Comm. v. Rowan & Nichols Oil Co., 310 U.S. 573 (1940); Railroad Comm. v. Humble Oil & Refining Co., 311 U.S. 578 (1941); Barr v. United States, 324 U.S. 83 (1945); Faitoute Iron & Steel Co. v. Asbury Park, 316 U.S. 502 (1942); Insurance Group Comm. v. Denver Rio Grande Rail Co., 329 U.S. 607 (1947); Secretary of Agriculture v. Central Roig Refining Co., 338 U.S. 604 (1950).

[53] Associated Press v. United States, 326 U.S. 1, 28 (1945).

when merely business relationships are involved, no area of the nation's life is beyond the purview of government action.

In treating Jehovah's Witnesses or labor unions, communities had been required to avoid discrimination. All regulations hemming in the activities of these groups had to have some very definite justification as judged by community welfare. In the treatment of business combines, the same kind of approach is utilized. They too must be protected within the limits of their rights. The Fifth Amendment's provision concerning just compensation has been given a very strict interpretation. While businesses must expect to suffer along with the rest of the community when generalized regulations make a change in the over-all economic position of the country, they can demand restitution when their particular property is singled out for community use. There is no doubt that the community can demand property or other economic assets from individuals or corporations, but it then must assume the responsibility of seeing that repayment is made. "When there is a taking of property for public use, whether in war or in peace, the burden of the taking is the community's burden." [54] Justice Frankfurter has been very staunch in his demands that the community shoulder such a burden. Other areas of business dealings that are vital to the maintenance of the economic system and that therefore indirectly concern the general public have also received sympathetic treatment in his hands.

To name but one area, he has been extremely active in the protection of bona fide trade-marks and patents. "The protection of trade-marks is the law's recognition of the psychological function of symbols. If it is true that we live by symbols, it is no less true that we purchase goods by them." [55] It is to the interest of the general public that they be not duped by false claims. Conversely, to merit a patent some genuine inventiveness must be shown, otherwise general progress may be curtailed through premature granting of legal and economic rights. In a different field, although very much in the same vein of thought, have been Justice Frankfurter's votes on stock reorganization plans. Although he

[54] United States v. Commodities Trading Corp., 339 U.S. 121, 134 (1950).
[55] Mishawaka R. & W. Manufacturing Co. v. S. S. Kresge, 316 U.S. 203, 205 (1942).

has written relatively few opinions on this question, those that he has composed have reiterated time and time again the fiduciary trust placed by stock-holders in boards of directors and the consequent necessity for directors to be above reproach in their dealings. Not only are their own reputations at stake, but also the future of a good many innocent people may be determined by their actions.

In January, 1929, Professor Frankfurter wrote to F.D.R. that "hydroelectric power raises without a doubt the most far-reaching social and economic issues before the American people, certainly for the next decade." [56] Hydroelectric power was but one of those many types of natural or manufactured products that were controlled by public utility companies. Professor Frankfurter's reference to it was merely indicative of his deep concern over the role that public utilities were playing in the economic life of the country. In the very next year he wrote a volume, one of whose major contentions was that "those economic services upon which public well-being is so dependent that they are deemed to be public callings although in private hands, present in many ways the most complex series of problems for government, and their complexity is not likely to be abated in the future." [57] In this he was most certainly correct. He thought then that both state and national governments should make sure that society secured the essential service of the public utilities, even if the latter had to be put under strict supervision. In helping to draft the Public Utility Holding Company Act in 1935, he was able to translate a good deal of his theory into practice. On the Supreme Court he has reiterated the dispersal theory of economic power upon which the Act was predicated, and he has required of public utilities more than he has required of any other type of corporation.

While probably the Court's most outspoken member on the necessity for curbing utility companies, Justice Frankfurter has been equally outspoken on the topic of administrative responsi-

[56] Frankfurter to F.D.R., January 5, 1929, Roosevelt Papers. Quoted in Arthur Schlesinger, Jr., *The Crisis of the Old Order* (Boston: Houghton Mifflin Co., 1957), p. 124.

[57] Frankfurter, *The Public and Its Government*, p. 3.

bility. "Who ultimately determines the ways of regulation, is the decisive aspect in the public supervision of privately-owned utilities." [58] This being so, the fact that Congress has delegated so much responsibility for regulation to the independent commissions and boards means that these agencies are in many instances the ultimate determinants. These professional administrative agencies through continuity of study, slow building up of knowledge, and initiative in enforcement then become the real protectors of the public interest and act as a counterweight to the economic pressures exerted by business organizations.

Over and over again the following theme, or some variation thereof, appears in his opinions: "Since these agencies deal largely with the vindication of public interest and not enforcement of private rights, this Court ought not to imply hampering restrictions, not imposed by Congress, upon the effectiveness of the administrative process." [59] In an oft-quoted passage Justice Frankfurter wrote that modern administrative tribunals were the outgrowth of conditions far different from those that gave rise to the judicial process. They were to be the transmitters of a social policy of social control. In the protection of both public and private interests and in the substantiation of a social policy of dispersal of economic control, administrative agencies are the organs of government through which business organizations are made to realize the vital, though limited, contributions that they can make to a responsible national life.

VI

The Supreme Court throughout its history has always been aware of the group conflicts that seethed under a good deal of litigation coming before it. While such conflict arose violently to the surface on a limited number of occasions—Dred Scott, Legal Tender, Income Tax Cases—it, nevertheless, remained as an unspoken consideration in many others. The changing social

[58] Federal Power Commission v. Hope Natural Gas Co., 320 U.S. 591, 625 (1944).
[59] Ashbacker Radio Corp. v. Federal Communications Commission, 326 U.S. 327, 335 (1945).

and behavioral pattern of modern society made the articulation of group interests a much more necessary ingredient of life in general and in Supreme Court opinions in particular. When the Court spoke of protecting property rights of business in the 1920's and 1930's, when it turned its attention to unions and the problems of labor in the 1940's, or when it agreed to the correspondingly new emphasis that should be given civil liberties of minority religious or racial factions, embryonic group interests were being taken into account. Like other members of the Court, although perhaps to a greater extent, Justice Frankfurter has accepted the fact that the law must accommodate itself to this new situation wherein groups often replace individuals as the central concern in ameliorating conflict. He has, however, added one very important qualification, which has not been wholly acceptable to some of the other justices. Given the fact that groups need to have their rights protected, the community as the greater whole must also have its day.

In a speech honoring the late Thomas Mann, Justice Frankfurter reminded his audience that "the essence of the democratic faith is the equal claim of every man to pursue his facilities to the humanly fullest—*for his own sake, but no less for the sake of society.*" [60] Individuals and groups in the pluralist tradition have worth and validity in and of themselves. But their greatest significance is gained when they can contribute their unique strengths to the social fabric that can be, although need not be, represented by some type of governmental arrangement. To dissipate this strength through violence or through stubborn attempts to revamp by indirect coercion the cultural patterns of an unwilling majority harms not only the groups but society as well. It is "Law alone [that] saves a society from being rent by internecine strife or rules by mere brute power however disguised." [61] Legislative judgments that certain actions must be prohibited or curtailed for the peace, security, and economic well-being of the community are passive statements of what the law should be. Coming from the truly representative branch of government they deserve serious consideration. It is up to the

[60] *New York Times,* June 26, 1945.

[61] United States v. United Mine Workers, 330 U.S. 258, 308 (1947).

courts and administrative agencies to make this passive law into an active force whereby strife and conflict can be mitigated if not entirely done away with. In concluding a recent article on his conception of the Court's function, Justice Frankfurter agreed that his insistence on government under law might be charged with being an old-fashioned liberal's view. But to this he replied, "I plead guilty."

> For the charge implies allegiance to the humane and gradualist tradition in dealing with refractory social and political problems, recognizing them to be fractious because of their complexity and not amenable to quick and propitious solution without resort to methods which deny law as the instrument and offspring of reason.[62]

No summation could better present the course that the Justice has followed in dealing with group conflicts in modern society.

[62] Felix Frankfurter, "John Marshall," in *Government Under Law* (Cambridge, Mass.: Harvard University Press, 1956), p. 30.

V

The Supreme Court and the
Interests of Society

No matter how well other governmental agencies have accomplished their tasks in protecting the public interest, when all is said and done, it is the Supreme Court that alone can give final legal satisfaction to both groups and society. It is the Supreme Court alone that becomes the ultimate keeper of the nation's legal conscience. Therefore, the way in which the Court looks at its function and the place of law in modern society, and the way in which the Court is looked at by society, become of the utmost importance in controlling the power of social forces for good or evil. In balancing the interests of society against the claims of special interests, be they individual or group, the Court has, consequently, somewhat of a symbolic role. With Paul Freund, "we accept the Court as a symbol in the measure that, while performing its appointed tasks, it manages at the same time to articulate and rationalize the aspirations reflected in the

Constitution." [1] Justice Frankfurter is acutely aware that a good deal of the Court's authority is intrinsic. It stems from the way in which the Court handles itself, from the types of cases that it permits itself to hear, and from its own consciousness of the moral nature of much of its work. While neither he nor anyone else has been able to define the essential nature of the Court, he has attempted to give an individualized image of some of its main characteristics. If he attempts any definition, it is of the role of the Court in a democratic society, not of its innate qualities.

I

Professor Frankfurter recognized as early as 1913 that if the Court's task was to be accomplished properly, "it is essential that the stream of the Zeitgeist must be allowed to flood the sympathies and the intelligence of our judges." [2] After becoming a member of the Court, he continued to insist that "the claims of dominant opinion rooted in sentiments of justice and public morality are among the most powerful shaping forces in law-making by courts." [3] Otherwise, in the balancing of social interests, those of the general public will be sacrificed to the interest of the few. Of course it is difficult to tell just what is "dominant opinion" or the "stream of the Zeitgeist." Public opinion polls, surveys, and interviews, while useful in other areas, are precluded when the Supreme Court is considering a case. But certainly the attempt to approximate public morality, within legal terms, is not precluded. The Supreme Court is inextricably an organ of statesmanship. In plying this art it tempers its own power by recognizing the organic relations of society and the consequent demands that arise from such relations. If these demands are most clearly articulated in the amorphous concept called "dominant opinion," then it is up to the Court to work with, although not be

[1] Paul A. Freund, "The Supreme Court and Civil Liberties," *Vanderbilt Law Review*, IV (April, 1951), 552.

[2] Felix Frankfurter, "The Zeitgeist and the Judiciary," *Survey*, XXIX (January 25, 1913), 544.

[3] National City Bank v. Republic of China, 348 U.S. 356, 360 (1955)

dominated by, the concept. The Court's work is the work of the law, and it is in the law that the clearest exposition on the rights of society is often found.

Government by law, as well as under law, means in reality that law is used as a social device for the satisfaction of social interests. Functionally, it is an attempt to satisfy and to adjust various claims and demands. The end result is, however, a social policy couched in legal terms. It follows that both law and the policy that it transmits are the products of the society that they in turn control. Variations in the legal structures of states and of nations stem from the fact that law and the policy that it contains have been shaped by the varying conditions of life found among different political communities. Law then not only reflects such diversities, it is also the reflection of them.

In a tribute to the late Justice Jackson, Frankfurter gave his own verbal picture of the symbolic function of the Supreme Court and the place of law in modern society.

> That law in its comprehending sense is at once the precondition and, perhaps, the greatest achievement of an enduring civilization since without it there is either strife or enslavement of the spirit of man; that law so conceived expresses the enforceable insights of morality and endeavors of justice; that law is not word-jugglery or the manipulation of symbols; that precedents, while not foreclosing new truths or enlarged understanding, are not counters to be moved about for preconceived ends; that this significance and role of law must particularly be respected in a continental federal society like ours; that the Supreme Court as the ultimate voice of the law must always be humbly mindful of the fact that it is entrusted with power which is saved from misuse only by a self-searching disinterestedness almost beyond the lot of men—these were convictions which Justice Jackson passionately entertained.[4]

They are no less passionately held by Justice Frankfurter. To fulfill the functions that he assigns it, the Supreme Court must be aware of its symbolic role as the interpreter and protector of social policy as expressed in legal terms.

Justice Frankfurter's interest in curtailing the jurisdiction of

[4] Felix Frankfurter, "Mr. Justice Jackson," *Harvard Law Review*, LXVIII (April, 1955), 937–38.

the Court is well known. His votes on writs of certiorari are no doubt influenced thereby. Mere avoidance of extra labor is obviously not the only reason for wishing to cut down on the number of cases coming before the Court. Beyond his stand on jurisdiction in general and on certiorari in particular lies a deeper philosophy as to the working of the Court. It is this philosophy, which sees the Court as a highly deliberative and contemplative body weighing and reweighing the social issues involved in all litigation, that justifies talking about the Court's symbolic role at all.

Society has a right to demand of the Supreme Court that it take cases only of general interest and that when it takes them real effort go into the decision, not just perfunctory performance. Because so much of its authority is intrinsic, the Court must rely heavily on prestige factors to have its decisions and itself honored. It must make the quality of its work obvious. Given the fact that only tremendous and delicate problems should reach the nation's highest tribunal, sufficient time should be allotted so that each and every aspect of a case can be thoroughly canvassed. If through rapid scanning of a case important aspects are overlooked or if through rushed composition slipshod opinions are handed down, the Court cannot possibly expect to remain the symbol of elevated integrity articulating and rationalizing the aspirations of the Constitution. If this should come to pass, the Court will suffer, but society will suffer more. As Thurman Arnold has demonstrated, symbols may be very illusive, but they may also be very necessary in the area of governmental operations.[5] In a society such as ours there needs to be some agency that can articulate deep-felt hopes and desires of a heterogeneous people. Traditionally, the Supreme Court through its decisions has held this position. To retain this place requires discrimination and reflection so that the myriad issues presented can be handled adequately.

After arguments have been listened to and records and briefs studied, there still remains the crucial period when each individual justice must commune with himself and try to reconcile

[5] Thurman Arnold, *The Symbols of Government* (New Haven: Yale University Press, 1935).

the issues presented with the law past and the law yet to come. "Reflection is a slow process. Wisdom, like good wine, requires maturing." [6] After the individual maturing process, the justices face the task of collective assessment since the judgments of the Supreme Court are collective judgments. Every participant has had to cover a large amount of material not found in the technical law books. The nature of the cases coming before the Court means conversance with the materials of economics, sociology, psychology, etc. It is in conference that the fruits of private study and reflection become of value. Such fruition is gained only by ample time. As Justice Frankfurter said early in his judicial career: "Without adequate study there cannot be adequate reflection; without adequate reflection there cannot be adequate discussion; without adequate discussion there cannot be that mature and fruitful interchange of minds which is indispensable to wise decisions and luminous opinions." [7] He has continued to say very much the same thing on other occasions.

While the Supreme Court may ask aid from others, it must shoulder a good deal of the responsibility for the way in which its time is spent. By refusing to indulge counsel in continuances, by demanding compact briefs, and by turning aside the too numerous requests for rehearings, the tribunal can allocate its time most profitably. Also since the passage of the Judiciary Act of 1925, the justices have been largely free to determine the dimensions of their docket. It is the discretionary writ of certiorari that brings most cases to the Court. Many years before he became a member of the High Tribunal, Frankfurter spoke out against the way in which the writ was being used. Before looking into the reasons he gave for thinking that the writ was being mishandled, it is necessary to look into the mechanism through which this type of review is gained, for differences over the use of the mechanism have caused as much trouble as differences over the writs themselves.

As explained at the hearings on the 1925 legislation, writs of

[6] Kinsella v. Kruger, 351 U.S. 470, 485 (1956).
[7] *Ex parte* Republic of Peru, 318 U.S. 578, 603 (1943). Cf. Dick v. New York Life Insurance Co., 359 U.S. 458–59 (1959).

certiorari were to be granted under "the rule of four." [8] By this is meant that when four members of the Court, after cursory examination of records and briefs, believe that a case warrants being brought before them, a writ will be issued allowing further documentations and perhaps oral argument. Parenthetically it should be noted that even in this early stage of the proceedings Justice Frankfurter differs from some of the other justices in the degree of documentation that he feels the Court should be called upon to cover. In an opinion in chambers, where he wrote only for himself, he said that "it does not require heavy research to charge the understanding of this Court adequately on the gravity of the issues on which review is sought and to prove to the Court the appropriateness of granting a petition for a writ of certiorari." [9] Requests of counsel for more research time would cause useless delay. In petitions, if not in briefs, brevity and conciseness are the most desirable traits.

The writ once having been granted, the matter is not closed. If, in the interim between the grant of the writ and counsel's presentation, five or more members of the Court remain or become convinced that the case does not merit Supreme Court review, the writ will be dismissed as having been improvidently granted. Thus it is possible that if five members of the nine were initially hesitant to take the case under consideration and they continue in their hesitancy, by a bare vote of five to four the writ could be dismissed and the case banished from the docket. Let it be understood that when real cause for dismissal becomes evident no criticism can be leveled for following that course. Nevertheless, there is a good deal of drama hidden behind the mere notation in memoranda cases that a writ has been improvidently granted. One never quite knows whether, after further consideration, a hearty majority of the Court was convinced that an original error in judgment had been made or whether five of

[8] See U.S. Congress. Senate. Committee on the Judiciary. "Hearings Before a Subcommittee . . . on S.2060 and S.2061," 68th Congr., 1st Sess., 1924, p. 29. For a full explanation of the "rule of four," see the article by that title by Joan M. Leiman in *Columbia Law Review*, LVII (November, 1957), 975–92.

[9] Brody v. United States, 1 L ed 2d 1130, 1131 (1957).

the justices are using their numerical superiority to defeat the wishes of four of their brethren. One never quite knows, that is, until a disgruntled justice decides to note his position or even to include a more extended statement of his reasons.

"Improvidently granted" is a unique escape clause. Its use has not caused much adverse comment when only a single controversy has been involved. It has come in for its greatest criticism when utilized against whole categories of cases, all involving the same basic issues. Justice Frankfurter has been one of the leaders in asserting that even if whole categories are thus precluded, a majority of the Court should be allowed to have the final say as to the types of controversies it wishes to consider. His deep sensitivity to maintaining the Supreme Court as the symbol of disinterested, generalized legal administration has made certain types of cases, which seem to stand in direct opposition to this symbol, anathema to him. Therefore he continues to insist that the rule of four is merely a guide line that has value in expediting some of the Court's business, but that the rule is not binding on other members of the tribunal after a case has been taken under advisement.

Paradoxically, when Justice Frankfurter is in the minority and cannot garner enough other votes to dismiss a writ that he thinks should not have been granted, he does not emphasize the right of the majority to have its say. He has even gone to the extreme of refusing to participate at all in the disposition of such a case after argument.[10] This is a rather questionable tactic. For Justice Frankfurter, however, judicial encouragement for disappointed litigants and losing lawyers to have another go at it will be the only result of the Court's taking cases that he feels are inherently trivial or that can be handled by lower state or federal courts. This is his justification for using the mechanism of certiorari, and it, in turn, depends upon his philosophy of certiorari.

Beginning in the late 1920's Professor Frankfurter contributed a yearly article to the *Harvard Law Review* appraising the work of the Court at the previous term. These articles were more

[10] See, for example, the opinion in Rogers v. Missouri Pacific Rail Co., 352 U.S. 500 (1957).

philosophic in tone than many of our present annual reviews. One of the topics for discussion that constantly appeared was that of certiorari. A characteristic statement of his understanding of the writ would run something like this:

> Clarification of the substantive law is . . . not an immediate objective in the disposition of petitions. Clarification of the canons which guide the Court's exercise of discretion, however, whether by grant or denial, is of the utmost importance. So long as these canons remain obscure and unfamiliar, so long will the Court be flooded with trivial and mistaken applications of its discretion.[11]

Frankfurter did all he could to clear up the obscurity and unfamiliarity. The canons by which the Court should be guided in granting writs were basically two: ". . . to compose conflict among lower courts and to invoke the voice of ultimate law on significant federal issues." [12]

In view of Justice Frankfurter's espousal of a symbolic role for the Supreme Court it is of some moment that he talked of "significant" federal issues rather than the more stereotyped designation, "federal questions." Significance is a matter of opinion. He measures it first by the degree to which the Supreme Court must apply generalized social values in contradistinction to the values or symbols held by more provincial groups. Second, he measures it by the degree to which the Supreme Court in the process of such application can articulate and rationalize the aspirations of the Constitution so that it deserves the symbolic designation so important for itself and for the good of society. It is possible to determine when a direct conflict in decision has evidenced itself between lower courts. At this time the Supreme Court should step in and clear up the confusion. While it is not as easy to rule on whether a "federal question" is involved in litigation coming from state courts, there are some general boundaries that guide discussion. Even if a "federal question" is involved, this does not mean that the Supreme Court should neces-

[11] Felix Frankfurter and Henry Hart, "The Supreme Court at October Term, 1934," *Harvard Law Review*, LXIX (December, 1935), 82–83.
[12] Felix Frankfurter and James Landis, "The Supreme Court at October Term, 1928," *Harvard Law Review*, LXIII (November, 1929), 52.

sarily take the case. The real meaning of the Judges' Bill as far as Frankfurter could discern it was that "litigation which did not represent a *wide public interest* was left to state courts of last resort and to the circuit courts of appeal, always reserving to the Supreme Court power to determine that *some national interest* justified invoking its jurisdiction." [13] Only by such an understanding could the Court remain the agency of government that legally cared for the interests of all.

Thus, in reviewing the actions of courts of appeal, the Supreme Court ought to have the final say but only when a general doctrine was being enunciated and not when the court below was dealing with the impact of a restricted set of circumstances. To have it otherwise would mean that the Court would be forsaking its major function as protector of the public interest and be descending into the realm of interesting and perhaps locally important controversies that, while telling enough in themselves, did not vitally concern the national well-being. When a comparison is made between the types of cases refused hearing by the Court and those accepted, Justice Frankfurter finds the contrast glaring.

The lower courts may make mistakes in their handling of cases. The Supreme Court might know that a mistake has been made and yet, in Justice Frankfurter's view, it would still not be authorized to call up the case. In his opinions he explains why.

> This Court is not a court to determine the local law of the forty-eight States. Error on the part of a Court . . . in applying the local law of any one of the forty-eight States involves injustice to a particular litigant. . . . If the claim of injustice . . . justifies review by this Court, it justifies it in every case in which on a surface view of the record this Court feels a Court . . . may have been wrong in its ascertainment of local law.
>
>   . . . The Supreme Court of the United States is designed for important questions of general significance in the construction of federal law and in the adjustment of the serious controversies that arise inevitably and in increasing measure in a federal system such as ours. These questions are more than sufficient in volume and

[13] Felix Frankfurter and James Landis, *The Business of the Supreme Court* (New York: Macmillan, 1927) p. 261. Emphasis added.

difficulty to engage all the energy and thought possessed by the Court; it should not be diverted by the correction of errors in local controversies turning on particular circumstances.[14]

It also follows for him that lower courts and the bar are not warranted in assuming either approval or disapproval of a decision when a writ of certiorari is denied. No judgment on the correctness of treatment should be implied. The only thing that can be understood is that the case did not have general significance. For the Court to make intelligible its canons of interpretation in certiorari cases Professor Frankfurter thought that some type of explanation was due the lower courts and bar. He suggested, therefore, "the value of an occasional full opinion upon the denial of a petition for *certiorari*." [15] He has heeded his own advice and since going on the Court has on numerous instances written notations explaining the basis for denial.

II

The cases that have provoked the greatest number of opinions from him on the philosophy of certiorari are those that have come up under the Federal Employers' Liability Act. Here, all the elements that he finds so disruptive to proper judicial administration become focused. Individual welfare rather than significant federal questions are involved. These cases do not require the enunciation of general principles. All they require is the application of settled doctrine to the special facts of a particular litigation. Conflict between the lower courts cannot be corrected because each lower court is dealing with a special set of conditions. Justice Frankfurter, consequently, finds that FELA cases contradict every canon for issuing the writ of certiorari, turning the Supreme Court from the nation's Highest Tribunal protecting the public interest into a compensation board adjusting the amount of money that an injured worker should receive. For this reason, time and time again he has noted dissent from the grant

[14] Gibson v. Phillips Petroleum Co., 352 U.S. 874 (1956).
[15] Frankfurter and Hart, "The Supreme Court at October Term, 1934," *loc. cit.*

of the writ or has absolutely refused to participate in decision
on the substantive issues presented. His personal crusade
against this type of case did not start with his elevation to the
Supreme Court. It started many years previously in his annual
articles on the Court. In 1929 he wrote that "one class of cases
that reaches the Court exclusively through *certiorari* is a heavy
drain on the Court's time, and a drain to which it should not be
subjected. These are controversies under the Federal Employers'
Liability Act." [16] At that time he thought it not dogmatic to assert
that writs in these cases were too readily granted. He certainly
feels that way today.

FELA is primarily an attempt to refine the common law's
definition of assumption of risk and employer liability. Traditionally, the common law found liability created only when, put
quaintly, an employer failed to "take care" so that injury could
be averted. Later variations found liability created only where
the employer did not fulfill a limited number of statutory requirements intended to protect an employee against very definite
types of injuries in fact incurred. As Justice William Brennan
says, "This limiting approach has long been discarded from the
FELA. Instead, the theory of FELA is that where the employer's
conduct falls short of the high standard required of him by this
Act, and his fault, in whole or in part, causes injury, liability
ensues." [17] This in turn means that whether fault is a violation
of the statutory requirement or of the more general requirement
to act with care, the employer becomes subject to legal sanctions. Correlatively, the assumption of risk by the employee is
reduced. No longer is he required to bear most of the incidental
injury burdens of employment. With all this Justice Frankfurter
would agree. However, early in his tenure on the bench, he
pointed out that " 'assumption of risk' as a defense where there
is negligence has been written out of the Act. But 'assumption
of risk' in the sense that the employer is not liable for those
risks which it could not avoid in observance of its duty to care,
has not been written out of the Act." [18]

[16] Frankfurter and Landis, "The Supreme Court at October Term, 1928," *loc.
cit.*, p. 51.
[17] Kernan v. American Dredging Co., 355 U.S. 426 (1958).
[18] Tiller v. Atlantic Coast Line Rail Co., 318 U.S. 54, 72 (1943).

When the Court tries to make the employer liable, even when no statutory negligence is apparent, the FELA is turned from a liability statute into a scheme for workmen's compensation. Or so thinks Justice Frankfurter. This is a second reason for his hesitance to deal with FELA cases. As are other members of the Court, he is fully aware that some type of compensatory scheme is necessary. He is, however, unwilling to see it brought about through a tortured construction of legislation.

> Legislation is needed which will effectively meet the social obligations which underlie the incidence of occupational disease. . . . The need for such legislation becomes obscured and the drive for it retarded if encouragement is given to the thought that here are now adequate remedies for occupational diseases in callings subject to Congressional control. The result of the present decision is to secure for this petitioner the judgment which the jury awarded him. It does not secure a proper system for dealing with occupational disease.[19]

Characteristically Justice Frankfurter was concerned with social obligations, but just as characteristically he did not feel that securing for a particular petitioner his rights would do much to bring about a proper system.

In liability litigation, juries are almost always used. Jurists have the prerogative to lessen or increase the amount awarded if they think jury determination is plainly wrong in either direction. As Justice Frankfurter said in another context, "every trial lawyer and every trial judge knows that jury verdicts are not logical products, and are due to considerations that preclude accurate guessing or logical deduction."[20] Juries are apt to be swayed by sympathetic considerations however much the presiding legal officer might caution against such a propensity. They are equally apt to award excessive compensation to an employee. Jurists then find themselves in the unenviable position of having either to reduce the amount or to deny that any negligence at all was involved. It is from the lower courts taking one of these two courses that many of the appeals in FELA cases stem.

Justice Black stands in direct opposition to Justice Frankfurter

[19] Urie v. Thompson, 337 U.S. 163, 197 (1949).
[20] Green v. United States, 355 U.S. 184, 214 (1957).

on almost all aspects of FELA litigation and, more generally, on certiorari policy. He does not believe the statute has been turned into a clumsy kind of workmen's compensation through undue stretching of negligence concepts. He feels instead that antipathy to the statutes rests on the mistaken assumption that juries will always decide against the employer. But, as James Conner has put it in a valuable study on this whole problem, ". . . Mr. Justice Black, who is a learned as well as passionate champion of trial by jury, must know that although juries may not *always* decide for the employee, they *almost* always will. This is certainly recognized by claimants' attorneys and by the railroad unions who prefer the present system to a bona fide compensation statute." [21] Justice Frankfurter inherently distrusts jury determinations; he favors a good deal of autonomy for lower courts in their actions; he does not think that particularized controversies should reach the Court. This chain of reasoning inevitably leads to a rejection of FELA cases.

In a series of cases coming to the Court in the 1956 Term he publicly displayed the pent-up annoyance and irritation engendered by this deep feeling.[22] In four cases decided at the same time the Court was variously called upon to decide whether damages were due in the following circumstances: first, a workman clearing weeds with a torch had, on the approach of a train, retreated to a culvert from which he fell when the flames fanned by the train came near him; second, a conductor on a train had been injured through the unexpected sudden stop of the conveyance to avoid hitting an automobile; third, a workman had fallen on a partially covered cinder in a roadbed that he was clearing; fourth and finally, a ship's cook had sustained severe cuts by using a knife to serve hardened ice-cream after the scoop that had been provided him failed to do the job. The Court in all instances decided that the employer was liable.

Justices Frankfurter and Harlan dissented in all. If these

---

[21] James C. Conner, "Supreme Court Certiorari Policy and the Federal Employers' Liability Act," *Cornell Law Quarterly*, XLIII (Spring, 1958), 467.

[22] See Rogers v. Missouri Pacific Rail Co., 352 U.S. 500 (1957); Webb v. Illinois Central Rail Co., 352 U.S. 572 (1957); Herdman v. Pennsylvania Railroad, 352 U.S. 578 (1957); Ferguson v. Moore-McCormack Lines, 352 U.S. 521 (1957).

could be called significant federal issues or even cases representative thereof, they remained unconvinced. It was not that these men did not need aid in their time of distress, but surely the Supreme Court was not the tribunal to dispense it. Lower courts, after hearing jury verdicts, were just as able to decide on an equitable arrangement as was the Supreme Court. An eye-witness in the Court's chamber on the day Justice Frankfurter delivered his dissenting opinion gives this account. "Frankfurter leaned forward and shouted at times. He grew red-faced when he discussed the facts of what he felt were ridiculous cases. He appeared to be lecturing not only his colleagues on the bench, but the crowded chamber, largely consisting of lawyers, as well." [23] The final insult seemed to be the case of the ship's cook. In discussing this case he roared that "My duty is not to concern myself with a stupid cook who used a butcher knife to take out ice cream."

Justice Frankfurter is very attuned to the duties, as well as the rights, surrounding a Supreme Court member. While this preoccupation may be compulsive, it is at least grounded in tradition. The symbolic role of the Court as the protector of social interests involves the duty of making sure that the Court does not become burdened with trivia. This desire to avoid trivia motivates his behavior on certiorari problems and on the FELA.

III

The philosophy of certiorari is here important because it pinpoints the justices' positions on the role of the Supreme Court. This limited area is, of course, only a part of each justice's larger philosophy concerning the function of the Court and the place of law in modern society. Justice Frankfurter does not believe the Court's major contribution to national welfare comes by individualizing performance, that is, by taking cases based on sympathy for one of the litigants. Obviously, most cases that the Court handles deal initially with individuals. Linda Carol Brown was a very particular young girl who wished admittance to the

[23] Peter J. Kumpa in *Baltimore Sun*, February 26, 1957.

schools of Topeka on an equal footing with others regardless of race. But Linda Carol Brown was more than an individual with an individual problem. She was representative of millions of other Negroes who wished to see an end to segregation in education. Even this would not have been enough to have the problem considered by the Supreme Court. Only because the problem was partially legal in nature could Linda Carol be heard.

It may seem harsh to say so, but fundamentally the Supreme Court is a court of law and not a court of justice. Due process concepts alleviate some of the tension that arises from this distinction, but they cannot relieve it all. Therefore, at times, the Court must reject cases based on sympathy for the unjust treatment meted out to some individual in his individual capacity or even in his capacity as representative of a larger group. In this sense, if the Court is concerned with justice at all, it is with societal justice, not individual justice. The role of the Supreme Court as a court of law takes precedence over all other consideration. In espousing this interpretation, Justice Frankfurter has put himself at variance with a number of his brethren.

He finds the identification of "justice" and "legality" false. While neither term is easy to define, justice is the more amorphous concept. When the Court in 1922 struck down the Federal Child Labor Tax Law,[24] many people were outraged. Frankfurter pointed out, however, that " 'humanity' is not the test of constitutionality. Recognition that a law enacted by Congress seeks to redress monstrous wrongs and to promote the highest good does not dispose of the Supreme Court's duty when the validity of such a law is challenged." [25] In ruling on legality, the Court cannot be swayed by the fact that the statute in question may be a good or just law in the sense that it is based on sympathy, compassion, and humanity. If, for instance, it tries to rearrange powers granted by the Constitution, it matters not that the end result may be a "just" one. The statute in question must fall.

Likewise, in ruling on claims, whether these arise in an individual or representative capacity, the Supreme Court should

[24] Bailey v. Drexel Furniture Co., 259 U.S. 20.

[25] Felix Frankfurter, "Child Labor and the Constitution," New Republic, XXXI (July 26, 1922), 248.

limit its attention to the legal issues involved. Many years before, he had written that "the romantic notion that the Supreme Court sits 'to do justice' in every case potentially within its jurisdiction dies hard." [26] Apparently the notion was hardier than expected, for it still had to be contended with when he took his place on the bench, leading him to say on one occasion that "this is a court of review not a tribunal unbounded by rules. We do not sit like a kadi under a tree dispensing justice according to considerations of individual expediency." [27] Legal rights, not justice, are the Court's consideration. It is unfortunate when the two do not coalesce, but at times it is unavoidable.

Even when legal rights proper may be present, if they are germane to the litigant solely as an individual, the Supreme Court may have to deny review.

> "Special and important" reasons imply a reach to a problem beyond the academic or episodic. This is especially true when the issues involved reach constitutional dimensions, for then there comes into play regard for the Court's duty to avoid decision of constitutional issues unless avoidance becomes evasion.[28]

Equally so in the use of the Court's equity powers, powers which were initially granted to soften the harshness of strictly legal determinations, Justice Frankfurter has not departed from his basic position that individual interest is not enough.[29] The Court cannot possibly hope to sit for the benefit of particular litigants if it expects to carry on its greater function of symbolizing to the nation a disinterested articulator of social values.

The way Justice Frankfurter looks at it, granting review on the basis of compassionate appeal of selected instances inevitably means that there will be a drain on the Court's time, time that could better be spent on cases of general interest that have unquestioned claims to full investigation, ample deliberation, and effective opinion-writing. He would agree that "where a statute permits either of two constructions without violence to language,

[26] Felix Frankfurter and Henry Hart, "The Supreme Court at October Term, 1933," *Harvard Law Review,* XLVIII (December, 1934), 264.

[27] Terminiello v. Chicago, 337 U.S. 1, 11 (1949).

[28] Rice v. Sioux City Cemetery, 349 U.S. 70, 74 (1955).

[29] See, for example, Rogers v. Missouri Pacific Rail Co., 352 U.S. 500, 544 (1957).

the construction which leads to hardship should be rejected in favor of the permissible construction consonant with humane considerations." [30] But individual hardship, in and of itself, would not warrant bringing a case before the Court, and twisting statutory language to arrive at a "compassionate" decision is also forbidden by the larger tasks of the Court.

It would be difficult to prove that Justice Frankfurter was not interested in the abstract quality called "justice." In his due process opinions he comes as close as any of the others to attempting a tentative definition for special circumstances. However, in the long run, generality and the maintenance of a legal system are necessary even for due process to operate. Justices Black and Douglas take a different view. They believe that the rule of four should be stringently upheld and that the individual nature of cases, even those as individual as that of the ship's cook, which was discussed in connection with FELA, should not count against bringing a case to the Supreme Court. While they would probably not identify legality with justice, they apparently can see no reason for the Court not to use its influence to bring about the identification, even if legal concepts have to be changed. In a study by Thomas Reed Powell he talks of Black and Douglas allowing the heart to rule the head.[31] He speaks of their "cardiac response" to fact situations, meaning that praiseworthy sympathy and compassion for personal misfortune often lead them to want cases brought before the Supreme Court because of their feeling "a sense of injustice" over the results reached below.[32]

To their credit they are interested in "goodness" and "justice." But since neither one of these concepts is expressible in a formula, there can be no one guiding rule. The criticism leveled at Justice Frankfurter's approach to due process, that it tends to foster confusion and instability in constitutional law, appears to be equally valid here. The only sure knowledge about the disposition of a case that anybody has is the knowledge gained

[30] United States v. Shaughnessy, 338 U.S. 521, 534 (1950).

[31] Thomas Reed Powell, "Behind the Split in the Supreme Court," *New York Times*, October 9, 1949.

[32] On this general topic, see Edmond Cahn, *A Sense of Injustice* (New York: New York University Press, 1949).

through familiarity with voting patterns, that those with a "cardiac response" are apt to vote in favor of what is colloquially known as the "underdog." Since, according to Justice Douglas, "common sense often makes good law," [33] common sense has decreed on more than one occasion that all interests "must yield where the interests of justice would make unfair the strict application of our rules." [34] No picayunish distinction or fancy dialectic, but bold assertion that the primary function of the Supreme Court is to dispense individual justice, irrespective of its effect upon society's legal structure.

The slogan that ours is a government of laws and not men has been so often attacked that we almost take the reverse of the proposition as true. Even devotees of the "Cult of the Robe" are aware that the personal traits of jurists do matter in dealing with legal issues. But personalizing all legal phenomena can be carried too far. If we are to retain even a semblance of government under law, there must be some general impersonal rules, formulated without regard to individual litigants, which can be applied with the same vigor to all. When courts feel free to concern themselves, not with social welfare, but with the welfare of even the most deserving person, we will indeed have a government of men, men irresponsible to the free play of political forces who yet may change legal rules with every change in fashion or mood. Judicial legislation has been excoriated by those with a "cardiac response" and by those who do not allow the heart to rule the head. It is difficult to see, however, how the former can reconcile their individualizing attitude with the fundamental tenet upon which our government is founded—that is, that the welfare of the people requires a change in the law to be made by the people through their representatives. By refusing to be bound by social concerns and by individualizing decisions, change is precluded not only for the present but also for the past and, perhaps, for the future. Supreme Court decisions have retroactive validity. The radiations of a decision based on individual considerations may rearrange legal relations and the rest of society will find itself so pulled along by the impetus of a decision that

[33] Peak v. United States, 353 U.S. 43, 46 (1957).
[34] United States v. Ohio Power Co., 353 U.S. 98, 99 (1957).

it can only change in the direction that the Court has indicated. Likewise, depending upon the outlook of future courts—whether precedents are important or immediacy takes precedence—there may be a stymying effect upon legal action.

Justice Frankfurter is primarily interested in method, secondarily in result, for it is only through the correct methods that the mystical prestige of the Supreme Court will be enhanced. When he uses the due process clause of the Fourteenth Amendment to interpose Supreme Court opinion on that of state courts in the so-called "shocking" cases, it is because he wants to vindicate the honor of the "judicial process," rather than to help a particular litigant, however personally worthy his cause may be. If in defining the role of the Court in modern society he at times appears cold and heartless toward individuals, the reason may lie, not in his own predispositions, but in the development of our legal tradition. As Roscoe Pound has said:

> Undoubtedly the quest of certainty, uniformity, and stability in the nineteenth century carried what might be called a hard-boiled attitude . . . too far. But that attitude had succeeded an era of individualized justice and overreliance on the personal feelings of the judge. It should be possible to avoid an extreme of counterreaction in zeal to be humane today. In an extreme of humanitarian thinking we may lose sight of the social interest in the security of the . . . order which is involved.[35]

There is reflected in the philosophy of Justice Frankfurter the faith that humanitarian ends can best be attained and the work of the Supreme Court as a constitutional court furthered by heeding the structure and processes through which society has traditionally searched for the ends of a democratic order.

IV

The position that he has taken regarding the symbolic role of the Court has implications beyond those dealing with individual litigants. His concern with retaining the traditional function of the

[35] Roscoe Pound, *Introduction to the Philosophy of Law* (New Haven: Yale University Press, 1930), p. 166.

Court as the protector of social interests means that certain types of activities are foreclosed. This has caused him to say on different occasions that "After all, this is the Nation's ultimate judicial tribunal, not a super-legal-aid bureau," [36] when cases arose on right to counsel contentions with the point being pressed that the Supreme Court should provide the aid requested if no other agency would assay the task. Or again, he has reminded the world that "we are not authorized nor are we qualified to formulate a national code of domestic relations." [37] The Court should not be turned into a divorce or probate court for the United States.

On this point of activities foreclosed, Justice Frankfurter is not entirely consistent. It would seem from his opinions in the Gobitis and Barnette cases that if the nation's Highest Tribunal cannot be a super-legal-aid bureau or a divorce court for the nation, it can in some ways assume the role of a national school board. However, as he must see it, the overriding importance of keeping national unity through the use of symbolic concepts such as the flag and public education, and the equally important mission of retaining the Supreme Court as an unbiased articulator of social hopes and fears, means that in the area of legal choice, certain ideals have perduring value and thus must be supported, while others, though of equal local or state significance, cannot command the attention of the Supreme Court.

Taking into consideration his feelings toward the judiciary, and particularly the Supreme Court, his votes in cases affecting the prestige of the legal hierarchy follow as a matter of course. In one of his opinions he said that "A timid judge, like a biased judge, is intrinsically a lawless judge." [38] Timidity may be induced by adverse criticism, backed by the force of modern modes of communication unchecked by any sense of self-restraint. In making criticism of the courts responsible, Justice Frankfurter has often had to face the radiations of the First and Fourteenth Amendments. He admits that in this area delicate issues are at stake. The Constitution itself, however, is not a doctrinaire docu-

[36] Uveges v. Pennsylvania, 335 U.S. 437, 450 (1948).
[37] Williams v. North Carolina, 317 U.S. 287, 304–305 (1942).
[38] Wilkerson v. McCarthy, 336 U.S. 53, 65 (1949).

ment, and the Bill of Rights is not a collection of popular slogans. The Court cannot, therefore, "read into the Fourteenth Amendment the freedom of speech and of the press protected by the First Amendment and at the same time read out age-old means employed by states for securing the calm course of justice." [39] States are not forbidden to prohibit expressions calculated to subvert the exercise of judicial power since "the administration of justice by an impartial judiciary has been basic to our conception of freedom ever since Magna Carta." [40] Even freedom of the press, which is so indispensable to a democratic society, cannot be maintained without an independent judiciary that will, when occasion demands, protect that freedom.

Justice Black, on the other hand, finds that any type of enforced silence solely for preserving the dignity of the bench would do more harm than good and would probably engender resentment, suspicion, and contempt. When this is done to protect the judiciary, insult is added to injury. The difference in approach between Justices Black and Frankfurter is immediately apparent. The latter's concern over limiting criticism of jurists *when they are considering a particular case* does not stem from the fact that he thinks jurists as persons are sacrosanct or that they are more apt to be influenced in their decisions than are other mortals. But the integrity of the judicial process must be protected. Any hint that a jurist might have been unduly influenced by remarks that were not in the best taste may so depreciate public confidence that the courts would no longer be able to carry out their functions as protectors of the public interest. Justice Frankfurter is not concerned with enforcing silence solely for the personal comfort of the individual judge, as Justice Black tends to suggest. His interest is the broader, deeper one of preserving intact judicial standards so that all freedoms—those of the press, as well as others—can be protected.

In dealing with instances of press obstruction to legal processes, the contempt power is often used. It is also used on other occasions when the behavior of counsel or witnesses may lower

[39] Bridges v. California, 314 U.S. 252, 283–84 (1941).
[40] *Ibid.*, p. 282.

the prestige of the court. The power of summary contempt is one of the most forceful weapons placed in the hands of the judiciary. The power of summary contempt entrusted to a judge "is wholly unrelated to his personal sensibilities, be they tender or rugged. But judges also are human, and may, in a human way, quite unwittingly identify offense to self with obstruction to law." [41] Therefore, as no man should be judge in his own case, no judge should be allowed to preside over the sentencing attendant to contempt in his presence. As newspapers can harm the function of the courts as impartial arbitors, so can the actions of the judiciary place doubt in the public mind. Contempt power is not given to courts so they can remain immune from the ordinary give and take of courtroom performance. Rather, it is the benefit of society that dictates that such a power should be held. As Justice Frankfurter has said on another occasion, "preserving and enhancing respect for law is always more important than sustaining the infliction of punishment in a particular case." [42] Respect for law means that jurists cannot descend to the forum of acrimonious recrimination and still hope to retain the elevated, disinterested position that a legal system, to be effective, calls for.

Taken out of the context of the contempt power, what Justice Frankfurter is striving to attain is a society under law as well as by law. To arrive at such a point, individual preferences must be foresworn and judicial prestige upheld. His major fear apparently is the degeneration of society into an anarchic situation where force and distrust of law will be predominant. In the Little Rock situation, he disclaimed any intention to prohibit adverse comment upon the Court's previous rulings. The point at issue was, not whether the Court was right or wrong, but whether society could withstand a challenge to the legal order.

> The duty to abstain from resistance to "the supreme Law of the Land," . . . as declared by the organ of our Government for ascertaining it, does not require immediate approval of it nor does it deny the right of dissent. Criticism need not be stilled. Active obstruction or defiance is barred. Our kind of society cannot endure

[41] Offutt v. United States, 348 U.S. 11, 14 (1954).
[42] Sacher v. United States, 343 U.S. 1, 33 (1952).

if the controlling authority of the Law as derived from the Constitution is not to be the tribunal especially charged with the duty
of ascertaining and declaring what is "the supreme Law of the
Land." [43]

The controlling authority of the law must be recognized if we are
to endure as a nation. Courts as the symbolic representatives of
that law must be unhampered in their functions. The Supreme
Court as the nation's Highest Tribunal has the highest responsibility. From these three premises flow Justice Frankfurter's votes
on issues that affect judicial prestige.

Perhaps a side issue, although one very much connected with
maintaining respect for legal processes, is the question of time,
time not only in the sense of giving jurists adequate periods for
reflection, but also time in the very real sense of the calendar
space between hearing and decision. In a statement reminiscent
of the phrasing in the desegregation opinion, Justice Frankfurter
remarked that "mere speed is not a test of justice. Deliberative
speed is. Deliberative speed takes time. But it is time well
spent." [44] In desegregating schools or in handing down decisions,
a certain amount of leeway must be provided if the outcome
is not to be disastrous. He does not advocate tardiness for tardiness' sake, indicating in several of his opinions that nothing has
disturbed him more than the length of time required to dispose
of a case after proper hearing. As a teacher, he remarked that
"expedition in decision is as much a condition as an end of justice." [45]

There are instances, however, when expeditiousness must yield
to consideration. This is a lesson that Justice Frankfurter has apparently learned since coming to the Court, and it is one that he
considers necessary to proper judicial functioning. His thought
that "surely the protection of the public interest in the special
keeping of the Court is more imperative than the dispatch of

[43] Cooper v. Aaron, 358 U.S. 20, 24 (1958).
[44] First Iowa Hydro-Electric Corp. v. Federal Power Commission, 328 U.S. 152,
188 (1946).
[45] Felix Frankfurter and Henry Hart, "The Supreme Court at October Term,
1932," Harvard Law Review, XLVII (December, 1933), 249.

judicial business . . . " [46] may explain in part his own procrasti-
nation in writing opinions. The load of the public interest is a
heavy one, and those to whom protecting this interest is of importance will be hesitant to settle too quickly the legal issues involved. This is contradictory if judged by the standard of preserving the Court's time; it is not contradictory if judged by
utilizing the Court's time as necessary for full and complete
consideration of all questions that affect society's interest.

One of the shortest, although one of the most complete, statements of Justice Frankfurter's judicial philosophy is that "Law is
a social organism, and evolution operates in the sociological domain no less than in the biological." [47] Change cannot be retarded,
but neither can change be given impetus through judicial behavior. The role that the judiciary holds in modern society is a
limited one. To preserve the limited function that it does have,
reliance must be placed on prestige factors. A society without
law, and an agency to articulate it, steps into mortal danger of
being a society no longer. The judiciary in the United States has
traditionally held the position of legal conscience. For the public
to remain convinced of the validity of this tradition, certain
modes of procedure must be adopted. Individual justice cannot
be allowed *if* social concerns thereby suffer. Decorous behavior
must be demanded from all agencies having to do with the
judicial process, be they professional or lay. Time and more time
is necessary for ample deliberation by the courts so that special
interests will not replace social interests as the main focal point
in legal proceedings. These are premises from which Justice
Frankfurter reasons. They are the premises that allow him to
think of the Supreme Court as a symbolic, almost mystical, institution in its preoccupation with the large concerns that make
any community living possible.

[46] Insurance Group Comm. v. Denver & Rio Grande Rail Co., 329 U.S. 607, 631
(1947).
[47] Green v. United States, 356 U.S. 165 (1958).

THREE

The Uses of History

The dual concept of "symbolism and social unity" has counted heavily with Justice Frankfurter in his disposition of cases. Another technique used by him in constitutional and statutory interpretation has been to consult history for insights into the solution of present problems. He believes one can gain from history not only an understanding of evolving legal concepts, but also, and more importantly, a grasp of the underlying premises that made the American system of government possible. Indeed, he has written that "the Constitution of the United States is most significantly not a document but a stream of history. And the Supreme Court has directed the stream. Constitutional law, then, is history. But equally true is it that American history is constitutional law." Neither lawyers nor historians have sufficiently shown how enmeshed the country's history is in the law of the Supreme Court. They have been apt to emphasize the spectacular decisions rather than the continuity of historical evolution. For Justice Frank-

furter this is an irreparable loss in understanding the nation's intellectual growth.

He has spoken largely in the area of civil liberties when discussing the uses to which history can be put in aiding constitutional interpretation. This type of analysis, however, becomes evident in other areas, too. Stare decisis is most obviously affected, while the not so obvious topics of statutory construction and constitutional doctrine also become involved. Since historical studies hold such a prominent place in Frankfurter's philosophy, they merit separate treatment.

VI
History and the
Bill of Rights

It may of course be objected that an understanding of history does not necessarily entail an understanding of the problems faced by government in mid-twentieth-century United States, especially those of a legal nature. But it is probably true, as Max Radin claims, that "every lawyer is a historian since to cite a case —any case—is to cite a historical document which ought to be dealt with as a problem in historical research." [1] The lawyer or judge as historian therefore truly does gain a deeper appreciation of his own profession by utilizing sister disciplines, and, given the predominant influence of lawyers on our governmental philosophy, a deeper appreciation of the values held by the legal profession leads inevitably to a more profound understanding of government in action. It is indeed true that each historical epoch is supercharged and overlaid with its own basic philosophical as-

[1] Max Radin, *Law as Logic and Experience* (London: Oxford University Press, 1940), p. 138.

sumptions. And it is agreed that history should not be used in an effort to escape present theoretical or philosophical difficulties. But being able to identify the common characteristics of many eras need not be made synonymous with indiscriminate amalgamation of their peculiarities. Justice Frankfurter's approach is to look for the ever-present—one hesitates to use the word "universal"—traits of human nature or human institutions that lend themselves to analysis so that the present may be more fully described and understood. He has insisted, both as teacher and jurist, that reverence for the past must be predicated upon the lessons the past can teach and that change in the law is necessary in order to put these lessons to use.

I

When Felix Frankfurter came to the Supreme Court in January, 1939, New Deal leaders of constitutional revolution had won their first battles but not the entire campaign. The new Justice was expected to join other Roosevelt appointees in breaking with supposedly stultified constitutional doctrines of the immediate past. There arose, however, for all the New Deal justices, a perplexing impasse, which has been aptly described by Robert McCloskey.

> One of the enduring premises of American constitutional jurisprudence is the ideal of continuity, and thus it was necessary for the new constitutionalism to march under a banner that proclaimed it, not an excursion into the untried future but a reversion to the tested verities of the hallowed past. . . . True to the law of its being, American constitutionalism fought history with more history, and this strangely unrevolutionary method of the revolution should be duly noted.[2]

It should also be noted that, after the initial success of New Deal history, the victors began to divide among themselves over the disposition of constitutional spoils. Justice Frankfurter had al-

[2] Robert McCloskey (ed.), *Essays in Constitutional Law* (New York: Alfred A. Knopf, Inc., 1955), p. 7–8.

ready indicated in his pre-Court writings that he would give heed to the dictates of history. His brethren on the bench likewise were forced to face up to the demands of the past. Many justices looked for historical allies in support of their particular constitutional interpretations. Indeed, much of constitutional development since the early 1940's can be explained in terms of this struggle between competing historical schools of interpretation.

No reading of history can be neutral in the sense that the reader makes no commitment to a particular version. The commitment may be made for many reasons—conquest by fact, philosophical prepossessions, historical imperative—but the commitment is, nevertheless, made. In the case of Justice Frankfurter his interpretation is motivated by the desire to prove that history places certain limitations on the Supreme Court when it deals with the various ideals that are enshrined in the Constitution. He thinks these ideals have survived because the Court has been wise enough to recognize that not all constitutional provisions have the same type of historical heritage. Different means are needed to work with these differences in background.

He recognizes at least a two-fold division of issues coming before the Supreme Court.

> Most constitutional issues derive from the broad standards of fairness written into the Constitution (e.g. "due process," "equal protection of the laws," "just compensation"), and the division of power as between States and Nation. Such questions, by their very nature allow a relatively wide play for individual legal judgment. The other class gives no such scope. . . . These had their source in definite grievances and led the Fathers to proscribe against recurrence of their experience. These specific grievances and the safeguards against their recurrence were not defined by the Constitution. They were defined by history.[3]

This statement was taken from a 1946 opinion. The paragraph itself, however, is almost a verbatim reproduction of views expressed on at least two separate occasions in his pre-Court writ-

---

[3] United States v. Lovett, 328 U.S. 303, 321 (1946). For a discussion of historical studies, see William Anderson, "The Intention of the Framers: A Note on Constitutional Interpretation," *American Political Science Review*, xlix (June, 1955), 340–52.

ings.[4] During this time Frankfurter has held to his conviction that constitutional issues can only be dealt with intelligently when this differentiation in background is understood. When the issues are based upon standards of fairness, he does not feel confined by exact historical limitations. When, on the other hand, vices of civilization have been overcome through specific historic legal techniques, the Justice remains unconvinced that any change in techniques is warranted.

In a sense, the real problem here involved is how much continuity is desirable in constitutional law? Granted that continuity and stability are prime requisites in a legal system, how are the demands of flexibility and elasticity to be met? Justice Frankfurter is not blind to the difficulties inherent in producing even a provisional answer to these questions. As early as 1923 he had written that "the eternal struggle in the law between constancy and change is largely a struggle between the forces of history and the forces of reason, between past reason and present needs." [5] But past reason and present needs are not mutually exclusive categories, as Felix Frankfurter knows. After admitting that, in studies on the interplay of continuity and change in law, the rate of change is the decisive factor, he has gone on to say that even that rate depends upon the momentum of continuity and therefore of resistance to change. He then raises the following significant question: "But may not one say with equal accuracy that the momentum of continuity, that is, resistance to change, depends upon the rate of change, and both the momentum of continuity and the rate of change within the law drastically depend upon the rate of change in forces—political, technological and psychological—outside the law?" [6] No one has given a totally satisfactory answer to this question. Frankfurter has, however, made an attempt, through historical analysis, to indicate when forces outside the law *should not* bring about

[4] Felix Frankfurter, "The Red Terror of Judicial Reform," *New Republic*, xl (October 1, 1924), 110–13 and Felix Frankfurter, *Mr. Justice Holmes* (Cambridge, Mass.: Harvard University, 1938), pp. 5–6.

[5] Felix Frankfurter, "Twenty Years of Holmes," *Harvard Law Review*, xxxvi (June, 1923), 931.

[6] Felix Frankfurter, "Law and the Future: Foreword," *Northwestern University Law Review*, li (May–June, 1956), 164.

changes in interpreting particular constitutional provisions. These analyses center mainly on two areas, the Bill of Rights and the Fourteenth Amendment.

II

A brief outline of the first of these topics, Justice Frankfurter's approach to the Bill of Rights, can be gleaned from the following quotation taken from one of his opinions:

> In the Bill of Rights, eighteenth-century statesmen formulated safeguards against the recurrence of well-defined historic grievances. Some of these safeguards such as the right to trial by a jury of twelve and immunity from prosecution unless initiated by a grand jury were built on experience of relative and limited validity. . . . Others like the freedom of the press or the free exercise of religion, or freedom from condemnation without a fair trial, express rights the denial of which is repugnant to the conscience of a free people.[7]

Two features stand out. The first is that all provisions of the Bill of Rights do not have the same historic pedigree. Different circumstances have brought these provisions into being. A second feature is that certain sections of the Bill of Rights are of fairly constant meaning while others are more indefinite in connotation —jury of twelve in contradistinction to freedom of the press. Justice Frankfurter does not place rigid terms lower on his hierarchy of values than those of indefinite dimensions. Both rigid and flexible terminology is needed, but each has its own separate and distinct function. Their adequacy in fulfilling these distinctive functions is his key to their acceptance.

The criterion used to differentiate rigid from flexible provisions is discovered by examining their origin. "Of compelling consideration is the fact that words acquire scope and function from the history of events which they summarize."[8] The Framers did not insert impractical ideals into the Fundamental Code;

[7] Malinski v. New York, 324 U.S. 401, 414 (1945).
[8] Phelps Dodge Corp. v. NLRB, 313 U.S. 177, 186 (1941).

they utilized words that in themselves summarized and carried a wealth of practical historical meaning. Part of this meaning was derived from the carry-over of English common law traditions and part from colonial experience. When Justice Frankfurter writes of the traditions of English-speaking people he has this heritage in mind. For him the task of Supreme Court members is to garner from history as much information about the meaning of the Constitution as can possibly be distilled from the records of the past. To do this a "higher criticism" of constitutional text and terminology may be necessary. Frankfurter as an exponent of such "higher criticism" has stated that "there are varying shades of compulsion for judges behind different words, differences that are due to the words themselves, their setting in a text, their setting in history." He elaborated by saying,

> . . . judges are not unfettered glossators. They are under a special duty not to over-emphasize the episodic aspects of life and not to undervalue its organic processes—its continuities and relationships. *For judges at least it is important to remember that continuity with the past is not only a necessity but even a duty.*[9]

His twist on Justice Holmes' pronouncement that necessity and not duty forces conformity to the past while stylistically a change in position for two words shows more than a slight difference in constitutional viewpoint.

In 1916 Frankfurter wrote that "the Constitution is a means of ordering the life of a young nation, having its roots in the past . . . intended for the unknown future. Intentionally, therefore, it was bounded with outlines not sharp and contemporary, but permitting of increasing definiteness through experience." [10] As a justice, Frankfurter has worked out a partial cataloging system wherein provisions of the Bill of Rights may be placed. He has developed this system to aid him in his search for a means to reconcile duty-continuity-change in constitutional law. Certain concepts are typed "specific" while others are labeled "generic."

[9] Felix Frankfurter, "Some Reflections on the Reading of Statutes," *Columbia Law Review,* XLVII (May, 1947), 531.

[10] Felix Frankfurter, "The Constitutional Opinions of Justice Holmes," *Harvard Law Review,* XXIX (April, 1916), 685.

Expressed differently, specific terms are analogous to the rigid concepts mentioned previously, while generic phrases may be compared to those formerly designated flexible. Within the specific grouping, for example, are found provisions dealing with double jeopardy, self-incrimination, and unreasonable searches and seizures. Although not within the Bill of Rights proper, prohibitions covering ex post facto laws and bills of attainder have been assimilated within the specific group. From the first eight amendments, the due process clause of the Fifth Amendment and the portions of the First dealing with freedom of speech, press, and religion fall squarely within the generic sphere.

In everyday parlance, Justice Frankfurter's use of specific as a designation indicates his acceptance of limitations on certain constitutional terms which are placed there by the accretions of history and are not to be removed by judicial interpretation. These terms were defined once and for all long ago and their definitions were known and accepted by the Framers of the Constitution. Arriving at such a conclusion, he refuses to alter their allegedly fixed content. His theoretical structure provides other mechanisms for change. Most important among these are the generic terms of the Constitution. These were originally left by the Framers to be filled by history and experience. They have not been strictly delimited by the situations in which they were applied. Definition of these generic clauses is a continuous, ongoing process. No point of finality can ever be reached. Contrasted with terms that were once and for all given a definite content by their own history and by the Framers' acceptance of the meaning of that history the generic terms are constantly free to make their own history, so to speak. Given this methodological background, only a case-by-case approach will demonstrate the translation of theory into practice.

A major difficulty in analyzing Justice Frankfurter's uses of history stems from an attempt to segregate cases based on the Bill of Rights from cases involving the Fourteenth Amendment. The tendency to insist that the Fourteenth Amendment makes the entire Bill of Rights applicable to the states means that discussion over definition of terms within the Bill of Rights can as easily come to the fore in state as in federal cases. Attention will therefore be focused on the constitutional terms themselves rather than on a fruitless struggle to distinguish federal from state cases.

III

Although Justice Frankfurter has not produced opinions dealing with all the first eight amendments, he has aired his views frequently enough to warrant a summary of his stand regarding specific and generic terms. On the whole, he has treated the First Amendment as a provision that allows for judicial leeway in interpretation, unshackled by exact historical standards. To speak of "freedom" of speech or of the press requires understanding as to what "freedom" entails. It is a commonplace that no words in the English language are more difficult to define than are "freedom" or "liberty." Because of the value judgments involved, words with such an emotional content will cause more trouble in application than will an expression like "jury of twelve." To avoid paralyzing the present by reverence for terms from the past that cannot be defined adequately and were not defined either by history or the Framers of the Constitution, Justice Frankfurter refuses to acknowledge that the First Amendment freedoms are specific and absolute.

Bridges v. California [11] determined the scope of freedom of speech and of the press in relation to judicial proceedings pending before the Court. A judge sitting on a case involving supposed crimes by labor leaders was informed via newspaper editorials of the undesirable impression their release would cause. After the defendants' conviction, Harry Bridges sent a telegram to the Secretary of Labor intimating dire consequences as a result of the case. With regard to these attempts to influence the outcome of judicial proceedings, Justice Frankfurter declared that "free speech is not so absolute or irrational a conception as to imply paralysis of the means for effective protection of all freedoms secured by the Bill of Rights." [12] He came to this con-

[11] 314 U.S. 252 (1941).
[12] Ibid., p. 282.

clusion by examining the times and ways in which attacks upon the courts had been controlled in the past. Freedom, because it is a generic term, must have the meaning of experience read into it. "Trial by newspaper" would not have been accepted by the Framers of the Constitution even at the time when that document was adopted; it could not be accepted today. By attempting to make too exact a definition for the inherently indefinable rights of "free" speech or "free" press, other rights may be lost. The Bridges case was one of the first to come before Justice Frankfurter involving First Amendment issues. The historical methodology employed there has been apparent on most occasions since, when questions concerning the Amendment have been raised. Justice Frankfurter finds his compulsion for interpreting freedom and liberty, not in the setting of the eighteenth century, but in the setting of today. Insisting that "the Constitution was not conceived as a doctrinaire document, nor was the Bill of Rights intended as a collection of popular slogans,"[13] he can see no valid reason for overburdening flexible freedoms with arbitrarily exact and confining qualifications.

In the Bridges case, Justice Black delivered the opinion of the Court over Frankfurter's dissent. Philosophic division among the New Deal justices had already made itself evident. In order to give his discussion as firm a foundation as possible, Black also turned to the past, but his purpose was to gather proof that an absolute prohibition against encroaching upon freedom of speech and press had been laid by the First Amendment—absolute in the sense that everyone (with the exception of the dissenters) was agreed as to the Framers' meaning.

> Ratified as it was while the memory of many oppressive English restrictions on the enumerated liberties was still fresh, the First Amendment cannot reasonably be taken as approving prevalent English practices. On the contrary, the only conclusion supported by history is that the unqualified prohibitions laid down by the framers were intended to give to liberty of the press, as to other liberties, the broadest scope that could be countenanced in an orderly society.[14]

[13] Bridges v. California, 314 U.S. 252, 283 (1941).
[14] *Ibid.*, p. 265.

The dissenters certainly did agree that the broadest scope possible should be given freedom of speech or of the press. They merely thought that the meaning assigned freedom in this case was historically untenable.

Main emphasis throughout the majority opinion went to establishing the unqualified and unqualifiable nature of the First Amendment. It was not pure chance that Justice Black wrote the opinion, for as John P. Frank, the Justice's biographer and ardent admirer, admits, "where freedom is involved, Black, unlike many liberals, is willing to embrace an absolute." [15] This he most assuredly did in the Bridges case. By contrast, the dissenting justices focused attention not on the negative aspect of prohibition—"Congress shall make no law . . . abridging freedom of speech or of the press"—but on the positive meaning of the First Amendment in various situations. The creative aspects of the First Amendment as a constitutional clause able to meet the emerging problems of a complex society were highlighted. The idealistic, absolutist-minded majority was counterbalanced by a strong, realistic, flexibly oriented minority. While many other cases involving freedom of speech or of the press have come to the Supreme Court in the interim, and the composition of both groups has changed with swings in personnel, the original two philosophic trends reflected in the Bridges case have appeared and reappeared. Once positions were taken on the specific or generic nature of "freedom" of speech or press, only the task of refining concepts remained. Refinements were often made on the basis of more extended historical analysis.

Perhaps at this time it should be stated that Justice Black has been chosen for placement in opposition to Justice Frankfurter, not because his talents or accomplishments as a jurist are any less notable than those of the former Harvard professor—indeed in some areas they surpass his adversary, but because he is the most articulate and mature in presenting the opposing views and he has written opinions in many of the cases in which divergence between members of the Court has been most evident. He most

---

[15] John P. Frank, "The United States Supreme Court: 1950–51," *University of Chicago Law Review*, XIX (Winter, 1952), 188. Cf. by the same author, *Mr. Justice Black, The Man and His Opinions* (New York: Alfred A. Knopf, Inc., 1949).

adequately represents a vastly different school of thought on constitutional interpretation and particularly on historical interpretation.

The difference between the two men over the nature of freedom and liberty is not one of mere semantics. The difference is fundamental. While both rely on history to provide guideposts for constitutional interpretation, Justice Black appears surer of his ability to recapture all possible eighteenth-century connotations in the use of those terms. Justice Frankfurter, on the other hand, agrees that eighteenth-century meaning for such phrases as "trial by a jury of twelve" can be understood. He is, however, hesitant to assert that nebulous and amorphous ideals such as liberty or freedom can be concretized in their twentieth-century setting, let alone in their eighteenth. "The language of the First Amendment is to be read not as barren words found in a dictionary but as symbols of historic experience illumined by the presuppositions of those who employ them." [16] The First Amendment is continually generating its own history out of unique experiences. While the presuppositions of Madison and Hamilton are important, they cannot be completely those of the Vinson or Warren Courts. Justice Frankfurter's historic approach admittedly allows for changing conditions to be taken into account when the First Amendment is discussed. Whether his correlation between conditions and freedoms is approved or not, the utility of the approach can be appreciated.

Justice Black, by attempting to equate twentieth-century freedom and liberty with that of the eighteenth, runs the risk of prejudicing the future of constitutional development. In practice, Justice Black has expanded the meaning of some words within the First Amendment. For example, speech has been made to include activities such as picketing, which could not possibly have been encompassed within the original meaning of the term. Frankfurter, of course, has done this very same thing, agreeing that picketing could be subsumed under the elastic freedom of speech conception that is basic to his historical approach. Black, however, refuses to accept the position that freedom has any other than a constant content. As with Frankfurter, the Framers are

[16] Dennis v. United States, 341 U.S. 494, 523 (1951).

often cited in support. Justice Black, nevertheless, has felt no such compulsion in changing the content for other terms in the Constitution, the Framers to the contrary notwithstanding.

Property has undergone enormous revision since the advent of the New Deal Court. No one bothers to quote John Adams to the effect that "Property is surely a right of mankind as really as liberty. . . . The moment the idea is admitted into society, that property is not as sacred as the laws of God, and that there is not a force of law and public justice to protect it, anarchy and tyranny commence." [17] For Frankfurter, property joins freedom and liberty as generic terms, all of which must be infused with meaning out of present experience. Contrariwise, Justice Black, while giving current connotations to property, has been adamant that freedom should be absolute and never change. As long ago as 1931 Professor Frankfurter noted that "those who chafe most against the governance of the present by the edicts of the past too frequently want the present to pronounce against the future, forgetting that for the future the present will be the past." [18] While his own insight may justly be turned against him on some counts, it also illumines Justice Black's difficulty. By handing the future a supposedly closed meaning for freedom in the First Amendment, Black may be defeating his own libertarian activist purposes if his definition is unable to cope with the problems that the future will surely pose.

The religion clauses of the First Amendment have provided other dividing points over constitutional interpretation for members of the present Court. The pattern of freedom of religion cases has followed closely the pattern of free speech and press cases, in that the division over the specific or generic nature of freedom has been evident. Different, however, are recent cases involving the establishment of religion clause. Two controversies especially present an interesting contrast in historical approach. Everson v. Board of Education [19] and McCollum v. Board of

[17] John Adams, *The Works of John Adams* (Boston: Little, Brown & Co., 1853), VI, 8–9.

[18] Felix Frankfurter, "When Justice Cardozo Writes," *New Republic*, LXVI (April 8, 1931), 211.

[19] 330 U.S. 1 (1947).

Education,[20] decided within a year of each other, illustrate the fact that even when agreement is reached on the specific-generic issue, there is no assurance that unanimity will be reached on the meaning of the specific terms themselves.

The decision in the Everson case turned on the question of whether a New Jersey law providing payment for transportation for children attending a parochial school in which religion was taught amounted to an unconstitutional "establishment of religion." Justice Black, in the majority opinion, found that "once again . . . it is not inappropriate briefly to review the background and environment of the period in which the constitutional language was fashioned and adopted"[21] before making any decision on the substantive point at issue. After surveying the meaning of "establishment," he ascertained that it meant in part no aid could be given a particular denomination in preference to others. In part it also meant that the state itself could not regulate organized religious activities. He concluded that neither situation occurred here.

Justice Rutledge delivered a dissenting opinion in which Justice Frankfurter joined. The Rutledge dissent, although utilizing much of the same historical material found in the Court's opinion, came to a different conclusion as to the meaning of "establishment." "No provision of the Constitution is more closely tied to or given content by its generating history than the religion clause of the First Amendment. It is at once the refined product and the terse summation of that history."[22] The only possible conclusion to be drawn from this history was that "not simply an established church, but any law respecting an establishment of religion is forbidden."[23] Therefore, the New Jersey statute should fall.

Justice Black in the second case, McCollum v. Board of Education, again presented the opinion of the Court. Here an Illinois law that permitted the use of public schools for the conduct of

[20] 333 U.S. 203 (1948).
[21] Everson v. Board of Education 330 U.S. 1, 8 (1947).
[22] *Ibid.*, p. 33.
[23] *Ibid.*, p. 31.

classes in religion supervised by different religious groups was judged by the standards of the First Amendment. Justice Black ruled that the released-time programs did come under the interdict of the establishment clause. The clause was exact enough to forbid such programs. In a concurring opinion Justice Frankfurter summed up his entire position by saying that "Separation means separation, not something less." [24]

For scholarly reasons it is unfortunate that he talked about "separation of church and state" since that phrase does not appear in the First Amendment. In the McCollum case he committed the cardinal sin against which he so often inveighs, that of interpreting the gloss on the Constitution rather than the Constitution itself. In any event, he made separation of church and state synonymous with the prohibition against an establishment of religion and found that there was no room left by history for judicial definition. The Framers had spoken and their commands must be obeyed. All the Justices seemed committed to this view. In both the Everson and McCollum cases, therefore, disagreement did not come over the theory of flexible versus absolute provisions but wholly over the problem of applying the absolute prohibitions. For Justice Frankfurter, the First Amendment presents two distinct types of historical terms: positive guarantees for freedom of speech, press, and religion, which he understands to be generic, fluid expressions; and a negative prohibition on the establishment of religion, which he understands to be a specific governmental response to a specific historic evil.

IV

With other amendments in the Bill of Rights, Justice Frankfurter employs the same technique of dividing terms and phrases on the basis of their specific or generic characteristics. The Fourth Amendment's declaration that "the right of the people to be secure in their persons, houses, papers and effects, against unreasonable searches and seizures" brought extended comment

[24] 333 U.S. 203, 231 (1948).

in the case of Harris v. United States.[25] The opinion of the Court upheld seizure by federal officers of selective service classification cards and registration certificates, illegally held by appellant, taken in the course of a search of his apartment without a warrant. Justice Frankfurter dissented. Declaring that "one's views regarding circumstances like those here presented ultimately depend upon one's understanding of the history and the function of the Fourth Amendment," he then went on to say that "a decision may turn on whether one gives the Amendment a place second to none in the Bill of Rights, or considers it on the whole a kind of nuisance, a serious impediment in the war against crime." [26] Frankfurter felt constrained to add that the Fourth Amendment was central to the enjoyment of the other guarantees of the Bill of Rights. Search and seizure was a phrase brought over from the common law. It carried with it a precise set of historical antecedents. If the police could, without a warrant, search houses from garret to cellar, then no safeguard for personal security would be found any longer in the Fourth Amendment. The prohibition against unreasonable searches and seizures would not be historically venerable; it would be antiquated.

Perhaps the clearest exposition of Justice Frankfurter's position concerning the Fourth Amendment came in United States v. Rabinowitz,[27] dealing with the search of a one-room business establishment, open to the public, by federal officers. The majority opinion upheld the search and seizure of forged ration stamps on the basis of prior knowledge that the defendant had such stamps in his possession. Justice Frankfurter again dissented. He acknowledged that such controversies often involve "not very nice people" and that in this particular case "a shabby defrauder" was the central figure. But these conditions did not authorize disregard of historic materials. For him, the central fact about the Fourth Amendment was that it safeguarded against abuses that helped lead to the Revolution. He then stated with precision its specific nature.

[25] 331 U.S. 145 (1947).
[26] *Ibid.*, p. 157.
[27] 339 U.S. 56 (1950).

Because the experience of the framers of the Bill of Rights was so vivid, they assumed that it would be carried down the stream of history and that their words would receive the significance of the experience to which they were addressed—a significance not to be found in the dictionary. When the Fourth Amendment outlawed "unreasonable searches" and then went on to define the very restricted authority that even a search warrant issued by a magistrate could give, the framers said with all the clarity of the gloss of history that a search is "unreasonable" unless a warrant authorizes it, barring only exceptions justified by absolute necessity.[28]

In order to appreciate the difference in constitutional interpretation between Black and Frankfurter, the following statement from one of the former's opinions should be compared with the quotation above:

> Some constitutional provisions are stated in absolute and unqualified language such, for illustration, as the First Amendment stating that no law shall be passed prohibiting the free exercise of religion or abridging the freedom of speech or press. Other constitutional provisions do require courts to choose between competing policies, such as the Fourth Amendment . . . .[29]

Justice Frankfurter finds the First Amendment a generic provision requiring definition by experience of today; the Fourth Amendment is specific, "unreasonable searches and seizures" being defined by the Framers as those conducted without a warrant. For Justice Black, the nature of these provisions is exactly reversed. The First Amendment is absolute, while the Fourth requires determination and definition.

Treating the Fifth Amendment's self-incrimination and double jeopardy clauses, Justice Frankfurter gives narrow, technical interpretations. One of his best expressions on self-incrimination came in the 1955 term in Ullmann v. United States.[30] In his opinion for the Court sustaining the validity of the Immunity Act of 1954, he agreed that the privilege was "an important advance in the development of our liberty." But this did not counteract the fact that the privilege had but a limited applicability. Such

[28] Ibid., p. 70.
[29] Rochin v. California, 342 U.S. 165, 176 (1952).
[30] 350 U.S. 422 (1956).

limits were set by the Constitution itself. "No person shall be . . . compelled in any *criminal case* to be a witness against himself." In the instance under consideration, Ullmann had refused to answer questions before a grand jury about his participation in and knowledge of subversive activities. This refusal came in spite of the fact that he was guaranteed immunity from future criminal prosecution under the 1954 statute.

In upholding the lower court's contempt conviction, Justice Frankfurter was most explicit. "The Fifth Amendment's guaranty against self-incrimination operates only where a witness is asked to give testimony which may possibly expose him to a criminal charge; if the criminality has already been taken away by an immunity statute, the Amendment ceases to apply." [31] Whether the individual was subjected to other types of nonlegal coercion, such as public condemnation, was immaterial. The investigation of the grand jury was not a criminal proceeding in the constitutional sense; even if it had been, immunity was granted. That was all the Constitution provided.

The privilege against self-incrimination has always been narrowly and strictly viewed by Justice Frankfurter. In cases coming before the Court early in his tenure he gave indication that he would sanction only the accepted historic uses to which the privilege had been put. For instance, in 1943 he wrote that "the duty to give testimony was qualified at common law by the privilege against self-incrimination. . . . But the privilege is a privilege to withhold answers and not a privilege to limit the range of public inquiry. The Constitution does not forbid the asking of criminative questions." [32] The only thing that the Fifth Amendment stipulated was that these questions did not have to be answered unless complete statutory immunity was given.

Or again, Justice Frankfurter did not think that self-incrimination resulted from an accused's refusal to testify in his own behalf when the trial judge specifically instructed the jurors that this failure "shall not create any presumption against him." [33] One of the troublesome issues growing out of a statutory grant

[31] *Ibid.*, p. 431.
[32] United States v. Monia, 317 U.S. 424, 433 (1943).
[33] Bruno v. United States, 308 U.S. 287 (1939).

of immunity is whether such immunity from prosecution, when given by the federal government, should be binding upon state authorities or vice versa. On many occasions Justice Frankfurter has indicated that he did not think protection against self-incrimination was transferable.[34] Inconveniences and embarrassments may result for the individual from such nontransferability, but these are prices that must be paid for a federal system. During the last few years pleading the Fifth Amendment has taken on notorious proportions, leading Justice Frankfurter to remark that the privilege against self-incrimination "has attained the familiarity of the comic strips . . . ."[35] But the number of times the privilege is invoked should not change its historic meaning or make it apply in cases precluded by the nature of our federal union.

In 1923 Professor Frankfurter had written that "Histories are not to be lightly swapped; a long course of history is apt to rest on humanly intrinsic considerations."[36] Many years later in a Supreme Court opinion he wrote: "In applying a provision like that of double jeopardy, which is rooted in history and is not an evolving concept like that of due process, a long course of adjudication in this Court carries impressive authority."[37] Justice Frankfurter in dealing with the double jeopardy clause of the Fifth Amendment has attempted not to swap or desert the historic meaning that he thinks the clause had for the Framers of the Constitution and that it held for previous members of the Court. United States ex rel. Marcus v. Hess,[38] although dealing with the fairly limited topic of the right to compensation under a federal fraudulent claims liability act, drew one of the earliest expressions of his views concerning double jeopardy.

Justice Black's opinion for the Court established that no double jeopardy was involved in an action for double damages against Hess, who had previously been indicted and fined for defrauding the government in connection with the same contested trans-

[34] Knapp v. Schweitzer, 357 U.S. 371 (1958).
[35] In re Groban, 352 U.S. 330, 337 (1957).
[36] Felix Frankfurter, "Enforcement of Prohibition," New Republic, xxxiii (January, 1923), 150.
[37] Gore v. United States, 357 U.S. 386, 392 (1958).
[38] 317 U.S. 537 (1943).

action. Concurring with the Court's findings, Justice Frankfurter corroborated their correctness by looking to the past and the past's treatment of comparable situations.

> Like other specific provisions of the Constitution, the double jeopardy clause must be read in the context of its times. It would do violence to proper regard for the framers of the Fifth Amendment to assume that they contemporaneously enacted and continued to enact legislation that was offensive to the guarantee of the double jeopardy clause which they had proposed for ratification.[39]

Satisfying himself once again that he was not countermanding the requirements of history, Justice Frankfurter acquiesced in the decision of the Court. During the 1959 term he expanded outward the implications of his views on double jeopardy by holding for the Court that subsequent state prosecution for an offense was not foreclosed by a prior unsuccessful federal attempt at conviction.[40] He held that although one act constituted both offenses, two separate statutes were involved, one each representing nation and state. As a generalization, with the Fifth Amendment, as with the First, distinctions can be drawn between the specific and generic characteristics of different provisions. In the former, double jeopardy and self-incrimination are in an equivalent specific classification with the establishment clause of the latter. Due process and just compensation can roughly be equated with freedom of speech, press, and religion on the basis of the generic attributes of all five terms.

Further detailed analysis like that employed above could be used to differentiate the specific and generic traits of other amendments in the Bill of Rights. The Sixth Amendment's declaration that "In all criminal prosecutions, the accused shall enjoy the right to a speedy and public trial, by an impartial jury . . . and . . . have the assistance of counsel for his defense" has been the basis for much litigation. While granting that, in general, the amendment is quite explicit in meaning, Justice Frankfurter has held that the right to a public trial does not preclude an accused from pleading guilty and thus foregoing

[39] *Ibid.,* pp. 555–56.
[40] Bartkus v. Illinois, 359 U.S. 121 (1959).

the trial stage.[41] The right to assistance of counsel, while again very specific in nature, must be applied in concrete situations. The fact that an accused was a competent, practicing lawyer and not a "helpless illiterate" made a difference when considering whether or not he had been denied assistance of counsel.[42]

Dennis v. United States [43] raised the question of what constituted an "impartial" jury. The Court upheld government prosecution of Communist leaders before a jury composed almost entirely of government employees or their close relations. Justice Jackson, in a concurring opinion, summed up the majority attitude by declaring that "so long as accused persons who are Republicans, Dixiecrats, Socialists or Democrats must put up with such a jury, it will have to do for Communists." [44] Justices Black and Frankfurter both dissented, feeling that the impartiality called for by the Constitution and given meaning by historical experience had not been attained. The Sixth Amendment's guarantee of a speedy trial has been extended through statute to include arraignment within a reasonable time before a competent federal judicial officer. While no precise historical definition can be given for a "speedy trial," Justice Frankfurter has indicated that there are limits inherent in even so nebulous a term. Just so, some proximate definition can be set for a "reasonable time" for arraignments, and he attempted to give such a definition in a recent case.[45]

In United States v. Lovett [46] the Court, in an opinion by Justice Black, treated a congressional statute depriving government employees of future government service through withholding of salary expenditures as a bill of attainder. The men involved were suspected of disloyalty. Justice Frankfurter, in a concurring opinion, refused to acknowledge the definition of the congressional

[41] Adams v. United States, 317 U.S. 269 (1942).
[42] Glaser v. United States, 315 U.S. 60 (1942).
[43] 339 U.S. 162 (1950).
[44] Ibid., p. 175.
[45] Mallory v. United States, 354 U.S. 457 (1957). Justice Frankfurter's opinion in this case has been made the basis for a proposed statute setting down with some precision a more lenient definition of "reasonable." See 104 Congressional Record 17036 and Baltimore Sun, August 20, 1958.
[46] 328 U.S. 303 (1946).

action as a bill of attainder, although he did agree that the men should be paid compensation for work already done. The prohibition against such a bill is not found in the Bill of Rights proper; nevertheless it is a specific historical term and is treated in that manner by Frankfurter. Professor Herman Pritchett thought that unquestionably Black's opinion "rested on an expansion of the old bill of attainder concept to cover a new situation." [47] Perhaps because of the comment that his opinion in the Lovett case caused, a few years later in another litigation purportedly dealing with bills of attainder—Justice Frankfurter again disagreeing on this point—Justice Black explicitly recognized that he was giving new meaning to a term that had a supposedly fixed content. "It is true that the classic bill of attainder was a condemnation by the legislature following investigation by that body. . . . But I cannot believe that the authors of the Constitution, who outlawed the bill of attainder, inadvertently endowed the executive with power to engage in the same tyrannical practices that had made the bill such an odious institution." [48] If the Framers had committed such an inadvertence, Justice Black was willing to rectify their mistake—and he was a perceptive enough historian to know that he was making changes. Action of this sort, however, raises questions of importance for the future of constitutional law.

What are to become of those portions of the Constitution whose meaning up to the present time has been definite, clear, and precise? It is all very well earnestly to desire to have the outcome in particular cases conform to laudable ideals of justice and fairness. But to twist defined constitutional terms out of their original shapes in order to arrive at such results probably does more harm than good. Just as the President often tries to disguise his source of power for certain actions by enumerating all different bases—his duties as Commander-in-Chief, the necessity to see that the laws are faithfully executed, etc.—so many of the activist justices try to pull in cases for review under as many clauses as possible—due process, bill of attainder, equal protec-

---

[47] C. Herman Pritchett, "The Political Offender and the Warren Court," *Boston University Law Review*, xxxviii (Winter, 1958), 110.

[48] Joint Anti-Fascist Refugee Committee v. McGrath, 341 U.S. 123, 144 (1951).

tion. Multiplicity of sources is often used when no one particular source definitely grants the power sought. In the judicial realm, this is especially dangerous, for constitutional terms, such as "bill of attainder," will be distorted to serve purposes for which they were not originally intended. Once new definitions are given, the historic worth of such terms may be lost.

Most important among the generic phrases of the first eight amendments is the due process clause of the Fifth Amendment. In 1924 Professor Frankfurter noted that "it cannot be too often made clear that the meaning of phrases like 'due process of law,' and of simple terms like 'liberty' and 'property' is not revealed within the Constitution; their meaning is derived from without." [49] Justice Frankfurter's extensive reliance on this philosophy and his constant use of "due process" to mitigate some of the harshness of specific clauses warrants brief examination here.

For him, the due process clause provides an extremely important *via media* between confining historic terms and the chaos of undirected self-indulgence. The phrase itself, although of imprecise historic content, relates surely to the maintenance of civilized and humane standards of behavior. Due process acts as a safety-valve. It takes the place of forcing undefinable circumstances into defined concepts. In Frankfurter's words,

> The Due Process Clause . . . has potency different from and independent of the specific provisions contained in the Bill of Rights. . . . The Fifth Amendment specifically prohibits prosecution of an "infamous crime" except by indictment; it forbids double jeopardy and self-incrimination, as well as deprivation of "life, liberty or property, without due process of law." Not to attribute to due process of law an independent function but to consider it a shorthand statement of other specific clauses in the same Amendment is to charge those who secured the adoption of this Amendment with meretricious redundancy by indifference to a phrase—"due process of law"—which was one of the great instruments in the very arsenal which the Bill of Rights was to protect and strengthen.[50]

Due process, therefore, takes its place beside freedom of speech, press, and religion as a clause that by its very generic nature allows present experience to translate itself into constitutional law.

[49] Frankfurter, "The Red Terror of Judicial Reform," *loc. cit.*, p. 112.
[50] Malinski v. New York, 324 U.S. 401, 414–15 (1945).

V

Instead of trying to seek solutions for twentieth-century problems in the straitjacket of eighteenth-century terminology, Justice Frankfurter admits that there are flexible, generic terms within the Bill of Rights that history has not defined. This admission has been noted and approved by others.[51] Such an admission is not professedly determined by convenience alone, but it is determined equally as much by the apparently sincere belief that expanding constitutional terms is historic sacrilege. Assuming that "law declared by this Court, in contradistinction to law declared by Congress, is something other than the manipulation of words to formulate a predetermined result," "judicial law implies at least some continuity of intellectual criteria and procedures in dealing with recurring problems."[52] When Justice Frankfurter can identify parallels with historic evils remediable by specific historic cures, he, as a member of the Court, administers the prescribed medicant, whether or not he would, as a private citizen, agree with the wisdom of the prescription. Otherwise, he looks to advances that time has brought to constitutional law through liberal doses of the due process clause and through judicial treatment of such terms as freedom and liberty. This approach was designed to combine the attributes of both continuity and change in constitutional interpretation. As one who is peculiarly sensitive to the nuances of factual and philosophic history, Justice Frankfurter apparently thinks that he avoids doing violence to the past by means of his specific-generic concept.

In fairness to the critics of this approach, a vast concession must be made. If agreement cannot be reached on the meaning of basic terms such as bill of attainder or ex post facto laws, there is considerable danger that the entire attempt to distinguish

[51] See Willard Hurst, "The Role of History," in Edmond Cahn (ed.), *Supreme Court and Supreme Law* (Bloomington: Indiana University Press, 1954), p. 57; Charles P. Curtis, "A Modern Supreme Court in a Modern World," *Vanderbilt Law Review*, IV (April, 1951), 431–32; Arthur E. Sutherland, *The Law and One Man Among Many* (Madison: University of Wisconsin Press, 1956), p. 71.

[52] Burford v. Sun Oil Co., 319 U.S. 336 (1943).

between specific and generic proves a hollow failure. When widely divergent interpretations of the same constitutional phrases appear in judicial opinions, no amount of subterfuge or explanation will hide that divergence. Over the years it has become clear that, at one time or another, most of the justices have disagreed over the creditability to be extended historical studies claiming to authenticate the meaning of even the most specific constitutional terms. Most obviously, Justices Black, Douglas, Murphy, and Rutledge have disagreed with the historical interpretations of Justice Frankfurter. This is not to imply that they did not have and use their own theory of constitutional history, but only that they refused to follow the Frankfurter analysis.

For all the justices, a warning by Carl Becker should be taken to heart: ". . . we shall not preserve our freedoms by resting in the comfortable conviction that they are secure because defined in the constitution. To revere the founding fathers is all very well but it would be better if we followed their example by re-examining the fundamental human rights and the economic and political institutions best suited to secure them." [53] Justice Frankfurter's specific-generic catalog will not by itself save him from this problem. It must be used as Becker suggests in order to be of enduring value. Even the most specific of terms in the Bill of Rights do not have the precise content usually attributed to mathematical symbols. In applying any terms, blurring is apt to occur. The main forte of Justice Frankfurter's historical approach is that it allows the Court to go a long way before blurring of many terms becomes necessary, and it takes into account the long line of growth for specific terms. For those others that are generic in nature, present experience may help to alleviate confusion and indecision. Flexibility replaces fixity as the polestar for constitutional interpretation, and thus the demands of both continuity and change are met. We are responsible for our own actions in important areas—freedom of speech, press, and religion—while we are able to sample and be nourished by the insights of our predecessors—unreasonable search and seizure, bill of attainder. Justice Frankfurter's system is far from perfect,

[53] Carl Becker, *Freedom and Responsibility in the American Way of Life* (New York: Vintage Books, Inc., 1955), p. 87.

but it does at least provide a framework for analyzing many of the most fundamental aspects of our constitutional system.

Judge Learned Hand, who stands very close to Frankfurter in philosophy and who has influenced Frankfurter in a great many ways, recently outlined the ways in which the Bill of Rights and the Fourteenth Amendment can be interpreted.

> First we may read them as embodying the limitations that were current in 1787, and so through their history to give them a more or less definite content. Second we may read them in the Jeffersonian or Thomistic idiom as postulates embodying the "inalienable rights" with which men "are endowed by their Creator" . . . Third we may read them as admonitory or hortatory, not definite enough to be guides on concrete occasions . . . .[54]

In interpreting the Bill of Rights historically, Frankfurter has combined, to a large degree, the first and third of these approaches. When we turn to the Fourteenth Amendment, as we shall now do, his historical analysis dictates a conjoining of the second and third constructions.

[54] Learned Hand, *The Bill of Rights* (Cambridge, Mass.: Harvard University Press, 1958), pp. 33–34.

VII

History and the Fourteenth Amendment

In the previous chapter Justice Frankfurter's treatment of the Bill of Rights was considered in terms of history. A survey was made of his specific-generic breakdown of amendments. As indicated there, the due process clause of the Fifth Amendment is, for him, the most important flexible provision allowing accommodation between the demands of the past and the needs of the present. Extended discussion of the philosophy of due process in the light of history was, however, foregone in order that that topic could be taken up under the present heading. As Justice Frankfurter once noted, "in the attempt to endow history with drama, different periods are too often conceived as duels between hostile champions." [1] Such has certainly been the situation for the last decade or so in the Black-Frankfurter debate on the meaning of the Fourteenth Amendment. In order to understand this debate,

[1] Felix Frankfurter, *The Commerce Clause Under Marshall, Taney and Waite* (Chapel Hill: University of North Carolina Press, 1937), p. 11.

it is necessary to recall that the "facts" of history appear simultaneously with and are an intrinsic part of the analysis that any individual follows. Selection of particular "facts" in any interpretive pattern can be useful in helping to clarify the philosophy of the interpreter. For Justice Frankfurter this is doubly true. His pattern was established many years before he became a member of the Supreme Court.

I

The *New York Times,* in editorializing on his appointment to that position, thought that the key to understanding his judicial philosophy lay in his deep reverence for those elements in the law that reconciled the freedom and dignity of the individual with the stability of society. "Over and over again he has stated his view of the law as an organic, growing thing, sharing in this respect the philosophy of two judges whom he seemed most to admire: Holmes and Brandeis." [2] Because he was deeply skeptical of panaceas or nostrums, the *Times* felt that the new Justice would provide a liberal view of constitutional interpretation. Frankfurter has partially fulfilled this expectation through his treatment of the due process clause. On the other hand, he has been equally insistent that, even for such an organic concept, there are basic historical limitations that must be observed.

Justice Frankfurter has eloquently recognized that "there is a deep need for harmony in man." [3] But, to borrow musical terms, harmony presupposes definiteness in tonal and value progression so that playing the same notes with the same force will produce the same sound. One of life's contradictions is that no such automatic reproduction is ever possible. We must face the fact that "the versatility of circumstances often mocks [man's] natural de-

[2] *New York Times,* January 6, 1939.

[3] "Music is the instinctive learning of the soul. It is an essential need of life, for there is a deep need for harmony in man. It cuts across all boundaries and national differences. In music one finds a greater hope for one world than in all the political mechanisms." From a speech delivered at Tanglewood, Massachusetts, and reported in the *New York Times,* August 4, 1948.

sire for definiteness." [4] The due process clause of the Fifth and
particularly of the Fourteenth Amendment comes as close to
providing a mechanism for dealing with the versatility of circumstance as is to be found in the Constitution. In cases depending
upon an interpretation of those clauses, the Court is called upon
to give transient definiteness to judicial concepts, however logically contradictory that may sound. An exercise of judgment is
called for, and "judgment is not drawn out of the void but is
based on the correlation of imponderables all of which need
not, because they cannot, be made explicit." [5] Certainly for Justice
Frankfurter two such imponderables are, first, the heritage that
historic experience has left the Court and, second, the pattern of
past decisions, especially by justices whom he venerates. For him
one of Holmes' outstanding traits was the intellectual's distrust of
exactitude and certainty when important legal controversies involving due process came before the Court. Frankfurter has simu-
lated Holmes' action by his insistence that in all due process cases
matters of degree are involved and often degrees of the nicest
sort.

Basically, then, what is the primary function of due process?
In 1932 Professor Frankfurter noted that "alternative modes of
arriving at truth are not—they must not be—forever frozen." [6]
Almost a quarter of a century later he wrote that " 'Due process'
is, perhaps the least frozen concept of our law—the least confined
to history and the most absorptive of powerful standards of a
progressive society." [7] It is the Court's means to arrive at approximate truth. It is the vehicle for growth and vitality in the law,
allowing for reasonable differences and shifting necessities. This
concept does not have a fixed nor finished content, since it merely
expresses an intuitive approach to law as mirroring deeply held
community ideals. The ideals themselves are composites of centuries of Anglo-American constitutional history and civilization,
strengthened by the evolution of democratic faith.

[4] Wiener v. United States, 357 U.S. 349, 352 (1958).
[5] Felix Frankfurter, "Some Reflections on the Reading of Statutes," *Columbia
Law Review*, XLVII (May, 1947), 532.
[6] *New York Times*, November 13, 1932.
[7] Griffin v. Illinois, 351 U.S. 12, 20 (1956).

Frankfurter's opinions often insist on the difference between his views held as an individual and those held as a jurist. In dealing with due process it has been hard for him to convince students of the Court that any such difference existed. To them, it is futile and perhaps not quite forthright, given his views expressed in pre-Court writings. Therein he wrote that through the use of due process the justices were able to read their own economic and social views into the neutral language of the Constitution.[8] On one point the Justice has been consistent over the years. Someone must put meaning into the Constitution when due process is involved. Relatively unrestricted notions of policy do matter when the justices are called to give temporary definiteness to a constantly changing scene, although they may be individual judicial notions rather than those conditioned by purely personal considerations. One may heartily disagree with the cartography of any particular Court without changing the fact that the due process clause is the instrument that allows boundaries to be drawn between permissive and nonpermissive conduct. Many years ago Professor Frankfurter thought that the Court was using its power to centralize control over the states to an excessive degree. He therefore advised that "the due process clause ought to go." [9] How different is this from the Supreme Court justice who finds due process "the most majestic concept in our whole constitutional system." [10] The difference seems to lie in the fact that, as a scholar, Frankfurter thought members of the Court were infusing their personal judgments too openly into constitutional adjudication. He does, however, have to face somewhat of a problem. Current due process standards may be subjective, but is this really an evil? Justice Frankfurter's knowledge concerning the uses to which due process can be put have led him at times to curse subjectivity as an evil, while at other times, though not accepting it as a virtue, at least to recognize the necessity for its existence.

[8] See, for example, Felix Frankfurter, "The Supreme Court and the Public," *Forum*, LXXXIII (June, 1930), 332–33.

[9] Felix Frankfurter, "Mr. Justice Brandeis and the Constitution," *Harvard Law Review*, XLIV (November, 1931), 16.

[10] Joint Anti-Fascist Refugee Committee v. McGrath, 341 U.S. 123, 174 (1951).

II

In statement of principle, Justice Black stands far from Frankfurter in his treatment of the Fourteenth Amendment. There are, however, similarities in that neither man boldly desires to assert that many cases hinge on five individual philosophies incidentally coalescing on some point so that a case can be decided. In order to avoid the appearance of personal participation Justice Black has gone farther than Justice Frankfurter with his manjurist dichotomy, which does acknowledge that some change in treatment of situations can be obtained through the due process clause of the Fourteenth Amendment. Black has advocated what is known as "incorporation." Desiring to protect civil rights in the most forceful manner possible, he believes this goal can best be attained by making the first eight amendments applicable against the states as against the federal government. Extended historical analysis has convinced him that the framers of the Fourteenth Amendment meant this addition to the Constitution to be the vehicle by which such application would become possible. Unlike Frankfurter, most of the provisions of the Bill of Rights are specific for Black, even to the First Amendment. By transposing them through the Fourteenth Amendment onto the states, he appears to desire a certainty in treatment of constitutional concepts, which admittedly cannot be gained by use of due process as a generic term. Supposed certainty in interpretation seems to Black equivalent to avoidance of the dangers inherent in judgment on the vague provisions of the Constitution. This, on the surface at least, is the rationale for his preoccupation with history to prove the specific nature of the Bill of Rights and to prove historically that the Fourteenth Amendment was meant particularly to have the Bill of Rights enforceable against state governments.

There are certainly many difficulties in the Black thesis and Frankfurter has pointed them out. For example, what part of the Fourteenth Amendment reaches down to the Bill of Rights for incorporation purposes? Or again, are all the amendments applicable, or is there some selectivity involved, necessitating the same type of judgment as a generic term. Black has been unable to give satisfactory answers to these and like questions. The reason is probably that he does not desire certainty *per se* in constitutional law, but only certainty when particular types of cases arise. His championship of the "preferred freedoms" doctrine, a subject that will be taken up in a subsequent chapter, was begun years before he made his incorporation proposals. Justice Black is deeply committed to the protection of civil rights. To justify the preferred position that he gives them, something more than personal choice seemed necessary. Justification on the basis of a variant natural law philosophy—Frankfurter's deep-felt convictions of the English-speaking people as expressed through due process—was supposedly uncongenial to the rest of Black's positions. Therefore he turned to the history of the Fourteenth Amendment in an effort to prove that his actions in elevating civil liberties protection against the states had been validated long ago. In that way he did not have to give reasons for his choices since they were predetermined and he could avoid the appearance of any personal involvement in holding state officials to account, since his actions were automatic responses to the defined specific clauses of the Bill of Rights.

Black is not alone in trying to conceptualize constitutional interpretation whereby legal terms are rigidified in terms of past legal experience. Most members of the Court, including Frankfurter, have taken part in such ventures. Once conceptualization has taken place, however, it becomes extremely difficult to revise the working bases for constitutional law. Conceptualization may, indeed, preclude development within a legal system of new techniques for meeting new problems that cannot be encompassed within time-honored patterns. It would be a very unusual person who would deny the great advance that the Bill of Rights represented at the time of its adoption or who would even question its present-day significance. But to suggest that the eighteenth-century ideals that are there incorporated represent the end-all and be-all of constitutional development is a refusal to face facts. The Supreme Court must deal with the problems of today in their own setting. As Charles P. Curtis has aptly remarked, there is no reason why we should not encourage the Court to do better by us than Congress saw fit to propose to our forefathers. We do not want to get stuck in the eighteenth century. Why should the Court's standards of political behavior . . . be forever eighteenth century? What Black proposes is an escape into the past for fear of the future. It is a little like a taste for antique furniture.[11]

Granting for the sake of argument that Black's historical analysis of the Fourteenth Amendment is beyond reproach, there are still difficulties in accepting incorporation. For one thing, the framers of the amendment certainly were not explicit in what they were doing if incorporation was to be the end result. Vast constitutional changes were hardly to be brought about by innuendo and indirection. A cardinal premise for legal interpretation is that attention must be focused on the words used rather than on the presumed intentions of the users. As for the Fourteenth Amendment, past Courts have repeatedly rejected incorporation proposals similar to Black's. The Court's own history cannot be totally ignored, and its pattern of interpretation should make some difference. Even if Black's scholarship is completely accurate, a second thought is required before established policies are overthrown. He must become aware that, however creditable his desire to protect civil liberties may be, there is more to constitutional government than protecting but one facet of life in an enormously complex scene.

In summary, both Black and Frankfurter rely heavily on historical data to substantiate their contentions regarding the Fourteenth Amendment, due process, and incorporation proposals. Both protagonists look to the past in an effort to explain the present. Justice Black with his more specific concept of all first eight amendments would bind the states to a respect for the federal absolutes of the 1790's—absolutes as he himself interprets freedom, liberty, etc. Justice Frankfurter, on the other hand, with his dual approach to the Bill of Rights has refused to acknowledge that even specific amendments thereof are automatically transported into the generic Fourteenth Amendment. Confusion over his position stems from the fact that a double set of factors is in-

[11] Charles Curtis, *Lions Under the Throne* (Boston: Houghton Mifflin Co., 1947), p. 289.

volved: (1) the initial specific-generic split within the Bill of Rights; (2) the wholly generic due process clause of the Fourteenth Amendment. Only by a survey of selected cases can the substantive nature of the due process be made evident and the differences in application of the Black and Frankfurter approaches exemplified.

III

Relating the specific terms of the Bill of Rights to the Fourteenth Amendment, Frankfurter admits that "each specific Amendment, in so far as embraced within the Fourteenth Amendment, must be equally respected." [12] His difference with Justice Black comes over the reasons why the ideals enshrined in certain amendments should be embraced while others are not. As far as the generic terms of the Bill of Rights are concerned, he takes an ambivalent position. There is little doubt that he finds freedom of speech, press, and religion protected against state action by the Fourteenth Amendment. This protection comes, however, not because of any absolute understanding as to the meaning of freedom, but because freedom of speech and other freedoms are characteristic of the civilized standards of English-speaking people protected by the legal term "due process of law."

Comparing due process of law as found in the Fifth and Fourteenth Amendments he stated that "of course the Due Process Clause of the Fourteenth Amendment has the same meaning. To suppose that 'due process of law' meant one thing in the Fifth Amendment and another in the Fourteenth is too frivolous to require elaborate rejection." [13] The paradox is that, in practice, Frankfurter himself has elaborately rejected such an identification. It is inconsistent to claim that the clause of the Fifth Amendment, which acts primarily as a fluid, supplementary mechanism to specific prohibitions in the protection of federal civil rights, is of the same range as the clause of the Fourteenth Amendment, which acts as a guarantee against state violation of civil rights

[12] West Virginia State Bd. of Education v. Barnette, 319 U.S. 624, 648 (1943).
[13] Malinski v. New York, 324 U.S. 401, 414–15 (1945).

solely on its ability to encompass selectively both specific and generic terms found in the Bill of Rights.

Which of the specific and generic guarantees does Justice Frankfurter think so vital that they have become an integral part of due process of law in the long course of its historical evolution? Cases involving coerced confessions, double jeopardy, self-incrimination, unreasonable searches and seizures, right to counsel, and the freedoms of the First Amendment have been mainly responsible for the statement of his views concerning their relation to due process. All these cases require some element of judgment on the part of Supreme Court justices. Especially is this so for those concerned with coerced confession. Legal systems cannot cope with the problems of free will and determinism; therefore, any line between voluntary and involuntary confessions will be very thin. Justice Jackson once remarked, in an opinion joined by Justice Frankfurter, that "custody and examination of a prisoner for thirty-six hours is 'inherently coercive.' Of course it is. And so is custody and examination for one hour. Arrest itself is inherently coercive, and so is detention." [14] Other considerations than mere length of time under questioning are the decisive factors in determining whether due process has been violated. Since ours is an accusatorial rather than an inquisitorial system, society carries the burden of proving guilt through evidence independently secured, but such a burden does not preclude all questioning of an accused when judicial safeguards are provided.

In Malinski v. New York [15] the question was raised as to the voluntariness of a confession obtained from a suspect held incommunicado by the police for a ten-hour span. Although it was established that Malinski was not physically assaulted, Justice Douglas, in the opinion of the Court, found that the prisoner's apprehension that he *might* be beaten was evidence enough to void the confession as coercively obtained. Justice Frankfurter concurred, but in his opinion he was at some pains to disavow Douglas' innuendoes concerning the direct and automatic applicability of the entire Fifth Amendment to the states.

[14] Ashcraft v. Tennessee, 322 U.S. 143, 161 (1944).
[15] 324 U.S. 401 (1945).

. . . the Fourteenth Amendment placed no specific restrictions upon the administration of their criminal law by the States. Congress in proposing the Fourteenth Amendment and the States in ratifying it left to the States the freedom of action they had before that Amendment excepting only that after 1868 no State could . . . "deprive any person of life, liberty or property without due process of law," nor deny to any person the "equal protection of the law." These are all phrases of large generalities. But they are not generalities of unillumined vagueness; they are generalities circumscribed by history and appropriate to the largeness of government with which they are concerned.[16]

These phrases of large generalities were meant to serve as vehicles for the protection of civil rights. Overlaying the states with Amendments First through Eight would not necessarily accomplish this protection. Looking back to the drafting of the Fifth Amendment, Justice Frankfurter was convinced that due process had then, and had at the time of the adoption of the Fourteenth Amendment, a singularly unique purpose: it was to express a demand for civilized standards of law. It was not a stagnant, rigid formula but a criterion for judgment. He was willing to admit that due process had in the instance of Malinski been violated; he was unwilling to agree that due process would always be violated in similar situations.

The best way to give full consideration to Justice Frankfurter's constitutional and historical philosophy in this area is to quote from the Justice himself. The excerpt given below is a lengthy one, but it contains many of his insights concerning due process, history, and the judicial function.

Judicial review of . . . the Fourteenth Amendment inescapably imposes upon this Court an exercise of judgment upon the whole course of the proceedings in order to ascertain whether they offend those canons of decency and fairness which express the notions of justice of English-speaking people even towards those charged with the most heinous offenses. These standards of justice are not authoritatively formulated anywhere as though they were prescriptions in a pharmacopeia. But neither does the application of the

[16] *Ibid.*, p. 414.

Due Process Clause imply that judges are wholly at large. The judicial judgment in applying the Due Process Clause must move within the limits of accepted notions of justice and is not to be based upon idiosyncracies of a purely personal judgment. The fact that judges among themselves may differ whether in a particular case a trial offends accepted notions of justice is not disproof that general rather than idiosyncratic standards are applied. An important safeguard against such merely individual judgment is an alert deference to the judgment of the state court under review.[17]

There has been evidence aplenty that judges do, in fact, differ among themselves as to whether a particular case offends "accepted notions of justice." Thus for some, Frankfurter included, historic due process does not always require the states to provide indictment by grand jury, or a jury trial, when the amount of suit at common law exceeds twenty dollars. These are specific requirements only for the federal government.

The states are under another compulsion, the compulsion of due process. Due process, then, is equivalent to "notions of justice," but it is justice under law. And law is here defined as the evolution of understanding concerning the historic rights attributable to individuals, whether these rights be implicitly or explicitly protected. Indeed, Justice Frankfurter has said that "Due process is that which comports with the deepest notions of what is fair and right and just. The more fundamental the beliefs are the less likely they are to be explicitly stated." [18] In the case from which these views were taken, the particular point under discussion was whether an insane person or one who claimed insanity could be executed. Justice Frankfurter held that such an execution would violate due process. He, among all the justices, has most staunchly maintained this position.[19]

The second case identifying the substantive content that Justice Frankfurter gives to due process is Louisiana v. Resweber.[20] The rather garish facts of this case often cause the statement of

---

[17] *Ibid.*, pp. 416–17.

[18] Solesbee v. Balkcom, 339 U.S. 9, 16 (1950).

[19] See Phyle v. Duffy, 334 U.S. 431 (1948); Leland v. Oregon, 343 U.S. 790 (1952); U.S. *ex rel.* Smith v. Baldi, 344 U.S. 561 (1953); Greenwood v. United States, 350 U.S. 366 (1956); Caritativo v. California, 357 U.S. 549 (1958).

[20] 329 U.S. 459 (1947). Cf. Brock v. North Carolina, 344 U.S. 424 (1953).

principle contained in the Supreme Court opinions to be overlooked. Justice Reed announced the judgment of the Court, which
was that constitutional prohibitions against cruel or unusual
punishment or double jeopardy were not violated by proceeding
with the execution of a death sentence by electrocution after an
accidental failure of equipment had rendered a previous attempt unsuccessful. Justice Frankfurter concurred. Reed's opinion
went into the general characteristics of due process and the uses
to which it had been put with respect to the states. Although
Louisiana's attitude toward Resweber might be vengeful, it was
not illegal. Due process was not now, and had not ever been, a
straitjacket into which state punitive measures could be pushed
by stringent, judicially created conditions.

Justice Frankfurter took up the gauntlet thrown down by
Justice Burton in a heated dissent. Referring to the due process
and equal protection sections of the amendment as "broad, in-
explicit clauses of the Constitution," he found that they had historic antecedents that "run back to Magna Carta." But he also
found that due process and equal protection "contemplate no less
advances in the conceptions of justice and fairness by a progressive society." [21] Advance is the key word in this quotation.
While quite agreeing that the Bill of Rights was of the utmost importance for the federal government, and that at the time of
drafting the first eight amendments the safeguards that they
contained were great strides forward in the protection of individual rights, Justice Frankfurter nevertheless pointed out that
"some of these safeguards have perduring validity. Some grew
out of transient experience or formulated remedies which time
might well improve." [22] All that the Fourteenth Amendment
required was that the states be not oblivious to the dignity of man.
This was, however, requiring a great deal. Determining what is
the dignity of man is no easy business, as Frankfurter is the first
to admit. During 1950 on a visit to Great Britain, he testified before the Royal Commission on Capital Punishment and made
mention of the Resweber case as one that "told on my conscience a good deal. . . . I was very bothered by the problem,

[21] Louisiana v. Resweber, 329 U.S. 459, 466–67 (1947).
[22] *Ibid.*, pp. 467–68.

it offended my personal sense of decency to do this. Something inside of me was very unhappy, but I did not see that it violated due process of law." [23] Frankfurter's vote in Resweber probably did cause him a good deal of personal anguish in view of his deep humanitarian instincts, but he has come to accept the fact that due process of law is meant primarily to maintain the integrity of the legal system. It is not to be used as a crutch for a particular defendant. It is this acceptance that sets him off from his brethren in so many cases that otherwise would find him voting in a more activist vein.

IV

Justice Black's incorporation proposals cannot be mentioned without treating the case of Adamson v. California.[24] Almost forgotten in the glare of battle between Justices Black and Frankfurter, which broke out clearly in this controversy, is the fact that Justice Reed delivered the opinion of the Court. Briefly, he declared that the provisions of a California law that permitted the failure of a defendant to explain or to deny evidence against him to be commented upon and considered by court, counsel, and jury did not amount to a violation of due process of law. Even granting for sake of argument that the prohibition against self-incrimination had been made applicable to the states, California's action was not equivalent to forcing self-incrimination in the traditional sense in which that concept was understood.

Justice Douglas joined Justice Black in an exasperated and protracted dissent. Taking violent exception to mention of natural law in the concurring opinion of Justice Frankfurter, they felt that the "decision and the 'natural law' theory of the Constitution upon which it relies degrade the constitutional safeguards of the Bill of Rights and simultaneously appropriate for this Court a broad power which we are not authorized by the Constitution to exercise." [25] To prove this assertion, Justice Black

[23] Testimony of July 21, 1950 given in Philip Elman (ed.), *Of Law and Men* (New York: Harcourt, Brace & Co., 1956), p. 98.

[24] 332 U.S. 46 (1947).

[25] *Ibid.*, p. 70.

appended to his opinion an elaborate history of the Fourteenth Amendment. His position in the Adamson case can be questioned on at least two counts. In the first place, the weakness of his historical exposition has been demonstrated in an extended study by Charles Fairman and Stanley Morrison, leading the latter to conclude that "the real significance of *Adamson v. California* is that four of the judges are willing to distort history, as well as the language of the framers, in order to read into the Constitution provisions which they think ought to be there. It is particularly regrettable that the great talents of Mr. Justice Black should be so misdirected." [26] One such appraisal, while worthy of note, would not be conclusive. However, the charge in some form or another has been leveled by innumerable commentators on constitutional development.[27] The general consensus of opinion seems to be that although accolades are usually due daring innovations they are not warranted for Supreme Court justices who must interpret, not create, constitutional terms.

As a second reason for close scrutiny of Black's Adamson opinion, it is suggested that his condemnation of Frankfurter's mention of natural law places him very much in the position of the man in the glass house who decided to throw stones. His plea for "judicial self-restraint" and abstention from natural law concepts is not entirely without contradictions. Protection from testimonial compulsion, whether framed in Fifth or Fourteenth Amendment terms, requires judicial definition and interpretation. Black's substitute for Frankfurter's adherence to a twentieth-century variant natural law position is the Bill of Rights, in some respects perhaps the eighteenth century's most complete expression of a natural law philosophy. However specific the Bill of Rights is and however specifically the Fourteenth Amendment made it applicable to the states, some judgment is needed to put theory into practice. Black's insistence on the validity of eighteenth-century philosophy as found in the Bill of Rights means that he must think it of enduring and timeless quality,

[26] Stanley Morrison, "Does the Fourteenth Amendment Incorporate the Bill of Rights? The Judicial Interpretation," *Stanford Law Review,* ii (December, 1949), 162.

[27] See, for example, Bernard Schwartz, *The Supreme Court, Constitutional Revolution in Retrospect* (New York: The Ronald Press Co., 1957), p. 167.

certainly one of the basic conditions for any natural law concept. To prefer eighteenth-century natural law philosophy is one thing; to deny the implications of such a preference is quite another.

Justice Frankfurter's concurring opinion was framed to meet certain objections posited by Justice Black. He met head on the contention that the Court was exercising too much discretionary power in its dealing with due process by returning once again to a statement of political and legal history surrounding that concept. Justice Frankfurter then went on to say that due process concepts had many characteristics usually attributed to natural law thinking. This reference did not enter his opinion by accident. Considering his specific-generic catalog of constitutional terms, he subsumes under natural law the flexible provisions that, although not completely definable, have, nevertheless, an enduring vitality for the American system of government.

In a recent article he referred to natural law as "not much more than literary garniture" and "not a guiding means for adjudication." [28] It is unfortunate that he feels constrained to recant his fomer comparison between due process and natural law, for candidness would surely require admission that "notions of justice of English-speaking peoples" comes very close to being a modern statement of a very old theme. In any event, the importance of the Adamson case lies in the forceful statement of principle concerning the historical interpretation to be given the Fourteenth Amendment, not in the novelty of the positions, since these can be traced back for many years. In some degree it is true that violent disagreement in the Adamson case over the historical meaning of the Fourteenth Amendment only highlights the depth of the problem involved instead of producing any solution. But it is equally true that even restatement tells much about the philosophic approaches of those concerned.

V

The "warped construction of specific provisions of the Bill of Rights" against which Justice Frankfurter warned in the Adamson

[28] Felix Frankfurter, "John Marshall," in *Government Under Law* (Cambridge, Mass.: Harvard University Press, 1956), pp. 15–16.

case came somewhat to pass in Rochin v. California.[29] Rochin was forcefully administered an emetic that made him disgorge morphine tablets swallowed in an effort to keep them from state officers. The tablets were admitted in evidence at Rochin's trial. In a concurring opinion, Justices Black and Douglas held that this action amounted to self-incrimination. In order to do this, however, they had to expand a concept that most cases and commentators have limited to testimonial utterances. Mechanical incorporation of the Bill of Rights concept was unable to avoid the vagueness of due process in this instance. Fundamental safeguards for individual liberty were at stake, but, instead of the "civilized standards" test that Justice Frankfurter proposed, Black and Douglas blithely shifted the meaning of self-incrimination and then continued to insist that they were applying it in a way that had been historically defined.

Justice Frankfurter delivered the opinion of the Court in the Rochin case, and he based his ruling on due process grounds. Many years previously he had written: "I deem a requirement as to the invasion of the person to stand on a very different footing from questions pertaining to the discovery of documents, pretrial procedure and other devices for the expeditious, economic and fair conduct of litigation." [30] The invasion of the person in Rochin's case could not be fitted into any specific category of prohibited actions found in the Bill of Rights. Justice Frankfurter thought that "in dealing with human rights, the absence of formal exactitude, or want of fixity of meaning is not an unusual or even regrettable attribute of constitutional provisions." [31] Inequities such as those in the case at hand could thus be taken care of without distorting the Constitution. Words are symbols, and the symbol of due process was quite adequate, since it covered that which offended a sense of justice without trying to define just what that intangible is.

Given Justice Frankfurter's feeling about personal inviolability as expressed in the Rochin case, his vote in the more recent case of Beithaupt v. Abrams [32] is difficult to explain. The controversy

[29] 342 U.S. 165 (1952).
[30] Sibbach v. Wilson & Co., 312 U.S. 1, 18 (1941).
[31] Rochin v. California, 342 U.S. 165, 169 (1952).
[32] 352 U.S. 432 (1957).

dealt with the legality of blood tests made to determine intoxication on an unconscious man. Since Warren and Black, along with Douglas, dissented from the Court's holding that due process was not violated, Justice Frankfurter was the senior member in the majority and had the privilege of assigning the opinion. It is somewhat odd that he assigned the task to Justice Tom Clark instead of writing himself in view of the fact that the dissenters relied heavily on the Rochin decision. Remaining silent in the majority, Frankfurter of course gave no indication as to his reasons for arriving at what appears to be two conflicting positions.

Wolf v. Colorado [33] and Irvine v. California [34] adequately present Frankfurter's views concerning the degree to which due process equals the protection against unreasonable searches and seizures that is given by the Fourth Amendment. While in federal cases he is one of the staunchest supporters of strictly applying the specific prohibitions of the Fourth Amendment, when comparable situations come up from states under terms of due process, another factor enters in, and that is his extreme deference to state judges in working out their own procedures. In the Wolf case, Frankfurter held for the Court that evidence seized in a search without warrant could be admitted in evidence at the state trial of an abortionist even though such evidence would have been excluded from federal proceedings. He followed a course that is very characteristic, that of citing numerous justices before him who had voted in similar cases the way he was now voting.

The case of Palko v. Connecticut,[35] one of the most extensive discussions and rejections of incorporation proposals before Frankfurter came on the bench, was reverently cited. "That decision speaks to us with the great weight of the authority, particularly in matters of civil liberty of a court that included Mr. Chief Justice Hughes, Mr. Justice Brandeis, Mr. Justice Stone and Mr. Justice Cardozo, to name only the dead." [36] Justice Cardozo in

[33] 338 U.S. 25 (1949). Cf. Francis Allen, "The Wolf Case," *Illinois Law Review*, XLV (March–April, 1950), 1–30.

[34] 347 U.S. 128 (1954). For a discussion of these cases see Emerick Handler, "The Fourth Amendment, Federalism, and Mr. Justice Frankfurter," *Syracuse Law Review*, VIII (Spring, 1957), 166–90.

[35] 302 U.S. 319 (1937).

[36] Wolf v. Colorado, 338 U.S. 25, 27 (1949).

the Palko case had spoken of the process of inclusion and exclusion by which certain concepts were encompassed within due process while others were not considered basic enough to warrant equal treatment. Frankfurter on many previous occasions had accepted the inclusion-exclusion terminology. In the Wolf case he made his acceptance very explicit indeed, saying, "basic rights do not become petrified as of any one time, even though, as a matter of human experience, some may not too rhetorically be called eternal verities." [37] The human desire for harmony and definiteness might call for a rejection of the inclusion-exclusion approach to due process, but all that such a rejection would accomplish would be to attempt satisfaction for the unsatisfiable longing for certainty, losing sight thereby of the fact that the law must deal with the evolving movements of a free society.

In the Irvine case, Justice Frankfurter dissented from the Court's holding that evidence secured against a gambler through use of concealed microphones located at various places in his home was admissible in a state court. Remarking that "observance of due process has to do not with questions of guilt or innocence but the mode by which guilt is ascertained," Frankfurter tried to explain how he could stand on opposite sides of the line in two cases as similar as Wolf and Irvine.

> Empiricism implies judgment upon variant situations by the wisdom of experience. Ad hocness in adjudication means treating a particular case by itself and not in relation to the meaning of a course of decisions and the guides they serve for the future. There is all the difference in the world between disposing of a case as though it were a discreet instance and recognizing it as part of the process of judgment, taking its place in relation to what went before and further cutting a channel for what is to come.[38]

Justice Frankfurter apparently did not make his distinction between empiricism and ad hocness clear to some of his compatriots. They chided him upon the difference in result between a slight and severe shock to the judicial conscience. They also questioned whether an empiric or an ad hoc approach would help shape the

[37] *Ibid.*
[38] Irvine v. California, 347 U.S. 128, 147 (1954).

conduct of local police at all. Some of these comments were extreme in implication, but they did pinpoint Justice Frankfurter's difficulty regarding search and seizure and the due process clause. The only thing that could be added is his insistence on due process as an historic term protecting basic liberties, which may change with time and circumstances. In this sense, a severe shock may very well have different repercussions and ramifications than a mild shock upon the judicial conscience.

The very recent case of Frank v. Maryland [39] in which Justice Frankfurter upheld a health inspection official's entry into a house without a warrant has occasioned a good deal of comment. This decision is, however, not at variance with his other votes. Leaving aside the community's legitimate interest in sanitary conditions and the fact that the procedure followed to gain entrance had long been established within the state, Justice Frankfurter was mainly concerned with showing that the protection against unreasonable searches and seizures was to protect individuals from having evidence that could be used in subsequent *criminal* proceedings taken from their dwellings. This is the exact emphasis used in discussing self-incrimination, whether in the Fifth Amendment proper or in its transcribed version in the Fourteenth. In each instance, history is relied upon to prove that the dual protections are limited to criminal cases. Since no criminality was involved under the contested ordinance, references to the concept of unreasonable searches and seizures were inappropriate.

Litigations concerned with right to counsel also become involved in the debate over the Fourteenth Amendment. Foster v. Illinois,[40] decided the same day as the Adamson case, displays once again the various positions. In the majority opinion Justice Frankfurter held that, although the record in a state court did not disclose an offer of counsel upon a plea of guilty to burglary and larceny by mature defendants, they were not denied a fair trial and had not suffered violation of due process of law. Taking into account that the men involved were both over thirty years old and both were mentally competent, he could find no extenuating circumstances that would allow the Court to overrule the state

[39] 359 U.S. 360 (1959).
[40] 352 U.S. 134 (1947).

decision, especially in view of the fact that the men had been advised of their rights of trial and of the consequence of a plea of guilty. Due process was, after all, itself, an "historical product" and should not, therefore, "furnish opportunities hitherto uncontemplated for opening wide the prison doors of the land." [41]

The dissenting quartet of the Adamson case remained intact. Justice Black's opinion almost vibrates with the intensity of his feeling.

> This decision is another example of the consequences which can be produced by substitution of this Court's day-to-day opinion of what kind of trial is fair and decent for the kind of trial which the Bill of Rights guarantees. This time it is the right of counsel. We cannot know what Bill of Rights provision will next be attenuated by the Court.[42]

Justice Black spoke almost exclusively in terms of the Bill of Rights. He did not bother to belabor his incorporation proposals but tacitly assumed that his position had been made perfectly clear in the past. In the Adamson and Foster cases he came closest to having these proposals accepted by the majority of the Court. Missing by just one vote in 1947, the Black tide slowly turned with changes in Court personnel and now, a little over a decade later, the recession has reached the point where only Justices Black and Douglas, and perhaps Chief Justice Warren, are definitely committed to the plan of making the first eight amendments completely and wholly binding upon the states.

Justice Frankfurter's reading of Fourteenth Amendment history has won out for the time being over the interpretation of his more activist brethren. Certainly this is true in right to counsel cases. In a relatively recent controversy the legality of an Ohio statute making "in camera" hearings by fire authorities standard procedure was challenged on the ground that the due process clause of the Fourteenth Amendment required the presence of counsel for the person under interrogation. The Court rejected this contention. Justice Frankfurter concurred. Since even the specific Sixth Amendment required assistance of counsel only in criminal

[41] *Ibid.*, p. 139.
[42] *Ibid.*, p. 140.

cases, he thought that even "the utmost devotion to one's profession and the fullest recognition of the great role of lawyers in the evolution of a free society cannot lead one to erect as a constitutional principle that no administrative inquiry can be had in camera unless a lawyer be allowed to attend." [43]

The dissenting opinion of Justice Black illustrates in another form the illusory precision of incorporation proposals. As with bills of attainder and self-incrimination, historic terms were distorted. The administrative hearing under the Ohio statute was treated as if it were a criminal proceeding in the constitutional sense. If the law is to be looked upon as a science of words, words to be used in their exact meanings, with all the precision that human utterance can give, then there does seem to be some difficulty in equating nonlegal conceptions with legal phraseology. Black was quite explicit in giving his reasons for such equalization.

> It may be that the type of interrogation which the Fire Marshall and his deputies are authorized to conduct would not technically fit into the traditional category of formal criminal proceedings, but the substantive effect of such interrogation on an eventual criminal prosecution of the person questioned can be so great that he should not be compelled to give testimony when he is deprived of the advice of his counsel.[44]

Once again Black the humanitarian has outvoted Black the historian and lawyer.

VI

Giving substantive meaning to due process entails infinite shades of interpretation for infinite circumstances. Justice Frankfurter's positions in several important fields have been cursorily surveyed. One could go on further to extended treatment of the relation of due process to almost any of the clauses in the Bill of Rights or to general notions inherent in a legal system. How far, for instance, is freedom of speech or freedom from censorship

---

[43] *In re* Groban, 352 U.S. 330, 336 (1957). Cf. Anonymous Nos. 6 and 7 v. Baker, 360 U.S. 287 (1959).

[44] *In re* Groban, 352 U.S. 330, 344 (1957).

protected by due process? [45] Can racial discrimination be handled under this concept as well as under equal protection? [46] These and other like questions would have to be answered if a complete appraisal of Frankfurter's philosophy in terms of the historical meaning of the Fourteenth Amendment were undertaken. Suffice it so say that he follows an empiric course and still holds fast in all due process cases to an opinion offered many years before he came to the Supreme Court. "Legal schemes often derive importance from what they do not formulate. Freedom for future needs is thus allowed." [47]

Much has been made of the supposed equivocation in Justice Frankfurter's treatment of due process. His gradual inclusion and exclusion of Bill of Rights guarantees on the basis of "civilized standards of behavior" has brought forth the charge that he fosters uncertainty in constitutional law. Held up for praise is the supposed certitude of the Black-Douglas interpretation. Accepting for the moment the Black-Douglas thesis, there is no assurance that here, too, equivocation will not be evident; it will be evident on the level of the Bill of Rights itself and may through incorporation also be removed to the level of the Fourteenth Amendment. With their emphasis on making specific most of the first eight amendments, Justices Black and Douglas presuppose that terms contained therein can be given a constant, defined historical meaning. Regardless of the amount of historical material that can be marshaled to their support, it is evident that all justices must frame constitutional definitions somewhat in terms of their own personal and experiential structures. When material is not originally encompassed within a definition (or is afterwards fitted in by mutilating the definition itself), self-effacement will not distort the fact that a discriminating choice has been made.

Again accepting for the moment the position that equivocation is a part of the Frankfurter treatment, is there any reason initially to remove that process one step from the Bill of Rights?

[45] See Bridges v. California, 314 U.S. 252 (1941) and Butler v. Michigan, 353 U.S. 380 (1957).

[46] See, for example, Railway Mail Association v. Corsi, 326 U.S. 88 (1945).

[47] Felix Frankfurter, *The Public and Its Government* (New Haven: Yale University Press, 1930), p. 62.

If the difficulty attendant on arriving at specific definitions for all Bill of Rights terms is recalled, and if the Frankfurter insistence on the use of generic terms as constitutional safety-valves is reconsidered, then some light is shed on his desire to have "inclusive and exclusive" associated with the due process clause of the Fourteenth Amendment. Feeling himself constrained by history to admit that certain prohibitions are specific, Justice Frankfurter wishes to avoid the artificially contrived difficulty of making the entire Bill of Rights a rigid construct. More important, since historic due process is for him anything other than a technically confining legal technique, he desires above all to allow free play and choice through the Fourteenth Amendment.

His understanding of the "civilized standards of English-speaking people" involves no more self-assertion or personal preference than do the Bill of Rights choices of Justices Black and Douglas. This is not to say that the choices that he does make will not be anathema to certain groups. It does, however, allow conjecture that the main distinction between Justices Black and Frankfurter is the latter's open admission that change and advance are necessary and possible in constitutional law without giving up all the benefits of continuity with the past. He then proceeds to furnish the reasons to prove his contention. Justice Frankfurter is not as candid as some would desire in recognizing his judicial influence in shaping that advance—but none of his fellows on the bench are overanxious to announce the fact that all constitutional interpretation contains a sizable amount of individual leaven.

The philosophies of history followed by Justices Black and Frankfurter are, in many respects, individualized manifestations of broader streams of jurisprudential thought. Much of current legal thought stems from orthodox historical jurisprudence of the nineteenth century, which denied jurists any creative role in formulating or applying the law. Legal precepts had binding force, for they were the expressions of principle discovered through human experience. The only task of the judge was to articulate these principles in the technical language of the courtroom. With the turn of the twentieth century, social standards of justice, which were the implicit bases for expressions of principle, took the limelight from the evolutionary emphasis of the historical school. In the United States, Roscoe Pound spearheaded the drive for the newer sociological approach. Once new ways of looking at legal materials became prevalent, there was a proliferation of speculative theories concerning the nature of legal phenomena. Legal realism and advanced analytical studies took on stature in the early decades of this century.

Justice Frankfurter utilizes an approach to constitutional interpretation drawn from many sources. From historical jurisprudence he takes the evolutionary views; from sociological jurisprudence, a fundamentally pragmatic attitude; from analytical jurisprudence, word skepticism and a disbelief in the fixity of concepts. The outcome of such an amalgam is a developmental view of the law that will by sympathetic to legislative attempts at revamping the content of vague constitutional provisions. Determining which are the vague provisions is done by historical research. Out of this position, however, grow several contradictions.

In the first place, Justice Frankfurter wants the flexibility traditional in the English system of government. This he attempts to gain through use of due process. But he also wants legislative responsibility, which would entail a full code of behavior in the Benthamite sense. This is almost an impossible combination, but it is a combination that he has tried to work out. In treating the flexible, generic provisions of the Constitution, he displays his Anglophile tendencies to their greatest extent. This may be mere personal preference, but others certainly not of Anglophile persuasion have also pointed out that "in a sense the United States has no written constitution. The great clauses in the Constitution . . . contain no more than an appeal to the decency and wisdom of those with whom the responsibility for their enforcement rests." [48] Justice Frankfurter would prefer the legislature to have such responsibility. But he is wise enough to know that because "in a sense the United States has no written constitution," and because no code of law can be entirely self-contained, the Supreme Court along with the legislature must act, and Justice

[48] Alexander H. Pekelis, *Law and Social Action* (Ithaca: Cornell University Press, 1950), p. 4.

Frankfurter acts largely through due process. He thereby impliedly rejects the limited role of the judge and legislator advocated by the historical school of jurisprudence. He accepts instead the more positive sociological and analytical interpretation.

A second apparent contradiction springs from the fact that rejection of the fixity of concepts would seem to rule out any proclivity toward a traditional "natural law" orientation. Yet Justice Frankfurter speaks of due process as enveloping the "eternal verities" of English-speaking peoples. Probably the clue to clearing up this misunderstanding lies in the fact that any description of social forces at work in a particular era and the way these forces interact is apt to be couched in terms of timeless abstractions. It is in this sense that Justice Frankfurter follows what may be called a natural law course. As long ago as 1913 he wrote that "if facts are changing, law cannot be static. So-called immutable principles must accommodate themselves to facts of life, for facts are stubborn and will not yield. In truth, what are now deemed immutable principles once, themselves, grew out of living conditions." [49] In trying to arrive at the consensus of society in the meaning of due process, Justice Frankfurter is utilizing the very essence of abstract notions and general concepts—immutable principles—in order to bring them up to date.[50] His metapsychotic method is, no doubt, open to question, but it is one facet of much current thinking about human perception in general. Jung's theory that long-range values of mankind can be distilled partly from the collective unconsciousness of the human race and the radically empirical, undifferentiated field consciousness that modern Confucian, Buddhist, and Hindu thought attribute in common to all persons are two manifestations of the same theme.[51]

Both Justices Black and Frankfurter came to maturity in the period when legal realism put many general principles under

[49] Frankfurter, "The Zeitgeist and the Judiciary," Survey, xxix (January 25, 1913), 543.

[50] For a highly critical evaluation of the Frankfurter position, see George Braden, "Objectivity in Constitutional Law," Yale Law Journal, lvii (February, 1948), 577–94. For other studies of this type, see G. Lowell Field, "Law as an Objective Political Concept," American Political Science Review, xliii (April, 1949), 229–49.

[51] See F. S. C. Northrop, "The Mediational Approval Theory of Law in American Legal Realism," Virginia Law Review, xliv (April, 1958), 347–64.

attack. Neither has completely escaped from the climate of opinion current in their developmental period. For this reason it is often difficult for them and others of their generation to feel comfortable in invoking universal principles of fundamental law. Justice Black has felt more at home with the stricter version of the historical school whereby the creative role of the judge is underplayed. Justice Frankfurter, on the other hand, has passed beyond strict adherence either to historical jurisprudence or to the legal realism in which he was raised. If, in trying to use history as one means of isolating the ultimate values in human personality and society, Justice Frankfurter appears to contradict himself in many instances, it is suggested that he is working on the frontiers of legal thought and that any advanced post is liable to the dangers of heavy frontal assault. But it is only by such expeditions, however tenuous they may be, that knowledge of the terrain ahead is gained.

VIII
Precedents, Doctrines, and Statutes

Justice Frankfurter's philosophy of history is largely motivated by a desire to account for the stresses in the law occasioned by the constant pull and tug of the forces of continuity and change. How to accommodate the legitimate demands of both is an oft-repeated question in his writings. His treatment of three such apparently diverse concepts as *stare decisis*, constitutional doctrine, and statutory construction reflects primarily an attempt to arrive at such an accommodation in widely differing sectors of the law. Basic postulates that became evident in analyzing his uses of history in dealing with the Bill of Rights and the Fourteenth Amendment will become evident again, although perhaps in slightly different guise.

I

He starts from the premise that the doctrine of *stare decisis* should, under all normal circumstances, be followed. Having said this, it is necessary to indicate briefly what the abnormal circumstances are in which he feels that divergence from the principle is warranted. Writing in 1915 he thought that "the doctrine of *stare decisis* has no legitimate application to constitutional decisions where the court is presented with a new body of knowledge, largely non-existing at the time of its prior decision." [1] When new medical studies showed the deleterious effect on both men and women of long hours and insufficient wages to maintain an adequate standard of living, the Supreme Court was free, indeed it was compelled, to overrule prior decisions that thwarted attempts to deal with these conditions. When advanced psychological and sociological studies showed the harmful consequences of keeping Negro children in segregated schools, the Court's decisions based on "separate but equal" reasoning had to fall. The Court may take judicial notice of advancements in sister disciplines and apply this new-found knowledge to its own area of specialization, the law. If in so doing a prior course of action is repudiated, it may be that only through change in particulars can continuity with the spirit of experimentation, which for Frankfurter characterizes our system of government, be maintained.

As a professor, he had written that "historic continuity in constitutional construction does not necessarily mean historic stereotype in application. To what extent respect for continuity demands adherence merely to what was, involves the art of adjudication—raises those questions of more or less that ultimately decide cases." [2] This is a generalized statement of his views. But the ways in which questions of more or less are answered depends heavily on each jurist's preoccupations. When questions of *stare decisis* come up, Justice Frankfurter finds the lore of the past hard to overlook.

A few years after taking his place on the Supreme Court, Frankfurter disclosed some of his beliefs about the bases for *stare decisis* in a letter to Chief Justice Stone.

[1] Felix Frankfurter, "The Present Approach to Constitutional Decision on the Bill of Rights," *Harvard Law Review,* xxviii (June, 1915), 791.

[2] Felix Frankfurter and Thomas Corcoran, "Petty Federal Offenses and Trial by Jury," *Harvard Law Review,* xxxix (June, 1926), 922

Law as a living force in society must make adaptation and from time to time slough off the past, but . . . law implies certain continuities, or, at the very least, a permeating feeling that stability as well as change is an element in law. Past decisions ought not to be needlessly overruled. If this is done with sufficient frequency, the whole notion of law is discredited.[3]

In treating the Bill of Rights and the Fourteenth Amendment, Frankfurter admittedly uses generic clause to bring law into conformity with the needs of the present. Likewise, in treating *stare decisis,* he has not denied that some revamping or overruling of prior decisions is necessary. As a matter of fact, soon after he had written the above-quoted letter to Stone, he again broached the same topic with the same correspondent and insisted that "Not a bit more than you do I believe 'it is a sin against the Holy Ghost ever to overrule a case.' That never has been, is not now, and never will be my outlook on law." [4] All that he does say is that Supreme Court justices cannot conjure up wholly new premises without taking into account the presuppositions of the legal system that underlies them. One of the most important sources of such existing materials is the web of precedents handed down to the Court. Following the principle of *stare decisis* is in many ways paying deference to the presuppositions of the legal system that it superintends. The problem of when to apply the doctrine is really the problem of how far the past should be allowed to control the present.

Beyond a philosophic propensity to honor the past, there are very practical reasons for the Justice's adherence to *stare decisis.* The lower courts must be given guidance for their decisions and one means by which the Supreme Court offers such guidance is through maintaining a fairly consistent course. Respect for continuity in the law means more than giving direction to subordinate tribunals. It means also that when no mischief for the legal system proper flows from a line of decisions, that line should be extended until injury manifests itself. As a supporter of and believer in the integrity of the judicial process as a whole, Justice

[3] Frankfurter to Stone, December 28, 1943. Quoted in Alpheus T. Mason, *Harlan Fiske Stone* (New York: The Viking Press, Inc., 1956), p. 610.

[4] Frankfurter to Stone, March 18, 1944. *Ibid.,* p. 613.

Frankfurter thinks that the Court can best protect itself and its reputation by minimizing the episodic nature of much of its work. "Especially ought the Court not reinforce needlessly the instability of our day by giving fair ground for the belief that Law is the expression of chance—for instance, of unexpected changes in the Court's composition and contingencies in the choice of successors." [5] By following precedent the very great role that fate can play in constitutional adjudication is at least contained within manageable limits. Certain ideas expressed by him in one of his earliest opinions are partially at variance with those quoted immediately above.

> The volume of the Court's business has long since made impossible the early healthy practice whereby the Justices gave expression to individual opinions. But the old tradition still has relevance when an important shift in constitutional doctrine is announced after a reconstruction in the membership of the Court. Such shifts of opinion should not derive from mere private judgment. They must be duly mindful of the necessary demands of continuity in civilized society. A reversal of a long current of decisions can be justified only if rooted in the Constitution itself as an historic document designed for a developing nation.[6]

He explicitly recognized that a reconstruction in the membership of the Court had led to abandonment of controlling precedents. It may be that his years on the Court have convinced him of the need to underplay such happenings.

Justice Frankfurter's early recognition that there are times when reconsideration and re-evaluation of constitutional precedents is in order stems oddly enough from the fact that so much of the Court's work *is* episodic and ad hoc. The implications of this fact for the legal system must be taken into consideration. Because the rationale expressed in opinions too often depends on unconscious factors and because the need to deal with immediate cases often accentuates ad hocness in the opprobrious sense, there is a point beyond which the Court cannot go on giving credence to precedents. Continuity with the past is no longer attained by following the principle of *stare decisis*. Rather it is

[5] United States v. Rabinowitz, 339 U.S. 56, 86 (1950).
[6] Graves v. New York, *ex rel.* O'Keefe, 306 U.S. 466, 487 (1939).

gained through stopping and thinking about what the Court has been doing. "There comes a time in the development of law . . . when a comprehensive survey must be made and the cumulative effect of episodic instances appraised to determine whether or not they reveal a harmonious whole." [7] The Court must decide whither it is going.

The survey that Justice Frankfurter proposes is of utmost significance when precedents dealing with constitutional issues are involved. When everyday, run-of-the-mill cases are involved, it is best to follow *stare decisis* and thus avoid instability. When, however, the time comes for important shifts in constitutional doctrine, it is best that each member of the Court be explicit on his own stand so that the public and members of the Court itself may judge the direction that it is taking and may approximate whether it is returning to or diverging further away from past historic interpretations. In this sense, his two statements on personal participation given above can be reconciled.

As would be expected, Justice Frankfurter thinks that when precedents that have long been a part of the law are repudiated, "it is better to do so explicitly, not by circumlocution." [8] He does not favor outright and immediate rejection on the slightest pretext when some particular holding is difficult, but not impossible, to reconcile with others. He is too much of a legal craftsman to disrupt the symmetry of the law by cutting out large clusters of cases at one fell blow. Distinctions have to be drawn and sometimes very fine distinctions to keep certain precedents intact. Following Cardozo and Stone, he prefers a gradual weakening of the weight of any case before it is finally discarded, but, once the decision to discard is made, there should be no doubt left about what has been done. While still at Harvard he wrote to Stone that "if only the theological tradition were not so strong upon our profession . . . things would be called by their right names instead of pretending that it is all a logical unfolding and that cases inconsistent with each other can be reconciled." [9] Forthrightness is

<hr/>

[7] Public Service Commission v. United States, 356 U.S. 421, 429–30 (1958).

[8] Scott Paper Co. v. Marcalus Manufacturing Co., 326 U.S. 249, 274 (1945).

[9] Frankfurter to Stone, September 28, 1933. Quoted in Mason, *Harlan Fiske Stone,* p. 356.

necessary to protect the integrity of the legal system. And so, many years after his letter to Stone, Frankfurter, now a member of the Court, wrote: "We should not indulge in the fiction that the law now announced has always been the law. . . . It is much more conducive to law's self-respect to recognize candidly the considerations that give prospective content to a new pronouncement of law." [10] As the specific terms of the Bill of Rights that have been defined by history should not be distorted by having new substance given them, so precedents that are conclusive only for particular circumstances should not be expanded or distorted in application. As it was far better to recognize that change can come in constitutional law through the generic terms of the Bill of Rights, so it is far better to acknowledge openly when new law is being made and new precedents created.

During the 1957 Term of the Court it was by coincidence that two unrelated but similarly titled cases, Green v. United States,[11] presented the forums through which various justices expressed themselves on the philosophy of *stare decisis*. The majority held that the constitutional prohibition against double jeopardy had been violated where a defendant, upon reversal of his conviction of second degree murder, was tried for first degree murder. Justice Frankfurter, feeling that "we should not be so unmindful, even when constitutional questions are involved, of the principle of *stare decisis*, by whose circumspect observance the wisdom of this Court as an institution transcending the moment can alone be brought to bear on the difficult problems that confront us," [12] dissented. When constitutional issues are involved, Frankfurter is more willing to re-examine controlling precedents. Yet even here judicial preoccupation with the claims of the immediate litigants should not be allowed to overshadow the fact that, in its institutional capacity, the Court must rise above the moment and think in terms of the continuing, organic nature of the law as tersely expressed in the principle of *stare decisis*.

In the second Green case, the Court held that criminal contempts are not subject to jury trial as a matter of constitutional

---

[10] Griffin v. Illinois, 351 U.S. 12, 26 (1956).
[11] 355 U.S. 184 (1957) and 356 U.S. 165 (1958).
[12] Green v. United States, 355 U.S. 184, 215 (1957).

right, nor does the Constitution require that contempts subject to prison terms of more than one year be based on grand jury indictments. Frankfurter wrote a concurrence, which emphasized that the past behavior of the Court as reflected in over two score litigations on the question of contempt power carried a good deal of authority. He even went to the length of including a roll of past Court members who had sustained the exercise of power that the Court was now reaffirming. In sum, while agreeing that the Court was always free to correct obvious mistakes or to revamp a rule of law that had been only occasionally applied, Justice Frankfurter thought to say that "everybody on the Court has been wrong for 150 years and that that which has been deemed part of the bone and sinew of the law should now be extirpated is quite another thing." [13]

The dissenting opinion of Justice Black represents a totally different orientation towards the deference that should be shown past Court action as found in precedents. From his first term on the bench, when he suggested overthrowing a half-century's interpretation that corporations were included within the meaning of persons in the Fourteenth Amendment,[14] Black has on many occasions advocated starting out on radically new tangents without so much as a by-your-leave to the vast number of cases that would thus be automatically overruled. Even a sympathetic observer of his actions noted that "he accorded to long established precedent a minimum of respect and showed scant compunction in overruling it. Moreover, his method of destroying that part of it that he considered wrong was by one lethal blow." [15] In the case at hand, Black thought that the interpretation of one hundred and fifty years was wrong and, therefore, notwithstanding the precedents, time had come for change. He agreed with Frankfurter that courts had a special responsibility to review ruling decisions when constitutional issues were at stake, but for a very different reason. Unless such review were undertaken, it would be needlessly difficult to alleviate the "errors" that his predecessors had made.

[13] Green v. United States, 356 U.S. 165, 193 (1958).
[14] See Connecticut General Life Insurance Co. v. Johnson, 303 U.S. 77 (1938).
[15] Charlotte Williams, *Hugo L. Black* (Baltimore: The Johns Hopkins Press, 1950), p. 83.

Both men would agree that abstract logical theories on the limits of *stare decisis* in and of themselves do not furnish adequate guides for action. There must, of course, be some consideration given to the wholesomeness of a particular change, at a particular time, in a particular society. When the Court disposed of a case on the basis of a precedent taken from the late nineteenth century, Justice Frankfurter felt compelled to say that the case relied upon "represents historically and juridically, an episode of the dead past about as unrelated to the world of today as the one-hoss shay is to the latest jet airplane." [16] The difference between the justices seems to lie in the degree of readiness with which they repudiate the past. For Black, history may have defined and made specific the Bill of Rights and may have dictated that the Fourteenth Amendment incorporates the Bill of Rights, but that is as far as it goes. When it comes to accepting or rejecting the precedents of the past, he desires complete freedom of choice.

Justice Frankfurter, on the other hand, recognizes that *stare decisis* embodies an important social policy in that it represents an element of continuity in law that is rooted in the psychological need to satisfy reasonable expectations. While Justice Black tried to make the Bill of Rights absolute, on many occasions Justice Frankfurter is more apt to make rules announced in previous decisions absolute. Yet he too admits that *stare decisis* is a principle of policy and not a mechanical formula. For him this also means that "adherence to the latest decision, however recent and questionable, when such adherence involves collision with a prior doctrine more embracing in its scope, intrinsically sounder, and verified by experience . . . ." [17] is not required. Thus longevity and repeated reaffirmation are weighty inducements to follow previous courts. Contrariwise, when a new position is recently taken, the judge is under far less compulsion to acquiesce. A judge should not persist in holding to views that have been repeatedly repudiated by his brethren, but "until then, full respect for stare decisis does not require a judge to forego his own convictions promptly after his brethren have rejected them." [18] In attempting to make history through *stare decisis* presently mean-

[16] Kinsella v. Kruger, 351 U.S. 470, 482 (1956).
[17] Helvering v. Hallock, 309 U.S. 106, 119 (1940).
[18] Radovich v. National Football League, 352 U.S. 445, 455 (1957).

ingful, Justice Frankfurter is tackling one of the most complex and difficult of jurisprudential problems. He is certainly not completely successful in the endeavor, but the attempt is much to be praised.

II

The use of doctrine in constitutional law can be of great aid to the courts, but it can also be a fetter whereby reliance on past experience serves as an excuse for present thinking. Justice Frankfurter in recent years has been increasingly dubious about the wisdom of allowing doctrinal short-hand statements of complicated ideas to rule the disposition of current cases. Scattered throughout his opinions are warnings to the effect that "in law as elsewhere words of many-hued meanings derive their scope from the uses to which they are put," [19] or "of compelling consideration is the fact that words acquire scope and function from the history of events which they summarize." [20] Since doctrines are really only the formal articulation of deeper experiences, they too must be treated in historical perspective. Doctrines often come into being as mere catchwords, passed over lightly in an opinion, which reappear later as full-fledged constitutional concepts. As in applying precedents, where the danger is that pronouncements in an opinion frequently exceed the justification of the circumstances on which they are based, so in using doctrines, Justice Frankfurter is wary of taking ideas out of their historical context and forcefully analogizing them to unanalogous situations.

In 1932 he had written that "in the domain of ideas, no less than in the biological world, an organism cannot be torn from the context of its environment without destroying its meaning." [21] He has held to this position in case after case that has come before the Supreme Court, reminding his brethren that "legal ideas like other organisms cannot survive severance from their con-

[19] Powell v. U.S. Cartridge Co., 339 U.S. 497, 529 (1950).

[20] Phelps Dodge Corp. v. National Labor Relations Board, 313 U.S. 177, 186 (1941).

[21] Felix Frankfurter and Nathan Greene, "The Labor Injunction," in *Encyclopedia of the Social Sciences* (New York: The Macmillan Co., 1932), viii, 653.

genial environment." [22] This is especially true when constitutional doctrines—clear and present danger, separate but equal—in contradistinction to other legal terms—situs, comity, jurisdiction— are involved. For here it is that the Court is most prone to disregard the limitations that it should take into account.

> Legal doctrines . . . have a specific juridical origin and etiology. They derive meaning and content from the circumstances that gave rise to them and from the purposes they were designed to serve. . . . Doctrines . . . must be placed in their historical setting. They cannot be wrenched from it and mechanically transplanted into an alien, unrelated context without suffering mutilation or distortion.[23]

Legal terms such as "situs" and "comity" are well defined and understood by the profession. For Justice Frankfurter, constitutional doctrines should be as specific and, as with the specific terms of the Bill of Rights, should not be extended in definition and thus distorted. Experience has, however, taught him that "legal doctrines have, in an odd kind of way, the faculty of self-generating extension." [24] Since this is so, and since the Court insists on using doctrines in a manner that he does not approve, the Justice has more counsel to offer his compatriots.

"The mobility of words at the present time brings in its train what might be called immobility of reflections." [25] This was the thought of Professor Frankfurter in 1930. Now, over a quarter of a century later, he would no doubt still agree and would likely think the sentence of such importance that it should be cast in bold type. During his long tenure on the Supreme Court he has seen many phraseological insights transmuted into definitive statements. The Court's duty does not end with the recitation of phrases that only summarize much more complicated historic processes. Recitation of that sort is merely an excuse for meditation and decision upon the unique circumstances presented by any litigation. Reflection is needed, not parroting of beautifully turned literary expressions. Parroting of doctrine without consideration

[22] United States v. Pink, 315 U.S. 203, 234 (1942).
[23] Reid v. Covert, 354 U.S. 1, 50 (1957).
[24] Texas v. Florida, 306 U.S. 398, 434 (1939).
[25] Felix Frankfurter, *The Public and Its Government* (New Haven: Yale University Press, 1930), p. 34.

of circumstances is apt to lead to atrophication of any critical sense. In order to avoid facing the unpleasant task of admitting that a favorite doctrine is simply not applicable, it is fitted to variant situations despite the contradictions. The end result is that, disregarding sound logic and good sense, juristic principles designed for the practical affairs of government are pressed to abstract extremes. And for Frankfurter, the Court "is under no duty to make law less than sound logic and good sense." [26]

Doctrines are symbolic concepts. When used correctly they telescope through one or two words understanding of specific circumstances into the present, thus making it available for similar current problems. When used incorrectly, even with the best motives, they confuse rather than help the situation for, "like all attempts to describe legal consequences through the use of inapposite concepts, the momentum of the symbolic concept may induce consequences beyond those which the true nature of the problem justifies." [27] The task faced here is very similar to that encountered in determining whether particular precedents should be allowed to dispose of a case when the historic nature of those precedents has been changed through ad hoc application. Case-by-case adjudication tends to change perspective. It makes the minute alterations wrought in doctrine seem minor until the entire consequences are suddenly thrust upon the Court's consciousness by the obvious degree of permutation that has resulted from the gradual accretion of symbolic nuances. When superannuated doctrines are used under such circumstances, "either lipservice will be paid . . . formulas while decisions are rooted in considerations outside them, or formulas not fitting practical circumstances will achieve impractical results." [28]

In recent years Justice Frankfurter's name has been tied to the school of thought that denies the efficacy attributed to certain doctrines by that group on the Court known as judicial activists. Many think that his denial of "preferred freedoms" or "clear and present danger" stems solely from a dislike of the meaning being given these formulas. While this may be partially true, the denial is based on something more than that. It is based on his entire

[26] New York v. United States, 326 U.S. 572, 577 (1946).
[27] Boston Metals Co. v. S/S "Winding Gulf," 349 U.S. 122, 127 (1955).
[28] United States v. Toronto, H. & B. N. Co., 338 U.S. 396, 408 (1949).

theory of the specific historical limitations that surround any doctrine. For example, " 'Clear and present danger' was never used by Mr. Justice Holmes to express a technical legal doctrine or to convey a formula for adjudicating cases. It was a literary phrase not to be distorted by being taken from its context." [29] Contrary to the impression often given in articles on the Court, Justice Frankfurter does not confine his criticism to the favorite doctrines of the activists. Quite technical formulas are treated in like manner.

The difficulty in criticizing the use of doctrines in constitutional interpretation is that they are necessary if some continuity with the past is to be maintained. If, as with precedents, at least some guidelines are not utilized, the ad hocness of litigation can turn into chaos. On the other hand, if doctrines are used with too much precision, changes in interpretation may be precluded and the law bound by ideas, valid in the past, but no longer of present vitality. When Justice Frankfurter speaks out against doctrine, he is often speaking out against doctrinal gloss on the Constitution being interpreted rather than the Constitution itself.[30] False doctrine as well as valid doctrine inappropriately used thus must be guarded against.

In the year preceding his elevation to the Supreme Court, Frankfurter had written an article entitled "Rigid Outlook in a Dynamic World" in which he said that the clue not only to the history of the last fifty years but also to the tensions of the future could be found in the reluctance of doctrines to pass from existence once they had become obsolete and no longer served society.

> One of the strange paradoxes about man is his disdain of theory as theory and the dominance of theory in practice. William James spoke of "irreducible and stubborn facts." But I think I can summon history to witness that theories can be even more stubborn than facts. . . . The elder Huxley once said there is nothing more tragic than the murder of a big theory by a little fact. But he hastened to add that nothing is more surprising than the way in which a theory will continue to live long after its brains are knocked out.[31]

[29] Pennekamp v. Florida, 328 U.S. 331, 353 (1946).

[30] See, for example, Graves v. New York *ex rel.* O'Keefe, 306 U.S. 466, 491 (1939).

[31] Felix Frankfurter, "Rigid Outlook in a Dynamic World," *Survey Graphic,* xxvii (January, 1938), 7.

These statements of James and Huxley are favorites of Frankfurter and have appeared in several of his opinions. Doctrines, beyond being symbolic concepts, are theoretical formulations, in that the Court's understanding of their implications must precede practical application. The Court, because it wields ultimate power to some degree, should be neither willful nor wooden: willful in the sense of following its own desires regardless of precedents and doctrines; wooden in the sense of relying uncritically on familiar formulas, refusing to acknowledge that other and newer ideas may have to come into play. Conflict of principle as this becomes apparent in divergent doctrines can only be resolved through an intelligent choice between doctrines, always keeping in mind the fact that the choice itself must be predicated upon understanding when a theory has had "its brains knocked out" and when it is still operative.

Speaking before the Federation of Bar Associations a few months before his appointment, Professor Frankfurter told his audience that "the history of the Supreme Court is . . . but the analysis of individuals . . . who make decisions and lay down doctrines, of other individuals, their successors, who refine, modify and sometimes even overrule the decisions of their predecessors, reinterpreting and transmuting their doctrines." [32] He has always been highly interested in the role that doctrines have played in the Court's history and for this reason has been sensitive to the means whereby a clearer comprehension of the meaning that any particular doctrine had at the time of its appearance can be gained: ". . . a hint here, a phrase there, an occasional letter appearing sixty years later, an innuendo in a public address, a revealing characterization of a departed colleague—these are aids to understanding that may impart meaning, if not always validity, to a seemingly wooden doctrine." [33]

As the history of the Supreme Court is always contemporary history, so doctrines must have current value to make them worth keeping. But value is not attained by forceably bringing up to date or giving new and perhaps contradictory significance to historic formulations. Validity cannot always be assumed, for many doctrines are only tentative thrusts put forth by the author with full realization that they may soon be discarded. If the reasons for their appearance are still valid, they may still be of present usefulness. Otherwise, constitutional law must break with them and find new methods to deal with the problems of today. Finally, regulations governing the use of doctrines are for Justice Frankfurter largely tied in with their generating history. The specific nature of much doctrine and the self-restraint that he advocates for the judiciary conjoin to make him extremely cautious in renovating obsolete formulas or promulgating new ones.

III

While canons of construction for statutes are necessarily different in many ways from those employed in constitutional interpretation, there are certain parallels in Justice Frankfurter's actions that indicate that history has meaning here too. As background, one should keep in mind that "legislative drafting is dependent on treacherous words to convey, as often as not, complicated ideas, and courts should not be pedantically exacting in construing legislation." [34] Thus Justice Frankfurter's distrust of treacherous words, whether they appear in precedents, doctrines, or statutes, leads him to deal with them very much in the same manner wherever found. Depending upon circumstances, he seeks aid from different sources—history, legislative intent—in taking the worst sting from treachery.

In treating statutes, where does one begin to look for such aid and what attitude of mind is conducive to finding it? Frankfurter's characterization of the Federal Employers' Liability Act is typical of the way he thinks of statutes even before attempting to apply them. This Act he called

the last in a series of consistently developing statutes. As such, it is an organism, projected into the future out of the past. It is not merely a collection of words for abstract notation out of the dic-

[34] United States v. Turley, 352 U.S. 407, 417–18 (1957).

tionary. The process of judicial construction must be mindful of the history of legislation, of the purpose which infused it, of the difficulties which were encountered in effectuating this purpose, of the aims of those most active in relieving these difficulties.[35]

Because of the vast complexities hidden behind the words of any statute, the Court should avoid grudging interpretation of legislation. In other words, the Court should realize that "laws are not to be read as though every *i* has to be dotted and every *t* crossed." [36] To do so would be to treat words as ends and not as vehicles to convey meaning. It would reflect a niggardly view of the legislative function. The plain words of a statute are often deceptively simple, just as terms within the Bill of Rights might at first glance seem quite clear and distinct until they have to be put to work. One, of course, begins with the words of a statute, just as one begins with the words of the Constitution, but the jurist cannot afford to stop there.

As certain words of the Bill of Rights are specific while others are generic, so a certain allowance must be made for the implementation of policy through flexible words that Congress is at times forced to use in drafting legislation. All language carries certain infirmities of inexactness. After the Court has made a real effort to ascertain what it is that Congress has enacted, it must apply the enactment as it understands it. This requires judicial judgment. Justice Frankfurter's rejection of the Bill of Rights as a completely defined and self-contained document and his insistence on the generic characteristics of the due process clause of the Fourteenth Amendment as allowing for judgment within the limits of civilized standards are here duplicated in some degree. He feels that "statutes . . . are not to be deemed self-enclosed instances, they are to be regarded as starting points of reasoning, as means for securing coherence and for effectuating purpose." [37] General words—generic if you will—must be allowed to draw nourishment from the program that they describe. The Court when dealing with terms of very limited specific meaning

[35] Reed v. Pennsylvania Rail Co., 351 U.S. 502, 510 (1956).
[36] U.S. *ex rel.* Knauff v. Shaughnessy, 338 U.S. 537, 548 (1950).
[37] Pope v. Atlantic Coast Line Rail Co., 345 U.S. 379, 390 (1953).

must abide by their limited qualities. On the other hand, when Congress chooses to write in a vague manner, the Court must, through empiric reasoning, give substance to the policy.

One aspect of Frankfurter's general philosophy of statutory construction may help to explain more clearly the relationship between Congress and the Court in this area. Congress gives the Court a heavy responsibility when it uses vague words; the Court in dealing with these generic terms sets up some sort of a pattern; if Congress wishes to change the pattern, it must do so explicitly. It is this third stage that sometimes causes misunderstanding, for the Court has changed generic concepts into specific ones through application. "Before a hitherto familiar and socially desirable practice is outlawed, where overreaching or exploitation is not inherent in the situation, the outlawry should come from Congress." [38] Once Congress has accepted an interpretation placed upon a statute by the Court, the Court cannot at will change that interpretation since that would amount to disregarding congressional pleasure. It is this twist that brings Justice Frankfurter's theory of statutory construction into line with his more pervasive theory of the judicial role as a very limited one and helps to mitigate the dangers that do stem from a breakdown of provisions on the basis of their specific and generic characteristics.

Certain terms within statutes can be likened to terms within the Constitution in the ways in which Justice Frankfurter treats them. In addition, there is the fact that entire statutes differ from one another on the basis of their drafting. Some statutes are meant to recite a broad policy, and it matters not in what terms the policy is stated because the very nature of the judicial task requires that the statute be treated as a generating document. Regulatory legislation is often of this type. On the other hand, some legislation is designed to deal with very narrow minute problems, and though it may have generalized provisions, giving meaning to these generalizations is only a prelude to dealing with its far more fundamental specific aspects. In a recent case

[38] Schulte v. Grangi, 328 U.S. 108, 121 (1946). For a discussion of how far Frankfurter has adhered to this policy, see Wallace Mendelson, "Mr. Justice Frankfurter on the Construction of Statutes," *California Law Review*, XLIII (October, 1955), 652–70.

involving governmental grants of privilege to private concerns,
Justice Frankfurter made this distinction quite unmistakably.

> Unlike constitutional provisions such as the Due Process Clause
> or enactments such as the Sherman Law that embody a felt rather
> than defined purpose and necessarily look to the future for the un-
> folding of their content, making of their judicial application an
> evolutionary process nourished by relevant changing circumstances,
> a specific grant . . . does not gain meaning from time. Its scope
> today is what it was in 1862, and the judicial task is to ascertain
> what content was conveyed by that section in 1862.[39]

For future reference it is important to note that history as an aid
in interpretation is valid whether broad or narrow statutes are
under consideration. Statutes, as the Constitution, cannot be read
in a vacuum. In plain speech, this means that judicial construction cannot be torn from its wider, nonlegal context.

Whether the Court is trying to determine the meaning of particular phrases within a statute or the nature of the statute itself,
common problems are involved. He has chastised as mechanical
jurisprudence attempts to make particular phrases such as "foreign country" or "possession" so precise as to preclude judicial
judgment.[40] They are terms that, unlike designations for weights
and measures, do not have scientifically determined meanings. It
then follows that "if individual words are inexact symbols, with
shifting variables, their configuration can hardly achieve invari-
ant meaning or assured definiteness." [41] Thus in determining the
nature of a statute, the problem is doubly confounded. Not only
must particular words be appraised, but also their cumulative
effect must be taken into account.

> . . . the significance of an enactment, its antecedents as well as its
> later history, its relation to other enactments, all may be relevant
> to the construction of words for one purpose and in one setting but
> not for another. Some words are confined to their history; some are
> starting points for history. Words are intellectual and moral cur-

[39] United States v. Union Pacific Rail Co., 353 U.S. 112, 122 (1957).

[40] United States v. Spelar, 338 U.S. 217, 223 (1949).

[41] Felix Frankfurter, "Some Reflections on the Reading of Statutes," *Columbia
Law Review*, XLVII (May, 1947), 528.

rency. They come from the legislative mint with some intrinsic meaning. Sometimes it remains unchanged. Like currency, words sometimes appreciate or depreciate in value.[42]

How then does Justice Frankfurter propose to find out whether appreciation or depreciation has occurred? As with constitutional terms, he turns to legislative history.

In treating such history Justice Frankfurter appears to be more cautious in imputing definitiveness to any term than is true with the specific phrases of the Bill of Rights. He does, however, continue to insist that legislative terms and legislation itself that can be correlated to relatively well-defined constitutional provisions should be shown comparable respect. However much one might disagree with the original interpretation, in dealing with specific terms and specific statutes, the uniform construction put by the Court upon any piece of legislation since its inception should carry preponderant weight. "The Court cannot . . . retrieve what Congress granted . . . . The hindsight that reveals [an act] as lavish or even profligate ought not to influence the Court to narrow the scope . . . by reading it in the light of a policy that did not mature until half a century thereafter." [43] Legislation of this type does not gain clarity with the passage of time since initially there could not have been too much leeway for judicial definition. The Court must face the fact that in certain instances it is presented with *fait accompli* and must acquiesce, as it should with specific constitutional terms, in the dispositions worked out by the past.

Although for the time of the adoption of the Constitution, and certainly for the period when the Fourteenth Amendment became a part of our fundamental code, records exist to intimate the major premises of participants in the drama, it is with statutory enactments that one is apt to have the most complete source materials in which to locate intention. With specific statutes these materials can be very telling. However, with statutes that are cast in vague terms or that are vague in the sense that they encompass a policy of an ongoing nature, considerable hesitancy is exhibited on the

[42] *Ibid.*, p. 537–38.
[43] United States v. Union Pacific Rail Co., 353 U.S. 112, 136 (1957).

part of Justice Frankfurter in making even official sources such as the *Congressional Globe* or *Congressional Record* conclusive. The Court must search out all relevant help in throwing light on a statute, even to examining the oral give and take of Congressmen studying the proposed legislation. But it is quite another thing to allow off-hand remarks to weigh more heavily than the words of the enactment or their encompassing history.[44] To make such a substitution would be spurious use of legislative history and, if followed too far, would conceal the real meaning of any enactment by presenting too much of a temptation for judicial policy-making, leading to the quip that only when legislative history is doubtful do you go to the statute. As Justice Frankfurter has put it, even for generic statutes, while courts are no longer confined to the language therein, they are still confined by it.

In an article dealing with the philosophy of statutory construction, he indicated that for him one of the most troublesome phases was to determine the extent to which extraneous documentation and external sources are absorbed by and become part of the text of a statute.[45] Administrative agencies and interested parties in general have perceived that loading the record with materials favorable to their demands may so confuse the issue that it is very difficult for the Court to disentangle relevant from irrelevant factors. "Since it is common practice to allow memoranda to be submitted to a committee of Congress by interests, public and private, often high-minded enough but with their own axes to grind," Justice Frankfurter finds that unless the Court is careful, "great encouragement will be given to the temptation of administrative officials and others to provide self-serving 'proof' of congressional confirmation for their private views through incorporation of such materials."[46] Consequently, innumerable opportunities will be provided for putting gloss upon innocent-looking legislation. The meaning of a statute often must be obtained by fashioning a mosaic of significance out of disjointed bits of history. But to say this does not mean that every bit of

[44] See Baltimore and Ohio Rail Co. v. Kepner, 314 U.S. 44, 60 (1941).
[45] Frankfurter, "Some Reflections on the Reading of Statutes," *loc. cit.*, p. 529.
[46] Shapiro v. United States, 335 U.S. 1, 49 (1948).

information is historically significant. Judgment is necessary to make history intelligible.

After much ground has been traversed, the starting point of this discussion of statutory construction is almost reached again. In the art of interpretation, there is no final, precisely defined meaning available. Looking outside the text, Justice Frankfurter finds meaning in history that is but the account of legislative compromise fashioned from social pressures. The purpose or command of the statute is merely the legalized statement of compromise. The Justice is the first to admit that no problem is really involved unless the Court is called upon to choose between two meanings for any term or statute, each of which comes with at least some degree of respectability. It must mediate in a contest between probabilities of meanings. At this point Frankfurter usually turns to history for aid in making a choice. In this he differs somewhat from his more activist brethren who tend to find meaning in the assumed hopes rather than in the expressed words of legislators.

Justice Frankfurter's philosophy of life and law is predicated upon a deep respect for the organic nature of both, whereby the evolving needs of society and of the individuals who compose it are best cared for by providing both stability and change. Continuity with past knowledge is gained through an understanding of history; but history is contemporary history when past insights are put to present uses. It is well to close this chapter and section with a quotation from Herbert J. Muller's *The Uses of the Past,* from which the section title is paraphrased.

> . . . the "wider self" is a sense of the past. It is a sense of the basic community beneath all the relativities of culture, the basic continuity beneath all the mutabilities of history. . . . The study of history must justify itself simply as an act of piety that deepens and widens this esthetic, spiritual, essentially religious sense of continuity and community.[47]

The past is prologue.

[47] Herbert J. Muller, *The Uses of the Past* (New York: Oxford University Press, 1952), pp. 372–73.

FOUR

The Constitution as an Instrument of Power

A third major operational technique that should be added to Justice Frankfurter's interest in symbolism and history is his concern with concepts of power. He is very fond of quoting John Marshall to the effect that "It is a constitution we are expounding." Being a constitution, it orders much of the life of society, not only through its expressed words but also through the radiations of its implied philosophy. Because it is a constitution, those who expound it must have a cohesive and mature approach to the document as representing the deeper, wider entity that is the United States. Justice Frankfurter looks at the Constitution as an organic whole, that is, he feels that all clauses are on an equal footing and should be so treated by the Supreme Court. Neither marked antipathy toward nor marked preference for certain clauses as the bases for the exercise of government power intrude into his judicial philosophy.

This conception of the Constitution has implications for several areas. Directly, it means rejection of a "preferred freedoms" position. It also colors Justice Frankfurter's thinking on such topics as the war power and the President's power as Commander-in-Chief. Self-perpetuation is one of the abiding concerns for any society. Catchy phrases like "clear and present danger" do not really serve to solve the problem of how far government must be in peril before positive action can be taken. Since the maintenance of society and coextensively of its constitutional system takes precedence, Justice Frankfurter's performance in this sector will be examined first before the other facets of his approach to the Constitution as an instrument of power.

IX Subversion and Self-Preservation

On an abstract scale of value, the completely unrestrained exercise of the "human" right, to say nothing of the "constitutional" right, of freedom of expression may outweigh all other considerations. This having been agreed to, it would be absurd in construing a constitution to admit any such priority without relating it to external factors. The preservation of the governmental system and of its particular constituent act from which government derives power is a value transcending all others in the scale used by a constitutional court. Talk of toleration assumes a common ground upon which uncoerced minds can meet. Coercion, whether it be of the psychological or physical variety, disrupts the accepted means of influencing opinion that is encompassed within the First Amendment. When the positive principle of accommodation and the search for agreement beneath diversity are anteriorly foresworn, government is presented with a dilemma that can be solved only with the greatest forbearance and self-restraint. Otherwise, innocent victims preaching an unpopular gospel will be hauled into the same net as those who are deliberately set upon the destruction of the governmental system that nurtured them.

I

Although government is not the only indispensable unity within the purview of modern man, its indispensability is obvious enough to rule out destruction. This recognition does not ignore the social value of smaller groups. It merely insists that smaller groups cannot exist without safety for the more inclusive whole. The fact that one recognizes a poiltical unity's peculiarly comprehensive membership and its special right to use social coercion as one of the means for retention of identity does not mean that any special claims for moral absoluteness or rightness are advanced. Subsocieties cannot be allowed to terrorize society as a whole, and coercion must remain under the control of Uncle Sam, or whatever other figurative personality symbolizes the nation as an ongoing concern. There are thus two sets of considerations: first, that innocent criticism is not banished at the same time that dangerous discussion or action threatening to the constitutional system is brought under restrictions; second, whether innocent or subversive groups are involved, that they are prohibited from the use of any type of coercion that must be centered in the government.

Even within the most dictatorial regime, an absolute ordering of human action is an impossibility. In a democracy, however much we strive for stability and order, we delude ourselves by thinking that it can be attained by making absolute any system or that the system can be protected by treating constitutional provisions as absolutes. To do so is to defeat the very purpose of a democracy. "Democracy is neither a mystical abstraction nor a mechanical gadget," Justice Frankfurter has said. "It is the teaching of experience. In the long course of human experience democracy has proven itself the only form of social arrangement which adequately respects, and by so doing helps to unfold, the richness of human diversity." [1] To remain such an arrangement, democracy must be able to make continual adjustments to different social pressures and above all to the new mechanisms of endangering security. Time-place factors, the degree of coercion evidenced, and the severity of the threat to social security all are important criteria in determining when government can intervene and exercise its power for self-preservation and self-perpetuation.

The most adequate index in determining whether social pressures are being taken into consideration is the volume and variety of legislation. Normally, legislation accurately reflects the range and intensity of governing political, social, and economic forces. One of the major concerns of society since the end of World War I has been to protect itself against destruction whether caused by internal or external enemies. Statutes passed by both federal and state legislatures have had as their main objective supervisory control over the activities of elements in the population dedicated to the forcible overthrow of government. To determine just how Justice Frankfurter has reacted to this climate and atmosphere over the long years of his public service, one must retrace some of his actions and positions before he became a member of the Supreme Court.

It will be recalled that Professor Frankfurter joined with others in a manifesto against the Red-baiting tactics of Attorney General Palmer in the years immediately following World War I. The hysterical outburst of fear and confusion displayed by both official and unofficial sources did little to enhance respect for law or legal authorities. The vehemence of response to a supposed threat was out of all proportion to the actualities of the situation. Palmer, while having some statutory backing for his actions, distorted their real significance through his fanatical behavior. It was against this distortion and not against the basic proposition that the government had a right to protect itself that Professor Frankfurter inveighed. In published articles on the opinions of Justices Holmes and Brandeis he was at some pains to express appreciation for their treatment of issues involving state or federal subversion or espionage statutes. The doctrine of "clear and present

[1] Felix Frankfurter, "On Being an American," *Survey Graphic*, xxxiii (June, 1944), 308.

danger" was a real advance, for it took into account the external time-place factors that are so necessary for an understanding of not *if* but *when* government can intervene. At the time of the announcement of the doctrine there was no question that the government had a right to act. Indeed, to the embarrassment of some of its later-day adherents, the first time the concept of "clear and present danger" was enunciated, it was used by Justice Holmes to uphold a conviction under an espionage statute.[2] This practical, empirical approach to the question of national security recommended itself to Professor Frankfurter.

As an academician, he often discussed how constitutionality was determined. In all crucial cases, including those that deal with the question of individual rights and national security, constitutionality resolved itself into a judgment upon circumstances. "Every tendency to deal with constitutional questions abstractly, to formulate them in terms of barren legal questions, leads to dialectics, to sterile conclusions unrelated to actualities."[3] To assert positively that it is a crime to cry "Fire!" in a crowded theater overlooks the fact that there may be fire. On the other hand, to assert just as positively that individual freedom would be violated by any restrictions on a shout of alarm would be disastrous. Carrying this over into the realm of national security, reasonable legislative attempts to deal with threats to society's future have been sympathetically discussed by Justice Frankfurter—as long as the procedural guarantees of due process of law are honored. As is his wont, he bows to legislative judgment even in this sensitive area when a correlation can be shown between cause—advocacy of overthrow—and effect—a real prospect of overthrow. Claims for absolute freedom of expression do not impress him if empirically it can be shown that some restrictions are necessary to retain a semblance of order and stability.

An opinion dealing with naturalization suggests Justice Frankfurter's criteria for dealing with national security. "Allegiance to this Government and its laws, is a compendious phrase to describe those political and legal institutions that are the enduring features

<hr />

[2] Schenck v. United States, 249 U.S. 47 (1919).

[3] Felix Frankfurter, "Advisory Opinions," in *Encyclopedia of the Social Sciences* (New York: The Macmillan Co., 1930), I, 478.

of American political society." Allegiance of some sort is "nothing less than the bonds that tie Americans together in devotion to a common fealty." [4] While allegiance must be measured in terms of very generalized formulations, there are boundaries beyond which behavior is obviously not that of respect, service, or obedi-ence. Accommodation of antithetical beliefs implies at least a willingness to work with the political and legal institutions that are the enduring features of American society. Unless a willing-ness for accommodation is exhibited by all parties, allegiance even in its most general guise cannot be attained, and if allegiance is no longer a rightful condition for participation within the body politic, then any ties of fealty are also broken.

Our political and legal institutions, which are the outward manifestations of constitutional democracy, are not always the easiest of man's social arrangements to manage successfully. They are, however, the arrangements that have grown from the soil that the Founders' provided, and the "Founders of this Nation were not imbued with the modern cynicism that the only thing that history teaches is that it teaches nothing. They acted on the conviction that the experience of man sheds a good deal of light on his nature." [5] If we are honestly to face up to our history and experience, we must admit that untrammeled free expression has never been a reality nor can it ever be if government is to remain relatively stable. Expression tempered by reason and affinity for allowing ideas that are not our own, but that may be based in reason, to influence us—that is, a willingness to accommodate on the intellectual level—is all that the First Amendment guarantees. While the Supreme Court is called upon for self-discipline in treating ideas that may be unpopular but that may very much be grounded in reason and present no threat to the national security, so those claiming protection for their right to free expression must show an equal self-discipline in the ways in which and the types of programs that they advocate.

Justice Frankfurter's position in cases involving the First Amendment, and especially in those cases where national security is involved, comes down to this, that reasoned argument, willing

[4] Baumgartner v. United States, 322 U.S. 665, 673 (1944).
[5] Youngstown Sheet and Tube Co. v. Sawyer, 343 U.S. 579, 593 (1952).

to have itself accepted in the market place of ideas solely on its own merit without any coercive features, should be tolerated even if it attacks some of our basic beliefs about the nature of man and government. When, however, there is apparent a deliberate rejection of the principle of accommodation and this rejection is tied not only to advocacy but also to action, Justice Frankfurter believes that the value scale of a constitutional court requires preservation of the government and its constituent act. The determination of whether accommodation has been by-passed is one that can only be made by the legislature on the basis of external factors and can only be validated by the judiciary by a correlation of legislative judgment with time-place features governing a particular litigation. Neither complete approval of governmental restriction on speech and actions nor complete disapproval of such restrictions will do.

The various approaches of Supreme Court justices to the problem of subversion and social self-preservation are extremely important, for it is on the level of the nation's Highest Tribunal that questions as to the constitutionality of statutes dealing with these issues usually receive fullest consideration. While we have been primarily concerned with the position of Justice Frankfurter, it is necessary to indicate a totally different school of thought on the topic. Once again Justice Black presents the most mature and articulate counterposition. It is difficult to choose from his many utterances on the topic of weighing individual freedom against national security. He and Justice Frankfurter are not at odds on all occasions. When either one of them is writing the majority opinion that is to be joined by the other, personal approaches are tempered and more stereotyped discussion ensues. Therefore, in choosing an expression of Black's one should look to a concurring or dissenting opinion for an uninhibited statement of his position.

For him,

> It seems self-evident that all speech criticizing the government rulers and challenging current beliefs may be dangerous to the status quo. With full knowledge of this danger the Framers rested our First Amendment on the premise that the slightest suppression of thought. speech, press, or public assembly is still more dangerous.

This means that individuals are guaranteed an undiluted and un-equivocal right to express themselves on questions of current public interests.[6]

Justice Black's admittedly uncompromising insistence on the right to individual expression over the right of society to protect its interests means a sharp division from other members of the Court. What Justice Frankfurter would call regulation, he would call suppression. While the former would rely on the courts to mediate the legal factors involved in national security, he would denounce any thought that courts, or any other governmental agency, have power to control utterances, even utterances that could be danger-ous. This difference of position is partially the cause of and par-tially the result of two other strands in Justice Black's judicial philosophy: the tendency to individualize justice, which was dis-cussed previously, and his reliance on an external objective stand-ard usually associated with the doctrine of "preferred freedoms," which will be discussed in a subsequent chapter.

II

The 1955 Term of the Court presents excellent material for a miniature study of various approaches to the problem of sub-version and social self-preservation. Enough variety of national security issues came before the Court to justify looking at the decisions of that session as being representative. However, one or two earlier cases must be slightly touched upon as background for that inquiry.

In American Communications Association v. Douds [7] the Court had under advisement the constitutionality of provisions within the Taft-Hartley Act that required union officials, if they wished their unions to gain the benefits of the Act, to file affidavits stating that they did not belong to nor were they affiliated with organiza-tions that taught, advocated, or believed in the overthrow of gov-ernment by force or violence. Only six members of the Court

[6] Wieman v. Updegraff, 344 U.S. 183, 194 (1952).
[7] 339 U.S. 382 (1950).

participated. For five of the six participants, Chief Justice Vinson held that the act was valid as to disclosure of membership in or affiliation with the Communist party. He was able to hold only two others with him when he contended that it was equally valid as to organizations that merely taught or believed in overthrow without any direct institutional relation between advocacy and overthrow. The two members of the original five whom he lost were Justices Frankfurter and Jackson. Both thought that the Act's requirements as to belief were too vague.

Justice Black was the only one of the six justices taking the case under consideration who dissented from the entire holding. He placed his holding solely on First Amendment grounds. Disagreement between the three dissenters or dissenters-in-part seemed to hinge on one point: was there a significant difference between actual participation in an organization that professedly advocated overthrow of governmental order and mere interest or attraction to organizations that might teach or believe abstractly in such a plan? Justices Frankfurter and Jackson agreed with legislative responses that would control the first type of activity; they reneged on restrictions as to the second.

Joint Anti-Fascist Refugee Committee v. McGrath,[8] decided in 1951, provides another comparison of views. Under authorization from a Presidential Order, the Attorney General, without due notice and hearing, placed certain organizations on a list of suspect associations. Membership by a government employee in an organization on the list could prove seriously detrimental, for, if any charge of disloyalty was brought against the individual, such membership was to be used as presumptive evidence of guilt. On very different premises five members of the Court agreed that the organizations placed on the Attorney General's list had standing to sue and were entitled to declaratory or injunctive relief in having their names removed from the list because of the resulting harm to their activities from such an identification.

The strange combination of Justices Douglas and Burton refused to consider initially any constitutional questions, feeling that a government admission in lower court proceedings established the arbitrary nature of the Attorney General's action. Justice

[8] 341 U.S. 123 (1951).

Douglas did, however, insert a separate statement to the effect that if the Court were going to treat constitutional questions he thought that due process had been violated. This was the basic position assumed by Justices Frankfurter and Jackson. The lack of notice and hearing particularly disturbed them and they consequently held that, under the circumstances described, the attempt to deal with subversion by the executive officer was not valid. They did *not* hold that if and when proper procedures were adopted, some like program would necessarily have to fall. Justice Black relied solely on the First Amendment, feeling that a direct violation of freedom of speech (and the absorbed, though more indefinite, freedom of thought) had resulted.

What comes out of these two cases is the fact that only Black of the participating Court members found reason to curtail government action in the field of subversion within the First Amendment. Justices Frankfurter and Jackson, while withdrawing from certain implications of the policies under consideration, relied on much more definite procedural regulations, hoping for the most part to by-pass direct challenges to legislative, ergo societal, responses to internalized threats. As Justice Frankfurter has said in another context, "The enemy is not so near the gate that we should allow respect for traditions of fairness, which has heretofore prevailed in this country, to be overborne by military exigencies. . . . In a country with our moral and material strength the maintenance of fair procedure cannot handicap our security." [9] When the Court has assured procedural regularity, it has done all it can to protect the individual. Yet this is doing a great deal. Procedural regularities having been ascertained, a constitutional court must then recognize that the overriding value that the legislature is trying to preserve is that of community existence and before this value the Court must yield. This is the belief that Frankfurter carried into the 1955 Term of the Supreme Court.

Six cases in the field of internal security dominate the scene. Taken chronologically, they deal with an immunity act, state sedition legislation, claims against self-incrimination under the Fifth Amendment, perjured testimony, dismissal from private employ because of suspect associations, and dismissal from public

[9] United States v. Nugent, 346 U.S. 1, 12–13 (1953).

employ for the same reason. In the first case, Ullmann v. United States,[10] Justice Frankfurter wrote the opinion of the Court over the dissent of Justices Black and Douglas. He found the Immunity Act of 1954 constitutional. It provided equal protection with the Fifth Amendment against self-incrimination for any witness called upon to disclose information in proceedings involving an interference with the security or defense of the United States by treason, espionage, or any other forms of subversion. "The Immunity Act is concerned with the national security. It reflects a congressional policy to increase the possibility of more complete and open disclosure by removal of fear of state prosecution. We cannot say that Congress' paramount authority in safeguarding national security does not justify the restrictions it has placed . . . ." [11] Adequate procedural protection was provided. Therefore, the government was entitled to the information elicited.

In the second and third cases Justice Frankfurter acquiesced silently in the majority holdings. He agreed that when the federal government enacted sedition legislation it pre-empted the field, thereby superseding any state statutes dealing with the same subject.[12] Parenthetically, it is necessary to note, however, that he has recently held that states were not foreclosed from legislating with regard to subversion within their own borders.[13] In this series of cases he also was in the majority, which said that a state statute denying employment in teaching solely on the basis of the individual's invocation of the Fifth Amendment was a violation of due process of law.[14] Justice Frankfurter wrote the Court's opinion in the fourth case. Here it was decided that the Subversive Activities Control Board, in considering whether the Communist party was a communist action organization within the meaning of the Subversive Activities Control Act, could not rely on the confessed perjured testimony of a government witness. Primarily, Justice Frankfurter wished to emphasize that "fastidi-

---

[10] 350 U.S. 422 (1956).
[11] Ibid., p. 436.
[12] Pennsylvania v. Nelson, 350 U.S. 497 (1956).
[13] Uphaus v. Wyman, 360 U.S. 72 (1959).
[14] Slochower v. Board of Education, 350 U.S. 551 (1956).

ous regard for the honor of the administration of justice requires the Court to make certain that the doing of justice be made so manifest that only irrational or perverse claims of its disregard can be asserted." [15] With this statement all the justices agreed, for none wished proceedings in the federal courts to be at all tainted.

In the fifth case, however, the split in philosophy once again reasserted itself. Justice Clark wrote for the majority, among whom Justice Frankfurter was numbered. He found no sufficient federal grounds for Supreme Court review of a California court holding that membership in the Communist party and not union activity had been the cause for dismissal from private employ.[16] Chief Justice Warren and Justice Black joined Justice Douglas in dissent on both jurisdictional and substantive grounds. Feeling that the California statute under which the dismissal was sought required a political oath from workers in private factories, Justice Douglas placed much of his reliance on the First Amendment as a bar to this sort of state legislation. Cole v. Young,[17] the final case to be surveyed here, dealt with the loyalty-security program of the national government.

The Summary Suspension Act of 1950 had given the chief officers within named agencies the right to dismiss or suspend from government employ any individual who they thought might be detrimental to national security. The officers had almost complete discretion in the matter. In 1953 under an Eisenhower Loyalty Order the discretionary suspension power was extended to government agencies not directly concerned with classified or important military information. It was on the basis of the extended loyalty order that Cole was dismissed from his civil service position as a drug inspector. The majority opinion centered on two main points: first, that the extension of the dismissal procedure to agencies not named in the original act was not warranted by the legislation itself; second, that dismissal or suspension without *prior* hearing so that the charges could be faced and answered

[15] Communist Party v. Subversive Activities Control Board, 351 U.S. 115, 124 (1956).

[16] Black v. Cutter Laboratories, 351 U.S. 292 (1956).

[17] 351 U.S. 536 (1956). Cf. Peters v. Hobby, 349 U.S. 331 (1955) and Vitarelli v. Seaton, 359 U.S. 535 (1959).

violated due process of law and therefore had to be changed. It is vital to note that no shadow of a doubt was cast on the government's power to find disloyalty, even disloyalty very broadly defined, a sufficient cause for dismissal. The opinion provided only procedural protection for the individual.

Abstracting the representative positions of Justices Black and Frankfurter in these cases, what is found? First and foremost, Justice Frankfurter, and he alone of all Court members, was in the majority in each and every case. As Robert McCloskey says, "he seems to represent with remarkable faithfulness the 'sense of the meeting' on the whole question." [18] The "sense of the meeting" seems to be that particularly in cases dealing with national security all that the judiciary can do is to provide procedural protection for individuals and groups under the due process clause either of the Fifth or Fourteenth Amendments. To question substantive policies inherent in legislation dealing with subversion is beyond the range of judicial power. Thus, in two instances, the Court held against the national government because of the defective nature of its hearing procedures and, in one instance, held for the government because adequate safeguards had been provided.

In the treatment of state action, the same procedural theme dominates. States were foreclosed from diminishing the Fifth Amendment's protection against self-incrimination by making the invocation of that Amendment a cause for dismissal. The remaining two cases are peripheral to the due process issue but central to the larger issue of basic responsibility for the maintenance of national security. The federal government is the major source of power here, and when it acts, its actions take precedence. When, however, there is apparently no direct conflict between federal and state programs, the latter may continue in existence, and the attempt to subvert the intentions of these programs by claims that federal rights have been violated will not be allowed.

Justice Black is so concerned with the very worthwhile preoccupation of protecting the individual against the coercive forces of society that he is apt to be oblivious to the reverse proposition. The First Amendment serves as one of the major protections for

[18] Robert McCloskey, "The Supreme Court Finds a Role: Civil Liberties in the 1955 Term," *Virginia Law Review*, XLIII (October, 1956), 758.

the individual when he is definitely and distinctly made the target for discriminatory or vengeful community action. It is a very different matter to use that same Amendment as a barrier against the state, when all procedural regularities have been met, in its drive to maintain itself. Individuals, then, are not protected from the state; they are placed above it. Justice Black's total reliance on the First Amendment irrespective of conditions was demonstrated in the Douds and McGrath cases before the 1955 Term. It has continued through and after that session of the Court.

While Justice Black has been the most consistent in turning to the First Amendment for guidance, other members of the Court operate under the same general persuasion. At the present time, certainly Chief Justice Warren and Justice Douglas would have to be counted in this group. It was the Chief Justice in the 1957 case of Sweezy v. New Hampshire [19] who tersely stated the basic position of all three. Certain questions had been put to Sweezy by the state's attorney general concerning associations and the content of a speech made at the state university. Relating political association and academic freedom to the Bill of Rights and the Fourteenth Amendment, Chief Justice Warren wrote that "we do not now conceive of *any circumstance* wherein a state interest would justify infringement of rights in these fields." [20] The absolute nature of the First Amendment as absorbed by the Fourteenth Amendment precludes any type of adjustment between individual utterances and community welfare. In this instance, Justice Frankfurter agreed that the state's actions were not justifiable, but he did so on totally different foundations. In what Professor Herman Pritchett has called "a considerably more persuasive opinion on the constitutionality of legislative inquiry," [21] Justice Frankfurter rejected both state contentions: first, that Sweezy's membership in certain groups on the Attorney General's list, the fact that he was a socialist, and his authorship of a controversial article, made it within legislative power to inquire as to whether he had advocated "violent overthrow of government"

[19] 354 U.S. 234.

[20] *Ibid.*, p. 251. Italics added.

[21] C. Herman Pritchett, "The Political Offender and the Warren Court," *Boston University Law Review*, xxxviii (Winter, 1958), 120.

in his university lecture; second, that his association with the Progressive party, which had supposedly been heavily infiltrated by Communists, made questions about the party relevant to state interests.

In rejecting these justifications, Justice Frankfurter did not say that under any and all circumstances questions such as those put to Sweezy would be unconstitutional.[22] While "inquiry pursued in safe-guarding a State's security against threatened force and violence cannot be shut off by mere disclaimer,"[23] in this particular case, the interest of New Hampshire in security was a meager countervailing claim to academic freedom or political association. The Supreme Court on the basis of massive proof and in the light of history could well appreciate the justification for not treating the Communist party as a conventional political party. But to extend this appreciation to the Progressive party would be foolhardy, since there was no documentary proof as to the latter's subversive doctrines or actions. Therefore, both New Hampshire contentions were lacking in force. As Justice Frankfurter said: "To be sure, this is a conclusion based on judicial judgment in balancing two contending principles—the right of a citizen to political privacy, as protected by the Fourteenth Amendment, and the right of the States to self-protection."[24] Somewhere some agency had to strike a balance, given a definite set of circumstances. It was difficult for Justice Frankfurter to override the preliminary determination made by New Hampshire's highest court that the inquiry was valid. "But," as he also said, "in the end, judgment cannot be escaped—the judgment of this Court."[25] Automatic or absolutist jurisprudence was not the answer when two such values as preservation of society and individual freedom clashed.

Most of the time, Justice Frankfurter places his emphasis on non-substantive considerations when possible. Procedural regularity is the hue and cry. The pivotal nature of his position on

---

[22] For later treatment of similar issues see, Barenblatt v. United States, 360 U.S. 109 (1959) and Uphaus v. Wyman, 360 U.S. 72 (1959).

[23] Sweezy v. New Hampshire, 354 U.S. 234, 265 (1957).

[24] Ibid., p. 266.

[25] Ibid., p. 267.

litigation dealing with national security means that other portions of his judicial philosophy take on greater import in this type of case. For example, his tendency to bow to legislative judgment on the basis of a theory of divided competence has meant that only extreme overbearance by the representative body would be struck down. Or again, his feeling that society should benefit by its own mistakes has meant that, unless procedural due process was violated and an individual harmed thereby, the Court should look dispassionately on even foolish attempts to preserve national security, since national security is one of the overwhelming concerns of any constitutional court. When substantive issues have to be faced, Justice Frankfurter becomes very aware of the clash of rights involved, rights of society and rights of the individual. In making his determination, he avoids generalization harmful to state power on the abstract notion that individual claims should always prevail. Thus, in the Sweezy case, he noted that "while the language of the Constitution does not change, the changing circumstances of a progressive society for which it was designed yield new and fuller import to its meaning." [26] These changing circumstances cannot be ignored, and, if in the area of national security they are ignored, Justice Frankfurter can foresee dire consequences for the future and well-being of our union.

III

Justice Frankfurter's pronounced antipathy to a doctrinal approach to constitutional law resulted in partial repudiation of a "clear and present danger" approach to questions of subversion. The doctrine was originally enunciated by Justice Holmes, although as Samuel Konefsky points out, even at that time Holmes was "not primarily concerned with propounding a new test of constitutionality." [27] He was merely placing, in very catchy terms, the basic contention that when individual rights and social interests collide a pragmatic determination of precedence had to

[26] *Ibid.*, p. 266.
[27] Samuel J. Konefsky, *The Legacy of Holmes and Brandeis* (New York: The Macmillan Co., 1956), p. 192.

be made. Justice Brandeis, according to the same commentator, "took the theory much more seriously than did Holmes." [28] It has thus resulted that treatment of "clear and present danger" is made in the light of the prestige that the names of both Holmes and Brandeis carry, while the latter gave it its most definite content.

Professor Frankfurter accepted the original Holmesian interpretation of the term as a guide for judicial judgment, not as an open sesame that would solve all problems. Even the modifications of Justice Brandeis, who carried the doctrine further toward a substantive concept than did its originator, never altered the basic point that time-place factors determined when governmental intervention was justified, not if it were ever justified. The latter was irrelevant, since it was an integral part of the initial formula that some restrictions on individual speech and actions were at times necessary in terms of the greater good. Justice Frankfurter stresses both aspects of the "clear and present danger" approach; that is, he has admitted that in certain instances legislative judgment concerning the threat to society has been exaggerated, and therefore unfettered individual expression should not be tampered with. But he has also accepted the other equally important part of the formulation, that when some reasonable case can be made for legislative fears that a direct and definite danger threatens social self-preservation, even individual actions may be curtailed.

His espousal of both parts of the formula accounts for the fact that he has repudiated the doctrine as doctrine, declaring that the treatment it has received at the hands of other members of the Court has turned it from its original meaning into a cheap imitation of the original. The criteria of judgment that he thinks Justices Holmes and Brandeis used, he has preserved. The identifying label of their contribution has been discarded because one of the equally important parts of the original formulation—the right of society to self-preservation—has also been discarded by other interpreters. The fact that the doctrine has now become identified mainly with protection of the individual irrespective of external circumstances has also meant that another damaging inroad into its usefulness has been made so far as Justice Frankfurter is con-

[28] *Ibid.*, p. 202.

cerned. Interest in protecting absolute freedom for individuals or groups has resulted in the transference of a concept initially used in the area of social security over into any other areas where individual or group rights might be at stake. For Frankfurter, this is so to falsify or pervert the doctrine as to render it virtually useless. In Dennis v. United States [29] the Supreme Court showed the utter confusion and inconsistency that can come from use of the doctrine of "clear and present danger" in its present guise within the field of national security. In myriad other cases, the second type of perversion can be discerned.

Many members of the Court seem more interested in what "clear and present danger" should mean than with what it did mean to its originators. It is quite all right to be interested in what the words should mean, but that is very different from parading this interest as an accepted fact. Those who are concerned with what the words should mean are apt to overlook the fact that the two intellectual giants of an earlier era saw both sides of the picture. The reverence that the names of Holmes and Brandeis elicit from present-day jurists, Justice Frankfurter included, activates them usually either to renounce any interference with governmental action in the field of national security or to reject the thought that even a very improbable attempt at overthrow could have serious repercussions on the community. The illustrious pair chose neither alternative. It is in the Dennis case that both extreme positions were championed and a middle ground proposed. While only eight members of the Court participated, five opinions were required to dispose of this litigation.

As is well known, the Dennis case concerned the prosecution of thirteen top-rung Communist leaders under the Smith Act of 1940. This Act made it unlawful to advocate or teach the overthrow of government by force or violence or to organize or help to organize an association to do such things. Because of the proliferation of opinions, there was no opinion of the Court, though Chief Justice Fred Vinson announced the judgment. Vinson held that a "clear and present danger" existed. The defendants had contended that their activities did not constitute such a threat and that limiting their activities would violate freedoms of the First

[29] 341 U.S. 494 (1951).

Amendment. The two dissenting opinions were written by Justices Black and Douglas. Neither found any semblance of "clear and present danger" that would validate the action of the government. Not unexpectedly, the First Amendment became their refuge. Finding adherence to his interpretation of that Amendment the key-stone and best insurance against destruction of all freedom, Justice Black spoke specifically for himself and in essence for Justice Douglas when he said:

> Public opinion being what it now is, few will protest the conviction of these Communist petitioners. There is hope, however, that in calmer times, when present pressures, passions and fears subside, this or some later Court will restore the First Amendment liberties to the high preferred place they belong in a free society.[30]

Justice Jackson wrote one of the concurring opinions. He agreed that the conviction under the Smith Act was valid, but he disagreed that reliance on "clear and present danger" was well placed. Thinking that the concept should be retained as "a rule of reason" in the type of case for which it was devised, Jackson contended that the Court was here dealing with a conspiracy statute that was constitutional in and of itself.

Justice Frankfurter, of all the participating justices, made no attempt to embrace or repudiate the Holmesian formula for this particular case. When he mentioned it, it was simply to deny that the formula, because of the various uses to which it had been put, was a usable concept any longer.

> It were far better that the phrase be abandoned than that it be sounded once more to hide from the believers in an absolute right of free speech the plain fact that the interest in speech, profoundly important as it is, is no more conclusive in judicial review than other attributes of democracy or than a determination of the people's representatives that a measure is necessary to assure the safety of government itself.[31]

Basically he felt that refusal to take into consideration the external factors that both Holmes and Brandeis found necessary to their doctrine when individual claims collided with community claims

[30] *Ibid.*, p. 571.
[31] *Ibid.*, p. 544.

invalidated its use entirely. Beginning his explanation with the thought that "just as there are those who regard as invulnerable every measure for which claims of national survival are invoked, there are those who find in the Constitution a wholly unfettered right of expression," Justice Frankfurter then went on to say that "the historic antecedents of the First Amendment preclude the notion that its purpose was to give unqualified immunity to every expression that touched on matters within the range of political interest." [32] After weighing the competing interests and stigmatizing all inflexible dogmas, Justice Frankfurter concluded that advocacy of overthrow deserves little protection.

The chain of reasoning and the decision caused many contradictory responses. According to John P. Frank, "This opinion is the very epitome of intellectual liberalism at its most ineffective." [33] Sidney Hook finds it a "remarkable concurring opinion," and would advise that "Justice Frankfurter's words . . . ought to be inscribed in letters of gold on the portals of the Supreme Court." [34] Whatever one might think about the opinion, it would be difficult to deny that it was characteristic of the Justice, embodying many of the major strains in his philosophy. The judicial function is a limited one and the limits of judicial power must be recognized. Legislatures are the proper forums for working out programs, especially when the question of national survival is at stake. Perhaps it is true, as Milton Konvitz suggests in an appraisal of the Dennis opinion, "Much of the trouble flows from the fact that Justice Frankfurter's mind in such cases works along legislative rather than judicial lines. . . . He thus places himself in the shoes of a legislator." [35] It is certain that as a teacher, Frankfurter called upon the law schools to produce lawyers more familiar with the legislative process. Writing in 1931 he said that

> Students today leave the law schools singularly innocent of, if indeed not hostile to, the legislative aspects of law. But competence

[32] *Ibid.*, p. 521.

[33] John P. Frank, "The United States Supreme Court: 1950–51," *University of Chicago Law Review*, XIX (Winter, 1952), 187.

[34] Sidney Hook, *Heresy, Yes; Conspiracy, No* (New York: The John Day Co., 1953), p. 105.

[35] Milton Konvitz, *Fundamental Liberties of a Free People* (Ithaca: Cornell University Press, 1957), p. 327.

to deal with legislation as part of the professional equipment of lawyers can be expected only if legal education will systematically concern itself with the characteristics and implications of the legislative process.[36]

If one steps into the shoes of a legislator, then one becomes familiar with the main concerns of such a person. Practical solutions for practical problems become of prime importance. These solutions can only be arrived at after a pragmatic weighing of interests. Preoccupation with theories, rules, and principles will confuse rather than illumine the solutions sought. Justice Frankfurter's understanding of the legislator's task makes him extremely wary of rejecting a solution once attained.

IV

The Dennis case showed what was for Justice Frankfurter one type of corruption of the "clear and present danger" doctrine. Another type involves applying the doctrine any time the First Amendment comes under consideration. For those who insist that the First Amendment *per se* is applicable against the states, the use of "clear and present danger" follows as a natural corollary. They are also the ones who champion a "preferred position" for the First Amendment. For those who have not accepted the suggestion that the Bill of Rights is applicable against the states or even that it is absorbed verbatim by the Fourteenth Amendment, using "clear and present danger" as a booster shot for the First Amendment doubly confuses the issue. Excerpts from several litigations may serve to indicate the problem.

Bridges v. California [37] involved the scope of permissible comment by the press upon a case already under advisement. Justice Black for the Court held that there was not enough of a "clear and present danger" to validate curbing the news reports. Well, of course there was not, and no one suggested that there was. Limitation upon press irresponsibility could be justified on far more relevant grounds. While Justice Black found it a trying task to choose between free speech and free trials, he managed to do so

---

[36] Felix Frankfurter and James Landis, "The Supreme Court at October Term, 1930," *Harvard Law Review*, XLV (December, 1931), 306.

[37] 314 U.S. 252 (1941).

in favor of the former on the basis of the absolute nature of the First Amendment and the Holmesian formula. The Bridges case was decided in 1941, very early in Justice Frankfurter's judicial career. Even at that day, however, he refused to accept what he thought was a change in his mentor's original emphasis.

Frankfurter would not be outdone in his profession of faith in the proposition that "public expression alone assures the unfolding of truth, it is indispensable to the democratic process." [38] But he was also convinced that a doctrinaire overstatement of the scope of free expression through "clear and present danger" gave the proposition an illusory absolute appearance. Free choice and responsibility in exercising the right to free speech were basic to a democratic society. To take away any need for choice or responsibility by encompassing all speech within the First Amendment and then treating "clear and present danger" as always applicable when the First Amendment was invoked would be a dangerous innovation. For himself, he thought that "The phrase 'clear and present danger' is merely a justification for curbing utterance where that is warranted by the substantive evil to be prevented." [39]

Taking the doctrine from its indigenous soil and transplanting it in foreign surroundings would only debilitate it. In another case involving press reporting of certain court actions as being too lenient toward criminals and gambling establishments, Justice Frankfurter explained:

> "Clear and present danger" was never used by Mr. Justice Holmes to express a technical legal doctrine or to convey a formula for adjudicating cases. It was a literary phrase not to be distorted by being taken from its context. In its setting it served to indicate the importance of freedom of speech to a free society but also to emphasize that its exercise must be compatible with the preservation of other freedoms essential to a democracy and guaranteed by our Constitution. When those other attributes of a democracy are threatened by speech the Constitution does not deny power to the States to curb it.[40]

This tendency to take the doctrine from its context has, on another occasion, prompted Justice Frankfurter to refer to it as a

[38] *Ibid.*, p. 293.
[39] *Ibid.*, p. 296.
[40] Pennekamp v. Florida, 328 U.S. 331, 353 (1946).

"felicitous phrase" having little or nothing to do with the question under consideration—whether school children could be required to salute the flag.

The difference in approach toward doctrine by Court members resolves itself into a difference on how far any constitutional concepts can be manipulated to serve as supports for a particular absolutist interpretation of the First Amendment. In almost any of the cases touching upon civil liberties that have been mentioned in this study, certain members of the Court were almost sure to have initiated argument on the basis of "clear and present danger." From cases involving Jehovah's Witnesses to those concerned with labor's right to picket, this has been true. But as Justice Jackson once remarked, "The choice is not between order and liberty. It is between liberty with order and anarchy without either. There is danger that, if the Court does not temper its doctrinaire logic with a little practical wisdom, it will convert the constitutional Bill of Rights into a suicide pact." [41] Very much in the same vein is Carl Becker's question: "Are we expected to be loyal to the principle of free speech to the point where, writhing in pain among its worshippers, it commits suicide?" As Professor Becker realized, "That is certainly asking a lot." [42]

It is in the fields of subversion and social self-preservation that this request is most dangerous. Refusal to acknowledge legislative ability to deal with the problems of subversion if any restriction is placed upon any individual can in a very real sense be suicidal. When the judiciary, and especially the Supreme Court, assures procedural protection for the people, they have done all they can. Beyond that they must recognize that within the Constitution there is legislative power to deal with the practical problems of life. Ruling on the substantive nature of policies is, or at least should be, outside the realm of judicial competence. For Justice Frankfurter, neither a false invocation of "clear and present danger" nor a judgment based on a particular interpretation of the Bill of Rights should be allowed to cloud this point.

[41] Terminiello v. Chicago, 337 U.S. 1, 37 (1949).

[42] Carl Becker, *Freedom and Responsibility in the American Way of Life* (New York: Vintage Books, Inc., 1955), p. 40.

X
"Preferred Freedoms"—
A Negative View

In discussing civil liberties a good deal of space is devoted to building out the implications of liberty *versus* order, freedom *versus* authority, as if each were mutually exclusive and mutually hostile categories. Concern for the individual takes a prominent place in any such discussion. There are times, however, when the claims of a politically organized society also have to be given credence. The fact that the United States works under a truly representative system does not mean that all problems of liberty *and* order, freedom *and* authority have been solved. Certainly the people must limit themselves or be limited by the Constitution under which they operate. To say this, however, is not to agree with the proposition that liberty totally excludes order or that freedom totally excludes authority.

We have been largely concerned with the proper place for liberty and authority in the clashes between individual rights and group or community interests. In addition, a conceptual scheme is needed for dealing, not with complications of social power and individual protection, but with the equally difficult area where individual freedoms collide with other such freedoms, individual rights clash with other such rights. In this area, too, questions of liberty and order are present, but they are present on a particularized lower level.

I

For Justice Frankfurter, the initial determination that must be made is that between the Bill of Rights and governmental power granted by the Constitution. As he has said, "Where the First Amendment applies, it is a denial of all governmental power in our Federal system." [1] Some other members of the Court, totally concerned with balancing rights against power and usually finding the first inviolate and the second foreclosed to use, stay at the point where one determination or judgment is necessary. Given their predisposition toward protecting the individual at all costs, that judgment is almost an automatic one. Thus in a deceptively easy manner, more difficult or trying problems are avoided.

We are apt to think of litigation as a clash between right and wrong with the judiciary primarily concerned with seeing that the former prevails. Unfortunately, things are not always this black and white. For Justice Frankfurter, the finding that some portion of the Bill of Rights is applicable is only the initial stage when various individual freedoms are at stake. It may be true that at times the Court can very clearly discern that an individual's right is being threatened by another individual totally in the wrong. More often than not, however, when governmental coercive power is not originally involved, there appears a clash of rights, freedoms, or whatever other term best describes the situation wherein no single correct disposition of a case can automatically be attained through saying that the Bill of Rights covers the situation. At this point a secondary determination between the freedoms involved has to be made. "When we are dealing with conflicting freedoms," Justice Frankfurter has noted, "we are dealing with large concepts that too readily lend themselves to

[1] Marsh v. Alabama, 326 U.S. 501, 511 (1946).

rhetoric."[2] Only a pragmatic judgment on the circumstances of the situation allows any accommodation between the conflicting set of individual freedoms.

It is on the reality and nature of this secondary determination that Justice Frankfurter differs from some of his brethren. Rhetorical eloquence he feels will not solve the judicial puzzle of having to weigh one right against another. In the pre-New Deal period, many of the justices could discourse with force and persuasion upon the magic phrase "freedom of contract," whose very mention seemed to them to settle any and all controversies. Current Court members who refuse to acknowledge that merely citing the Bill of Rights is not enough to work out practical arrangements are not acting very differently from earlier justices whom they chastised for their championing of economic rights to the possible exclusion of other considerations. It is necessary to recognize that within the covering protection of the Bill of Rights there may still be clashes of individual freedoms, clashes that the judiciary must moderate, neither side being completely right or completely wrong. Any formula or approach to the Constitution and the Bill of Rights that sees them as self-contained entities that do not allow for any conflict once they are in operation is beguiling and mischievous. Especially is this so "when contending claims are those not of right and wrong but of two rights, each highly important to the well-being of society. Seldom is there available a pat formula that adequately analyzes such a problem, least of all solves it."[3] To deny the reality of this secondary determination between rights is to deny much of the judicial function.

Although society's power does not immediately make itself felt, after the judgment as to which freedom should be favored in particular instances has been made, this power may be called upon by the judiciary to reassert itself on behalf of the right adjudged predominant. With this reassertion comes considerable confusion. Those who find only one judgment necessary—is or is not the Bill of Rights applicable—seem unable to distinguish between the original rejection of governmental power as antithetical to the Bill of Rights and governmental power invoked to aid, after a secondary determination, the predominant right. As Frankfurter

[2] American Communications Association v. Douds, 339 U.S. 382, 418 (1950).

[3] Pennekamp v. Florida, 328 U.S. 331, 351 (1946).

said in 1929, "Legal rights do not necessarily define moral claims. Legal rights are not even the measure of equitable relief. A wise social policy may well consider the manner in which parties exercise their legal rights before putting the coercive powers of society behind those rights." [4] Once again, it bears repeating that the Supreme Court is a court of law, not primarily justice or morality. Those who find within the Bill of Rights a complete moral decalogue would have difficulty in recognizing that individual legal rights covered by that document could clash. In the clash of rights some judicial choice as to the more worthy must result, and, depending upon the manner in which those rights are exercised, society may have to lend aid to one individual. This is all that Professor Frankfurter was trying to say; it is all that Justice Frankfurter claims.

This completes one half of the conceptual scheme when governmental power is balanced against the Bill of Rights and the latter prevails, although perhaps with incidental reinsertion of the first quality. The other half of the scheme is not so complicated or involved, even though some confusion may result from the fact that those who rely on a single determination when the Bill of Rights proper is under consideration apparently seem bound to refuse the second part of the equation. There are certain instances when a clash between individual freedoms is not possible because governmental power is already available to enact general legislation, which in turn might incidentally favor one right over another. Take, for example, the classic situation in which claims to religious liberty under the First Amendment collide with individual claims to privacy that can be provided under the police power of states as encompassed within the Tenth Amendment. While the legislature may decide that special consideration is due religious scruples in the example given above, it need not do so. This certain members of the Court seem unable to grasp.

II

There is a good deal of absolutism in portions of today's constitutional approach. Terms within the Bill of Rights may be

[4] Felix Frankfurter, "Labor Injunctions and Federal Legislation," *Harvard Law Review*, XLII (April, 1929), 788–89.

absolutely defined, and these terms are absolutely binding upon the states. It is somewhat amusing that within the Bill of Rights certain portions are held to be more absolute than others, bringing to mind the quip that everything is relative except relativity. The most absolute portion apparently is the First Amendment, providing the basis for interpretations of "preferred freedoms" to which we will soon turn. Before doing this, it is well to recall certain of the strengths and weaknesses of any generalized absolute interpretation.

Writing in 1927, Professor Frankfurter said: ". . . 'principles' are rarely absolute. Usually they are sententious expression of conflicting or at least overlapping policies. The vital issue is their accommodation. Decisions thus become a matter of more or less, of drawing lines." [5] There is nothing new or startling in this quotation. It merely points up the attitude that Justice Frankfurter carried into the New Deal period. Attempting an intellectual characterization of that period, one might say that the search for immediate solutions, rather than an inquiry into the longer-range implications of problems that had to be faced, intrigued the creative mind as this became evident in policy decisions or constitutional doctrines. Perhaps because he did not exactly fit into this pattern Justice Frankfurter was criticized for his attention to detail, for his preoccupation with procedural regularity, and for his insistence on keeping constitutional holdings as narrow as possible.

The New Deal Court as a whole displayed disarming enthusiasm towards the task of clearing away the holdings of previous Courts. Opinions had not only a communicative but also an emotive function. Very little attempt was made to reduce the emotional element. Evocation of a sense of fairness seemed a very legitimate aim. In place of the rather cold and austere emphasis on economic rights came a new, youthful liveliness directed towards that ever shining goal, human rights. And in no way was it easier to evoke an emotional response towards this goal than by citing the Bill of Rights and treating it as though it captured the absolute essence of human rights for all times and all places.

This rather engaging enthusiasm for certain assumed absolute

[5] Felix Frankfurter, "Mr. Justice Holmes and the Constitution," *Harvard Law Review,* XLI (December, 1927), 133.

values did, however, have one major drawback. Because conclusions rather than legal reasoning were sought, the doctrines enunciated to rationalize these conclusions often had to be of an absolute nature to cover the absolute values. "Preferred freedoms" was changed from its original form as a suggestion of attitude toward certain provisions of the Bill of Rights into a self-contained and very definite constitutional concept. The concept has remained static. The New Deal initiated vast changes in American constitutional development. But, just as the New Deal Court was the example, par excellence, of changing times, it was not the agency that could arrest further development. The world in which it operated continued to show different traits and attitudes. Thus the attempt to make the Bill of Rights absolute in eighteenth-century terms and the attempt to make more absolute still certain portions thereof by a concept that is static and unbending led to futility and frustration.

To their credit, the judicial activists are interested in seeking out the essence of human existence. They have a well-defined and well-articulated approach to this quest. The only difficulty is that, as members of the Supreme Court, their approach is basically not a legal one. It is much more tempered by political-humanitarian considerations in the widest sense of the term. The desire to have the Supreme Court give something beyond legal protection means that, when the inevitable clash of absolute rights occurs, they are pushed to utter subjectivity on the basis of political-humanitarian considerations. This may or may not be fortunate. But, similar subjectivity on the basis of other considerations helped destroy the Nine Old Men. When absolutes tumble, the destruction that they wreak is apt to be fairly complete.

Justice Frankfurter in his treatment of the Bill of Rights does not lean toward an absolute position. His statement that "many a decision of this Court rests on some inarticulate major premise and is none the worse for it"[6] may open him to the charge of subjectivity that has been raised against Justice Black. The subjectivity is, however, of a slightly different kind. It is not a subjectivity forced by a breakdown of a supposedly self-contained system that should mechanically provide answers to any conflict.

[6] Nietmoko v. Maryland, 340 U.S. 268, 285 (1951).

It is self-assumed on the understanding that clashes of legal, not political-humanitarian, rights must be mediated by the judiciary and that no single standard, absolute, or concept can serve in place of pragmatic determination.

Writing after fifteen years on the Supreme Court, Justice Frankfurter still showed that his abiding interest was in judicial technique and method rather than conclusions: "Alert search for enduring standards by which the judiciary is to exercise its duty in enforcing those provisions of the Constitution that are expressed in what Ruskin called 'chameleon words,' needs the indispensable counterpoise of sturdy doubts that one has found those standards." [7] Although Justice Black may not entertain doubts about the absolutes that he champions, Justice Frankfurter entertains them for him. When the absolutes are all in the area of civil liberties, the doubts take on larger proportions. Three decades ago the absolutes were in the area of "property" or "freedom of contract." Today they all abide in the Bill of Rights. Who can say where they will be located five or ten years from now? If absolutes tend to paralyze thought and imprison their holders in a straitjacket of their own making, then the trial and error that is the very basis for accommodation within democratic society will be abandoned to the detriment of all. The judiciary demands tough-minded relativists, not soft-hearted absolutists. It is in the light of this contrast that "preferred freedoms" must be examined.

III

To retell in full the story of the appearance of "preferred freedoms" is unnecessary, since this has been done very successfully on many occasions and the tale is one that is now well known. It has, of course, been done most successfully by Professor Alpheus T. Mason in his biography of Harlan Fiske Stone, from whose opinion the doctrine stems. In what Professor Mason

[7] Felix Frankfurter, "John Marshall," in *Government Under Law* (Cambridge, Mass.: Harvard University Press, 1956), p. 21. For discussion of the Justice's position on this type of issue, see Wallace Mendelson, "Justice Frankfurter and the Process of Judicial Review," *University of Pennsylvania Law Review,* CIII (December, 1954), 295–320.

calls the "otherwise obscure case of United States v. Carolene Products Co.," [8] there appeared a footnote written by Louis Lusky, Justice Stone's law clerk at the time, which made some interesting, although novel, suggestions. Since "it was not unusual for Stone to allow his law clerks to use footnotes as trial balloons for meritorious ideas," [9] the uniqueness of Footnote Four was not immediately apparent. It was only after it was picked up and used as a rationalization for the primacy of civil liberties, particularly as found in the First Amendment, over other constitutional rights, that discussion of its implications became numerous.[10]

In its original formulation by Lusky, Footnote Four contained only two paragraphs. It is assumed that the first paragraph, as the footnote appears in the Court reports, was superimposed by Chief Justice Hughes. The complete footnote reads as follows:

> There may be narrower scope for operation of the presumption of constitutionality when legislation appears on its face to be within a specific prohibition of the Constitution, such as those of the first ten amendments, which are deemed equally specific when held to be embraced within the Fourteenth . . . .
>
> It is unnecessary to consider now whether legislation which restricts those political processes which can ordinarily be expected to bring about repeal of undesirable legislation, is to be subjected to more exact judicial scrutiny under the general scrutiny of the Fourteenth Amendment than are most other types of legislation . . . .
>
> Nor need we inquire whether similar considerations enter into the review of statutes directed at particular religious . . . or national . . . or racial minorities . . . whether prejudice against discrete and insular minorities may be a special condition, which tends seriously to curtail the operation of those political processes ordinarily to be relied upon to protect minorities, and which may call for a correspondingly more searching judicial inquiry.[11]

[8] Alpheus T. Mason, *Harlan Fiske Stone* (New York: The Viking Press, Inc., 1956), p. 512.

[9] *Ibid.*, p. 513.

[10] For a listing of the early cases in which preferred freedoms were mentioned, see Kovacs v. Cooper, 336 U.S. 77, 90–96 (1949).

[11] United States v. Carolene Products Co., 304 U.S. 144, 152–54, note 4 (1938).

No one is as qualified to explain the meaning of this footnote as is its author. In an article devoted to this task, it is a fairly telling point that the first paragraph was not even mentioned, leading to the speculation that the originator of the larger idea thought Chief Justice Hughes' addition unimportant or unnecessary. Of the third paragraph Lusky says in part: "Where the regular corrective processes are interferred with, the Court must remove the interferences; where the dislike of minorities renders those processes ineffective to accomplish their underlying purpose of holding out a real hope that unwise laws will be changed, the Court must step in." [12] In a consideration of the original meaning of "preferred freedoms" these are the raw materials with which one has to work—the footnote itself and its author's explanation of a portion thereof.

Justice Frankfurter has never rejected the pristine meaning of paragraphs one and two of this footnote, which say *only* that legislation relating to the Bill of Rights, and in particular to the First Amendment, should be subject to "more exact judicial scrutiny" than other legislation. Before becoming a member of the Court and in defending the proposition that economic rights could be considered a function of personality, Professor Frankfurter admitted that "the various interests of human personality are not of equal worth. There is a hierarchy of values." [13] Even in his Supreme Court opinion that is considered the epitome of anti-preferred freedoms philosophy, he said that "those liberties of the individual which history has attested as the indispensable conditions of an open as against a closed society come to this Court with a momentum for respect lacking when appeal is made to liberties which derive merely from shifting economic arrangements." [14]

Whether a society is open or closed depends to a good extent upon the capacity of a representative body to reflect the felt needs and desires of the people. So that a relatively exact reflection can become evident, keeping the channels of public pres-

[12] Louis Lusky, "Minority Rights and the Public Interest," *Yale Law Review*, LII (December, 1942), 20–21.

[13] Felix Frankfurter, *Mr. Justice Holmes* (Cambridge, Mass.: Harvard University Press, 1938), p. 49.

[14] Kovacs v. Cooper, 336 U.S. 77, 95 (1949).

sure open is of utmost importance. This is apparently what Justice Frankfurter thought the second paragraph of Footnote Four to mean, for he wrote to Justice Stone shortly *before* the decision in one of the first cases invoking the "preferred freedoms" concept, "I am aware of the important distinction which you so skillfully adumbrated in your footnote 4 (particularly the second paragraph of it) in the *Carolene Products Co.* case. I agree with that distinction; I regard it as basic." [15] He complimented Stone for his understanding that, even in dealing with civil liberties, the Supreme Court was not "in the domain of absolutes. Here, also, we have an illustration of what the Greeks thousands of years ago recognized as a tragic issue, namely the clash of rights, not the clash of wrongs." [16] The Supreme Court in its judicial scrutiny was, however, guided by an understanding that it was not the primary resolver of conflict. This role was assigned to legislative assemblies freely influenced by various portions of the population. As long as representatives could be informed of desires or removed from office through political processes, the courts had done their job in seeing that the processes themselves were not corroded or legal rights denied. Whether this is a correct interpretation of Stone's position or not, it is, at least, Justice Frankfurter's understanding of that position.

Justice Frankfurter's difficulty in following the course of development for "preferred freedoms" taken by the Court links with the inversion of meaning given paragraph one and the judicial interpretation of paragraph three rather than with what paragraph three itself says. The initial section by Chief Justice Hughes speaks of a narrower scope for the presumption of *constitutionality* when a statute could conceivably invade the freedoms of the *first ten amendments*. In the application of the doctrine, first a subtle and then not so subtle change occurred, ending with the meaning that there was a presumption of *unconstitutionality* for any statute even remotely related to the *First Amendment*. With this position and the extreme statement of "preferred freedoms" even Stone himself disagreed.

If it is a wise man who knows his own children, Stone in deny-

[15] Frankfurter to Stone, May 27, 1940. Quoted in Mason, *Harlan Fiske Stone*, p. 218.

[16] *Ibid.*

ing paternity of this offspring exhibited a good deal of discernment and discretion. Both he and Justice Frankfurter worked within the accepted scheme where legislation is presumptively valid although "more exact judicial scrutiny" may be needed to establish this validity when the Bill of Rights is involved. This is not to say that the two men always agreed. Quite obviously, as the flag salute cases show, they did not. Their disagreement came, however, not on the absolute nature of the First Amendment, or even of the Bill of Rights itself, but on the value choices necessary to establish validity. Neither ever accepted the implications of presumptive invalidity. On the other hand, those who have made the "preferred freedoms" doctrine into a concept that challenges all legislation and places the complete burden of proof upon representative assemblies have placed themselves in the position of Platonic guardians exercising discretion over absolute values protected by an absolute doctrine.

Louis Lusky's explanation of paragraph three of the footnote—that when there is little hope that "unwise" laws will be changed, the Court must step in—shows an orientation completely different from that of Justice Frankfurter. Subsequent action by the Court has shown that many of the justices at one time or another have accepted the Lusky explanation. Unwisdom, then, becomes dependent upon the degree to which a statute deviates from the preconceived notion held by the justices as to the absolute content of First Amendment rights. Under this interpretation the Court should not hesitate to act as a superlegislature, automatically turning aside any statute that incidentally collides with the absolutist judicial interpretation of the First Amendment. To this Justice Frankfurter takes very marked exception. Since "the function of this Court does not differ in passing on the constitutionality of legislation challenged under different Amendments," he has told his brethren that

> The right not to have property taken without just compensation has, so far as the scope of judicial power is concerned, the same constitutional dignity as the right to be protected against unreasonable searches and seizures, and the latter has no less claim than freedom of the press or freedom of speech or religious freedom.[17]

[17] West Virginia State Board of Education v. Barnette, 319 U.S. 624, 648 (1943).

The Justice's very pronounced views on the fact that due deference should be paid by the judiciary to the legislature did not keep him from agreeing that "more exact judicial scrutiny" might be called for to prove the constitutionality of legislation touching the Bill of Rights, but the presumption of validity stayed with the legislature. Judicial determination of "unwisdom" was totally out of the question for him as the basis for striking down a statute. Because the Bill of Rights warranted extra study did not mean that it should be elevated over other constitutional provisions, and it certainly did not mean that one portion of that section should be "preferred." Justice Frankfurter's conception of the nature of the Constitution is extremely important here, and it is the crux of the difference over the "preferred freedoms" doctrine.

This conception is that "the Constitution is an organic scheme of government to be dealt with as an entirety. A particular provision cannot be dissevered from the rest of the Constitution." [18] Constitutional powers and provisions are intrinsically of equal worth. To suggest that, on the basis of judicial supremacy, one cluster of constitutional rights should be favored at one time, while, at another time, a totally different set could be substituted, is, in the words of Justice Frankfurter, "to disrespect the Constitution," and coincidentally to deny its organic nature. "As no constitutional guarantee enjoys preference, so none should suffer subordination or deletion. . . . To view a particular provision of the Bill of Rights with disfavor inevitably results in a constricted application of it." [19] As there can be no second-class citizens, so there can be no second-class rights.

The constricted application that Justice Frankfurter fears is one that rigidly insists on a preconceived absolute value scale and ignores the fact that our constitutional system is one identified by the diffusion of power. In the last century, jurisprudence tried to solve the problems of law by a theory of natural rights that held that those rights were absolute and could not conflict. The individual in the enjoyment of these rights was placed above state and society. In gaining such enjoyment, neither adjustment nor compromise was recognized. It is true that economic rights largely over-

[18] Reid v. Covert, 354 U.S. 1, 44 (1957).
[19] Ullmann v. United States, 350 U.S. 422, 428–29 (1956).

shadowed what we would call civil rights. Nevertheless, no agency of government was ever equal to giving them the precise delimitation in practice that theory demanded. It was against this emphasis that the mid-twentieth century reacted. But what had been the difficulty for the nineteenth century in turn became the difficulty of the twentieth.

Justice Frankfurter's name cannot be disassociated from a variant natural law position in that he thinks due process of law approximates the enduring values of human existence, or, at least, human existence in the Anglo-American world. This, however, is more expressive of a feeling than of an absolute commitment. Those who make the Bill of Rights absolute through definition and then try to concretize the absolutes by a doctrine that gives prominence to one portion thereof come closer to the nineteenth-century conceptions—and with the same drawbacks. The validity of adjustments and compromises is never recognized. Walton Hamilton and George Braden, two subsequent defenders of the libertarian-activist approach, wrote in 1941 that "the several ancient liberties [enshrined in the First Amendment] were never absolutes; and, as caught in the generic term liberty, they do not completely escape the finite. The Court has never said, the current bench is unlikely to say, that executive and legislature may never interfere with a person's freedom." [20] This was a sanguine appraisal that was disproved by many cases following shortly after 1941.

The opinions of Justices Black, Douglas, Rutledge, and Murphy are especially significant for their very forthright espousal of the position that Hamilton and Braden thought the Court would never take. Justice Douglas, for instance, has written that "The First Amendment is couched in absolute terms—freedom of speech shall not be abridged. Speech therefore has a preferred position as contrasted to some other civil rights." [21] He is not entirely consistent on this point, however, as a few years earlier he had said that "freedom of speech, though not absolute . . . is nevertheless protected against censorship or punishment, unless

[20] Walton Hamilton and George Braden, "The Special Competence of the Supreme Court," *Yale Law Journal*, L (June, 1941), 1351.

[21] Beauharnais v. Illinois, 343 U.S. 250, 285 (1952).

shown likely to produce a clear and present danger of a serious substantive evil . . . ." [22] Since a clear and present danger rarely if ever exists for those who hold a "preferred freedoms" position, the end result is very much the same as when the First Amendment is given an absolutist interpretation.

Again, it was Justice Douglas who suggested recently that there might be areas outside the First Amendment that should also be elevated. According to him, "Citizenship, like freedom of speech, press, and religion, occupies a preferred position in our written Constitution, because it is a grant absolute in terms." [23] It seems reasonable to question just how many absolutes the present Court is going to be able to find. Another question may be raised: Are any of the "preferred freedoms" more preferred than others? Stated hierarchically, we have seen a section of the Constitution, the Bill of Rights, given prominence over other sections of the same document, and then a portion of the section, the First Amendment, elevated and absolutized. In some of the cases the suggestion was made that a segment of the portion of the section held top position. Justice Murphy, for example, implied that freedom of religion was the most precious of all rights and should be given ultimate preference over all others. To this even Justice Rutledge, another very staunch supporter of the absolutist interpretation, could not agree, "If . . . appellant seeks for freedom of conscience a broader protection than for freedom of the mind, it may be doubted that any of the great liberties insured by the First Article can be given higher place than the others. All have preferred position in our basic scheme." [24] While the Court as a whole has not taken the last step and agreed on any particular freedom as being ultimately indispensable, the tone of certain of its opinions dealing with subversion leads one to wonder whether freedom of speech has not implicitly been given this distinction.

As there have been many opinions written on the need to elevate the First Amendment, so there have been many written to denounce such a course. It is in the case of Kovacs v. Cooper,[25]

[22] Terminiello v. Chicago, 337 U.S. 1, 5 (1949).
[23] Perez v. Brownell, 356 U.S. 44, 84 (1958).
[24] Prince v. Massachusetts, 321 U.S. 158, 164 (1944).
[25] 336 U.S. 77 (1949).

however, that the most articulate and complete rejection of the doctrine of "preferred freedoms" comes. At question was a city's power to prohibit the use of sound amplifying devices on public streets when they emitted "loud and raucous" noises. Justice Murphy alone of the nine members held that even reasonable regulation was not consonant with the First Amendment. Justices Black, Douglas, and Rutledge did not take this extreme view but did hold that, since speech was a "preferred freedom," the city had to prove without a shadow of a doubt what constituted "loud and raucous" noises and then show that the sound device involved was definitely emitting such a noise. This they did not think had been done in this case, and so they dissented. The judgment of the Court was announced by Justice Reed. His opinion upheld the ordinance against charges of indefiniteness and violation of the First Amendment.

Justices Frankfurter and Jackson went further than others in the majority and held that the use of sound trucks in the streets may be completely prohibited without violating the constitutional right to free speech. Beginning with the proposition that "wise accommodation between liberty and order always has been, and ever will be, indispensable for a democratic society," [26] Justice Frankfurter thought that to favor the former over the latter through a doctrinaire approach to constitutional issues simply disregarded reality. Of "preferred freedoms" proper, he had this to say:

This is a phrase that has uncritically crept into some recent opinions of this Court. I deem it a mischievous phrase, if it carries the thought, which it may subtly imply, that any law touching communication is infected with presumptive invalidity. It is not the first time in the history of constitutional adjudication that such a doctrinaire attitude has disregarded the admonition most to be observed in exercising this Court's reviewing power over legislation, "that it is a *constitution* we are expounding," . . . I say the phrase is mischievous because it radiates a constitutional doctrine without avowing it.[27]

[26] *Ibid.*, p. 89.
[27] *Ibid.*, p. 90.

Calling for clarity and candor in the treatment of the doctrine, Justice Frankfurter then proceeded to a long, historical account of its appearance, uses, and perversion.

The significance of the Kovacs opinion for a study of Justice Frankfurter's judicial performance is immense. The opinion is almost a compendium of his major views. Insistence on the Constitution as an organic document, acceptance of governmental power to deal with social problems, and recognition of liberty *and* authority as valid concerns for legislatures would have to be listed on the positive side of the ledger. Rejection of an absolutist interpretation of constitutional terms with its own implied avoidance of pragmatic solutions, denial of ultimate provisions in one portion of the Constitution in preference to others, and refusal to acquiesce in furthering the use of a doctrine all of whose major implications were not articulated are the negations that the opinion contains. While the decline and fall of a doctrine are not easy to trace, it would seem that Frankfurter's broadside against "preferred freedoms" in the Kovacs case inflicted enough damage and was so well placed that the Court as a whole has never again adopted that concept as the deciding factor in a case.

IV

Justice Frankfurter has leveled serious criticism at his colleagues on the issue of absolutism and preferred treatment for constitutional terms. He, in turn, has not escaped unscathed. The most obvious criticism is that he has been in the majority in some cases where a modified "preferred freedoms" position was taken. What considerations prompt him to yield concurrence to an approved result reached through inapposite doctrine? Many years ago he speculated how this could happen to members of the Court: "Long-term strategy, or immediate fatigue, hopelessness of opposition or depreciation of the importance of the pronouncement, *bonhommie* of common labors or avoidance of undue division—such are the factors that may restrain the expression of individual views." [28] Whether one or more of these factors were

---

[28] Felix Frankfurter, *The Commerce Clause Under Marshall, Taney and Waite* (Chapel Hill: University of North Carolina Press, 1937), p. 57.

operative, Justice Frankfurter has at times not opposed the "preferred freedoms" approach.

More serious consideration must be given the comparative performances of Justices Black and Frankfurter in their respective treatments of the Bill of Rights and the Fourteenth Amendment. Recalling the incorporation proposals of Justice Black, one can say that when the absolute provisions of the Bill of Rights are made applicable to the states, they are made applicable equally. None can suffer subordination or deletion. No selectivity is advanced. Yet, when the Bill of Rights is proposed as a barrier against federal action, there is a very definite grading process in which the First Amendment becomes the most important civil rights guarantee. The perspective of Justice Frankfurter is almost the reverse. In determining what portions of the Bill of Rights are encompassed within the more general concept of due process as found in the Fourteenth Amendment, he automatically acknowledges that a choice is involved and that the jurist in trying to approximate an understanding of the traditions of English-speaking peoples is the agency for such a choice. On the other hand, when the Bill of Rights proper is under consideration, he discounts attempts to elevate one section of the Constitution over another, and he is particularly adverse to having one portion of that section given prominence.

The choice factor based on pragmatic value judgments plays an inordinately important part in assessing the opposing philosophies of Justices Black and Frankfurter. From his recorded votes, the suggestion has been made that the latter has his own set of "preferences," which he consistently champions. Preoccupation with national security and unity has been proposed as one of these, public education as another. It is true that on one occasion he said that "national unity" is an interest "inferior to none" in the hierarchy of legal values.[29] But he did not say that it was an interest superior to all others. Unfettered public education, at the elementary, high school, or college level, seems to come closer to being an absolute for him. To protect this interest, he has turned certain provisions of the Bill of Rights into very rigid concepts. Thus, in the released-time cases, involving an interpretation of the establishment clause of the First Amendment, he found the

[29] Minersville School District v. Gobitis, 310 U.S. 586 (1940).

statutes providing for released time unconstitutional, for they violated "the basic constitutional principle of absolute separation" between church and state.[30]

It may be noted that, in part, Justice Frankfurter was not trying to protect religion or the state *per se*, but was using available constitutional tools to fashion protection for broader considerations that cannot be captured in any phrase or cliché. Separation of church and state was picked up and used, in the particular circumstances presented to the Court. There was no automatic elevation of constitutional provisions nor obstinate holding to an absolute that must be applied in all situations. This selectivity can be disagreed with on the basis of end result; the process itself, however, should not be confused with the process that accepts a closed set of values and sets out to defend them at all costs. This is a like confusion to that found in freedom of speech cases. No differentiation seems to be made between restrictions on the means by which information is disseminated and restrictions on the actual information being disseminated.

Of the other broader considerations that weigh heavily with Justice Frankfurter and that he finds worthy of judicial protection, the integrity of the political and democratic process and the ultimate responsibility of the legislature for social well-being must be numbered. To insure integrity, freedom of speech and press might have to be strictly applied and, in this instance, for particular cases, the applicable part of the Bill of Rights becomes absolute. But the Bill of Rights does not give total insurance, and so, in other situations, the right to suffrage takes on greater import. As a counterweight to the libertarian-activists' faith in the absoluteness of freedom over authority, liberty over order, Justice Frankfurter suggests faith in legislative competence to work out accommodations between the two sets of concepts. Pushed to its logical extreme, it would be very difficult to prove that there was not some basis in reason for all legislative acts. Although Justice Frankfurter has come very close to expressing the view that judicial review of legislative determinations, especially those of

[30] McCollum v. Board of Education, 333 U.S. 203 (1940). For discussion, see Alexander Meiklejohn, "What Does the First Amendment Mean?" *University of Chicago Law Review*, xx (Spring, 1953), 475.

the federal government, should be abolished altogether, he has not carried the doctrine of presumptive constitutionality to the point where it has been turned into legislative absolutism. His judicial philosophy is a profession of faith that neither the Court nor any other nonrepresentative body can completely or adequately correct the evils of our day. If faith in the legislature and concern for democratic processes are absolutes, they are absolutes with a venerable tradition, which cannot be preserved by automatically invoking concepts to fit a preconceived set of values.

"Preferred freedoms," whether as the cause or corollary of incorporation proposals, bring into use certain parts of the Bill of Rights more than others. It must be admitted that in his pragmatic search for accommodation of clashing interests, Frankfurter calls upon one constitutional concept more than upon any other. His view of due process, whether found in the Fifth or Fourteenth Amendment, is that here is to be located a source of fluidity and flexibility with which the judiciary can work. Due process of law, then, because of its wider, more inclusive nature, becomes the over-all safeguard for a democratic form of government. It is the "preferred" instrument by which the automatic preference for arbitrary absolute values can be avoided. It is the alternative to treating liberty and order as opposing forces. This awareness has not escaped members of the Court who find it necessary to make the Bill of Rights specific and specifically binding upon the states. Justice Douglas has complained that

> The decision we render today exalts the Due Process Clause of the Fifth Amendment above all others. Of course any power exercised by the Congress must be asserted in conformity with the requirement of Due Process. . . . But the requirement of Due Process is a limitation on powers granted, not the means whereby rights granted by the Constitution may be wiped out or watered down.[31]

Justice Douglas is correct that whether the federal government or state authorities are involved, due process is procedural—or, at least, should be. Being procedural, it should not concern itself

[31] Perez v. Brownell, 356 U.S. 44, 83 (1958).

with limiting power, but should see that power is exercised only in certain ways. Contrariwise, it should not be used as a supplementary mechanism to enforce absolute values—rights, if you prefer—against any government. Justice Frankfurter is not blameless in his substantive use of due process. The substances that he does propose are, however, variables and not predetermined choices. For him also there is a hierarchy of values, but this hierarchy is not absolute and is constantly changing as the needs of society change.

V

There are other hierarchical tendencies in the thought of Justice Frankfurter. He said at one time that "decisions of this Court do not have equal intrinsic authority." [32] Such authority apparently derives from the length of time the decision has stood in good stead. Decisions of long validity cannot be disregarded. Neither can those that have recently been handed down, but the latter do not have the encrustation of prestige or demonstrated workability that older decisions hold. Conjointly, in deciding which precedent should govern the disposition of a current case, choice is normally involved. With choice comes an infusion of considerations that influence personal judicial performance. For Frankfurter, the longevity of a precedent is one of these considerations, its originator another. If either Justice Holmes or Justice Brandeis can be cited, he seems to feel that extra weight is given the correctness of his choice. Holmes and Brandeis are the outstanding examples of judicial authority, but there are others, Judge Learned Hand among them. Quite frankly, he has listed those past members on the Supreme Court whom he thinks rank high in the hierarchy and thus deserve careful attention to their opinions. "It would indeed be a surprising judgment that would exclude Marshall, William Johnson, Story, Taney, Miller, Field, Bradley, White (despite his question-begging verbosities), Holmes, Hughes, Brandeis and Cardozo in the roster of distinction . . . I myself would add Curtis, Campbell,

[33] Adamson v. California, 332 U.S. 46, 59 (1947).

Matthews and Moody." [33] Many times in his opinions one will find a list of the justices who have supported the position that he is backing. Joined to such a list or perhaps in place of it will be a long citation of cases supposedly leading up to the disposition that he favors.

In assessing the work of administrative agencies Justice Frankfurter initially showed somewhat of an hierarchical approach. Extreme politeness to the Interstate Commerce Commission was a noticeable trait, while the Federal Trade Commission, among other agencies, was subjected to more rigid scrutiny. This tendency has now somewhat abated and all areas of administrative action are held strictly to account. In a much more technical vein, he still follows the hierarchical course that he explained as a professor. In relation to judicial review of administration he wrote that the topic "must be studied not only horizontally, but vertically, e.g., 'judicial review' of Federal Trade Commission order, 'judicial review' of postal orders, 'judicial review' of warrants." [34] Judicial review is not an absolute concept. It is colored by the whole structure of the agency over which it is exercised. Therefore, while an agency-by-agency approach is basic, within each agency the treatment of a concept must be vertical.

These are but a few of the obvious hierarchical elements in Justice Frankfurter's philosophy. They are all predicated upon a continuing process of choice, which can be revamped when shown to be in error. They are not absolutized after the initial choice has been made. They do show preferences. They do not show automatic, unreflecting preferences that are good for any time or place. Realizing that if the law is not to become static, contemplative choice must be allowed the judiciary, Justice Frankfurter also believes that such choice should be allowed the legislature. [35] While the priority of civil rights may be the

[33] Frankfurter, "The Supreme Court in the Mirror of Justice," *University of Pennsylvania Law Review*, cv (April, 1957), 783. Cf. the charming and informative "Chief Justices I Have Known," *Virginia Law Review*, xxxix (November, 1953), 883–905.

[34] Felix Frankfurter, "The Task of Administrative Law," *University of Pennsylvania Law Review*, lxxv (May, 1927), 620.

[35] See Wallace Mendelson, "Mr. Justice Frankfurter—Law and Choice," *Vanderbilt Law Review*, x (March, 1957), 333–50.

treasured personal belief of all the justices, except on transcendental, abstract grounds, that priority cannot be proved. No less powerful rational arguments can be put forth to back the priority of economic interests. If the legislature decides to give heed to the latter rather than the former, courts should not overrule this decision—unless, of course, some explicit constitutional provision is violated. If personal rights are to be given priority, it is for the legislature to indicate which ones. Judicial elevation of the rights of the First Amendment through "preferred freedoms" runs counter then not only to the proper limited role of the judiciary but also to the organic nature of the Constitution.

Justice Frankfurter recently wrote that "as good a test as I know of the significance of an opinion is to contemplate the consequences of its opposite." [36] This is an especially good insight in comparing his position on "preferred freedoms" with that of Justice Black. In their assertion of judicial power, the Black-Douglas group appears logically indistinguishable from the pre-New Deal Court. They do not strike down directly as many federal statutes as did their predecessors, but they do rather freely exercise a constitutional veto over state enactments. Upholding mild to severe economic regulation, they are staunchly opposed to any regulation, federal or state, which they consider to touch upon the sensitive area of personal liberty. To fashion protection for civil rights they have been thrown into conflict with the legislatures, and to justify this conflict they have taken a doctrine and turned it into an absolute barrier. "Preferred freedoms" and the corollary incorportion proposals are the outcome. So fearful of having individual freedom limited, a fear that is quite plausible within reasonable bounds, Justices Black and Douglas often see freedom as being antithetical to order, liberty, antithetical to authority. In their zeal to promote freedom and liberty, they deny that governmental power as lodged in the Constitution can ever be operative when a claim that they recognize under the Bill of Rights, especially the First Amendment, is made. They deny that governmental power may be subsequently inserted to back the right that has been wronged in a clash of rights, for, in their philosophy, no such clash can occur.

[36] Frankfurter, "John Marshall," loc. cit., p. 8.

Put briefly, those who champion "preferred freedoms" appear to be more interested in the microcosm than in the macrocosm, seeming to forget that the former cannot exist without the latter. Their zeal for the individual is understandable and praiseworthy. When, however, it is taken to extremes and made the absolute basis for all existence, the zeal is misplaced. Justice Frankfurter, on the other hand, is interested in the macrocosm of representative government. His insistence on the competency of the legislature and his rejection of absolute solutions to any problems, or even absolute values for their solution, are necessary adjuncts to his faith in a politically mature and responsible people.

XI

"It Is a Constitution We Are Expounding"

Justice Frankfurter has said of the Marshall statement that serves as the title of this chapter that "it bears repeating because it is, I believe, the single most important utterance in the literature of constitutional law—important because most comprehensive and comprehending." [1] He has repeated it on many occasions and each repetition helps to make clearer his own understanding of the nature of the Constitution. In the previous chapter we quoted him to the effect that the Constitution was an organic document that would suffer irreparable harm by having particular provisions dissevered from the entity. To pick and choose from among the provisions, whether they deal with rights or with power, and make the scope of judicial review over legislative action vary with the provision under consideration, seems to him irreverent and self-defeating. We have considered this subject as it related

[1] Felix Frankfurter, "John Marshall," in *Government Under Law* (Cambridge, Mass.: Harvard University Press, 1956), p. 8.

to civil liberties and incidentally to governmental power. It is now time to investigate the Constitution directly as an instrument of power.

I

Justice Frankfurter in a 1956 opinion [2] referred to an address by Senator Albert Beveridge in which the Senator castigated the mutilating effects upon the Constitution of a policy of selectivity. The Justice remarked on Beveridge's appeal to the whole Constitution and not those parts of it that for the moment find favor. This was not, however, the first instance on which he quoted approvingly the sentiments expressed by the eminent legislator. During the hearings on his nomination to the Supreme Court, Professor Frankfurter tried to make plain his own position by referring to the Beveridge remarks.

> In a speech by the late Senator Beveridge, whose friendship I had the honor to enjoy, before the American Bar Association in 1902 [sic, 1920?] he stated in effect that he was, of course, a staunch defender of the Constitution, a supporter of the document that established this country and maintained it, but that he was in favor of supporting the Constitution as a whole and not selectively. I was then 20 years younger than I am now, and this address and attitude by Beveridge made an even greater impression upon me than it would now.[3]

The impressions made on the young man continued to carry weight, and they explain in part his treatment of the Constitution after becoming a member of the Supreme Court.

There are two distinct power concepts in the judicial philosophy of Justice Frankfurter. One sees government, labor, business, minority groups as power blocs. The other sees the Constitution as a document containing enumerated and implied powers, all of which are of equal merit, none of which can be deleted or elevated. Thus, the war power or the power over immigration

[2] Ullmann v. United States, 350 U.S. 422, 428–29.

[3] U.S. Congress. Senate. Committee on the Judiciary. "Hearings on the Nomination of Felix Frankfurter," 76th Cong., 1st Sess., January 11 and 12, 1939, p. 111.

and naturalization deserves as much consideration as the taxation or commerce powers. Holding the legitimate possessors of power to account for the ways in which they carry out their functions differs from denying that power exists or from being selective in the types of power judicially approved. With Justice Holmes, he finds it ironic that "we fear to grant power and are unwilling to recognize it when it exists." [4]

In an address in the fall of 1942, Justice Frankfurter told his audience that the war against the Axis was the paramount task for all free men and free nations. Until this supreme task was brought to successful conclusion, any interest or issue that stood in its way must be put aside. This expression brought comment from certain liberals that he was so interested in winning the war that he relegated to the background things that people call social gains or a better world. The *New York Times,* in editorializing on this complaint, remarked somewhat sarcastically that possibly Justice Frankfurter was neglecting "the major issue, a new social system, for the minor issue, the task of saving the world from Hitler." [5] It suggested that the "major" issue could not be accomplished without the "minor" one, and that while both tasks should be kept to the forefront wherever possible, various advanced sections of American opinion would have to accommodate themselves to the fact that war existed and the government had to deal with it before further social reforms could be undertaken.

The advanced sections of American opinion as personalized in certain Supreme Court justices soon had an opportunity to rule on legislative and executive actions growing out of the war situation and based on the war power or military necessity. Treatment of Japanese-Americans on the West Coast has been subjected to severe and warranted criticism. In the first case touching this group, the Supreme Court unanimously upheld a curfew order issued by military authorities requiring enemy aliens or persons of Japanese heritage to remain in their homes during certain hours of the day. [6] In the next case, taken chronologically,

[4] Tyson v. Banton, 273 U.S. 418, 445 (1927).
[5] *New York Times,* October 3, 1942.
[6] Hirabayashi v. United States, 320 U.S. 81 (1943).

Korematsu v. United States,[7] the Court upheld, over vigorous dissents, a more drastic military order that excluded Japanese-Americans from certain areas altogether. The dissent by Justice Jackson is the most important in the position that it takes and in its possible ramifications for constitutional development.

Jackson seemed almost unconcerned with the particular order under consideration. His major point was that, if the Court passed either positively or negatively upon such orders under due process or other constitutional provisions, it would fasten them upon constitutional law for good and all. While "a military order, however unconstitutional, is not apt to last longer than the military emergency . . . ," Justice Jackson thought that "once a judicial opinion rationalizes such an order to show that it conforms to the Constitution or rather rationalizes the Constitution . . . the principle then lies about like a loaded weapon ready for the hand of any authority that can bring forward a plausible claim of an urgent need." [8] What he seemed to be suggesting was that actions taken under the war power, or, perhaps, even the war power itself, are in many respects extraconstitutional and, as such, should not be fitted by the judiciary into the normal pattern of constitutional law.

The answer to Justice Jackson came in the concurring opinion of Justice Frankfurter. Leaving the explanation of the validity of this particular order to the majority opinion, Frankfurter set out to explain the Constitution as a source of power adequate for peace or wartime use and to outline his own belief that the Court could not be selective in its judgment of various portions.

> The provisions of the Constitution which confer on the Congress and the President powers to enable this country to wage war are as much part of the Constitution as provisions looking to a nation at peace. . . . If a military order such as that under review does not transcend the means appropriate for conducting war, such action by the military is as constitutional as would be any authorized action by the ICC within the limits of the constitutional power to regulate commerce.[9]

[7] 323 U.S. 214 (1944).
[8] *Ibid.*, pp. 245–46.
[9] *Ibid.*, pp. 224–25.

The Court was the agency to determine the authorized limits of the war power as well as any other. It might be a very trying occupation and mistakes might be made. If so, the Court must take the burden and responsibility upon its shoulders. Inserted then is the characteristic thought that "to find . . . the Constitution does not forbid the military measures now complained of does not carry with it approval of that which Congress and the Executive did. That is their business, not ours." [10] The business of the Supreme Court was to deal with a Constitution adequate to the demands of war and peace, all of whose powers were on a par, only having to be kept within the bounds of their constitutional limits.

Justice Frankfurter has not treated the Constitution as a fair-weather document, and he has insisted that in times of stress the government under the war power can institute programs as varied as price restrictions, control of contracts, and supervision over state militia.[11] He has concurred, either expressly or silently, in the Court's rulings in treason cases [12] and on appeals growing out of military trials for defeated enemies.[13] In these cases, he voted to uphold government power and denied pleas by citizens or aliens that constitutional rights were being violated. With the Court, he reacted against sending Americans of Japanese background to relocation centers,[14] but he differed with the majority on the question of military trials for civilian defendants in a semi-war zone while hostilities were still under way, as this issue was presented in the Kahanamoku case.[15] Here the majority re-

[10] *Ibid.*, p. 225. For an appraisal of these respective positions of Justices Frankfurter and Jackson, see Charles Fairman, "Government Under Law in Times of Crisis," in *Government Under Law*, p. 265.

[11] For cases in which Justice Frankfurter has expressed these views or concurred in their expression, see: United States v. Bethlehem Steel Corp., 315 U.S. 289 (1942); Priebe & Sons v. United States, 322 U.S. 407 (1947); Yates v. United States, 321 U.S. 414 (1944); Bowles v. Wallingham, 321 U.S. 503 (1944); Woods v. Miller, 333 U.S. 128 (1948); Lichter v. United States, 334 U.S. 742 (1948); Burns v. Wilson, 346 U.S. 137 (1953).

[12] See Cramer v. United States, 325 U.S. 1 (1945); Haupt v. United States, 330 U.S. 631 (1947).

[13] See *Ex parte* Quirin, 317 U.S. 1 (1942); *In re* Yamashita, 327 U.S. 1 (1946); Hirota v. McArthur, 338 U.S. 197 (1948); Johnson v. Eisentrager, 339 U.S. 763 (1950).

[14] *Ex parte* Endo, 323 U.S. 283 (1944).

[15] Duncan v. Kahanamoku, 327 U.S. 304 (1946).

fused to sanction imprisonment by a military board of two civilians whose offenses had been brawling with sentries and embezzlement in the Hawaiian Islands during World War II.

Speaking through Justice Black, the Court based its holdings on the premise that the power to declare martial law does not include the power to supplant civilian laws by military orders and to supplant courts by military tribunals, where conditions are not such as to prevent the enforcement of laws by the courts. With this, no member of the Court disagreed. The concurring opinions of Chief Justice Stone and of Justice Murphy merely reiterated or embroidered on this theme. Even the dissenting opinion of Justice Burton, in which Justice Frankfurter joined, did not deny that where conditions are not such as to prevent law enforcement by the courts, military tribunals should not be in operation. The difference between those in the majority and those dissenting, and it was a major difference, was over the question of who was to determine where such conditions prevailed and when they came to an end. The former thought the judiciary should have such power; the latter thought that right belonged elsewhere, with the executive or legislature.

Alexander Pekelis has said that "the vitality of a country, like the youthfulness of an individual, can be revealed by the constructive use it makes of the crises and emergencies through which it lives." [16] No greater crises or emergencies were presented to the United States than those that became evident during World War II. In terms of legal development, the constructive use to which Justice Frankfurter directed his votes and the attention of his colleagues was that of a Constitution geared and ready to provide the sources of power with which the nation could defend itself, a Constitution establishing agencies of government capable and authorized to take over this task, a Constitution that did not call for nor validate excessive judicial interference with the proper exercise of power.

As Professor Clinton Rossiter remarked, the several opinions of Justices Frankfurter, Jackson, and Burton in the Korematsu and Kahanamoku cases, along with their general demeanor in other controversies involving the war power or powers closely related

[16] Alexander H. Pekelis, *Law and Social Action* (Ithaca: Cornell University Press, 1950), pp. 96–97.

thereto, showed a movement away from fatuous indignation over the civilian-military question toward a tough-minded recognition that, in the words of Justice Stephen J. Field spoken many years ago, "the medicine of the Constitution has now become its daily bread." Given the changing milieu in which the Constitution has to work, Professor Rossiter thought that this was a beneficial trend.

> Increasingly the justices are speaking and interpreting in terms of "the *fighting* Constitution," and this trend, if not carried too far, could be a welcome departure. If the Court would be a little more clear voiced about the general power of this nation to make war, it could then turn around and deliver a great deal more relief in the specific instances of individual injustice, which was all it was supposed to do in the first place. In short, the less it pretends, the more it can defend.[17]

In their zeal to give relief in individual instances of injustice, several members of the Court so confused the situation that they almost made it appear as if there was no such thing as the war power. Justice Frankfurter, on the other hand, and those who voted with him, were primarily interested in preserving the vitality of the war power and were not particularly concerned with righting all wrongs that could flow from its exercise. Only as each side gave some attention to the preoccupations of the other could the situation that Professor Rossiter describes come about.

The Constitution to survive must be a fighting Constitution. Many years after the termination of World War II, Justice Frankfurter reiterated the thought that the judiciary must allow the executive and legislative branches to utilize the war power and others relating to it if we are to have our fighting Constitution. "Although these specific grants of power [Article 1, Section 8, clauses 11 to 14 and 18] do not specifically enumerate every factor relevant to the power to conduct war, there is no limitation upon it (other than what the Due Process Clause commands). 'The power to wage war is the power to wage war success-

---

[17] Clinton Rossiter, *The Supreme Court and the Commander-in-Chief* (Ithaca: Cornell University Press, 1951), p. 130.

fully.' " [18] Discretion must be given those to whom the Constitution gives it. Judicial picking and choosing over the power clauses is just as erroneous as selectivity between the rights provisions. The war power is an integral part of the Constitution. It must be valid if the Constitution itself is valid, and its effective exercise must be unhampered by the Court as other powers are unrestrained, with the notable exception that it too must be exercised according to due process of law. Here, and only here, to secure procedural regularity, does the judiciary have a right to intrude upon the scene.

While the war power cannot be deleted from our Fundamental Law on the whim of Supreme Court members, neither can it be elevated over other provisions on the assumption of its excessive importance.

> . . . even the all-embracing power and duty of self-preservation is not absolute. Like the war power, which is indeed an aspect of the power of self-preservation, it is subject to applicable constitutional limitations. . . . Our Constitution has no provision lifting restrictions upon governmental authority during periods of emergency, although the scope of a restriction may depend upon the circumstances in which it is invoked.[19]

This explanation by Justice Frankfurter is very close to that given many years before by Chief Justice Hughes, to wit, that "while emergency does not create power, emergency may furnish the occasion for the exercise of power." [20] War is the extreme emergency. Its existence brings into play a power that lies dormant during times of peace. This power, like all others, comes under judicial scrutiny for its legal, though not for its political-social, ramifications. Justice Frankfurter would have the Court indicate that applicable constitutional limitations should be as strict, though no stricter, than they would be were any other claims before it. Unfamiliarity with the war power because of its sporadic activation may cause it either to be interpreted away altogether or made the basis for excessive and questionable actions. Justice

---

[18] Trop v. Dulles, 356 U.S. 86, 120–21 (1958).
[19] Dennis v. United States, 341 U.S. 494, 520 (1951).
[20] Home Building and Loan Association v. Blaisdell, 290 U.S. 398, 426 (1934).

Frankfurter through his opinions and votes has suggested that neither exclusive approach is desirable and that, in dealing with the war power, courts should recognize the organic nature of the Constitution.

II

With his personal background, Justice Frankfurter's performance in cases involving aliens or naturalized citizens should present telling commentary on how far he allows personal sympathy and identification to influence his decisions. It should also indicate how far he retains his view of the Constitution as an instrument of power all of whose provisions, even those concerning immigration and naturalization, should be treated with equal deference by the judiciary. It would be quite natural for him to feel sympathy for those seeking to gain or retain American citizenship, since he himself had attained that status derivatively through the naturalization of his father. Yet the Constitution is very clear in Article 1, Section 8, that it is Congress that is to have power "To establish a uniform rule of Naturalization." The conflict, if any, between individual heritage and constitutional mandate seems to have been resolved in favor of the legal standards. He has probably leaned over backwards to avoid the charge of discrimination in favor of those with a similar foreign background.

This is not to say that Justice Frankfurter has disavowed his own heritage. On the contrary, many of his public utterances show extreme awareness and appreciation of this background. But he also is well aware of the contribution that life in the United States has made to his development. In his private activities he has been a supporter of programs or organizations that attempt to integrate the new arrival into the fabric of American life. In accepting the scroll of honor from the National Institute of Immigrant Welfare, he explained some of his inner feelings. "Gratitude," he said, "is one of the least articulate of the emotions, especially when it is deep. I can express with very limited adequacy the passionate devotion to this land that possesses millions of our people, born, like myself, under other skies, for the privilege that this country has bestowed in allowing them to partake of the fellowship." [21] Believing that nothing is more uniquely American than hospitality to the human spirit whatever its source, he said on another occasion that "to make Americanism turn on blood instead of on completeness of devotion to the spirit of the Declaration of Independence, the Second Inaugural, and the Four Freedoms, is to come dangerously near the abyss into which Nazism finally fell." [22] Regard for the inherent worth of the individual and not for the accident of birth should be the criterion by which any person is judged. While, therefore, Justice Frankfurter has high praise and interest in the alien and the naturalized citizen within our midst, he does expect of them, as well as others, complete devotion to the principles and precepts of democratic government. This dual perspective, colored by personal experience, explains in part his actions in cases involving them.

Before he became a member of the Supreme Court, that tribunal had decided on numerous occasions that pacifists were excluded from naturalization, because they refused to take the required oath calling for participation in the defense of the country against its emenies.[23] In the case of Girouard v. United States [24] the New Deal Court reversed this policy and Justice Frankfurter joined Chief Justice Stone in dissent. Justice Frankfurter, in a commencement address delivered a few years previously, had said that "I respect the conviction of a conscientious objector to war and I believe I understand the philosophy underlying Gandhi's nonresistance. But the relentless choice events may force on every individual cannot be met by such a fair-sounding pernicious abstraction as that 'war never settled anything.' " [25] In the case at hand, Stone and Frankfurter were not so much concerned with disproving the proposition that war never settles anything as they were with proving that congressional belief in

[21] *New York Times,* May 12, 1938.
[22] Felix Frankfurter, "Thomas Mann," in Philip Elman (ed.), *Of Law and Men* (New York: Harcourt, Brace & Co., 1956), p. 350.
[23] United States v. Schwimmer, 279 U.S. 644 (1929); United States v. Macintosh, 283 U.S. 605 (1931); United States v. Bland, 283 U.S. 636 (1931).
[24] 328 U.S. 61 (1946).
[25] *New York Times,* June 19, 1941.

the efficacy of an oath to defend the country had a basis in reason and that that belief still prevailed. Court action in overriding the necessity for such an oath ran counter to legislative desires and legislative approval of prior decisions. Justice Frankfurter, therefore, joined Stone in reaffirmation of congressional power as he had joined him three years previously in the case of Schneidermann v. United States.[26] There their dissenting opinion insisted that Congress had the power to make membership in the Communist party at the time of naturalization grounds for revoking citizenship.

In the 1948 case of Ludecke v. Watkins [27] Justice Frankfurter wrote the opinion of the Court and incorporated in that opinion thoughts on both the war power and congressional power over immigration and naturalization. A German enemy alien, after a hearing held under authority of the Attorney General, a hearing not required by any provision of the Alien Enemy Act, was directed to be deported from the country upon a finding that he was dangerous to the public peace and safety. His petition for habeas corpus was denied by the lower courts, and it was this denial that Justice Frankfurter upheld. Countering suggestions that the petitioner was not dangerous and that the war was over in all but a technical legal sense, he decided that the Attorney-General's decision to direct removal was justified as part of the executive's prerogative and that it was up to the executive and legislature to inform the courts as to the end of the war. Finding the fact that the President chose to have a nonreviewable war power exercised within narrower limits than legislatively authorized not sufficient cause for judicial intervention, Justice Frankfurter concluded, "we hold that full responsibility for the just exercise of this great power may validly be left where the Congress has constitutionally placed it—on the President of the United States." [28] This power might be abused, but that did not

---

[26] 320 U.S. 118 (1943).

[27] 335 U.S. 160.

[28] *Ibid.*, p. 173. For other cases in which Justice Frankfurter has voted against the claims of individuals and in favor of the government, see: Bridges v. Wixon, 326 U.S. 135 (1945); Klapportt v. United States, 335 U.S. 601 (1949); Perez v. Brownell, 356 U.S. 44 (1958); Bonetti v. Rogers, 356 U.S. 691 (1958); Trop v. Dulles, 356 U.S. 86 (1958).

sanction judicial review until some flagrant violation had occurred. Congress unquestionably had the power to draw up schemes for naturalization; the President was the primary holder of the war power; both had some responsibility for aliens within our gates; conjoined, these powers were more than adequate to justify deportation when both popular branches of government thought that step necessary, the one directly, the other indirectly through delegation of part of its power.

Let it not be assumed for a moment that Justice Frankfurter always agrees with the ways in which aliens or naturalized citizens are treated. He has sounded wistful in many of his writings over the ways in which constitutional power was handled. But he has steadfastly warned that "whether immigration laws have been crude and cruel, whether they may have reflected xenophobia in general or anti-Semitism or anti-Catholicism, the responsibility belongs to Congress. . . . One merely recognizes that the place to resist unwise or cruel legislation touching aliens is the Congress, not this Court." [29] Even in what must be a very sensitive area personally he holds to his philosophy that when power exists it is obligatory for the judiciary to recognize it and that if the public desires a substantive change in its exercise, this change should be sought at the polls and not at the bar of the Supreme Court. This point is illustrated very well in the case of Galvan v. Press [30] in which Justice Frankfurter wrote for the Court that support, or even demonstrated knowledge, of the Communist party's advocacy of violence is not a prerequisite to deportation under the Internal Security Act of 1950, which provides for the deportation of aliens who had been members of that party at any time. Courts in the past had recognized unlimited congressional power over immigration and naturalization. Aliens, as well as naturalized citizens, were accorded all the procedural protections of the Constitution. On the policy level, however, Congress remained unchecked and the statute being applied in the Galvan case contained very definite policy implications.

Justice Frankfurter appeared tempted to correct what he

[29] Harrisiadis v. Shaughnessy, 342 U.S. 580, 597 (1952).
[30] 347 U.S. 522 (1954).

thought was the exceedingly harsh basis of the statute. He wrote that

> In light of the expansion of the concept of substantive due process as a limitation upon all powers of Congress, even the war power . . . much could be said for the view, were we writing on a clean slate, that the Due Process Clause qualifies the scope of political discretion heretofore recognized as belonging to Congress in regulating the entry and deportation of aliens.[31]

After going this far, he pulled himself up short with the reminder that "the slate is not clean." Not being clean, the Court would have a lot of erasing to do before it could write its own policy, a type of composition it was never intended to undertake in the first place. Thus, not even the stupidity of this program for dealing with aliens could make Justice Frankfurter swerve from the main point, the uncontested right of Congress to act stupidly if it so desired. Justices Black and Douglas dissented separately. Justice Black could not make up his mind whether the legislation was a bill of attainder, an ex post facto law, a violation of the First Amendment, or a denial of due process or equal protection of the laws. Of one thing he was quite sure, however. Congress in causing a man to be deported from the country solely because of past membership in the Communist party was somewhere, somehow, violating, if not a constitutional right, then the spirit of the Constitution. This tendency on the part of the more activist members of the Court to strike down legislation under very broad and ambiguous citation of clauses comes very much to the fore in cases involving aliens, for in this area congressional power over the years has been undoubted and the attempt to forestall it now must be based on a new and inexact form of interpretation of the Constitution.

Discussing Justice Frankfurter's performance in cases where the substantive use of congressional control over denaturalization and deportation is under consideration may lead to the erroneous impression that he never votes against the government. Such is not the situation. Indeed, he has voted in favor of individual litigants in more alien cases than he has voted to uphold

[31] *Ibid.*, pp. 530–31.

some particular government action.[32] The difference is that when the government is brought to task it is usually on a question of procedural regularity and not substantive power. He has refused, for example, to honor the government's claims that it could deny admission to the wife of an American citizen merely on the basis of information supplied by an unidentified informer; that it could disregard in deportation proceedings the explicit provisions of the Administrative Procedure Act to the effect that those who investigated a cause could not be the ones to serve as hearing officers on its merits and disposition; and that it could ask aliens, subject to deportation, any type of question about past activities, not those relating only to continued availability for departure.

The 1956 case of Jay v. Boyd [33] places the procedural-substantive question in perspective very well. The Court held that the due process clause of the Fifth Amendment was not violated by interpreting the Immigration and Nationality Act of 1952 in such a way as to sanction a subordinate officer's determination that discretionary suspension of deportation was not warranted. The determination had been based on confidential information, which supposedly disclosed a threat to the interest, security, or safety of the United States. Chief Justice Warren and Justices Black, Frankfurter, and Douglas reacted warmly against this decision, each writing a separate dissenting opinion. The Chief Justice thought that this type of proceeding was not an administrative hearing in the American sense. Justice Black felt that the prestige of the courts was at stake. Justice Douglas inveighed against faceless informers.

Justice Frankfurter limited his ruling to the administrative law aspects, concluding that the Attorney General might be given

---

[32] See Kessler v. Stretcher, 307 U.S. 22 (1939); Baumgartner v. Unted States, 322 U.S. 665 (1944); Savorgnan v. United States, 338 U.S. 491 (1950); United States v. Shaughnessy, 338 U.S. 521 (1950); U.S. *ex rel.* Knauff v. Shaughnessy, 338 U.S. 537 (1950); Bindezck v. Finucane, 342 U.S. 76 (1951); Carlson v. Landon, 342 U.S. 524 (1952); Heikkela v. Barber, 345 U.S. 299 (1953); Shaughnessy v. U.S. *ex rel.* Arcardi, 349 U.S. 280 (1955); Marcello v. Bond, 349 U.S. 302 (1955); United States v. Minker, 350 U.S. 179 (1956); United States v. Witkovich, 353 U.S. 194 (1957); Rowoldt v. Perfetto, 355 U.S. 115 (1957).

[33] 351 U.S. 345.

discretion by Congress to withhold clemency. In thus forcing deportation, however, the Attorney General personally, and no subordinate official, had to make the final decision. This was the fatal flaw in the Jay case—that the Attorney General had delegated his powers to members lower in the hierarchy without congressional authorization. Justice Frankfurter's attention to procedural regularity here can be taken as representative of his approach to most controversies involving aliens or naturalized citizens.

III

The 1951 Term of the Supreme Court presented Justice Frankfurter with one of the most trying personal cases of his career, trying in the sense that various facets of his judicial philosophy seemed to be in conflict. The so-called Steel Seizure Case, Youngstown Sheet and Tube Company v. Sawyer,[34] contained within its myriad ramifications untold complications for members of the Court. During the Korean war, President Harry Truman directed his Secretary of Commerce to seize the steel mills in order to avert a threatened major strike. He by-passed the Taft-Hartley Act, the Selective Service Act of 1948, and the Defense Production Act of 1950, possible sources of authority for such action, and relied for support solely on his position as Commander-in-Chief of the armed forces and other like broad executive powers. Justice Frankfurter was painfully and acutely aware of the conflicting values, need for action at this critical juncture of American history and the need to reconcile executive and legislative power. In the final analysis, he rejected the executive's claims to an inherent source of power for seizure in disregard of legislative competence. Arriving at the final determination meant, however, subordinating one prime judicial consideration, executive responsibility for the nation's welfare in time of strain, to another, legislative predominance in the field of remedial action.

The Youngstown case, if noted for nothing else, gained wide comment for the number of opinions that it elicited. For the nine justices, seven opinions were necessary to cover all nuances of

[34] 343 U.S. 579 (1952).

approach. In what is technically the opinion of the Court, Justice Black proceeded on the theory that the President was without power to seize private property, even though an emergency might exist. He had no compunction against using judicial power against the executive and found his actions totally beyond the bounds of the acceptable, either on the basis of inherent power or any supposed, although not claimed, legislative authorization.

For Justice Frankfurter the important point was arbitrating the division of functions between the executive and legislative branches. He was not so interested in proving or disproving the President's rectitude. His concurrence attached great significance to the congressional policy that could be found in the interstices of labor and related legislation. This stress was quite different, therefore, from that of Justice Black, who set the problem up as one of presidential action taken in the absence of congressional consideration. The dissenters upheld the seizure as an appropriate method, not prohibited by the Taft-Hartley Act or any other legislation, of faithfully executing and preserving the defense program enacted by Congress, until the latter could take needed action.

While Justice Frankfurter thought that the principle of separation of powers was more complicated and flexible than appeared in Justice Black's opinion, he agreed thoroughly with the application of the principle to the case at hand. Characteristically, early in his opinion he referred to Marshall's polestar for constitutional adjudication, "it is a *constitution* we are expounding." Because it is a Constitution, the Court had to take a spacious view of the powers it contained, but it also had to limit as narrowly as possible, under the circumstances, the constitutional issues that it permitted itself to examine.

> We must therefore put to one side considerations of what powers the President would have had if there had been no legislation bearing on the authority asserted by the seizure, or if the seizure had been only for a short, explicitly temporary period, to be terminated automatically unless Congressional approval were given. These and other questions, like or unlike, are not now here. I would exceed my authority were I to say anything about them.[35]

---

[35] *Ibid.*, p. 597.

The Framers of the Constitution had presented to the nation a document "made for an undefined and expanding future." They had not tried to bind the actions of generations coming after them. While, therefore, Justice Frankfurter found that the executive in the particular instance did not have the power claimed, he was unwilling to state unequivocally that that power could never be gained through agreement with the legislature. As the Framers had not put fetters upon the future, it was no less encumbent upon the Court to avoid ruling on issues that were not before it and by these needless pronouncements to forestall future programs.

Justice Frankfurter recognized that on many occasions a plaintiff with an otherwise acceptable claim is refused equitable relief because of countervailing public interest. The steel companies in this instance were demanding such relief from the actions of the Secretary of Commerce. If this had been the end of the matter, he might have decided that the relief should be refused because of the overriding importance of national security. He saw this dispute, however, as one of separation of powers, with the executive attempting to cross the line into legislative territory without a green light from the representative body or, perhaps, even against the red warning signal contained in some statutes. The major public interest was to be found not in the issue of executive seizure versus the claims of the steel companies but in the broader issue of executive-legislative relations and competences. The executive could not show a particularly strong public interest for the enhancement of its prerogatives at the expense of those belonging to another branch of government. Nor could it even show that previous like actions had been acquiesced in by Congress, thereby becoming part of the undefined sections of "executive power" as found in Article 2. This was the initial assertion by the executive, and it was one that ran counter to legislative will, as well as that will could be determined from pre-existing statutes. Consequently, the assertion had to be denied.

Finding that in the particular circumstances, given the network of legislation already on the books, the President could not deal with the situation in the way he chose, Justice Frankfurter went on to say that "absence of authority in the President to deal with a crisis does not imply want of power in the Government." [36] While it was inconceivable that the executive branch should absorb power that was not directly or indirectly its own without congressional consent, it was equally inconceivable that the government could not deal with a crisis or emergency because of lack of constitutional sanction somewhere. The Constitution was an instrument of power, strong alike in peace or times of disturbance. Congress could, but had not, authorized the type of procedure followed by President Truman. Until Congress acted, the power was dormant, but it was still there. Bowing graciously to the executive, Justice Frankfurter reminded him of the existence of the other co-ordinate branch and suggested that if the two could compose their differences, action such as the steel seizure could be authorized by legislative power.

As to the other opinions, that of Justice Jackson came very close in spirit and statement to that of Justice Frankfurter. Citing the numerous occasions on which the government had evolved techniques to expand normal executive powers to meet an emergency, Justice Jackson said of these techniques that "they were invoked from time to time as need appeared. Under this procedure we retain Government by law—special, temporary law, perhaps, but law nonetheless." [37] This portion of his opinion is very reminiscent of his performance in Korematsu, where he suggested that many actions taken under the constitutionally recognized war power might be extraconstitutional, and that it was far better for the Court not to treat of these situations in legal terms. In any event, the final result was that the President as ultimate representative of the executive branch could not rely solely on inherent, unmentioned power but must consult and gain consent from the legislature. To this combined approach of the majority, Chief Justice Vinson in dissent replied: "Those who suggest that this is a case involving extraordinary powers should be mindful that these are extraordinary times. A world not yet recovered from the devastation of World War II has been forced to face the threat of another and more terrifying global conflict." [38] For Justice

[36] *Ibid.*, p. 604.
[37] *Ibid.*, p. 653.
[38] *Ibid.*, p. 668.

Frankfurter, the fact that these were perilous times made the decision between legislative and executive power that much more difficult. But in keeping with his view of the Constitution as an organic whole, he traced the source of control in this instance to the legislature and abided by the finding that the President, for all his inherent resources to meet emergency situations, had to accommodate himself to statutory direction.

IV

President Truman's bid for power in the Youngstown case was turned down, but presidential powers not in conflict with legislative competence and constitutionally founded have been consistently given recognition by Justice Frankfurter. Control over foreign relations and all subjects incidental thereto has received his unqualified judicial approval.[39] The problem of foreign relations became more diversified as the armed forces of the United States took up positions around the world after the termination of World War II and at the beginning of the Cold War period. No longer was it sufficient to decide that the executive branch had supervisory control over our relations with foreign nations. Now the Court was faced with the problem of how far any branch of government could determine the fate of American citizens in overseas bases, citizens both in and out of the armed forces.

There was scant doubt that in its power "To make Rules for the Government and Regulation of the land and naval Forces," Congress could provide for court-martial proceedings for those in the military. Even the Constitution itself, through the Fifth Amendment, recognized that all procedural safeguards usually accorded citizens were not requisite for those serving in a branch of the military. In an unusual summer session, the Supreme Court decided that a soldier could be turned over to civilian authorities for trial of an offense committed within their area of jurisdiction even though he was in that area only by virtue of the fact that he was serving with United States military contingents. With Justice

---

[39] See his votes in United States v. Pink, 315 U.S. 203 (1942) and Republic of Mexico v. Hoffman, 324 U.S. 30 (1945).

Frankfurter in the majority, the Court upheld executive orders, made in pursuance of a duly executed treaty, that provided for this transfer.[40]

Problems relating directly to citizens within the armed forces have not, therefore, caused too much trouble for the Court. It is when persons indirectly involved with the military—wives of servicemen, employees on government bases—have become embroiled in legal difficulties that the Court has had to fashion new remedies. The Uniform Code of Military Justice, the latest in a series of congressional enactments governing judicial procedure in the armed forces, provided for military trial of persons within certain categories who were not members of the military. Like trials for civilians had received adverse criticism in the Kahanamoku case. In the interim between the Kahanamoku case and litigation coming up under the new Code, the Court had held, with Justice Frankfurter once again in the majority, that the military could not constitutionally try a civilian for an offense committed earlier when he had military status.[41]

It was in the 1955 Term that the Court was called upon to decide whether the Constitution requires a trial of an American civilian before a Court, established under Article 3, in a foreign country for offenses committed by him.[42] In this instance, two companion cases revolving about the murder of military personnel by their wives were the vehicles for judicial expression. The majority decided that it was within legislative competence to establish legislative courts for this type of situation. Dissents were noted and Justice Frankfurter entered a reservation, stating that he wanted more time to consider all the implications. The use of special legislative courts, such as courts-martial, in contradistinction to tribunals falling within the established judicial hierarchy, meant that all legal safeguards usually accorded a defendant were not necessarily applicable. This gap was one of the major sources of dissension.

Before the opinions could be entered, and after considerable

[40] Wilson v. Girard, 354 U.S. 524 (1957).

[41] United States *ex rel.* Toth v. Quarles, 350 U.S. 11 (1955).

[42] Kinsella v. Krueger, 351 U.S. 470 (1956); Reid v. Covert, 351 U.S. 487 (1956). Cf. Madsen v. Kinsella, 343 U.S. 341 (1952).

change in Court personnel, the issue was brought up for rehearing. During oral arguments the suggestion was made that Congress had provided for trial of Americans by Americans because the standard of justice in foreign countries was not equal to ours. To this suggestion, Justice Frankfurter reacted with gusto. Fuming from the bench, "where do these men live?" he lectured counsel on the relative merits of different legal approaches.[43] The final outcome was that the Court reversed itself within a year and held that legislative power did not extend to creating legislative courts, courts-martial, for the trial of civilian dependants of members of the armed forces overseas who were charged with offenses committed while abroad.[44] Of those in the majority, Justices Frankfurter and Harlan limited their holdings to capital cases, while Chief Justice Warren and Justices Black, Douglas, and Brennan, in an opinion by Black, expressed the broader view that military trial of civilians is, in any case, inconsistent with the Constitution. Justices Clark and Burton retained the position that they had taken the year before, that under certain circumstances Congress could provide for military trials of civilians.

Beyond the interest in this case as a determinant of civil-military relations and as a guide for estimating the role of the military in our scheme of government lies its importance in focusing the justices' conception of power and in translating other aspects of their judicial philosophies over into an area of only recent emergence. Justice Frankfurter limited his holding to capital cases, for he was unwilling to say that congressional power might not at some time and if properly exercised be sufficient to regulate judicial procedures overseas. Life is the ultimate possession of any human being, and to protect it every judicial safeguard and legal advancement should be brought to bear. But as with due process, judicial decision may determine which rights are so fundamental that they should be included within judicial scrutiny and which are peripheral enough to be excluded and left to non-Article 3 courts. As Justice Black has rejected the interpretation of the due process clauses as flexible mechanisms for individual

[43] Heard in courtroom at rehearing, February 27, 1957.
[44] Reid v. Covert, 354 U.S. 1 (1957).

protection in favor of an absolutely defined Bill of Rights absolutely binding upon the state and national governments, so he rejected the contention that civil courts should not supervise all trials of civilians, saying that he could "find no warrant, in logic or otherwise, for picking and choosing among the remarkable collection of 'Thou shalt nots' which were explicitly fastened on all departments and agencies of the Federal Government by the Constitution and its Amendments." [45]

Most members of the Court seemed to feel that Congress either had the total power to establish legislative courts for civilians, or it had none. The dissenters thought the power existed and that Congress was free to use it. Justice Black thought that no such power existed and that the total Bill of Rights and all constitutional provisions applied. Justice Frankfurter took his characteristically middle stance, a stance that is also becoming identified with Justice Harlan. This impression is further increased by this duo's performance in the 1960 case of Kinsella v. United States *ex rel.* Singleton [46] wherein other members of the Court radically changed sides on the issue of military trial for civilian defendants and employees, but Frankfurter and Harlan held fast to their conviction that such trials were only precluded when capital offenses were involved.

He is not as leery of governmental action as are some of his brethren. If it can be demonstrated that power belongs to one of the co-ordinate branches, he does not hesitate to recognize it. It matters not what power clause is under consideration, all deserve equal respect, none deserves to be selectively treated. In recognizing the existence of power, he shies away from giving approval for its exercise in all places and at all times, preferring to take the specific instance with all its attendant specific circumstances into view. While other members of the Court either approve or disapprove absolutely of power conceptions and their implications, Justice Frankfurter pursues a pragmatic path to the decision of a case at hand. Meticulously careful that procedural guarantees are respected when governmental power is being

[45] *Ibid.*, p. 9.
[46] 4 L ed 2d 268.

utilized, he leaves substantive questions of policy to those whom the Constitution has appointed, the executive and the legislature. These are traits that crisscross his judicial philosophy as it touches many subjects. They are traits that come clearly to view in his treatment of the Constitution as an instrument of power.

FIVE
Decentralization and
Dispersal of Control

Justice Frankfurter's name is associated with the theory of judicial self-restraint. He has often been praised or blamed, depending upon the analyst's findings as to how far in practice he has lived up to his theory. Studies have been made of his use of the self-restraint standard in relation to civil rights or taxation or commerce cases, as if each type of litigation was a closed category and called for a different type of restraint. Such investigations have value in pin-pointing the problem, but they do not go to the heart of the matter. Judicial self-restraint cannot be discussed in a vacuum, for it is not a self-contained concept. It is merely the short-hand way of expressing more fundamental and long-maturing aspects of Justice Frankfurter's judicial philosophy. These fundamental aspects appear in the guise of techniques of interpretation—the uses of history—and in substantive considerations—symbolism and social unity, the Constitution as an instrument of power. This section investigates the self-restraint standard in terms of Justice Frankfurter's understanding of the role of the Supreme Court in the American system of government.

His basic premise is that each agency of government has a fairly well-defined area of competence in which it should work and to which it should limit itself. The width and depth of such areas differ with the various units. Legislatures, for example, have greater leeway in controlling the destiny of the nation than does the judiciary. Further refinement shows that the competence of the national legislature precludes state legislative activity on certain matters. Within the area of its competence, however, each governmental unit, be it a state regulatory commission or the Supreme Court of the United States, should be autonomous in the performance of its duties. Decentralization and dispersal of control is, therefore, a dual-pronged theory. It deals with the relations between units of the federal government, and it concerns itself with the proper balance between nation and states.

XII

The Court and Congress

Many times during our history the Supreme Court and Congress have been at odds. Charges that the Court is usurping and exercising legislative power are not of recent origin, although they have certainly become prevalent over the last decade or so. Legislative competence is jealously guarded by those to whom it is entrusted, and rightly so. It is equally true that no member of the Supreme Court would deny the primacy of Congress' legislative function or intimate that the High Tribunal is better equipped to carry on such an activity. The trouble lies in defining the boundaries between legislative and judicial competence in that misty area where the two are apt to meet. Justice Frankfurter uses certain guideposts in keeping the judiciary on its side of the boundary line. Proper jurisdiction and avoidance of constitutional issues weigh heavily with him. His conception of the legislative function and his theory of representative government are here also directly relevant.

267

I

"Putting the wrong question is not likely to beget right answers in the law," [1] for "it is also true of journeys in the law that the place you reach depends on the direction you are taking. And so, where one comes out on a case depends on where one goes in." [2] Realizing this, Justice Frankfurter has been at some pains to have the Court define exactly where it intends to enter a case. In other words, he localizes the issues upon which the Court will rule.

Writers on the judicial process often give the impression that once the opening statement has been made, logic will inevitably lead to but one result. They center attention on following this logical unfolding and tend to overlook the fact that the choice of a starting point is often the most important element in any case. Hidden behind this choice are the major premises of the jurist. Frankfurter's choices are extremely revealing. His first concern in cases that come before the Court is whether that tribunal has properly assumed jurisdiction. It is, of course, natural that he should be interested in such an issue, since he taught jurisdiction of the federal courts and co-authored a study entitled *The Business of the Supreme Court*. Fred Rodell suggests that his interest in this type of issue stems from his desire to be the legal profession's Emily Post. This seems unfair. Writing in 1927 Professor Frankfurter argued that "so-called jurisdictional questions treated in isolation from the purposes of the legal system to which they relate become barren pedantry. After all, procedure is instrumental; it is the means of effectuating policy." [3] Many years later in a Supreme Court opinion he wrote: "The law of the jurisdiction of this Court raises problems of a highly technical nature. But underlying their solution are matters of substance in the practical working of our dual system and in the effective conduct of the

[1] Vanston Bondholders Protective Comm. v. Green, 329 U.S. 156, 170 (1946).

[2] United States v. Rabinowitz, 339 U.S. 56, 69 (1950).

[3] Felix Frankfurter and James Landis, *The Business of the Supreme Court* (New York: The Macmillan Co., 1927), p. 2.

business of the Court." [4] The solution of jurisdictional problems is important, yes, but only as these solutions lead to a fuller understanding of the legal system and of the Court's place therein.

Over the years there has been a general contraction of the Court's jurisdiction. In order to warrant the nation's confidence, the Supreme Court must adequately dispose of cases presented to it. If it goes too far afield, it cannot fulfill this duty. How then is the Court's jurisdiction defined? Broadly, the Constitution provides the answer. For Frankfurter, "No provisions of the Constitution, barring only those that draw on arithmetic . . . are more explicit and specific than those pertaining to courts established under Article 3." [5] By Article 3, the Framers made clear the definition and limitation of judicial power; therefore, "however circumscribed the judicial area may be, [the Court] had best remain within it." [6]

While the general contours of this area were set down many years ago, Congress, by the terms of the Constitution, can do some revamping. Any legislation dealing with the courts is, however, under two limitations. First, the types of cases coming before the Court are determined by the predominant concerns of contemporary life. Second, as with all legislation, statutes dealing with courts will operate slightly differently in practice than they would appear to do on paper. Because legislators cannot possibly encompass within a statute all the various ramifications of judicial power for contemporary life and because only as a statute becomes a working document do its strengths and weaknesses appear, the Court must be its own guardian in jurisdictional matters. And this the Court has always deemed itself peculiarly qualified to do. Justice Frankfurter has taken a limited view of the Court's competence. The prime reason for this is his fear of compromising the powers that duly belong to the judiciary. As he has noted, jurisdictional questions are questions of statecraft. But they are also inevitably questions of power in which each department of the federal and state governments is interested. If the Supreme

---

[4] Flournoy v. Wiener, 321 U.S. 253, 263 (1944).

[5] National Mutual Insurance Co. v. Tidewater Trade Co., 337 U.S. 582, 646 (1949).

[6] United States v. Bethlehem Steel Corp., 315 U.S. 289, 312 (1942).

Court claimed for itself certain kinds of power, other units of the government would resist, probably forcing the Court to back down, thus lowering its prestige and hindering its effective operation. In order to avoid such a clash, the justice has at times engaged in what critics call jurisdictional dialectics.

Growing out of such "dialectics" is Frankfurter's insistence that the Court should allow itself to be activated only when a case or controversy, in the strictest sense, is up for consideration. His reasons for this are not hard to find. The Court "escapes the rough and tumble of politics . . . largely because [it moves] only when invoked and then only under the guise of settling a lawsuit." [7] This statement came in the late 1920's. He recognized that the Court exercised political functions but he wanted to keep the Court out of politics. After he took the Scholar's Seat, Frankfurter continued to insist that judicial power could come into operation only "as to issues that the long tradition of our history has made appropriate for disposition by judges." And again the reason is given. "This restriction . . . reflects respect by the judiciary for its very limited, however great, function in the proper distribution of authority in our political system . . . ." [8] It is quite apparent how much this sounds like his pre-Court writings.

If the Court were not dealing with a real conflict of interest, it would be merely rendering advisory opinions. Such opinions are particularly to be avoided when sought on congressional enactments for they tend to weaken legislative and popular responsibility. "Legislatures and executives may inform themselves as best they can; but the burden of decision ought not to be shifted to the tribunal whose task is the most delicate in our whole scheme of government." [9] This was the Harvard professor's position in 1934; it is the position of the Supreme Court Justice in 1960.

While most cases before the Court have a statutory or constitutional background, there are certain instances when its equity

[7] Felix Frankfurter, "Mr. Justice Holmes and the Constitution," *Harvard Law Review,* XLI (December, 1927), p. 122.

[8] American Communications Assoc. v. Douds, 339 U.S. 382, 416 (1950).

[9] Felix Frankfurter, "Advisory Opinions," *Encyclopedia of the Social Sciences* (New York: The Macmillan Co., 1930), I, 478. Cf. by the same author, "A Note on Advisory Opinions," *Harvard Law Review,* XXXVII (June, 1924), 1002–1008.

jurisdiction comes into play. Characteristically, Justice Frankfurter calls for extreme scrutiny before the tribunal can be invoked in this way. "To require a court to intervene in the absence of a statute . . . in the exercise of inherent equitable powers, something more than adverse personal interest is needed." [10] This is a blunt statement, but it is very much in keeping with the tenor of articles written before Frankfurter's elevation to the bench. Over a period of time he produced a series of annual pieces for the *Harvard Law Review* evaluating the work of the Court in the term just ended. In all these evaluations considerable space was given to discussion of the broader issues behind jurisdiction. The article of 1928, for example, carried the comment that "Considerations for abstention from decision, unless technical equity requirements are satisfied, are met with the temptation to make use of the flexible facilities of equity for prompt allaying of uncertainty." [11] Professor Frankfurter made it entirely clear that he did not think easy-going attitudes toward equity jurisdiction helped the Court in the least. As a critic of the Court on jurisdictional matters, he was not gentle; as a self-critic of the institution on which he serves, he has been even more uncompromising.

II

Jurisdiction ascertained and a case or controversy identified, the next step in Justice Frankfurter's attempt to avoid clashes with other government units is to have litigants define exactly what it is they want the Court to do. He is impatient with buckshot blasts of charges that cover the whole legal target without ever coming to the central point. Indefiniteness forces the Court to cull out the decisive points based solely on its own judgment. This is but an invitation for the Court to give full reign to its own preferences unbounded by even the flimsiest barriers. Such a situation is dangerous enough when only private litigants are involved; it can be fatal when some other governmental agency

[10] Joint Anti-Fascist Refugee Comm. v. McGrath, 341 U.S. 123, 151 (1951).

[11] Felix Frankfurter and Adrian Fisher, "Supreme Court—1935 and 1936 Terms," *Harvard Law Review,* LI (February, 1938), 624.

is concerned. Specificity in attacking legislation or governmental action cuts down on broad charges of unconstitutionality and thus allows the Court to deal with its heaviest responsibility, that of ruling on the competence of a co-ordinate branch, only when absolutely necessary. As charges must be definite, so the record of the case must be complete and only challenges to the law considered in the courts below can be entertained. Justice Frankfurter once admitted that "exercises in procedural dialectics so rampant in the early nineteenth century still hold for me intellectual interest . . . ." [12] It is perhaps in the area of charges and records that such an interest comes most to the fore. But it may well be that, at times, extreme formalism helps to protect the Court.

Previous avenues explored for escaping conflict between Court and Congress have been limited and technical in nature. When Justice Frankfurter turns to the "political questions" doctrine, he leaves narrow confines for broad expanses. Because of its very nature, litigation that may involve "political questions" does not fit nicely into any breakdown of Court cases. It must be handled ad hoc. Judges' personal idiosyncrasies and evaluations assume vast proportions, for there is a very fine line "between cases in which the Court [feels] compelled to abstain from adjudication because of their 'political' nature and the cases that so frequently arise in applying concepts of 'liberty' and 'equality.'" [13] Liberty and equality must have meaning read into them. So must the concept of "political questions." When no neutral meaning can be devised, Justice Frankfurter will go out of his way to avoid even the appearance of questioning legislative competence on matters that do not fall definitely within the purview of the judiciary.

The "political questions" concept is a very necessary adjunct to one of his main contentions that we have considered, that no part of the Constitution which can be judicially applied or interpreted is of more value than another. There are, however, some portions of the Constitution and state constitutions that are not

[12] Chicago R.I. & P.R. Co. v. Stude, 346 U.S. 574, 586 (1954).
[13] Felix Frankfurter, "John Marshall," in *Government Under Law* (Cambridge, Mass.: Harvard University Press, 1956), p. 19.

judicially enforceable. In large measure, the parts concerning redistricting or the status of constitutional amendments are some of these. In cases such as these Frankfurter will concede judicial impotence rather than draw legislative fire. This is not because Congress or any other legislature warrants undue deference. It is because the judiciary is supposedly the weakest branch of the government. Its meager prestige and power must be protected at all costs. This may be fact or fiction, but it is an integral part of Justice Frankfurter's philosophy.

Justice Frankfurter believes that the Court's heaviest responsibility comes with ruling on the competence of other branches of government. Whether state or national power is at stake, he prefers to forego constitutional adjudication when other grounds are available. Avoidance of constitutional issues was an integral part of James Bradley Thayer's teaching. On the Supreme Court both Holmes and Brandeis advocated such a policy. One of Justice Brandeis' best known opinions was a reasoned but eloquent plea for restraint on constitutional rulings.[14] Frankfurter finds Brandeis' position "frequently cited and always approvingly . . . ."[15] As a scholar he had written that "not to decide, especially constitutional questions, until issues are ripe for the judicial process as tested by traditional canons of adjudication, is as important a function of the Supreme Court as to decide when an issue is inescapable, no matter how difficult or troubling."[16] Thus even before he became a member of the Court he was convinced that settled principles of constitutional adjudication required the Court to forego constitutional issues if any other way was open.

The case of United States v. Rumely[17] illustrates how this philosophy is put into operation. The Court was asked to rule whether a House Committee had infringed First Amendment freedoms in putting certain questions to witnesses. Frankfurter, writing the opinion of the Court, refused to be drawn into constitutional controversy. He based his ruling wholly on the ground

---

[14] Ashwander v. Tennessee Valley Authority, 297 U.S. 288 (1936).

[15] Staub v. Baxley, 355 U.S. 313, 330 (1958).

[16] Felix Frankfurter and James Landis, "The Supreme Court at October Term, 1931," *Harvard Law Review,* XLVI (December, 1932), 260.

[17] 345 U.S. 41 (1953).

that the Committee had exceeded the grant of authority contained in the House authorizing resolution. Therefore, because of this defect, witnesses were under no obligation to respond. "Grave constitutional questions are matters properly to be decided by this Court but only when they inescapably come before us for adjudication. Until then it is our duty to abstain from marking the boundaries of congressional power or delimiting the protection guaranteed by the First Amendment." [18] The avoidance of constitutional issues can be used as a manipulative device by justices who, fearing the outcome of present litigation, prefer to have the issues treated at a later time by a different Court composed of different members. Some of the present justices do not subscribe to the avoidance theory at all, preferring to meet constitutional objections head on. Justice Black, for example, differed strongly with Frankfurter in the Rumely case and wished to have the ruling based on First Amendment grounds. His reasoning is that, however wise avoidance of constitutional issues may be at times, there is too much of a tendency to turn avoidance into judicial self-abnegation. It may well be that Justice Frankfurter never faces this central point.

Being a constitutional historian, he knows that in many periods the Court has invalidated legislation whose only infirmity was that the Court thought it unwise. The outcome of such invalidation was, not loss of prestige for Congress, but loss of prestige for the Court. And so to escape "self-inflicted wounds," Frankfurter abstains from constitutional adjudication by various devices, statutory construction primarily. He feels that any statutory question that is not frivolous must be met before constitutional issues can be taken into consideration. As it is the duty of the legislature and executive to inform themselves so that advisory opinions will not be necessary, so it is the Court's responsibility, once a statute is on the books, to be very careful in its treatment. "To allow laws to stand is to allow laws to be made by those whose task it is to legislate." [19]

When cases come up that must be decided on constitutional grounds, Justice Frankfurter makes his holdings as narrow as pos-

[18] *Ibid.*, p. 48.
[19] Tax Commission v. Aldrich, 316 U.S. 174, 185 (1942).

sible. He is reluctant to lay down absolute rules without qualification. Everything cannot be settled at one time. There must be gradations in treatment. A recent book on *Desegregation and the Law* gives Frankfurter considerable credit for the way in which the initial desegregation decrees were drafted. The authors especially pointed out that the way in which the decrees were announced allowed the Court to escape an "either/or" dilemma.[20] What the writers of this volume did not pick up was the fact that on three separate occasions [21] the term "with all deliberate speed" had appeared in his opinions. Before the desegregation decisions, such an expression had not come to light in the opinions of any of the other current justices. During hearings on integration, a participating lawyer remarked that "tough problems" were involved. Frankfurter replied immediately, "That is why we are here." [22] He understands full well that the Court must deal with hard constitutional problems. But he also knows that the quiet surrounding the Court is the quiet of a storm center. He is not about to undertake the role of rainmaker. The Court might thereby be inundated.

There is another reason beyond protecting the Court that makes Justice Frankfurter wary of touching constitutional questions. That is the outlook of the American people on constitutional rulings. Roscoe Pound once thought that the nineteenth-century conception of legal rights was but a disguised version of the natural right and moral duty found in earlier philosophic jurisprudence. People were convinced that if what they did was morally correct, it must also be legal. Twentieth-century Americans are apt to give the reverse interpretation. Most of them believe that if some action is constitutional then it must be correct. The Court has become the oracle defining "correctness," whether it wishes to be so or not. One can gather from certain of Justice Frankfurter's intimations that he is not really too certain that it is best for the Court to adjudicate constitutional questions at all. Since the Court

[20] Albert Blaustein and Clarence Ferguson, *Desegregation and the Law* (New Brunswick, N.J.: Rutgers University Press, 1957), pp. 32–33.

[21] Addison v. Holly Hill, 322 U.S. 607, 619 (1944); Chrysler Corp. v. United States, 316 U.S. 556, 568 (1942); Radio Station WOW Inc. v. Johnson, 326 U.S. 120, 132 (1945).

[22] *New York Times*, December 10, 1952.

has, from Marshall's time, called this prerogative its own, there is little to be done about it. But reading into constitutional rulings moral approval or disapproval is another matter. He has always been strongly against the tendency to equate "constitutional" with "right."

To show the consistency in this matter over the years, even as to phrasing, two of his statements should be compared.

> It must never be forgotten that our constant preoccupation with the constitutionality of legislation rather than its wisdom tends to preoccupation of the American mind with a false value. Even the most rampant worshipper of judicial supremacy admits that wisdom and justice are not the basis of constitutionality.[23]

> Preoccupation by our people with constitutionality, instead of with the wisdom, of legislative or executive action is preoccupation with a false value. . . . Focusing attention on constitutionality tends to make constitutionality synonymous with wisdom.[24]

The first statement came from his pen in 1925, and the second in 1951, over a quarter of a century later. He has taken every available opportunity to stress this theme because it is extremely important from his viewpoint. People must be made to realize that courts cannot be responsible for the deeper, moral life of any group. Only as citizens themselves take responsibility for the Constitution and its working will a well-integrated society result. The Court can do only so much to protect civil rights or economic opportunities. The rest is up to the people. "Holding democracy in judicial tutelage is not the most promising way to foster disciplined responsibility . . . ."[25] In constitutional adjudication the Court is of course passing on policy matters, but it is doing it in a highly technical and limited way. Responsibility for the broader ramifications of legislation should not be placed on the Court. It is not the proper forum. While it is true that, at times, constitutionality and wisdom coalesce, Frankfurter's conception of a liberal judge in the tradition of Holmes and Brandeis will not allow him to unite them. It must be a natural mating.

[23] Felix Frankfurter, "Can the Supreme Court Guarantee Toleration?" *New Republic*, XLIII (June 17, 1925), pp. 85–87.

[24] Dennis v. United States, 341 U.S. 494, 555–56 (1951).

[25] Frankfurter, "John Marshall," in *Government Under Law*, p. 20.

III

Jurisdiction, political questions, and constitutional issues are the specific aspects of Justice Frankfurter's reasoning that allow him to avoid clashes with the legislature. These aspects are, however, but parts of his general philosophy of judicial review. Since in the Justice's writings the concepts of judicial review and self-restraint are so often intertwined, it is almost impossible to separate them. For analytical purposes, however, they must be dealt with consecutively. The basic point in his conception of judicial review is that a politically unresponsible branch of government is sitting in judgment on the competence of a co-ordinate politically responsible branch. Since "legislation is the most sensitive reflex of politics," and is "most responsive to public ends and public feelings," [26] the Court in exercising judicial review calls to account not only the legislature but also the people. For someone who is a majoritarian, as Frankfurter is, this is a most awesome duty. Believing that, with scant exceptions, the will of a majority should prevail in the electorate or in the legislature or even in the courts, he is faced with the prospect of seeing perhaps five men thwart the desires of the nation. However much he might like to circumvent this impasse, the fact remains that it must be faced. And he faces it in much the way in which he imagines Holmes and Brandeis to have faced the same dilemma.

The touchstone of judicial review is establishing the "reasonableness" of legislation under consideration. Frankfurter is convinced in theory that when even the slightest scintilla of evidence can be adduced for the reasonableness of legislative action, such legislation must be allowed to stand. However noble of statement and however consistently adhered to in application such a theory is, it is at least open to some question. Reasonableness and wisdom need not be and often are not synonymous. This is true enough, but it is difficult to define for purposes of judicial review the one without the other. One may argue cogently that the very

[26] Felix Frankfurter, *The Public and Its Government* (New Haven: Yale University Press, 1930), p. 10.

attempt to estimate "reasonableness" may be the way in which legitimate judicial creativity can affect the course of law. Reasonableness may be nothing more than a short-hand formula for balancing social interests. Justice Frankfurter is certainly conversant enough with the sociological theories of Pound and others to recognize that in accepting or rejecting a claim of reasonableness he is at the same time directing to some degree the path that legislation should follow. For policy reasons, this admission is not too readily made in his Supreme Court opinions, but it certainly has an extensive place in his pre-Court writings. No less a person than "our great master of constitutional law," James Bradley Thayer, recognized that "the difference, then, in the crucial cases is apt to resolve itself not really to a difference about law, but to a difference in knowledge of relevant facts." [27] Professor Frankfurter understood this in 1924. He has not lost that understanding.

When he went on the Court, Felix Frankfurter had a background that made him especially conscious of the complexities of modern life. Working with Brandeis he understood how to use the factual method. He knew that while such material had to be presented to courts it was mainly in the legislature that factual findings could most directly be put to work. With growing regularity the theory that appellate courts will rule only on points of law and not on facts has been honored more by its breach than by its fulfillment. "Judicial notice" has become very wide indeed, but it seems true to say that between the judiciary and the legislature, the latter still is more intimately involved with the complex facts of modern society. This being the case, review of legislation on factual, usually termed reasonable, grounds is open to two dangers. In the first place, "judicial attempts to solve problems that are intrinsically legislative—because their elements do not lend themselves to judicial judgment or because the necessary remedies are of a sort which judges cannot prescribe—are apt to be as futile in their achievement as they are presumptuous in their undertaking." [28] In the second place, the fast-moving tempo of twentieth-century life demands immediate relief for many of its

[27] Frankfurter, "A Note on Advisory Opinions," *loc. cit.*, pp. 1003–1004.
[28] Williams v. North Carolina, 317 U.S. 287, 305 (1942).

pressures. This the judiciary cannot provide. It can merely stultify the present and bind the future when disallowing legislative action without itself being able to provide any positive relief. Congress, on the other hand, can immediately change its course of direction or the people can change that course by choosing other representatives. Therefore, Justice Frankfurter would insist, judicial review must be narrowly exercised if there is to be any free play for the present, let alone for the future. In addition, opinions themselves in such cases must be couched in the most guarded language, for there is great potential danger that language broad and sweeping in nature will later be applied by false analogy to cases in which it really does not fit.

Justice Frankfurter's opinion in the case of Trop v. Dulles [29] contains many of his important insights concerning judicial review. That this case was of some moment can be gathered from the justices' behavior. Anthony Lewis, *New York Times* correspondent, commented that "the members of the court put their deep philosophic differences on vivid display . . . in their written opinions and even more in their oral comments. Their remarks in the courtroom verged on the bitter, even waspish." [30] The Trop case concerned expatriation and denaturalization and the power of Congress to legislate concerning them. Chief Justice Warren wrote the opinion of the Court. He found it beyond the power of Congress to require denationalization because of wartime desertion from the armed forces. Such a power was not included in the control of citizenship. There was another infirmity. The legislation conflicted with the Eighth Amendment's prohibition of cruel and unusual punishment. Justice Frankfurter dissented. As important as the substantive holding is for constitutional law, major interest at this point is on the rationale for judicial review as expressed in Warren's and primarily in Frankfurter's opinion.

Warren's opinion was premised upon the fact that, for the majority, the Constitution clearly forbade the type of legislation under review. As for the power of judicial review, he noted that "in some 81 instances since this Court was established it has deter-

[29] 356 U.S. 86 (1958).
[30] *New York Times,* April 3, 1958.

mined that congressional action exceeded the bounds of the Constitution. It is so in this case." [31] The Chief Justice's reference to the eighty-one instances in which legislative competence had been denied apparently annoyed Frankfurter considerably. In the oral presentation of his own opinion he interpolated a direct answer to the reference. Commenting rather caustically that holding eighty-one acts of Congress unconstitutional was nothing to boast about, he went on to remark that many of these same decisions had since been overruled.[32]

Frankfurter maintained that there was a difference between limits of power and authority and wise or prudent exercise of power. However subtle the distinction, the Court could oversee only the former category. After quoting Madison to the effect that all power is of an encroaching nature and noting that judicial power could also be thus characterized, he insistently called to the Court's attention the fact that it was sitting in judgment upon a co-ordinate branch of government. Near the end of his opinion he entered the warning that "the power to invalidate legislation must not be exercised as if, either in constitutional theory or in the art of government, it stood as the sole bulwark against unwisdom or excesses of the moment." [33] This sentiment is very much in keeping with his view of the legislature and of the people in a democracy. Trop v. Dulles is not unusual in any way; it is quite characteristic of Frankfurter's opinions. He has been so articulate on the subject of judicial review that almost any of his opinions would have served just as well. If articulateness can be equated with deep preoccupation, then Justice Frankfurter's basic interests are openly on display.

IV

His theory of judicial self-restraint follows as a very natural corollary to his conception of judicial review. In sum, he wants the judiciary to exercise as much self-control as possible, not be-

[31] Trop v. Dulles, 356 U.S. 86, 104 (1958).
[32] New York Times, April 3, 1958.
[33] Trop v. Dulles, 356 U.S. 86, 128 (1958).

cause complete disinterestedness can ever be attained, but precisely because it cannot. He realizes full well that "in law also men make a difference," [34] and that "five Justices of the Supreme Court *are* molders of policy, rather than impersonal vehicles of revealed truth." [35] Once again these are not thoughts that make their appearance often in Court opinions, but the opinions calling for restraint cannot be understood without this underpinning. One may regret the fact that Justice Frankfurter does not many times see fit to include such statements and thus opens himself to charges of inconsistency and self-delusion. But, in view of his pre-Court writings, his calls for judicial self-restraint should not have naïveté attributed to them.

When Justice Black was appointed to the Supreme Court, Justice Stone wrote to Frankfurter inquiring how well he knew the new member and remarking that Frankfurter might be able to give Black some assistance. The Harvard scholar responded to this plea with a memorandum for Black on the art of judging. "Writing in the same spirit and for the same academic purposes as I would were I writing a piece as a professor in the *Harvard Law Review*," [36] he informed his supposedly less knowledgeable student that a lack of candor often obscured from public view exactly what judges were about in their profession. Thereby, he wrote, the people were miseducated and failed to understand their own or their representatives' responsibilities for bringing about change in judge-created law. Here was no philosophic treatise on the meaning of self-restraint but a very practical appraisal of the judicial process by a practical observer. Black may have learned the lesson too well for Frankfurter's comfort, for, in later years when the two had served together on the Supreme Court, it has often been Justice Black who has reminded his former instructor that "in law also men make a difference." In fairness, however, it should be recalled that Supreme Court opinions are not meant to be political tracts, and if the tone of Frankfurter's

[34] Felix Frankfurter, "Justice Holmes Defines the Constitution," *Atlantic Monthly,* CLXII (October, 1938), 485.

[35] Felix Frankfurter, "The Supreme Court and the Public," *Forum,* LXXXIII (June, 1930), 334.

[36] Frankfurter to Black. Quoted in Alpheus T. Mason, *Harlan Fiske Stone* (New York: The Viking Press, Inc., 1956), p. 470, note.

opinions seems perhaps too lofty and withdrawn from reality, it is because his conception of the function of an opinion differs substantially from that of other members of the Court.

In Frankfurter's pleas for self-restraint, as in his discussion of judicial review, one must go behind the immediate formulation to earlier statements in order to understand the premises from which he is working. Doing this, one becomes familiar with several themes. One of these is the preponderant weight that individual preference, *if unchecked,* can have upon constitutional law. Also prevalent is the thought that if the Court is to be effective it must interfere with legislative competence only at crucial times when its action can have some real meaning. Too frequent and strenuous assertion of power, even that which duly belongs to it, will make any assertion of power suspect. Self-restraint has therefore a positive as well as a negative aspect. It saves the Court's prestige so that when it acts, its actions will be decisive; it is the "one quality the great judges of the Court have had in common."[37]

While these aspects are important, Justice Frankfurter's primary motivation for self-restraint is his theory of democratic government and the preponderant role that the politically responsible legislature plays therein. This theory of democratic government is majoritarian. He feels that "judicial review is a deliberate check upon democracy through organs of government not subject to popular control."[38] Except when explicit limitations are placed by the Constitution upon the will of the majority, it is the better part of valor for the Court to refrain from intervening. The distinction is often made that what Frankfurter desires is popular government, but what the Framers of the Constitution created was limited government. This seems but a play on words, much like the fruitless arguments over absolute versus conditional majoritarianism. In the United States with its Bill of Rights obviously some limitations are placed upon popular will. The real question is where the limitations are set and how far the legislature can legislate undeterred by the particular views of particular justices at a particular time. What Frankfurter is concerned with

---

[37] United States v. Lovett, 328 U.S. 303, 319 (1946).
[38] Frankfurter, "John Marshall," in *Government Under Law,* p. 19.

in judicial self-restraint is reconciling democratic ideals with partial judicial control.

The opinion that he wrote in American Federation of Labor v. American Sash and Door Company [39] is probably one of his finest expositions on the necessarily limited role of the judiciary in a democracy. The Court, unlike Congress, cannot bow to every change in popular fancy. Unless its judgments are shaped by communicable, rational standards, it tends to become despotic. Therefore, because matters of policy are by definition matters that require the resolution of largely imponderable value clashes, "assessment of their competing worth involves differences of feeling; it is also an exercise in prophecy. Obviously the proper forum for mediating a clash of feelings and rendering a prophetic judgment is the body chosen for those purposes by the people." [40] Like Judge Learned Hand, who does not wish to be ruled by a bevy of Platonic guardians, and like Thayer, who warned that under no system of government could courts go far to save a people from ruin, Frankfurter believes it debilitating to democracy when the legislature and people of a nation refuse to face up to their responsibility.

On more than one occasion Frankfurter has quoted Thayer to the effect that correcting legislative mistakes from the outside has two evil consequences: The people lose political experience and capacity, and they forego the moral education and stimulus that comes from fighting the questions of values out in the ordinary way, thus correcting their own mistakes. It has been said of Frankfurter's performance as a judge that his "contextual method of interpretation, his accentuation of historical perspective and his deliberate judicial humility provide the essentials for the difficult task. He is handicapped only by his inability to admit the reality of unwanted responsibility." [41] But the situation is not so simple. For Frankfurter, it is not a matter of having the judiciary avoid unwanted responsibility; it is a matter of placing responsibility where he thinks it belongs—in the legislature.

[39] 335 U.S. 538 (1949).
[40] *Ibid.*, p. 557.
[41] Clyde W. Summers, "Frankfurter, Labor Law and the Judge's Function," *Yale Law Journal,* LXVII (December, 1957), 290.

He has a great deal of faith in Congress as an institution. Even in the controversial area of investigations he has leaned over backwards to sustain congressional action. In view of the decision in Watkins v. United States,[42] which, at the time of its announcement, supposedly curtailed the investigatory powers of Congress, a good deal of notoriety has come from the fact that as a teacher he wrote an article entitled, "Hands Off the Investigations." [43] The primary purpose of the article was to ward off attacks on studies of governmental corruption. While the disparity between his votes in the Watkins case and his sentiments in the article cannot be explained completely, it is true that in neither instance did he deny congressional power. The Frankfurter opinion in United States v. Rumely, discussed above, is an important bridge between the two so-called contradictory positions. Unlike the majority in the Watkins case, Frankfurter merely concurred on the ground that the scope of an inquiry must be defined with sufficient clarity to protect a witness from the dangers of vagueness in the enforcement of sanctions against him. It was quite natural for him, therefore, to join the 1959 holding in Barenblatt v. United States [44] in which the Court confirmed committee questioning of a witness as to his associations. The Court felt that the questions asked were germane to the subject under investigation, the relationship was made very clear to the witness, and he was protected against any misunderstanding as to his rights.

Early in the New Deal Frankfurter remarked that no body of men worked harder or with more intelligence than the Senate.[45] These are still apparently his feelings. He accepts legislating as a highly deliberative process. When during the course of argument before the Court Solicitor General Lee Rankin intimated that Congress passed a statute without realizing its full implications, an annoyed Frankfurter remarked, "You think then that legislation by Congress is like the British Empire, something that is acquired in a fit of absent-mindedness?" [46] Other lawyers have found that

[42] 354 U.S. 178 (1957).

[43] Felix Frankfurter, "Hands Off the Investigations," *New Republic*, xxxviii (May 21, 1924), 329.

[44] 360 U.S. 109 (1959).

[45] *New York Times*, February 23, 1933.

[46] *Ibid.*, December 9, 1953.

questioning legislative competence or the legislative function is not the best way to win approval. In the hearings on desegregation at Little Rock, one of the council suggested that perhaps a public opinion poll reflected the will of the nation more accurately than did legislative judgment. This was too exasperating for Frankfurter, who acidly commented, "I sometimes wonder why we have elections, and do not turn it all over to the polls." [47]

Instances such as those recounted above and the tone of the Justice's writings, both pre- and on-Court, have led to the speculation that he is a believer in legislative supremacy, in the very special sense in which that term refers to British governmental practice. Frankfurter has not gone out of his way to dispel such a notion. A believer in the empiric approach to problem-solving, he probably also believes that the linguistic absolutes of the Constitution can only be mitigated by the legislature. From his knowledge of and association with persons like Thayer, Pound, and Hand, he has perhaps absorbed much of the sociological jurist's distrust for written guarantees of fundamental community-centered values. And it must be remembered that the whole sociological approach is not unlike that of the more historically minded British school of constitutional law, represented par excellence by A. V. Dicey, a writer often referred to by the former law professor.

One does not have to look far in Justice Frankfurter's writings to find at least tacit approval if not preference for the British approach. The most superficial examination of his judicial philosophy reveals self-professed Anglophilism. Its roots trace back to many important figures in English thought. For example, Jeremy Bentham's dislike for judge-made law and his insistence on the completeness of legislative statement of purpose through codes echo to some degree in Frankfurter's opinions. Harold Laski and the whole English pluralist school have had their effect, an effect that shows up much more clearly in discussion of geographical disbursion of control and responsibility and in analysis of group theory as related to the concept of social unity.

It is perhaps in this area of bowing before congressional will and advocating self-restraint that Justice Frankfurter comes clos-

[47] *Ibid.*, August 29, 1958.

est to the British legislative supremacy tradition. The case of
Perez v. Brownell [48] found him holding for the Court that Congress had power in the Nationality Act of 1940 to declare that a
person voting in a foreign election forfeited citizenship. Justice
Douglas in dissent called attention to what he thought was a serious flaw in the majority opinion.

> The philosophy of the opinion that sustains this statute is foreign
> to our constitutional system. It gives supremacy to the Legislature
> in a way that is incompatible with the scheme of our written Con-
> stitution. A decision such as this could be expected in England
> where there is no written constitution, and where the House of
> Commons has the final say. But with all deference, this philosophy
> has no place here. By proclaiming it we forsake much of our con-
> stitutional heritage and move closer to the British scheme. That
> may be better than ours or it may be worse. Certainly it is not
> ours.[49]

Justice Douglas could better have said that certainly the philosophy displayed was not his, for on many occasions Justice Frankfurter has been able to carry a majority with him in sustaining,
against vehement protest, congressional competence based on the
philosophy expressed in the Perez case.

V

A good deal of the criticism of Justice Frankfurter's positions
on judicial self-restraint and legislative competence comes from
those who desire a variant of judicial supremacy—at least at this
particular juncture in constitutional development. Justice Jackson,
in his posthumously published work on *The Supreme Court in the
American System of Government*, pointed out one of the contradictions of the last three decades. "A cult of libertarian judicial
activists now assails the Court almost as bitterly for renouncing
power as the earlier 'liberals' once did for assuming too much
power." [50] Professor Herman Pritchett is not quite so blunt, but

[48] 356 U.S. 44 (1958).

[49] *Ibid.*, p. 79.

[50] Robert Jackson, *The Supreme Court in the American System of Government*
(Cambridge, Mass.: Harvard University Press, 1955), p. 57.

he does indicate the difference in perspective between the goal-orientation of the activists and the functional-orientation of Frankfurter and others.[51] One of the primary differences, of course, is that in emphasis as to how far the Court should sally forth to protect certain interests, especially in the field of civil rights. Because of Frankfurter's conception of the Constitution as a source of power, he is unable to don the crusader's garb. While he has not and would not subscribe to the theory that we have un-limited trust in the majority, neither could he wholeheartedly endorse the view that the function of the Court varies with the types of congressional enactment under consideration. Majority rule, limited only by the Constitution, can be as responsible in the civil rights field as it is in the area of economic supervision.

Those members of the Court who are functionally oriented are more apt to talk in terms of objective standards, thus underplay-ing the personal contributions of particular justices and empha-sizing the continuing role of the Court as an institution. Frank-furter tends to follow this course through most of his opinions. The judicial activists, or absolutists as they have been called, tend to think that it is psychologically impossible even to approximate objectivity and impartiality. Since someone, somewhere, has to make a decision as to what aspects of a civilization's values should be protected above all others, they are willing to undertake the task. In doing this, however, they are driven to an individual-rather than a law-centered philosophy. Justice Frankfurter has suggested that certain decisions, especially those involving the Bill of Rights, could only have been made because certain of the justices were convinced that everyone was completely motivated solely by their own personal ideas of The Just. One may happen to agree with their ideas, as Frankfurter does in many cases, with-out being convinced that their actions help to dignify law as a social phenomenon. Individual justices dispensing individualized justice, in the sense that each case is determined wholly on dis-guised sympathy, leaves much to be desired for those who are functionally oriented.

Such an orientation is not itself without limitations. Frank-furter's deference to legislative judgment presupposes that con-

[51] See C. Herman Pritchett, "Libertarian Motivations on the Vinson Court," *American Political Science Review,* XLVIII (June, 1953), 321–36.

gressional acts coming before the Court should be of the kind that would eliminate, as much as possible, any temptation for judges to become lawmakers. The trouble is that, however desirable such legislation might be, there is precious little of it on the statute books today. His insistence that the legislature assume its responsibilities and not attempt to impart segments of its competence to the judiciary should indicate to him that there is somewhat of a practical contradiction in the functionally oriented philosophy. By saying on the one hand that the dictates of Congress as contained in legislation must be followed, while, on the other hand, complaining that Congress often does not provide any policy to be followed, one is left in a no man's land of doubt and consternation. Many people would agree with the proposition that *if* Congress completely fulfilled its competence obligations, *then* the courts should respect the limits of their own area of power. Unfortunately, the first part of the proposition is not always fulfilled, thereby invalidating the second.

Justice Frankfurter's self-restraint, in the light of his views on Congress, comes in for the fairest and most telling criticism, not because he will not assay an activist role but because others do. By theoretically refusing to assert himself in the face of strong and pronounced views on the part of other members of the Court, Frankfurter is in the dangerous position of losing the match by default, so to speak. Indeed, in the judgment of Professor Pritchett, "Frankfurter, by his conscientious efforts to apply the restraint idea, has carried it to a logical extreme and thereby demonstrated its hollowness as a guide for action." [52] While his cohorts on the bench may and do question whether the Justice has carried restraint to the extreme where his own personal views have not been infused into decisions, yet Professor Pritchett's criticism seems sound. If the so-called activists unashamedly show preference for certain programs, FELA and FLSA, and for certain values, "preferred position" of the First Amendment, may it not be better openly to have another set of conceptions vying for prominence?

But Justice Frankfurter is caught in the web of his own theo-

[52] C. Herman Pritchett, *Civil Liberties and the Vinson Court* (Chicago: University of Chicago Press, 1954), p. 245.

retical formulations. It would be an almost impossible task for him to break, if this were desirable, with the positions that have been a lifetime in developing. A basic formulation of this position holds that "the powers exercised by this Court are inherently oligarchic . . . ." [53] This is true whether humane ends are being served or not. Being inherently oligarchic, it is important to lessen rather than to increase the control that the judiciary exercises. As Roscoe Pound thinks of law as only one element in social control, so Justice Frankfurter thinks of the judiciary as only one, and perhaps a minor, element in a democratic society. By dispersing responsibility and making each agency of government assume the responsibility that duly accrues to it, the nation will be more fully served.

[53] American Federation of Labor v. American Sash and Door Co., 335 U.S. 538, 555–56 (1949).

XIII

The Institutional Role of the Court

The Supreme Court stands in a unique relation to administrative agencies and lower courts, be they federal or state. To some extent it must supervise their activities, but it must also be sure that in such supervision it does not encroach upon their prerogatives nor stifle their initiative. In the previous chapter we were concerned with certain elements of Justice Frankfurter's judicial philosophy as these became articulate in demands for decentralization and division of responsibility in the federal government between Court and Congress. In the next chapter attention will be focused on geographical dispersal of control. With the Court's institutional role, there is conjoining of functional and geographical reasons for dispersing competence throughout various governmental units. It should be made clear at the outset that in talking of an institutional role we are not basically concerned with the Supreme Court's own primary jurisdictional position or with the Court's symbolic role in instances of appeal. What we are attempting here is a discussion of the juridical premises of decentralization and dispersal of control from which Justice Frankfurter reasons in dealing with units in some degree subordinate to the Supreme Court.

I

There are definite parallels between Justice Frankfurter's views concerning the relation of the legislature to the judiciary and his views concerning the relation of the Supreme Court to administrative agencies and the lower courts. Once again the major theme is that courts, and especially the Supreme Court, are not the only units of government that can protect the public interest. Others can fulfill part of this function better. As the Court was not to interfere with congressional policy, so the policy of administrative agencies should go largely unchallenged. When a challenge is unavoidable, the concept of expertise replaces the concept of reasonableness as the basis for judgment. The insistence that, before judicial action can be invoked, a real case or controversy must exist is translated into the demand that, before a challenge to administrative action is heard, it must be shown conclusively that the challenger has the correct standing. In reviewing the competence of the legislature, emphasis was placed on allowing it to correct its own errors. In reviewing administrative and state court action, emphasis is placed on finality of rulings and on exhaustion of remedies and procedures. Legislative purpose and intention should be clearly stated in the statutes; the records of administrative agencies and lower courts should be complete and concise. These are but a few of the intertwining themes in Justice Frankfurter's preoccupation with establishing the role of the Supreme Court vis-à-vis other agencies of government.

His position in specific cases and his treatment of technical administrative law concepts such as substantial evidence, primary jurisdiction, and the intricacies of notice and hearing have been ably covered elsewhere.[1] A distillation of such materials presents,

[1] See Wallace Mendelson, "Mr. Justice Frankfurter on Administrative Law," *Journal of Politics,* xix (August, 1957), 441–60; Nathaniel L. Nathanson, "Mr.

however, a philosophy of administration and administrative law. Since he has written opinions in most of the important cases in this field—often the majority opinion, it might even be contended that an understanding of his philosophy would approach an understanding of the developing administrative philosophy of the last quarter century, thus throwing light upon a good deal of the American governmental scene.

"So far as administration decisions are concerned, it would seem that if this headless fourth branch has a head, it must be the Supreme Court." [2] Justice Jackson's description of administration as a fourth branch of government was not new nor was his recognition of the fact that the Supreme Court had to be the directing force above that branch particularly startling. He was not trying to enunciate a new theory; he was merely stating a commonplace. The trouble with such commonplaces is that they often obscure the very real difficulties that do occur when the Supreme Court tries to exercise supervisory power. Justice Frankfurter, since the days when he taught administrative law at Harvard, has been stressing the point that the Supreme Court, because of its very nature, could not oversee all action. Attitudes that were conducive to individual and group rights had to be made part of the creed of administration itself. The first task was to make administration responsible for its own actions; the second was to make courts accept their limited but important role. Only after these feats were accomplished could the courts be effective in their anatomical function of being heads for the headless fourth branch.

One day when hearing a tax case argued, Justice Frankfurter leaned back in his chair and asked counsel, "And what is your philosophy of administrative law?" [3] Perhaps fortunately, in view of the time limit set for argument, his question went unanswered. The question, however, was quite typical of the questioner. Unless administrative agencies can produce rational arguments for

Justice Frankfurter and Administrative Law," *Yale Law Journal*, LXVII (December, 1957), pp. 240–65; Bernard Schwartz, "The Administrative World of Mr. Justice Frankfurter," *Yale Law Journal*, XLIX (June, 1950), pp. 1228–65.

[2] Robert Jackson, *The Supreme Court in the American System of Government* (Cambridge, Mass.: Harvard University Press, 1955), p. 48.

[3] See Alpheus T. Mason, *Harlan Fiske Stone* (New York: The Viking Press, Inc., 1956), p. 603.

their existence and exercise of power, they cannot expect other agencies of government, and particularly the courts, to respect or tolerate them. Justice Frankfurter had his own philosophy of administration, which he tried to impart to his young men who went to Washington. One of the cardinal tenets of this philosophy was that "although the administrative process has had a different development and pursues somewhat different ways from those of the courts, they are to be deemed collaborative instrumentalities of justice and appropriate independence of each should be respected by the other." [4] Courts and agencies should compliment, not contradict, one another.

The Justice has been interested in all aspects of administrative functioning. With his background and training, the legal and philosophic side has held the most interest for him. In 1927 he wrote that "in administrative law we are dealing pre-eminently with law in the making; with fluid tendencies and tentative traditions. Here we must be especially wary against the danger of premature synthesis, of sterile generalizations unnourished by the realities of 'law in action.' " [5] Premature syntheses were to be avoided because they would stultify the growing capacity of administrative agencies to assume their peculiar and particular responsibilities. Administration was reprimanded for its tendency to copy inapplicable legal concepts and procedures. Because administrative law was "law in action," it had to fashion its own tools. Its real strength was its adaptability. It would only dissipate this strength by trying to manipulate unsuited concepts and procedures. Administrative law was free and yet confined at the same time. Its confinement came from the fact that, while it did not have to use any predefined rules, it nevertheless had to provide the same protection for individual and group rights as did the normative legal order. These were Frankfurter's views as a scholar. They have been translated into his votes on the Supreme Court. He has insisted that transplanting judicial procedures onto administrative agencies is not wise. The specific interests entrusted to an agency, its history, structures, or enveloping environ-

---

[4] United States v. Morgan, 313 U.S. 409, 422 (1941).

[5] Felix Frankfurter, "The Task of Administrative Law," *University of Pennsylvania Law Review*, LXXV (May, 1927), 619.

ment are apt to preclude the transplant from taking root. There has, however, been a growing insistence on his part that whatever the administrative procedure chosen, it does provide substantially the same protection that would be given by judicial procedure.

The main function of administration is to provide flexibility denied courts in dealing with problems of a complex yet vital nature. Just as administration must be familiarized with its strengths and weaknesses, so courts must come to accept the fact that they are not all-powerful and that administrative agencies and tribunals are here to stay. Such acceptance does not mean that courts become "administrative adjuncts" or "automata carrying out the wishes of the administrative agency." [6] They continue their own independent existence but simply become more attuned to the fact that certain specialized factors have to be taken into account. The factor of expertise is perhaps the most obvious and important.

Because "problems of law became problems of administration," Professor Frankfurter wrote, "new instruments for expertness and precision were needed. Law had to meet the demands of the age of specialization." [7] The specialist, the expert, the professional administrator came to assume new prominence and their skills became the skills that would shape the future. During his first few years on the Court, Justice Frankfurter emphasized this point again and again. Indeed, many of his best-known opinions stand out for their discussions of the role of expertise in helping to bring about responsible administration.[8]

In decentralizing responsibility within a democracy, courts were warned not to interfere with legislative policy. Any reasonable recommendations emanating from the experts must weigh heavily with courts, for the latter can only, as in their dealings with the legislature, deny action without being able to fashion an

[6] Penfield v. Securities and Exchange Commission, 300 U.S. 585, 604 (1947).

[7] Felix Frankfurter and James Landis, *The Business of the Supreme Court* (New York: The Macmillan Co., 1927), p. 146.

[8] Rochester Telephone Corp. v. United States, 307 U.S. 125 (1939); Federal Communications Commission v. Pottsville Broadcasting Co., 309 U.S. 134 (1940); Phelps Dodge Corp. v. National Labor Relations Board, 313 U.S. 177 (1941); Scripps-Howard Radio Inc. v. Federal Communications Commission, 316 U.S. 4 (1942).

acceptable alternative. Expertise and specialization are thus a very necessary part of the division of labor that underlies the whole theory of decentralization and dispersal of control.

On more than one occasion critics of Justice Frankfurter, both on and off the bench, have charged that he has not paid the deference to expertise that he professes. Throughout the twenty years that Frankfurter has been on the Court, there is no doubt that his votes have not always followed his speeches. In one of his early opinions, however, he gave a clue as to when a claim of expertise would not be enough to validate administrative action. His dissent in Federal Power Commission v. Hope Natural Gas Company [9] directs itself to this point. "Expertise is a rational process and a rational process implies expressed reasons for judgment. It will little advance the public interest to [encourage] conscious obscurity or confusion in reaching a result, on the assumption that so long as the result appears harmless its basis is irrelevant." [10] In a different context, Frankfurter told his colleagues that "Courts can fulfill their responsibility in a democratic society only to the extent that they succeed in shaping their judgments by rational standards, and rational standards are both impersonal and communicative." [11] Therefore, in asking the experts in administrative agencies to spell out in complete detail the bases for their findings, he is asking of them no more than he requires of courts proper. No question of their competence need be involved.

The judiciary in its opinions has to justify its exercise of supervisory power over legislative or administrative actions. What Frankfurter primarily requires is that administrative agencies in their findings and orders show that they too are working within the confines of the congressional statutory framework that created them in the first place. Once this is done, technical rulings go largely unchallenged. Beyond the immediate necessity of establishing title to subject matter, there is a second imperative behind demanding clarity in statement. If administration does

[9] 320 U.S. 591 (1944).
[10] *Ibid.*, p. 627.
[11] American Federation of Labor v. American Sash and Door Co., 335 U.S. 538, 557 (1949).

not fulfill its duty of laying out findings and the evidence gathered to support such findings, courts in their opinions must undertake such a task, for it is inherent in due process that the parties moved against understand exactly the reasons for administrative rulings. An integral segment of Justice Frankfurter's theory of decentralization is that the legislature should not place upon the courts duties that they cannot possibly fulfill. Likewise, it is an imposition for the courts to have administration burden them with chores from which they should be protected. As he said in a controversy involving railroad rates,

> When regard is had for the complicated technical nature of the problems and voluminousness of the records in the important cases that come before the Commission, a fair discharge of its function precludes casting upon a reviewing court the task of quarrying through a record to find for itself adequate evidence to permit effectuation of orders of the Commission.[12]

Unlike the lower courts, which also deal in materials familiar to the average lawyer or jurist, administrative agencies go far afield from known legal terrain. Unless the agency gives aid to the Court in explaining its highly technical materials, the Court will be left with the formal power to give or withhold assent, but in reality they will have their important supervisory function curtailed. For someone as sensitive to the prestige of courts as is Frankfurter, this indirect whittling away of power is unthinkable.

His recognition of the administrative process as a necessary adjunct to democratic government holds a central place in his judicial philosophy. His insistence that judicial review of administrative action be severely limited is equally basic. This is so because, "to the extent that a federal court is authorized to review an administrative act, there is superimposed upon the enforcement of legislative policy through administrative control a different process from that out of which administrative action under review ensued."[13] Technical rules that work well enough under a unified command may, when taken out of their environ-

[12] Denver & Rio Grande W.R. Co. v. Union Pacific Rail Co., 351 U.S. 321, 340 (1956).

[13] Federal Communications Commission v. Pottsville Broadcasting Co., 309 U.S. 134, 141 (1940).

ment, tend to stifle legislative power as exercised by a designated agency. Courts should only review administrative action under express congressional authorization. Statutory provisions granting review must be beyond question. There can be no implied grant; it must be explicitly stated.

While Frankfurter has rejected any implied congressional authorization and has advocated a like course for the Court, many of his brethren have not adopted a similar attitude. Reflecting activist tendencies, they have found as much authorization for review in the silence of Congress as they have found when Congress spoke. They argue that there are basic principles of our law that must be respected by administration and that it is up to the Court to exact such respect. One may wonder whether, in the light of the Frankfurter and activist positions on "basic principles" inherent in due process of law, either side is entirely consistent. In reviewing administration action, Frankfurter demands explicit provisions upon which to work; in dealing with the Fifth or Fourteenth Amendment he rejects absolute infusion of the specific provisions of the Bill of Rights. The activists merely reverse the process. These dual positions of both parties can be reconciled only by recognizing that each has a totally different conception of the role of the judiciary in democratic government.

Overemphasis on Frankfurter's insistence on authorization for review tends to distort the picture. Once the Court's competence has been established, he does not think the judging process automatic nor the end result foreclosed. There are too many impalpable factors involved to give any definite content to any theory of judicial review. There is a good deal of ad hocness in the relation of the Supreme Court to administrative agencies. Claiming that "since the precise way in which courts interfere with agency findings cannot be imprisoned within any form of words, new formulas attempting to rephrase the old are not likely to be more helpful than the old," the Justice has gone on to say that "there are no talismanic words that can avoid the process of judgment. The difficulty is that we cannot escape, in relation to this problem, the use of undefined defining words." [14]

[14] Universal Camera Corp. v. National Labor Relations Board, 340 U.S. 474, 489 (1951).

Judicial review of administrative action is an evolving concept. Its finished contours have not and cannot be put down. Old doctrines are discarded while new ideas take on life.

One of Justice Frankfurter's very first opinions, Rochester Telephone Corporation v. United States,[15] laid to rest the "negative order" doctrine. A negative order has been defined by the Court as one

> which does not command the carrier to do, or to refrain from doing anything; which does not grant or withhold any authority, privilege or license; which does not extend or abridge any power or facility; which does not subject the carrier to any liability, civil or criminal; which does not change the carrier's existing or future status or condition; which does not determine any right or obligation.[16]

If such an administrative order was involved, the Court refused review. Calling this doctrine "obfuscating," Justice Frankfurter in the Rochester case made it plain that the availability of review in any given case no longer depended upon the form of order. On the surface it appeared that the Justice, who was most anxious to limit the breadth of judicial review, was extending an open invitation for its extension. Such was not true, however, for Frankfurter was primarily concerned with the proper allocation of power between administration and the courts.

He has always insisted that, as courts must have their competence granted by Congress before administrative action could be reviewed, standing to challenge such action could only be gained by express statutory statement. In the case under discussion, he thought that persons who had duly been given such standing were being denied access to judicial review merely by an outmoded formulation of the Court. Thus the negative order doctrine had to fall. His opinion showed quite distinctly the interrelation of two of his main concerns. Maintaining the integrity of administration meant that it was not to be interfered with unless Congress so ordered. But maintaining the integrity of the Court's jurisdiction through exercising judicial review

---

[15] 307 U.S. 125 (1939).

[16] United States v. Los Angeles & Salt Lake Rail Co., 273 U.S. 299, 309–310 (1927).

when granted was equally important and in this instance took precedence. Legislation leads to a right of challenge; the concept of standing is but part of a larger case or controversy issue; establishment of a case or controversy determines whether judicial power can come into play; identifying the area of judicial power is merely identifying one of the areas created by the separation of powers doctrine; and separation of powers is the external manifestation of decentralization and dispersal of control, which are necessary in the United States. Stated in this fashion, the hierarchical nature of Justice Frankfurter's thought becomes evident.

When the Rochester decision was handed down, there was some speculation that the prime motivation for the abandonment of the negative order doctrine came from a desire to have greater leeway in correcting hardships that might stem from administrative action. Some members of the Court might have preferred to read the opinion that way, but Justice Frankfurter did not. Solely mitigating hardship was not the Court's concern. Some definite legal right had to be infringed before judicial power for correction was available. He quickly established this point with considerable force: ". . . to slide from recognition of a hardship to assertion of jurisdiction is once more to assume that only the courts are the guardians of the rights and liberties of the people." [17] Availability of judicial review could not be made to depend on the justices' sensibilities. Even when review was available in theory, it could not be used until irreparable or immediate harm was threatened. A definite legal right had to be involved. This is a harsh position and in many respects Justice Frankfurter has not always been as harsh in action as he has been in theory. The theoretical statement on the availability of review, however, is completely in harmony with the rest of his judicial philosophy.

Some of the sternness has been tempered with the passage of the Administrative Procedure Act of 1946. Since Congress has seen fit to extend the scope of judicial review of administrative actions, Justice Frankfurter wrote, with what seemed to be a sense of relief, "the Administrative Procedure Act should be treated as a

[17] Columbia Broadcasting System v. United States, 316 U.S. 407, 446 (1942).

far-reaching remedial measure affording ready access to courts for those who claim that the administrative process, once it has come to rest, has disregarded judicially enforceable rights." [18] It is perhaps well that Congress was thus able to reassure Justice Frankfurter and allow his conscience to remain clear while exercising wider reviewing powers. Although his hesitation to interfere with administrative competence is eminently praiseworthy, it does increase the danger that if the Court does not review, absolutely no review at all will be available.

While he has previously been much concerned over preventing personal conceptions of fairness from becoming the basis for review, he has also been aware that for administrative agencies themselves, "determination of what is 'fair and equitable' calls for the application of ethical standards to particular sets of facts." [19] Since these standards were not static, an agency was not bound by settled judicial precedents in evolving its concepts of fairness and equity. Here again was one of the strengths of administration coming to the fore—the ability flexibly to apply concepts of fairness and justice in fashioning its remedies or policies for current situations. But even for administrative agencies, fairness and equity alone were not enough. Factual justification must also be present.[20]

Since judicial review is predicated upon Justice Frankfurter's theory of decentralization and dispersal of competence and its corollary proposition that responsibility for actions must be attributed to the various units of government, his insistence on administrative finality, before judicial intervention, comes as no surprise. He feels that "for purposes of appellate procedure, finality . . . is not a technical conception of temporal or physical termination. It is the means for achieving a healthy legal system." [21] In order to have finality, administrative remedies must be exhausted. Unhesitatingly, he has fought against the abandonment of the exhaustion rule.[22]

[18] Heikkila v. Barber, 345 U.S. 229, 238 (1953).

[19] Security and Exchange Commission v. Chenery Corp., 318 U.S. 80, 89 (1943).

[20] See the second Chenery case, Security and Exchange Commission v. Chenery Corp., 332 U.S. 194 (1947).

[21] Cobbledick v. United States, 309 U.S. 324, 326 (1940).

[22] See Columbia Broadcasting System v. United States, 316 U.S. 407, 446 (1942).

Such a self-denying ordinance for the judiciary implies a very circumscribed—some would term it abject—attitude toward congressional grants of power to administration. Justice Frankfurter has written no opinions directly indicating the lenience he would accord legislative delegation of power. Probably a wide allowance would be approved. "Necessity . . . fixes a point beyond which it is unreasonable and impractical to compel Congress to prescribe rules; it then becomes constitutionally sufficient if Congress clearly delineates the general policy, the public agency which is to apply it, and the boundaries of this delegated power." [23] Freedom and trust for administrative agencies also bring obligations. First and foremost, since the enabling legislation of Congress may be broad in scope, they must stay within the standards created thereby. Procedures may take due account of administrative needs, but they cannot be used as excuses for not complying with congressional and judicial standards. For instance, the elements that guarantee a fair hearing in administration must be those encompassed within the elements that guide courts in ruling on due process. In the last several terms Justice Frankfurter has become more and more insistent on this point.

The Justice also vehemently dislikes the constitutional-jurisdictional fact doctrine enunciated in Crowell v. Benson.[24] The classic distinction between law and fact forms an integral part of his philosophy. The Crowell doctrine to his mind completely distorts this distinction, allowing the Court to turn into legal issues what are normally factual determinations. By this twist of words the Court thus may assume jurisdiction over administrative actions and rule directly on the validity of administrative findings. For Justice Frankfurter, " 'jurisdiction' competes with 'right' as one of the most deceptive of legal pitfalls. The opinions in Crowell v. Benson," he has written, "bear unedifying testimony of the morass into which one is led in working out problems of judicial review over administrative decisions by loose talk about jurisdiction." [25] When legal rights are truly involved, he is one of the first to de-

[23] American Power & Light Co. v. Security and Exchange Commission, 329 U.S. 90, 101 (1946).
[24] 285 U.S. 22 (1932).
[25] City of Yonkers v. United States, 320 U.S. 685, 695 (1944).

mand wide judicial review. Otherwise, he feels that it is best for the Court to exercise limited review under the dictates of the "substantial evidence" rule.

To sum up, Justice Frankfurter's view of the relation between courts and administration is conditioned by his more complete theory that competence should be decentralized and dispersed in a democracy. He has not become disillusioned by the obvious faults of administration. No branch of government ever completely fulfills its theoretical role. As long as an attempt is made to approach the theoretically perfect, the Justice is satisfied. Moreover, Frankfurter, in trying to ascertain the proper relationship between judicial and administrative power, is as interested in the former as he is in the latter. He wants to define the role of courts within a democratic society and in order to do this he must define the roles of other agencies. To avoid absolute positions, which might later prove untenable, he has gone out of his way to forego broad constitutional rulings on the power of administration. He prefers to deal with particular situations through specific holdings. He does not start with a bias in favor of judicial review, but, when Congress makes plain its desire to have the judiciary supervise, he does not side-step the responsibility. Indeed, in recent years, he has been more willing than some other members of the Court to find directives for judicial review in congressional enactments. Utilizing the concept of due process to absorb the strictly legal doctrines of *res judicata* and *stare decisis*, he had made administration mindful of its responsibilities to the present and to the future. Upholding administrative discretion to the limit, he has faltered in his admiration for the "fourth branch" of government only when it has collided with the lower courts, another of his intense interests.

II

Maintaining the integrity of the lower courts, and especially those in the federal system, has been one of Justice Frankfurter's deepest concerns. Even before going on the Supreme Court he evidenced, in his books and articles, an awareness that, however excellent the job that the Court itself was doing, it of necessity relied heavily upon the wisdom of the lower courts. Two factors conditioned all of the federal judiciary acts—that the United States was a federation and that it covered a continent. In whatever manner Congress dealt with these issues, the Supreme Court remained the vital center of all judicial activity. Therefore, while relying on the lower courts, it also largely determined the mode in which they worked. It set the standards of judicial conduct, especially for the federal hierarchy. "In so doing it acts less as an organ of technical law than as exemplar of the highest ethical sense realizable through political institutions. What is decisive is the Court's feeling for the integrity of the judicial process." [26] These were the views of Harvard's Frankfurter in 1933; his opinions for the Court reiterate the same philosophy. One thing is clear. The Justice considers his supervisory power with respect to the lower federal courts different from that exercised over state courts. His position is most clearly articulated in cases involving review of criminal trials held under federal auspices.

He begins with a disposition favorable toward lower federal judges. As he said in one of his very first opinions for the Court in 1939, "Such a system as ours must . . . rely on the learning, good sense, fairness and courage of federal trial judges." [27] As with administrative agencies, the lower courts, having been granted a great deal of freedom in their actions, should feel responsible for the way in which their power is exercised. While the Supreme Court can only require of state courts that they enforce "fundamental principles of liberty and justice" through the Fourteenth Amendment, its role in relation to the federal courts is not thus constitutionally circumscribed.

> Judicial supervision of the administration of criminal justice in the federal courts implies the duty of establishing and maintaining civilized standards of procedure and evidence. Such standards are not satisfied merely by observance of those minimal historic safe-

[26] Felix Frankfurter and James Landis, "The Supreme Court at October Term, 1932," *Harvard Law Review*, xlviii (December, 1933), 277.
[27] Nardone v. United States, 308 U.S. 338, 342.

guards for securing trial by reason which are summarized as "due process of law" and below which we reach what is really trial by force.[28]

Federal justice cannot rely on minimal historic safeguards; it had to pass beyond this point to a full protection of individual and corporate rights. But, and here is the important element, the Supreme Court cannot provide such protection by itself. The lower federal judges have to co-operate.

In recent proposals to have the Judicial Conference change the rules of criminal procedure, Justice Frankfurter was much against the Supreme Court justices participating in any such venture. "The Justices have become necessarily removed from direct, day-to-day contact with trials in the district courts. To that extent they are largely denied the first hand opportunities for realizing vividly what rules of procedure are best calculated to promote the largest measure of justice." [29] Even in the federal courts, the High Tribunal can but interpose a veto on flagrant violations. Otherwise, it must allow the lower tribunals to work out their own destinies on the basis of rules instigated and promulgated by members thereof.

While lower federal judges are responsible for their conduct and cannot shirk the praise or blame that stems from such conduct, other general circumstances also have to be taken into account. Courts of law are not the only instruments of adjustment for the contending forces within society. The range of their authority and, indeed, even their structure, is determined to a large extent by contemporary considerations. Since the Supreme Court has become the focus of national attention, the vital functions that the lower courts perform are often overlooked by the public. To compensate for this oversight, Justice Frankfurter's opinions often allude to and uphold the prerogatives of the lesser tribunals of the federal hierarchy. These tribunals must gain recognition in their own right. Final appeal to the Supreme Court, while necessary in certain instances, will not encourage a healthy judiciary and may even prove deleterious to the Supreme Court itself.

[28] McNabb v. United States, 318 U.S. 332, 340 (1943).
[29] *New York Times*, May 12, 1958.

Equally undesirable is the effect, however insidious, upon Courts of Appeal. If, barring only exceptional cases, they are to be deemed final courts of appeals, consciousness of such responsibility will elicit in them, assuming they are manned by judges fit for their tasks, the qualities appropriate for such responsibility.[30]

"Courts of Appeal are human institutions," but, unless some abusive excess of discretion is evident in the record, institutional foibles must be tolerated. For the Supreme Court needlessly to rebuke lower federal judges weakens the entire judiciary.

Even in a sensitive area affecting foreign relations, Justice Frankfurter has not hesitated to uphold the powers of the lower courts. When foreign nations seek standing to sue in American courts, ticklish issues of international prestige often become involved, and the Supreme Court is pressed to assume immediate jurisdiction. While the Court relies heavily on State Department advice in such matters, when indefinite advice is forthcoming, Justice Frankfurter prefers that regular channels be followed before the Court takes a case. As he said in *Ex parte* Republic of Peru, "To require a foreign state to seek relief in an orderly fashion through the circuit court of appeals can imply an indifference to the dignity of a sister nation only on the assumption that circuit courts of appeals are not courts of great authority." [31] He was quick to add that our system presupposes the contrary.

The Justice has amply demonstrated his faith in the competence of the lower federal courts. As with administration, such a faith does not justify any or all actions that these tribunals may wish to take. On matters of criminal procedure, the lower courts must take the initiative in promoting high standards. The Supreme Court, however, remains the ultimate arbitor on questions of responsibility. When the lower courts seek to exceed their power through the use of such writs as injunction or habeas corpus, the High Tribunal must call a halt. When a circuit court judge does not follow the distinction between "law" and "fact" and attempts to exercise independent judgment on facts as though he were sitting in a district court, he is called to account. There are cer-

[30] National Labor Relations Board v. Mexia Textile Mills, 339 U.S. 563, 574 (1950).
[31] 318 U.S. 578, 602 (1943).

tain institutional requirements for lower courts, both federal and state. These requirements parallel demands made upon administrative agencies and stem far back into Frankfurter's writings as a teacher. Explaining the Judiciary Act of 1925, he thought it extremely important that "carefully framed findings by the lower courts should serve as the foundation for review, leaving for the Supreme Court the ascertainment of principles governing authenticated facts, the accommodation between conflicting principles, and the adaptation of old principles to new situations." [32] In his book on the business of the Court, considerable space was given to explaining why the justices should not have to disentangle confused testimony or to pass on questions of evidence. These things were for the lower courts. Like emphases have reappeared in the Justice's opinions.

In addition to institutional requirements for the federal judiciary there are personal requirements of equal importance. Often tucked away in the midst of his opinions are little essays on the need for federal judges to remain above reproach personally and in the conduct of their official business. In Sacher v. United States [33] Justice Frankfurter was one of the dissenters from the majority, holding that Judge Harold Medina could summarily punish for contempt lawyers representing the thirteen Communist leaders in the Dennis case.[34] He felt that Judge Medina had not shown himself completely objective and therefore should have disqualified himself from deciding guilt and punishment. The Sacher dissents have been called "the most severe scolding for judicial misbehavior ever given a lower federal judge by a bloc of Supreme Court Justices." John P. Frank thought "the rebuke was all the more striking because its most comprehensive statement was by Justice Frankfurter, noted for his almost extreme courtesy to the lower federal bench." [35] In recent years one federal judge, smarting under a verbal spanking administered by

[32] Felix Frankfurter, "The Judiciary Act of 1925," *Harvard Law Review,* XLII (November, 1928), 23.

[33] 343 U.S. 1 (1952).

[34] Dennis v. United States, 341 U.S. 494 (1951).

[35] John P. Frank, "The United States Supreme Court, 1951–52," *University of Chicago Law Review,* XX (August, 1952), 43.

Justice Frankfurter, spoke out against the latter's action on the bench.

District Judge Alexander Holtzoff of the District of Columbia was apparently quite annoyed that the Supreme Court did not approve of his use of the summary contempt power, and he was quite indignant over the reprimand that Frankfurter had administered for the majority of the Court.[36] In one of his opinions rendered soon thereafter, he, in turn, upbraided Frankfurter for the many times and the many ways in which he thought the Justice was overruling previous decisions without explicitly mentioning them.[37] He also complained bitterly about disregard of the principle of *stare decisis* and abandonment of precedents. Some questions can be raised about Holtzoff's interpretation of Frankfurter's devotion to *stare decisis*. In any event, Justice Frankfurter has probably found that teaching etiquette to lower court judges can at times be painful. However, given his deep insistence on personal integrity for the federal judiciary, there is little probability that in the future he will forego his instruction.

The Supreme Court and other courts in the federal hierarchy are joined by certain other tribunals established under general legislative power and not covered by Article 3 of the Constitution. At one time or another these tribunals have included those devoted to patent problems, tax litigation, and cases growing out of interstate commerce. While the personnel requirements for these courts are the same as those applicable to regular federal courts, Justice Frankfurter combines in his treatment of them attitudes previously noted as being directed to the administrative agencies and lower courts. He is impressed with the expertise they display. "To hold that . . . this Court, must make an independent examination of the meaning of every word of tax legislation, no matter whether the words express accounting, business or other conceptions peculiarly within the special competence of the Tax Court, is to sacrifice the effectiveness of the judicial scheme designed by Congress . . . ."[38] Likewise he feels that appellate court intervention will deprive these special courts of confidence

---

[36] Offutt v. United States, 348 U.S. 11 (1954).

[37] Union Producing Co. v. Federal Power Commission, 127 F. Supp. 88, 93 (1954).

[38] Bingham's Trust v. Comm. Internal Revenue, 325 U.S. 365, 380 (1945).

in their own abilities and thus psychologically will destroy their reason for being. In his treatment of legislative courts, with the very important exception of courts martial, Justice Frankfurter shows a considerable tendency to accept them as reliable partners in his campaign to carry out decentralization of function.

III

In one of his opinions Justice Frankfurter said somewhat hopefully that "an Act for the elimination of diversity jurisdiction could fairly be called an Act for the relief of the federal courts." [39] His preoccupation with ridding the federal judiciary of cases arising solely from diversity jurisdiction is one of long standing. Back in 1927 he had thought that reducing the range of business of federal courts was extremely necessary and one of the prime ways in which to relieve the overburdening then visible was to refuse to hear arguments based on diversity of citizenship.[40] Litigation of essentially a federal nature was growing by leaps and bounds. State judicial reforms were making those courts more reliable. The historic reasons for diversity jurisdiction were no longer valid. Therefore it seemed best, for both state and federal courts, to do away with this category of cases. Each judicial hierarchy would consequently fulfill the functions for which it was truly suited and thus responsible administration of justice would ensue. Justice Frankfurter's desire to have diversity jurisdiction abandoned has not been fulfilled, but this desire is a very natural accessory to his judicial philosophy with its veneration of the federal hierarchy and its growing appreciation of the worth of state judicial power.[41]

[39] National Mutual Insurance Co. v. Tidewater Trade Co., 337 U.S. 582, 651 (1949).

[40] See Frankfurter and Landis, *The Business of the Supreme Court.*

[41] For an excellent appraisal of Justice Frankfurter's thought on judicial power, see Wallace Mendelson, "Mr. Justice Frankfurter and the Distribution of Judicial Power in the United States," *Midwest Journal of Political Science,* II (February, 1958), 40–61. Cf. Felix Frankfurter, "Distribution of Judicial Power Between Courts of the United States and Courts of the States," *Cornell Law Quarterly,* XIII (June, 1928), 499–530.

Professor Frankfurter in 1929 wrote an article for the *New Republic* entitled "Federal Courts" [42] in which he expressed the view that the distribution of judicial power between nation and states was perhaps the most delicate of all recurring problems that had to be faced. Geographical dispersion of function assumes a place second to none in his philosophy. In his treatment of state courts there is a coalescence of his views on geographical dispersion with his general veneration of the judicial process. The role of the Supreme Court is narrowly limited in reviewing state court action. Only in guaranteeing substantive and procedural due process, and then mostly in criminal cases, does the Justice feel that interference with state competence is warranted. Even here care must be taken before attributing to him overzealousness for Supreme Court action. Once again, more than one reason is apparent. State courts should be respected; the Supreme Court should not allow itself to be drawn away from its primary responsibilities by undertaking tasks for which it is not suited.

Back in 1932 Frankfurter noted that "the Court, though it will continue to act with hesitation, will not suffer, in its own scathing phrase, 'judicial murder.' " This comment was on the Court's handling of the Scottsborro case, Powell v. Alabama.[43] But he also felt that "in no sense is the Supreme Court a general tribunal for the correction of criminal errors. . . . On a continent peopled by 120,000,000 that would be an impossible task; in a federal system it could be a function debilitating to the responsibility of state and local agencies." [44] Such debilitation was to be avoided at all costs. As he wrote in a case late in 1959, "something that thus goes to the very structure of our federal system in its distribution of power between the United States and the States is not a mere bit of red tape to be cut, on the assumption that this Court has general discretion to see justice done." [45] On procedural matters Justice Frankfurter has been even stauncher in his sup-

---

[42] Felix Frankfurter, "Federal Courts," *New Republic*, LVIII (April 24, 1929), pp. 273–74.
[43] 287 U.S. 45 (1932).
[44] *New York Times*, November 13, 1932.
[45] Irvin v. Doud, 359 U.S. 408.

port of the states. Even though state court methods and procedures may appear outmoded, awkward, or finicky, "this Court is powerless to deny a State the right to have the kind of judicial system it chooses and to administer that system in its own way." [46] This, of course, was stated with the provisions that no federal claims were stifled.

Justice Frankfurter, on one of the first days in which he was a member of the Court, was questioning a lawyer as to the procedures for getting a case to the Court. "How did you get here?" he quizzed. Apparently quite flustered, counsel replied, "I came in on the B. & O." [47] This certainly was not the explanation expected. The initial question of the Justice did, however, highlight one of his main interests. He is always at some pains to discover whether the Supreme Court's jurisdiction has been properly invoked, and this is especially true when a question of federal-state judicial relations is involved. He will not be lulled into having federal courts adjudicate cases that are basically local in nature through the mere claim of a litigant that a federal right has been violated. Violation has to be conclusively demonstrated. Federal courts cannot intervene on the basis of a federal right when state courts have not made any ruling on the issue. Even in the event that a valid federal question is present, state court remedies must be exhausted before the federal courts intervene. Justice Frankfurter does not, however, flinch from upsetting state court procedures and remedies when it is evident that they are being used to circumvent rather than to aid the course of law. All things considered, one cannot help but agree with Wallace Mendelson that within the broad range of discretion that Congress has left to the courts, "Mr. Justice Frankfurter has drawn lines for a modus vivendi that would leave to state judges the broadest range of competence consistent with full respect for national interests." [48]

[46] Staub v. Baxley, 355 U.S. 313, 329 (1958).

[47] See Fred Rodell, "Felix Frankfurter—Conservative," *Harpers*, CLXXXIII (October, 1941), 456–57.

[48] Mendelson, "Mr. Justice Frankfurter and the Distribution of Judicial Power," *loc. cit.*, p. 60.

IV

One further topic needs to be mentioned and that is the role of the bar in our system of government. Strictly legal competence relations are not involved, but members of the bar do have functional responsibilities toward administration, the court, and the public. Responsibility rather than prerogative should be the keynote of the lawyer's creed. From the public defender to the Solicitor General, lawyers must be made aware of the fiduciary nature of their profession.

Since membership in the bar is largely governed by state regulations, Justice Frankfurter has been tolerant of obligations imposed by the states in their attempts to ascertain the responsibleness of candidates for admission. During the 1957 Term two cases of interest on this topic were heard and both were decided on the same day, Schware v. Board of Bar Examiners [49] and Konigsberg v. State Bar of California.[50] They involved state requirements that candidates show "good moral character." Frankfurter did not join the Court's opinion in either case, for he thought that even an implied rejection of the conception of moral character for indefiniteness was unwarranted. The basic outline of moral character—a high sense of honor, granite discretion, and observance of fiduciary responsibilities—was readily understood and states should be able to exact it. Justice Black, who wrote the majority opinion in both cases, inserted in his Konigsberg opinion an answer to Justice Frankfurter. He thought little of the term "good moral character," even though states had used it for many years. "Such a vague qualification, which is easily adapted to fit personal views and predelictions, can be a dangerous instrument for arbitrary and discriminatory denial of the right to practice law." [51]

As is true with so many of these issues, there was no disagree-

---

[49] 353 U.S. 232.
[50] 353 U.S. 252.
[51] *Ibid.*, p. 263.

ment between Black and Frankfurter on the question whether a state could establish some criterion for admission. Disagreement came over giving substance to the criterion. Justice Black rightly thought that the prejudices of the definer of necessity entered the picture. What Frankfurter was trying to do was to make sure that these were not the prejudices of the Supreme Court. Since the bar must serve the state, the latter must be able to judge the qualifications of its servants. Only when excessively harsh and unreasonable conditions are imposed is it up to the Supreme Court to interfere.

While the states are primarily responsible for the character of the bar, all units of government have a right to make certain demands upon the legal profession. The state and federal courts are, of course, most directly concerned. As a scholar, Frankfurter complained that the empiricism characteristic of Anglo-American lawyers prevented them from systematically presenting information to the Courts. To remedy this situation the "Brandeis Brief" was evolved.[52] This technique, partly originated by Frankfurter, has continued to find favor in his eyes. Lawyers, by presenting courts with adequate information on all facets of a case and by knowledgeable and relevant arguments on the issues involved, can do much to aid the judiciary in fulfilling its responsibilities. At the same time they, as lawyers, carry on the vital function of indicating possible lines of development for the legal system. Courtroom performance is probably of some value when basic constitutional issues are at stake, but one may speculate that extensive briefs and records are of even more value. Certainly for the Supreme Court, counsel's arguments in ordinary cases weigh heavier than when great national questions are under consideration. For the bar, then, as for administration and the lower courts, there is a functional relationship with the Supreme Court.

There could be scant disagreement with Justice Frankfurter's opinion that "if lawyers are good, if lawyers have range, if lawyers are true to their functions, then they are what I venture to call

[52] See Marion E. Doro, "The Brandeis Brief," *Vanderbilt Law Review*, xi (June, 1958), 783–800.

experts in relevance." [53] And his reliance on and encouragement of the "Brandeis Brief" as a means of informing the Court would draw few criticisms. But the question can be raised whether, in some instances, lawyers can be experts in relevance when the Brandeis technique is used. When Frankfurter argued before the Court, he presented briefs of over a thousand pages. While the briefs were no doubt very scholarly pieces of work, may it not be that such extreme length defeats its own purposes by making everything and anything relevant information? Justices may be impressed by the massiveness of material gathered; but they are not thereby induced to go through and absorb its content. In the period since the inauguration of the Brandeis brief, judges, and especially Supreme Court justices, may be trapping themselves by demanding too much information.

In other words, they are finding it impossible to deal with all the facts and conflicting precedents and citations given them. They are being forced in many instances almost to the position of having to act on personal predelictions, since they cannot disentangle the vast network of authorities with which they are presented. Justice Frankfurter's desire to cut down on the number of cases that the Supreme Court hears is at least in part conditioned by the fact that lawyers have learned their lessons too well. Sensitive to the reality that only if materials are read and contemplated can they be of any use at all, Justice Frankfurter now finds himself faced with a plethora of information provided by each lawyer for every case and apparently finds it an impossible task to inform himself intelligently from such an abundance. It may well be, consequently, that the Court in the future will have to emphasize extensive briefs only in rare instances, as in establishing the historic meaning of the Fourteenth Amendment for desegregation, while on other occasions warning lawyers that relevance means relevance and not mere accumulation of statistics or citations.

However the Supreme Court works out its difficulties with the bar, one thing is certain. Justice Frankfurter will continue to

[53] Felix Frankfurter, "Personal Ambitions of Judges: Should a Judge Think Beyond the Judicial?" *American Bar Association Journal,* xxxiv (August, 1948), p. 747.

strive for some reasoned workable relation, as he has striven for accommodation between the judiciary and other arms of government. His treatment of administration and the lower courts is predicated upon the pattern of competence that he discerns. This pattern of competence is diffused geographically and decentralized functionally. For competence to remain dispersed, however, requires that the recipients thereof exercise it with understanding and responsibility. Otherwise, by the natural need to fill a vacuum, the Supreme Court will be drawn in, to its own detriment and to the detriment of democratic government. It is to infusing understanding and responsibility, therefore, that Justice Frankfurter has devoted himself in his dealings with administration, lower courts, and the bar.

XIV
The Court between Nation and States

Justice Frankfurter's theory of decentralization and dispersal of control is completed by infusion of a geographic element. He wrote in 1930 that "this element of size is perhaps the single most important fact about our government and its perplexities." [1] In a volume dedicated to studying the demands of modern society upon government, he outlined some of the difficulties that our federal system would face in the decades ahead. In general, the refusal, rather than the inability of state governments to cope with the myriad pressures of industrial life, was one of the causes forcing the federal government to assume greater burdens. Suggesting that perhaps the desire to protect regional interests would reinvigorate the feeling of state responsibility, and that such reinvigoration would be a healthy sign, he recognized that certain services and powers could only be handled in Washington.

[1] Felix Frankfurter, *The Public and Its Government* (New Haven: Yale University Press, 1930), p. 8.

Such a division of labor, while guided by the traditional break-down between delegated and reserved powers, would not be limited by it. A pragmatic division based on day-to-day experience was what was needed. He had seen the destructive tendencies inherent in the too centralized enforcement of prohibition and had spoken against it: "I cannot help but wonder whether those who suggest [centralizing all administration in Washington] have ever had the slightest opportunity to gauge the absorptive power of the federal government in the assumption of increased burdens." [2] This inarticulate fear of absorptive power led him in 1930 to advocate pragmatic-functional division of labor.

Professor Frankfurter thought that the Framers fortunately provided for just such an occurrence, having been aware that for federalism to retain its vitality, "the division of power between states and nation . . . should in the main not be spelled out with particularity, but be derived from the general political conceptions regarding the purposes of the Constitution and their achievement." [3] These views were expressed before the New Deal came into being. Frankfurter probably did not foresee how completely the Nine Old Men would imperil state and federal attempts to deal with the economic crisis, thus triggering the Court Packing plan and leading eventually to the accretion of power in Washington. Questions that he raised in 1930 and before were picked up and amplified after the full impact of the New Deal became visible. He stands as a forerunner of and yet as a present-day participant in the movement that would re-examine the basic premises of federalism in order to retain as much of our traditional system as is feasible.

I

References to the fact that Justice Frankfurter is deeply concerned with maintaining the states as workable units of govern-

[2] Felix Frankfurter, "Enforcement of Prohibition," *New Republic*, xxxiii (January, 1923), 150. Cf. Felix Frankfurter, "National Policy for the Enforcement of Prohibition," *Annals of the American Academy of Political and Social Science*, cix (September, 1923), 193–95.

[3] Frankfurter, *The Public and Its Government*, p. 73.

ment are legion. Hardly a commentator passes up mention of this interest, and the Justice himself reiterates it in his opinions whenever possible. But why such an interest? Beyond his reverence for traditional ways lie other reasons. He is familiar with the pluralist approach to political organization, a familiarity perhaps gained in the early period of his friendship with Harold Laski. Pluralism basically holds that the state, while the most inclusive of all associations, is not the only nor even the prime group through which individual self-realization is reached. Smaller autonomous units must be present in order for a society to be deemed democratic. Frankfurter has absorbed much of this philosophy and has applied it in pure form. He has also exhibited a transcribed version of the pluralist creed in his accommodation of state and national interests, merely substituting states for the smaller autonomous units in the formula. The United States, then, is federalistically plural in outlook and structure. It is partially this dualism that Frankfurter's writings reflect.

His association with Laski probably only brought to fruition his inarticulated philosophic leanings. Growing to maturity when the pragmatism of James and Dewey was setting the tone for an age, Frankfurter could not have avoided, however unconsciously, making some of their teaching his own. In the Justice's opinions praising federalism as the system most adaptable to geographic division of function and competence, various strands of pluralism and pragmatism are interwoven. It is important that the semi-autonomous units known as states be maintained in order that governmental experimentation can be carried on. And for Frankfurter, government means primarily experimentation. Federalism depends upon local experience to provide the answers to local problems. Such an emphasis certainly did not originate with Frankfurter. Indeed, he would be happy to acknowledge an intellectual debt to Holmes and Brandeis on this matter.

While the romanticist would picture a defender of state integrity against the supposed predatory forays of the federal government as a defender of states' rights, the identification would be largely inaccurate. States are important in and of themselves and as areas for the necessary experimentation that may lead to the good society. In addition, however, they provide at a lower level the fluidity that is necessary for unity at the national level. Federalism is one of the devices whereby the tensions of a heterogeneous society can be ameliorated and co-operation can take its place alongside of competition as a unifying force. With but one exception, compromises and adjustments have been worked out without rending the fabric of national life.

A further reason for geographical dispersion is that, to paraphrase Lord Acton, centralization of power tends to corrupt, absolute centralization of power to corrupt absolutely. It has often been charged that Frankfurter has confidence in the disinterestedness and ability of all branches of the government except the judiciary. Such charges would have to be revised to take into account his hesitation about giving to any level of government complete power, no matter how disinterested or able it may prove itself. State power acts as a medicant, keeping the national government from becoming too corrupted or polluted by an overdose of power. This concern for the health of the national government, as well as that of the states, places Frankfurter not in the camp of states' righters but in the circle of those who desire a totally well-integrated body politic.

Fundamentally, this is the rationale behind geographic decentralization of function, competence, and control. In reality, of course, delicate gradations make applying theory to practice a hazardous business. One of Justice Frankfurter's favorite expressions is that "a line has to be drawn" somewhere indicating the difference between permissible or nonpermissible conduct, authorized or unauthorized exercise of power. Nowhere does the line have to be drawn with greater care or more exactness than in this area of state-federal competence relations. Precise formulation of issues and due regard for the present significance of past decisions would help to lessen the contest between centralization and local rule. After he came to the Court, Frankfurter told his brethren that "the autonomous powers of the states are those in the Constitution and not verbal weapons imported into it." [4] In the very difficult task of ruling on state power, constitutional provisions should be the basis for judgment and not the commentary that time has placed upon these provisions. Each case presents

[4] Wisconsin v. J. C. Penny Co., 311 U.S. 435, 444 (1940).

varied circumstances and the demarcation line between permissive and nonpermissive conduct is variously drawn. There are no fixed points. Wherever the line is drawn, it is bound to appear arbitrary judged solely by the bordering cases. Rational considerations must determine where the line is to be placed. Drawing a line is, therefore, an exercise of judgment in each particular case. All that the judiciary must recognize is that the line "must follow some direction of policy, whether rooted in logic or experience. Lines should not be drawn simply for the sake of drawing lines." [5]

II

When Justice Frankfurter took his place on the Supreme Court, many of the most important cases dealing with New Deal legislation had already been litigated. The competence of the national government to shape economic destinies had been largely recognized. Of the important cases dealing with economic issues in the early part of his tenure he wrote the opinion of the Court in only one, the Fair Labor Standard Act case of Kirshbaum v. Walling.[6] Otherwise he acquiesced silently in the majority's vast extension of federal power to all fields and aspects of economic life.[7] By this early display, one would have been justified in assuming that he was a staunch supporter of increasing centralization. However, it is probably true for most of the justices who participated in these decisions that none was concerned with deliberately making a Goliath of the national government; they were instead either motivated by strictly legal competence considerations or by non-legal policy desires to see economic imbalance righted.

Diminution of state power had not been planned. It had come as the consequence and aftermath of interpretations given to federal legislation. The Court since the New Deal has been

[5] Pearce v. Comm. Internal Revenue, 315 U.S. 543, 558 (1942).

[6] 316 U.S. 517 (1942).

[7] See United States v. Darby, 312 U.S. 100 (1941); Wickard v. Filburn, 316 U.S. 517 (1942); Mulford v. Smith, 307 U.S. 38 (1939); Sunshine Anthracite Coal Co. v. Adkins, 310 U.S. 381 (1940); United States v. Appalachian Electric Power Co., 311 U.S. 377 (1941).

criticized for its handling of legislation directed at economic evils, but it must be remembered that the Court inherited many rulings on the statutes it was to apply. The Sherman Act and the Interstate Commerce Act were direct precursors of many New Deal enactments. Tentative approval had already been given much federal regulation. When statutes dealing with every conceivable subject under the sun were added to the vast array already on the books, it is small wonder that an incidental lessening of state competence ensued. Justice Frankfurter has not been entirely happy about the process. Recognizing that it was inevitable that the federal government would move into more fields, he has desired explicit congressional statement when state power was to be displaced. Pre-emption could be a dangerous weapon unless properly controlled. "To hold . . . that paralysis of state power is somehow to be found in the vague implications of the federal . . . enactments, is to encourage slipshodness in draftsmanship and irresponsibility in legislation." [8] Justice Frankfurter is not as apt to think that Congress specifically desires state dislodgment as are some other members of the Court. His general insistence on legislative responsibility becomes even stronger when state powers are under attack.

In 1928 he had written to Justice Stone complimenting him on one of his opinions. The behavior of the Court was worrying the scholar, however. He feared that "the due process clause will be used as an instrument of restriction upon the area of discretionary power of the states over local matters, and whatever may not be susceptible of curbing through the due process clause will be restrained by the requirement of equal protection of the laws." [9] The decade of the 1930's gave ample proof that his fears were well grounded. After he traded his academic gown for the jurist's robe, he found that members of the Court were still using due process and equal protection to invalidate state action. He has called the veto that the Supreme Court exercises over the socio-economic legislation of states through the due process clause the most vulnerable aspect of undue centralization. Not only does it

[8] Cloverleaf Butter Co. v. Patterson, 315 U.S. 148, 178 (1942).
[9] Frankfurter to Stone, June 6, 1928. Quoted in Alpheus T. Mason, *Harlan Fiske Stone* (New York: The Viking Press, Inc., 1956), p. 240.

prevent an increase in social knowledge but it also turns what are really policy determinations into false legal issues by having the Court rule on matters outside its field of special competence. Frankfurter has, of course, joined in striking down state legislation based on due process claims and perhaps at times he has done it merely because of personal notions as to the wisdom or unwisdom of the legislation. On theoretical grounds, however, he has upheld the principle that geographic dispersal of competence and function should not be disturbed. Thus he has approved state schemes for regulation of insurance, liquor, marketing agreements, and prices,[10] against the charge that regulation violated due process of law.

On the whole, claims brought to the Court declaring that equal protection of the laws has been denied have received short shrift from the Justice. They have not warranted the attention given to due process allegations. Equal protection considerations are often tied to schemes of classification used by the states. Frankfurter has been lenient in his treatment of those schemes, thinking that sectional or state practices should be accepted unless a definite infringement of constitutional rights was involved. Equal protection could not be used to force unnecessary conformity. He has warned time and time again that "the equal protection clause was not designed to compel uniformity in the face of difference" [11] and that "the Equal Protection Clause did not write an empty formalism into the Constitution. Deeply embedded traditional ways of carrying out state policy . . . are often tougher and truer law than the dead words of the written text." [12]

Classification of persons, occupations, etc. on a rational basis by state legislatures, while affecting the concept of geographic dispersal of function and control but indirectly, does bring into question state competence, which is tied very closely to the dis-

[10] See, for example, Mayo v. Lakeland Highland Can Co., 309 U.S. 310 (1940); Osborn v. Ozlin, 310 U.S. 53 (1940); Pacific Coast Dairy v. Dept. of Agriculture, 318 U.S. 285 (1943); Johnson v. Yellow Cab Transit Co., 321 U.S. 383 (1944); Rice v. Sante Fe Elevator Corp., 331 U.S. 218 (1947); Algona P. & V. Co. v. Wisconsin Employee Rel. Bd., 336 U.S. 301 (1949).

[11] Whitney v. State Tax Commission, 309 U.S. 530, 542 (1940).

[12] Nashville, Chattanooga and St. Louis Railway v. Browning, 310 U.S. 362, 369 (1940).

persal argument. Early in his judicial career Justice Frankfurter set forth with some bluntness his conception of the equal protection guarantee.

> . . . laws are not abstract propositions. They do not relate to abstract units A, B, and C, but are expressions of policy arising out of specific difficulties, addressed to the attainment of specific ends by the use of specific remedies. The Constitution does not require things which are different in fact or opinion to be treated in law as though they were the same.[13]

The treatment that the equal protection clause should receive would be pragmatic and empirical to the core. As in due process, there are minimal limits below which state action cannot descend and still be acceptable, but the descent has to be judged one step at a time. In this way invalidating state legislation can often be avoided and the pristine geographic division maintained. According to Justice Frankfurter neither due process nor equal protection should be allowed to stifle experimentation within the states that does not run counter to very explicit and expressed constitutional prohibitions—otherwise the real worth of the federal system will be lost.

III

Of all the clauses in the Constitution that have provided the legal bases upon which an adjustment between federal-state functional relations are carried out, those dealing with interstate commerce and taxation are cited most frequently. It is perhaps fitting that Justice Frankfurter's first opinion for the Court, Hale v. Bimco,[14] discussed interference with interstate commerce. Florida had provided that all cement imported into the state should be inspected and that the firms affected pay an inspection fee. No such requirement was set up for Florida producers. The Court struck down the statute as being discriminatory. Ironically, in his debut, Justice Frankfurter thus found himself on the side of those who denied rather than upheld state competence. The

---

[13] Tigner v. Texas, 310 U.S. 141, 147 (1940).
[14] 306 U.S. 375 (1939).

opinion in the Hale case was not very long, barely four pages, but either the issues involved or the fact that he was performing for the first time as a member of the Court intrigued the Justice enough so that on opinion Monday he delivered his initial offering verbatim without looking at any notes.[15]

Frankfurter's interest in issues growing out of the commerce clause has been one of long-standing. As a teacher he wrote a notable volume on *The Commerce Clause Under Marshall, Taney and Waite*. Devoted to a study of the changing patterns of interpretation that the clause had received and to a discussion of the fluctuations in the nation's economic life that motivated such changes, this book may give the fullest account of his own conceptions of this important constitutional provision. Fortunately the Justice has the ability, when he so desires, to condense the essence of material into very limited space. The following quotation amply catches the mood and meaning of his study.

> The history of the commerce clause . . . is the history of imposing artificial patterns upon the play of economic life whereby an accommodation is achieved between the interacting concerns of states and nation. The problems of the commerce clause are problems in this process of accommodation, however different the emphasis or preference of interest, and however diverse the legal devices by which different judges may make these accommodations.[16]

Frankfurter wrote his study on the commerce clause in 1937, scarcely two years before he took his place on the Supreme Court and joined in the statecraft which that body fashioned. For him, any accommodation between nation and states has been premised upon mutual respect growing out of the geographic and functional division of labor.

His 1937 statement of principle is valuable because of its proximity to the time of his appointment and because of the fullness of its nature. But it is merely the culmination and compilation of previous views. Exactly a decade before he had warned

---

[15] See "Frankfurter, J.: His First Opinion," *Baltimore Evening Sun*, March 2, 1939.

[16] Felix Frankfurter, *The Commerce Clause Under Marshall, Taney and Waite* (Chapel Hill: University of North Carolina Press, 1937), pp. 21–22. Cf. Ernest J. Brown, "The Open Economy: Justice Frankfurter and the Position of the Judiciary," *Yale Law Journal*, LXVII (December, 1957), 219–39.

that members of the Supreme Court must be not just statesmen but "industrial statesmen." [17] Wisdom in political adjustment would no longer be enough. An understanding of economic and industrial facts was also necessary. Frankfurter wrote that perhaps no greater responsibility had ever confronted a judicial tribunal, but the responsibility was unavoidable, given the nature of industrialized American life in the twentieth century. The Court had always been faced with the political problems of federalism and the consequent need to protect the integrity of both nation and states. Now it was called upon to arbitrate more subtle conflicts. And again the integrity of both levels of government had to be maintained. After he took his place on the bench, Frankfurter continued to stress the fact that decisions concerning the commerce clause ultimately depend on judgment in balancing considerations as to whether a particular field of legal control could best be cared for by state or national action. No automatic answer in favor of either side was available. When "the requirements of an exclusive nationwide regime" do not have overriding backing in law and fact, "respect for the allowable area within which the forty-eight States may enforce their diverse notions of policy" [18] must be granted.

To make the words "interstate commerce" encompass all aspects of business transactions was to turn the concept into a shibboleth. The geographic division of function and competence that underlay the federal system precluded complete centralization unless the system itself was to be sabotaged. "Scholastic reasoning may prove that no activity is isolated within the boundaries of a single State, but that cannot justify absorption of legislative power by the United States over every activity." [19] In interpreting the interstate commerce clause, Justice Frankfurter has not always avoided the "scholastic reasoning" that he criticized. His voting record could be used either to prove or disprove that he was deeply committed to geographical decentralization and maintenance of the states as useful and necessary units of government. Justice Frankfurter's jurisprudence generally, however, is characterized

[17] Felix Frankfurter and James Landis, *The Business of the Supreme Court* (New York: The Macmillan Co., 1927).

[18] United Mine Workers v. Arkansas Flooring Co., 351 U.S. 62, 76 (1956).

[19] Polish National Alliance v. National Labor Relations Board, 322 U.S. 643, 650 (1944).

by a balance of interest approach. In the weighing of claims of state and national governments under the commerce clause, this approach is visible in one of its most pronounced forms.

Many state claims to competence are put forward under the traditional plea for state police power. Frankfurter has treated this concept as a fertile doctrinal source for accommodation of local interest with those of national importance as included within the rubric of interstate commerce. As the commerce clause is not a static but a dynamic section of the Constitution, so police power, because of the dynamic qualities, eludes attempts at definition. Only a case-by-case treatment can indicate even its broadest contours. Justice Frankfurter has found that "even in matters legal some words and phrases, though very few, approach mathematical symbols and mean substantially the same to all who have occasion to use them. Other law terms like 'police power' are not symbols at all but labels for the results of the whole process of adjudication." [20] The results at which he has arrived in police power litigation show him sympathetic to local responsibility for vast areas of public health and welfare. While the concept has gradually diminished in scope under the impact of problems national in dimension—and some even predict its total demise— it has weathered the storm and remains as a vital ingredient in Justice Frankfurter's recipe for maintaining geographic dispersion of function and control.

Appeals to state police power, while in the finest tradition of American constitutional development, are often last ditch efforts to prevent complete centralization of some activity in Washington or to forestall federal negation of an activity particularly important to a state or local community. Frankfurter is perhaps outstanding in his willingness to heed such appeals. Certainly in his early years on the bench this was so. As the terms have passed, he has become more sensitive to the idea that interstate commerce needed some protection and that automatic appeals to police power arguments would not bring automatic solutions for value clashes.[21]

[20] Felix Frankfurter, "Some Reflections on the Reading of Statutes," *Columbia Law Review*, xlvii (May, 1947), 527–46.

[21] For a discussion of this change in emphasis, see Louis Jaffe, "The Judicial World of Mr. Justice Frankfurter," *Harvard Law Review*, lxii (January, 1949), 395.

IV

Running a close second to the commerce clause as a source of conflict between nation and states are the portions of the Constitution dealing with taxation. Excise, use, and sales taxes have joined with levies on income to present a confusing array of categories under which the theory of taxation is discussed in Supreme Court opinions. Justice Frankfurter certainly is not an expert in the intricacies of tax law and does not write as many opinions in this field as do some of his brethren. He is, however, interested in the philosophy behind the taxing power as this affects competence relations of national and state governments. There should be a general view as to the purposes of taxation and the ends to which the fruits thereof will be used before a ruling can be made on the particular exercise of the power.

Justice Frankfurter had been acquiring such a view many years before he became a member of the Supreme Court:

> Taxation is perhaps the severest testing ground for the objectivity and wisdom of a social thinker. The numerous increases in the cost of society and the extent to which wealth is now represented by intangibles, the profound change in the relation of the individual to government and the resulting widespread insistence on security, are subjecting public finance to the most exacting demands. To balance budgets, to pay for the costs of progressively civilized standards, to safeguard the future and to divide these burdens fairly among different interests in the community, put the utmost strain on the ingenuity of statesmen.[22]

In dealing with federal and state taxation schemes, the Justice has voted for adequate latitude of power. He has been sympathetic to experimentation within constitutional limits. As with the commerce clause, local issues and needs may dictate any number of different types of schemes, each unique and yet each within the bounds of competence. With the nation moving further into the twentieth century, heavier demands have been placed upon

[22] Felix Frankfurter, *Mr. Justice Holmes* (Cambridge, Mass.: Harvard University Press, 1938), p. 42.

all governments. To finance services, revenues must be obtained; to obtain revenue, legislative plans of taxation must be drawn up; to validate these plans, the judiciary must show an understanding of the world in which it operates. Thus runs his reasoning in most taxation cases and thus his motivation for approving most governmental action in this field.

The federal government, through the Sixteenth Amendment and other constitutional provisions, has an obvious advantage over the states in gaining revenue. Unless the states have as much latitude in tapping sources of income as is in any way permissible, they may become captives of Washington. Grants-in-aid programs, while judicially approved, cause many people today to fear that the traditional geographic division of function and competence has already been fatally undermined. Justice Frankfurter is certainly not among the group who fear federal aid to the states on principle, but he is, and has been, concerned to see that state taxing power remains as a source of strength against undue federal financial encroachment. Early in his career on the Court he wrote that "each State of the Union has the same taxing power as an independent government, except insofar as that power has been curtailed by the Federal Constitution." [23] Once again the parellel between treatment of commerce clause cases and those involving taxation becomes evident. When the federal government wishes to replace state competence in gathering revenue, the displacement must be very explicit. It will not do for the Court to say that there is a conflict between state policy and that proclaimed by Congress unless Congress has made the pronouncement unavoidable.

But even the importance of geographic decentralization and of maintaining state taxing power will not excuse action that is clearly violative of some specific federal function. As the commerce and taxation clauses are usually the sources of greatest conflict between state and national authorities, so there can be conflict between the two concepts themselves. The Court can be called upon to decide, not whether some particular area of taxation is foreclosed either to state or national authorities, but whether state taxation interferes with interstate commerce. Jus-

[23] Tax Commission v. Aldrich, 316 U.S. 174, 182 (1942).

tice Frankfurter has made it very plain that "a burden on interstate commerce is none the lighter and no less objectionable because it is imposed by a State under the taxing power rather than
under manifestations of police power in the conventional sense." [24]
His dispersal of control theory makes overruling state claims difficult; yet when particular occasions arise, his personal preferences
fall before the greater claims of national competence. The theory
of intergovernmental tax immunity has also provided him some
basis for calling the states to account. States, in their zeal to
garner all revenue possible, have often tried to bring within their
taxing powers operations that were performed under the auspices
of the federal government and that therefore should have remained immune.[25] Valid intergovernmental tax immunity, especially for the national government, represents for him a very important part of our federal system.

Justice Frankfurter has recognized the provisional nature of all
attempts completely to define spheres of competence. Commerce
and taxation are not terms like "jury of twelve" "bill of attainder," which can be given a specific meaning. He is reluctant
to admit that individual philosophic leanings have such a large
part in constitutional determinations, and he tries to cover up
this fact in some of his opinions, but in his more forthright moments this understanding is articulated. In a case involving Nebraska's ad valorem property tax on an airline doing business
within the state but not having its home base there nor being
incorporated within the state, the Court upheld the tax against
claims that the due process clause of the Fourteenth Amendment
had been violated. Justice Frankfurter dissented and, after re-
counting all the factors that he thought necessary for consideration, closed his opinion with the observation that "I am not unaware that there is an air of imprecision about what I have written.
Such is the intention." [26] Complete precision and definition would
foreclose future experimentation, thus defeating one of the major
purposes for geographic dispersal of governmental authority.
Thomas Reed Powell, one of the Justice's most outspoken sup-

[24] Freeman v. Hewit, 329 U.S. 249, 253 (1946).
[25] For a recent example, see Detroit v. Murray Corp., 355 U.S. 489 (1958).
[26] Braniff Airways Inc. v. Nebraska State Board, 347 U.S. 590, 609 (1954).

porters, agreed that "imprecision is better than a delusive effort at precision, or than competing and contradictory delusive efforts for absolutes and generalities where particulars are so variegated in various respects." [27] In preference for imprecision in cases involving commerce and taxation, Justice Frankfurter's deepest philosophic leanings are evidenced.

In the first half of his service on the Supreme Court, he hesitated to substitute the New Deal concept of liberal nationalism for the dual federalism of Justice George Sutherland and other members of the earlier conservative group. He, and to some extent Justice Black, protected state power for two reasons. In the first place, liberalizing the Supreme Court meant that progressive state programs would not automatically be struck down. Since progressive state programs could be obtained, one of the main reasons for advocating national action was no longer valid. In the second place, most members of the Supreme Court accepted the idea that the states could regulate certain aspects of economic life, not by right, but by sufferance, with the judiciary holding arbitral control. While Frankfurter's receptivity to state claims has not been greatly altered, there has been a growing awareness on his part that, in a limited number of instances, the federal government needed protection from the states.

As is his wont, he often cites authorities among past members of the Court to bolster his own position. In dividing taxation competence he has relied heavily upon Justice Joseph Bradley, "whose penetrating analysis, particularly in this field, were in my view second to none." [28] Bradley was very conscious of the need for federal action in the post-Civil War period. Perhaps Frankfurter has absorbed more of Bradley's positions than he realizes or perhaps the press of circumstances over the past decade has made him more pliable when federal claims arise. In order to have geographic dispersal, both the major and minor governments must be retained, and this retention assumes financial solvency on the part of both.

[27] Thomas Reed Powell, *Vagaries and Varieties in Constitutional Interpretation* (New York: Columbia University Press, 1956), p. 203.
[28] Detroit v. Murray Corp., 355 U.S. 489, 497 (1958).

V

During recent arguments before the Court, Justice Frankfurter complained that "lawyers always want to deal in abstractions." He then went on to warn counsel that in dealing with the concept of state competence they should remember that "our federalism does not stop a state from being benighted." [29] Praising state competence in abstract terms did nothing to clarify the issues under consideration. The issue here was whether the state of Washington could challenge the city of Tacoma's right to condemn fish-hatcheries under a license issued by the Federal Power Commission. Because the question of municipal incapacity had not been raised adequately below, the Court refused to consider it. The basic point under the technical ruling was that a state could not interfere with the national policy of power development that was incorporated in the Federal Power Act and that the FPC administered. Justice Frankfurter concurred in the majority opinion, agreeing in this instance that the state of Washington had been "benighted." Not so many years previously, however, he had written:

> . . . the national policy for water power development formulated by the Federal Power Act explicitly recognizes regard for certain interests of the States as part of that national policy. This does not imply that general, uncritical notions about so-called "States rights" are to be read into what Congress has written. It does not mean that we must adhere to the express Congressional mandate that the public interest which underlies the FPA involves the protection of particular matters of intimate concern to the people of the States in which proposed projects requiring the sanction of the Federal Power Commission are to be located.[30]

These views are more in line with his general philosophic position.

The control of power and other public utilities, while of necessity national in scope to some degree, should be decentralized

[29] Heard in courtroom, April 30, 1958.
[30] First Iowa Hydro-Electric Corp. v. Federal Power Commission, 328 U.S. 152, 183–84 (1946).

wherever feasible. His connection with the drafting of the Public Utilities Act has been mentioned. The philosophy of that Act, with its insistence on dispersal of control among private utility companies, reflects the general desire to avoid centralization. Making the states partially responsible for power control reflects the desire to avoid geographic centralization. In his book on *The Public and Its Government,* Professor Frankfurter devoted considerable space to examining the function of public utilities and the ways to supervise them. He concluded that "local administration should be charged with responsibility for such matters of essentially local concern as the regulation of local public utilities." [31] Interference by the federal courts, and especially the Supreme Court, would do little to make the states conscious of their responsibilities and obligations. Control of public utilities in some ways touches the very heart of twentieth-century economic life. Infusing a sense of responsibility here would not solve all the problems of a federalistically plural society, but it would be a long step along the road.

The privileges and immunities clause of the Constitution has often been thought of as an untapped source of strength in bringing orderliness out of the supposed chaos of individualized state practice. Justice Frankfurter has not been openly hostile to use of the clause in litigation, but he has resisted attempts to enforce conformity just for the sake of conformity.

> It is not conceivable that the framers of the Constitution meant to obliterate all special relations between a State and its citizens. This Clause does not touch the right of a State to conserve or utilize its resources on behalf of its own citizens, provided it uses these resources within the State and does not attempt a control of the resources as part of a regulation of commerce between States. A State may care for its own . . . . [32]

A state by caring for its own may incidentally appear to discriminate against others. This, however, is one of the prices we must pay for our federalism. The privileges and immunities clause, because of its checkered history, would not be used by Justice

[31] Frankfurter, *The Public and Its Government,* p. 121.
[32] Toomer v. Witsell, 334 U.S. 385, 407–408 (1948).

Frankfurter to solve difficulties that could be handled by other constitutional provisions.[33] The concept is so indefinite and has been rejected by previous Courts on so many occasions that only misunderstanding can come from its use. It is far better to acknowledge openly our pluralist heritage and to remedy faults that may stem from it in a pragmatic manner, than to try for absolute perfection through defining privileges and immunities.

Discussion of Justice Frankfurter's concept of the role of the Supreme Court as mediator between states and nation may lead to the mistaken conclusion that his desire to retain both types of government as viable units would make him unduly hesitant to call them to account for any reason. While he is certainly reticent about intervening when substantive policy decisions are at stake, he has advocated making all governments, both state and national, legally responsible for their actions. Neither functional nor geographic competence need be threatened by making government liable for its misdeeds. Finding the doctrine that the United States or the states cannot be sued without their consent "an anachronistic survival of monarchical privilege" which "runs counter to democratic notions of the moral responsibility of the State," [34] he has warmly praised the liberalizing tendencies of the Federal Tort Claims Act. Consent to be sued does not have to depend on some ritualistic formula, however. He quite readily recognizes that "courts reflect a strong legislative momentum in their tendency to extend the legal responsibility of Government and to confirm Maitland's belief . . . that 'it is a wholesome sight to see "Crown" sued and answering for its tort.' " [35] One is not left in any doubt that Frankfurter is wholeheartedly in agreement with Maitland.

Interweaving the various strands of Justice Frankfurter's theory of decentralization and dispersal of control as reflected in its geographic element is a difficult task, for so many of the topics that must be mentioned—commerce, taxation, public utilities—can be treated as specific problems demanding attention in their own right. Nevertheless, certain characteristics stand out. Justice

---

[33] See his concurrence in Edwards v. California, 314 U.S. 160 (1941).

[34] Kennecott Copper Corp. v. State Tax Commission, 327 U.S. 573, 580 (1946).

[35] Great Northern Life Ins. Co. v. Read, 322 U.S. 47, 59 (1944).

Frankfurter has emphasized responsible action on the part of Congress, administrative agencies, lower courts, and state governments. He has bowed before the concept of expertise in the many ways in which it makes itself manifest. In the division of competence between national and state governments, expertise appears in treating local or sectional questions with intimate knowledge and feeling. This explains Justice Frankfurter's willingness to back state solutions unless explicitly prohibited by the Constitution. The experimentation that can be carried on in the states is partner in the geographical area to the fluidity that administration and the national legislature can provide in contradistinction to the rather limited answers that the judiciary can provide. Underlining all the accommodations that geographic division of competence entails is, of course, Justice Frankfurter's implicit faith in the pluralistic society that is the United States.

In reaching the accommodations necessitated by geographic decentralization, the Justice is guided basically by a pragmatic philosophy. At any given time, a specific adjustment may be arrived at for a specific problem, but no all-encompassing solution valid for all time and any situation can be obtained. The commerce and taxation clauses, for example, are so indefinite that no final answers to the central issue of federalism can be worked out through them for posterity. The issues raised under these clauses are continuous, on-going problems. For Justice Frankfurter, the best method of dealing with them is to arrive at the balance best suited to the time, leaving as much state power intact as is at all possible. Such a course would protect not only the state but, ultimately, the federal government as well.

In a 1925 article, Professor Frankfurter put forth some of his fundamental notions concerning the nature of our federalistically plural system. Basically he felt that

> The combined legislative powers of Congress and of the several States permit a wide range of permutations and combinations for governmental action. . . . Political energy has been expended on sterile controversy over supposedly exclusive alternatives instead of utilized for fashioning new instruments adapted to new situations.[36]

[36] Felix Frankfurter and James Landis, "The Compact Clause of the Constitution —A Study in Interstate Adjustments," *Yale Law Journal*, xxxiv (May, 1925), 688.

With just slightly different emphasis, he wrote in a 1959 opinion that

> Diffusion of power has its corollary of diffusion of responsibilities with its stimulus to cooperative effort in devising ways and means for making the federal system work. That is not a mechanical structure. It is an interplay of living forces of government to meet the evolving needs of a complex society.[37]

What Justice Frankfurter proposes, therefore, in his insistence on geographic dispersal and decentralization, is a co-operative venture in democratic government by both state and national authorities. Stylistically, he is one of the few writers who frequently capitalizes the word "State." Such capitalization is more than an effective literary device; it is a telling sign of the importance that he gives to states as partners in the search for the Good Society.

[37] New York v. O'Neill, 359 U.S. 11.

SIX

The Role of the Judge

Of all the members of the Supreme Court serving during his ten-ure, Justice Frankfurter has probably been the most acutely aware of that elusive concept called "the judicial function." This is a topic that has intrigued jurists and laymen alike. For those with a philosophic bent, examining the processes by which any in-dividual reaches a decision and placing the judicial hierarchy in its proper relation to other co-ordinate branches of the govern-ment become of the utmost importance. In his writings both be-fore and after his elevation to the Supreme Court and in his pro-nouncements issued both on the bench and off it, Justice Frank-furter has shown keen attention to the function of a judge in modern society.

His courtroom behavior and his conference room performance, his many individual opinions and his style for expressing such opinions, all are related to a broader interest in the judicial func-tion. All must be summarily covered before passing on to a final evaluation of Justice Felix Frankfurter as the scholar on the bench.

XV   *"The Man Who Talks So Much"*

During oral arguments of a recent case before the Supreme Court, a visitor to the imposing and impressive courtroom turned to the small boy beside her to explain that "the man who talks so much is Justice Frankfurter." [1] The Justice's loquaciousness has drawn comment not only from this visitor but also from students of the Court. If he is prodigious in the quantity and intensity of his oral performance, his written contributions are no less diffuse and numerous. He freely uses all forms of communication to put across the points that he thinks are important. It is difficult to assess the work of some of his judicial compatriots because they have written or spoken so little; it is equally puzzling to deal with Justice Frankfurter because he has written or spoken so much. In a facetious introduction to a technical legal lecture before the New York City Bar Association, he disclosed that he had his wife "blue-pencil all my non-judicial writings." "When I told that to

[1] Heard in courtroom, February 26, 1957.

337

Justice Jackson," he continued, "he said, 'why don't you extend the censorship?'" [2] Doubtless others would echo this question.

I

A growing backlog of pronouncements was available when Professor Frankfurter became Justice Frankfurter. Although he is in many ways an enigma because of his prolificness, those who have been disappointed over his showing should find the fault to lie not in his past but in their premises. He defies classification in terms of "liberal" or "conservative" concepts—coffins, as Professor Louis Jaffe has called them. He is an exceedingly complex man as his myriad pre-Court and Court writings show. His long and intricate opinions often sound like professional lectures, which, in some sense, they are supposed to be. Justice Frankfurter's work includes a recurring theme and that is the justification for writing opinions at all and the functions of opinions after they are written. His perhaps too numerous contributions to the field of legal literature cannot be dissevered from this facet of his judicial performance.

The Justice has issued a warning to anyone who would attempt an appraisal of a jurist solely through his opinions. As an analyist of the Court, he had written that "inferences from opinions to the distinctive characteristics of individual justices are treacherous, except in so far as a man's genius breaks through a collective judgment, or his vivid life before he went on the bench serves as commentary, or as he expresses individual views in dissent or through personal writings." [3] Certainly the interaction of the conference room is beyond the ken of the ordinary observer. Changes noted on the margin of slip opinions, the nuances of inserting one word for another, subtle variations that do not appear in published opinions, all these must remain outside the area of knowl-

[2] *New York Times,* March 19, 1947.

[3] Felix Frankfurter, *Mr. Justice Holmes* (Cambridge, Mass.: Harvard University Press, 1938), p. 13. Cf. Felix Frankfurter, "The American Judge," *New Republic,* XXXVIII (April 23, 1924), 236–38 and Felix Frankfurter, "The Job of a Supreme Court Justice," *New York Times,* November 28, 1954.

edge held by non-Court members. But as Justice Frankfurter himself has also reminded us, "a judge of marked individuality stamps his individuality on what he writes, no matter what the subject." [4]

Soon after he came on the Court he indicated that when important shifts in constitutional doctrine were to be consummated, he thought that each justice should express his own feelings. The early practice of seriatim opinions he thought at times had real value.[5] Since then he has said on many occasions that "when the way a result is reached may be important to results hereafter to be reached, law is best respected by individual expression of opinion." [6] Respect for law prompts him to limit or clarify the more sweeping holdings that some of his more expansive brethren would perpetuate. The law is an on-going concern of society. Not only must it tie in with precedents, but it must also provide the seed-bed for future decisions. When language is not carefully chosen, when mistaken assumptions can be drawn from ambiguity, when dramatic exposition may end in ultimate confusion, Justice Frankfurter thinks that it is incumbent upon some member of the Court to mitigate the disastrous consequences that can flow from too absolute pronouncements.

On the rationale for dissent he has been quite clear. Justice Frankfurter often uses dissenting opinions to forewarn future justices that all is not as settled as appears in the majority opinions. The frequency with which concurring or dissenting opinions are cited instead of the supposed holding within any case suggests that the Justice's efforts are not completely in vain. In 1929, before any positive suggestion of his elevation to the Supreme Court may have intruded upon his objectivity, he wrote that by doing away with dissenting opinions, "American law, particularly constitutional law, is deprived of one of the most wholesome elements in its growth." [7]

On becoming a member of the Court, Justice Frankfurter continued the campaign, begun as a professor, against crowding the

[4] Felix Frankfurter, "Some Reflections on the Reading of Statutes," *Columbia Law Review*, XLVII (May, 1947), 531.

[5] See Graves v. New York *ex rel.* O'Keefe, 306 U.S. 466 (1939).

[6] Nietmoko v. Maryland, 340 U.S. 268, 273 (1951).

[7] Felix Frankfurter and James Landis, "The Supreme Court at October Term, 1928," *Harvard Law Review*, LXIII (November, 1929), 47.

court's docket and in favor of allowing ample time for reflection. Both these conditions were prerequisites for the leisure necessary if worthwhile concurring or dissenting opinions were to be written, opinions that might help to focus attention on the continuity or changes being wrought in the law. The focusing process, against charges of repetition, might have to be repeated over and over again. In 1932 Frankfurter communicated with Stone, chiding him for an apology that his dissents only reiterated earlier views. "For Heaven's sake," he answered, "don't get the notion that you are 'repeating the old story' or, in the alternative that it does not need to be repeated. After all, you are an educator, even more so on the Supreme Court than you were off it. . . . The whole nation is your class. . . . Don't let yourself get weary of well-doing." [8] This conception of a Supreme Court justice as educator has colored Justice Frankfurter's oral and written performance on the Court.

His numerous dissenting expressions over the last two decades often obscure the fact that from his appointment to the Court in January, 1939, until the end of the Court's work in June, 1941, he had written but two dissents and these came fairly well along in the latter year.[9] His other separate expressions were just as scarce.[10] With the addition of more justices with a libertarian-activist bent, the Court set out on its course of protecting the individual above all else. Justice Frankfurter did in some respects then become the great dissenter. His exercise of this right was based on the philosophy of dissent expressed before going on the bench, a philosophy that he continued to expound now through his opinions. While fighting to curtail his colleagues' tendency to bring up cases of less than national importance, he has insisted that once a case is before the tribunal, he has a right

[8] Frankfurter to Stone, March 28, 1932. Quoted in Alpheus T. Mason, *Harlan Fiske Stone* (New York: The Viking Press, Inc., 1956), p. 310.

[9] Palmer v. Connecticut R. & Light Co., 311 U.S. 544 (1941); Sibbach v. Wilson, 312 U.S. 1 (1941).

[10] He wrote four concurrences, Graves v. New York *ex rel.* O'Keefe, 306 U.S. 466 (1939); Driscoll v. Edison Light & Power Co., 307 U.S. 104 (1939); Coleman v. Miller, 307 U.S. 433 (1939); Deputy v. Du Pont, 308 U.S. 488 (1940): and entered three "separate" opinions designated neither dissents nor concurrences, Texas v. Florida, 306 U.S. 398 (1939); Mayo v. Lakeland Highlands Con. Co., 309 U.S. 310 (1940); L. Singer & Sons v. Union Pacific Rail Co., 311 U.S. 295 (1940).

to speak his mind—"the same considerations which made the case one of general importance for review here made it appropriate to spell out the grounds of dissents." [11] Dissents were used to point out faults in the Court's procedure as well as fallacies in the substantive reasoning. Justice Frankfurter is a man with a good many deep convictions about constitutional law, the place of the Court in modern society, and last, but not least, the judicial function. His belief that dissents are vitalizing influences, that they provide wholesome elements to legal growth, and that though the Court is ultimately operated by majority rule each individual member must be true to his own conscience, prompted him in the middle years of his tenure to attack vigorously the actions being taken.

There are drawbacks, however, to appearing in print so often. Justice Jackson once noted that "each dissenting opinion is a confession of failure to convince the writer's colleagues, and the true test of a judge is his influence in leading, not in opposing his Court." [12] Justice Frankfurter has been to the confessional often. In addition, prolificness, whether warranted or unwarranted, evokes a good deal of irritation from persons on and off the Court. Explanations for Frankfurter's frequent contributions range from a superficial desire for vanity satisfaction to a deep-felt psychological need for articulateness. Not all discussion of the proliferation of opinions stems from personal irritation. Some of it is prompted by reflective concern for the welfare of the Court as a governmental institution putting into words the enduring interests of society. As one critic of the move away from unanimity to individuality, Carl B. Swisher, has put it, "When a judge speaks officially he speaks in the name of the law and his words carry a weight not derived from other positions in officialdom." [13] Suggesting that for the general public, overtones of natural law, fundamental rightness, even deity, are found in Supreme Court pronouncements, Professor Swisher, as do many other qualified observers, seems to feel that, in the normal run of events, mono-

[11] Johnson v. New York, New Haven & Hartford Rail Co., 344 U.S. 48, 54–55 (1952).

[12] Robert Jackson, *The Supreme Court in the American System of Government* (Cambridge, Mass.: Harvard University Press, 1955), p. 19.

[13] Carl B. Swisher, *The Supreme Court in Modern Role* (New York: New York University Press, 1958), p. 145

theism is to be preferred to polytheism. He finds that much personal responsibility for the present pantheon must rest with Justice Frankfurter. It is true that Frankfurter's frequent expressions cause other members to take up the cudgels in defense of a favorite position. This cause and effect sees two or more opinions being written in a case when one would probably have served. The basic division then seems to be over the question of how beneficial or harmful to constitutional law is this proliferation.

Most persons who have occasion to use the reports of the Court would agree that quantity has often replaced quality. But are there not equal drawbacks in having but a single opinion for all nine men? As Alexander Pekelis says, "the very conception that a court—or a country—to be dignified, orderly, and authoritative, must speak as a unit assumes that harmony, progress, and order can be achieved only through unity or uniformity." [14] To present a false front of accord when there are deep cleavages present, to stifle individual expression on the theory that only in unity can the Court articulate the ethical underpinning of constitutional law, or to make greater the possibility of violent disagreement erupting by postponing its initial appearance, seems just as doubtful as writing opinions on picayune topics or the casting of personal aspersions in those opinions, which we sometimes find. In a different context, Justice Jackson once remarked that you can attain unanimity through eliminating dissent, but it will be the unanimity of the graveyard. However much some people may think the Supreme Court building looks like a mausoleum, its occupants are very lively spirits.

In our idealized picture of the Court, we see it translating into words and decisions what are inarticulate premises and feelings. We are attuned to "the spirit of the Constitution" and are pleased when nine men sitting in Washington are able, preferably through one voice, to give substance to the spirit. Yet in our sophisticated way, we reject any notion of an automaton, mechanically receiving the right answer to all questions merely by comparing a statute or behavior with the text of the Constitution. We recognize that judges are men, not gods, that they are heir to all the

[14] Alexander H. Pekelis, *Law and Social Action* (Ithaca: Cornell University Press, 1950), p. 196.

sins of the flesh, that they are fallible. When, however, they exhibit their mortality and, either through egotism or genuine mistakenness, find that it takes more than one voice to give homage to "the spirit of the Constitution," we are slightly disgruntled. There is more than a little irony here.

II

Stylistically, how do Justice Frankfurter's opinions compare with others? What is his own conception of their purpose? Shortly after he went on the Supreme Court, an appraisal was made by a newspaperman covering the Court's work.

> Press excitement over the first opinions handed down by Justice Frankfurter cooled noticeably when the reporters began to read them. They were tough going . . . .
> Big words do not necessarily strangle reporters. Most of them know a few themselves. But the job of converting big words into little ones for clear and quick newspaper reading, without losing a shade of the proper meaning, was an extra task that the reporters did not relish.[15]

Put briefly, Justice Frankfurter did not write to be understood by newspaper readers. His conception of a Supreme Court opinion is far different from this.

Justice Frankfurter's opinions are the repositories for some of the most exotic words in the English language. His interest in words, their history and slightest gradations in meaning, finds an outlet in his writings. It is not unusual to come across such brain-teasers as "palimpsest" or "gallimaufry" in the middle of a technical dicussion. He also loves figures of speech that are colorful but at the same time meaningful. His references range from the nautical Plimsoll line to Elizabethan sonnets.[16] A voracious reader, who, unlike Justice Holmes, does not find it necessary to

[15] Preston Grover, "Frankfurter Gives Reporters Bad Time," *Baltimore Evening Sun,* April 12, 1939.

[16] For a wry and amusing criticism of some of these sources, see Richard H. Field, "Frankfurter, J., Concurring," *Harvard Law Review,* LXXI (November, 1957), pp. 77–81.

cover an entire book in order to extract its essence, his taste runs from works on *Jeremy Bentham and the Law* to *Einstein, His Life and Times*.[17] In rhetorical form he at one time questioned, "How can we possibly lay claim to being a learned profession unless we have an avid interest in books and so order our lives that somehow or other we wrest time from the demands upon us to keep the mind alive as only books can?"[18] Maintaining an interest in scholarly production (Mark DeWolfe Howe has recently said that "so many authors have expressed their gratitude to Mr. Justice Frankfurter that it is becoming almost a ritual of scholarship to acknowledge indebtedness"[19]) he brings all these forces to bear in his composition.

It may be said of his style that it is dangerously attractive. His writing is so quotable that even those who disagree with his positions find it difficult to avoid the temptation of utilizing his elegance and eloquence. Tidiness and precision normally characterize his prose. He is agile in shifting ground in an argument, being able to bring about changes in ideas without appearing to do so. Justice Frankfurter's opinions are at times dulling in their enormity and eternity of references. His elongated appendices, although of use in research and analysis, make difficult reading. Granting all this, are there any redeeming features that, while not dispensing with merited criticism, help to explain the situation? The Justice's own impressions on the matter of opinion-writing should carry some weight. As he perceives it,

> style reflects the writer's notions of the form in which an opinion should be cast or his desire to promote one purpose rather than another. . . . Again it makes a difference whether an opinion-writer consciously aims to be understood by the casual newspaper reader, or whether he has a strong sense of the educational function of an opinion within the profession, and more particularly among law teachers, or writes merely to dispose of the case.[20]

[17] See Felix Frankfurter, "My Current Reading," *Saturday Review of Literature*, xxix (October 26, 1946), 21, and Walter P. Armstrong, "What Do The Justices Read?" *American Bar Association Journal*, xxxv (April, 1949), 296.

[18] Armstrong, "What Do The Justices Read?" *loc. cit.*

[19] Mark DeWolfe Howe, *Justice Oliver Wendell Holmes* (Cambridge, Mass.: Harvard University Press, 1957), p. vii.

[20] Felix Frankfurter, "Mr. Justice Jackson," *Harvard Law Review*, lxviii (April, 1955), 938.

This latter alternative can be discounted in the case of Justice Frankfurter. If one recalls the newsman's lament and the Justice's own communication to Justice Stone on the importance of the educational function of opinions, there can be little doubt about what he considers the prime motivation for expression. He has not shaken the teacher's prejudice that communicating information to the young, especially in the law schools, is of vital importance to the future of the nation.

Justice Frankfurter's writings are not meant for those untrained in the law or its sister disciplines. Within that limitation he feels free to soar to unlimited heights in his use of allegorical or figurative references in his opinions. When he wishes to write for the general public, something he has done and continues to do quite successfully, he uses other media, such as articles and letters to newspapers, to transmit his message. In his off-the-bench contributions he can be as eloquent as any libertarian-activist member of the Court. In writing opinions for the Court, in contradistinction to writing for popular consumption, he is much more careful in what he has to say. Because of his style, his opinions cannot help but be emotive in part, but their major purpose is communicative and educational.

Even when using colorful language, he appears quite circumspect in what he has to say. Familiar with the innuendos of past opinions, possessing a fund of knowledge on their appearance and meaning, and seeing the exact shading that seems to elude some of the brethren, he strives in his own work for clarity of statement through the use of words with exact meanings. His interests span the world. If he finds a British or Australian case applicable, he does not hesitate to cite it, nor do foreign courts hesitate to cite him. Chief Justice Sir Owen Dixon of the High Court of Australia has said: "You will see Frankfurter's name again and again in the reports of the constitutional decisions of the High Court. When you find in judicial writings repeated reliance upon the words of a contemporary judge, especially of another country, you may safely infer that his opinions tend to throw new light in dark places . . . ." [21]

In the attempt to attain clarity, exactness, and precision of

[21] Sir Owen Dixon, "A Tribute from Australia," *Yale Law Journal,* LXVII (December, 1957), 181.

statement and holding, there is a good deal of danger, however, in relying too heavily on comparative law. The examples taken may be selective and not representative. To be really meaningful, there must be comparable economic, social, and political conditions in which the decisions are rooted. Too easily to assume such comparableness is to disregard basic tenets of sociological jurisprudence with which he is familiar.[22] This is one of the weakest links in Justice Frankfurter's armor. Acknowledging that exactness is a prime requisite for a Supreme Court opinion, he seems tempted by his interests to include at times not really analogous foreign citations. His belief that opinions also have to be educational probably prompts him to extend the field of that education. At times he does it successfully, at other times not, often to the considerable annoyance of other members of the High Tribunal.

Criticism of the Court over its myriad opinions has probably had an effect upon the way in which they are now written. Since the advent of Earl Warren's Chief Justiceship, opinions for the Court have been more general and vague. Because the Court is more conscious of the need for unanimity, and in order to gain the greatest consensus possible, broad generalizations have become frequent. Alexander Bickel, a former law clerk of Justice Frankfurter, has interestingly noted that current opinions have the "vacuity characteristic of desperately negotiated documents." [23] Not all those who advocated cutting down on the number of opinions foresaw this untoward turn of events. Broad generalization often means, in addition to inexactness, absoluteness. These are two fatal sins for Justice Frankfurter. The fact that they have appeared together with more frequency in recent years accounts somewhat for the number of his concurring and dissenting opinions.

Another reason for his frequent appearance in print is his dislike for *per curiam* opinions. As a scholar in his annual articles on the Court he excoriated their use, finding that they did not give sufficient direction to the lower courts and bar and that often, by mere citation of cases, they confused rather than clarified the

---

[22] For discussion, see Edward McWhinney, *Judicial Review in the English-Speaking World* (Toronto: University of Toronto Press, 1956), p. 182.

[23] Alexander Bickel and Harry Wellington, "Legislative Purpose and the Judicial Process," *Harvard Law Review*, LXXI (November, 1957), 3.

situation.[24] He thought it far better that review be denied entirely if the Supreme Court, through specifically spelling out the grounds for its decision, could not edify the profession. Justice Frankfurter has carried this conviction with him to his work on the Court. While the writer's personality has a great deal to do with it, to account for his style and opinions as mere ego-satisfaction or as an off-shoot of vanity is far too simple an explanation.

Perhaps the overriding distinguishing characteristic of Justice Frankfurter's opinions is the amount of space he gives to speculation on the nature of the judicial function after the particular points at issue have been decided. Of all the justices since Cardozo he typifies the deepest philosophic approach to the problem. Others may use Supreme Court opinions as tracts for the propagation of political theories; he uses them as vehicles of expression for the distillation of a lifetime's preoccupation with the essence of a judge's role and tasks. His observations on this topic are provocative and profound. Being included in official writings, they have the aura of having been pronounced from the bench and thus psychologically seem to carry more weight. If the function of an opinion is to communicate and educate on the technical points of law, it is no less important to Justice Frankfurter as the means to familiarize the lower courts and bar with the agony of judging, an agony that is at the core of the judicial function for him.

III

Justice Frankfurter has quoted approvingly Justice Holmes' *aperçu* to the effect that law becomes more civilized as it becomes more self-conscious.[25] But he has also recently complained that, with the notable exceptions of Justices Holmes and Cardozo,

> The power of searching analysis of what it is that they are doing seems rarely to be possessed by judges, either because they are lacking in the art of critical exposition or because they are inhibited

[24] See, for example, Frankfurter and Landis, "The Supreme Court at October Term, 1928," *loc. cit.*

[25] Felix Frankfurter, *The Commerce Clause Under Marshall, Taney and Waite* (Chapel Hill: University of North Carolina Press, 1937), p. 31.

from practicing it. The fact is that pitifully little of significance has been contributed by judges regarding the nature of their endeavor . . . .[26]

Following in the steps of his predecessors, Justice Frankfurter is not inhibited in discussing this subject. For any practicing jurist, a discussion of the judicial function must contain a large measure of introspective material. As is fashionable, terms have been coined to cover this type of performance, and we now speak of introspective or psychological jurisprudence.

If there is one word that Justice Frankfurter uses more than any other, even than "self-restraint," it is "disinterestedness." Of course, the two are intimately related in his judicial philosophy, but it is telling that his drive to transcend personal limitations should loom so large in his perspective. Knowing his intense and vivid interest in so many topics, one may surmise that he reacts quickly to policy decisions. He must struggle hard not to become a partisan and allow his partisan feelings to be translated into his opinions. Perhaps his honest recognition of this temptation prompts him to insist that strict observance of the law be put before the strongest of personal sympathies or biases. In any event, he has reiterated the disinterestedness theme times without number.

He is realist enough to acknowledge that "of course, individual judgment and feeling cannot be wholly shut out of the judicial process." The main point, however, is that "if they dominate, the judicial process becomes a dangerous sham." [27] A jurist's conception of the scope and limits of his role can exert both intellectual and moral force on the development of the law. As for Justice Frankfurter, "the duty of Justices is not to express their personal will and wisdom. Their undertaking is to try to triumph over the bent of their own preferences and to transcend, through habituated exercise of the imagination, the limits of their direct experience." [28] Although he does not always conform to this ideal

[26] Frankfurter, "The Judicial Process and the Supreme Court," in Philip Elman (ed.), *Of Law and Men* (New York: Harcourt, Brace & Co., 1956), p. 32.

[27] Felix Frankfurter, "John Marshall," in *Government Under Law*, (Cambridge, Mass.: Harvard University Press, 1956), p. 21.

[28] Frankfurter, "Mr. Justice Jackson," *loc. cit.*, p. 439.

in practice, his theoretical attachment to what he has called "dominating humility" must be understood as background for discussion of the judicial process.

"There is a good deal of shallow talk," Justice Frankfurter has written, "that the judicial robe does not change the man within it. It does." [29] This expression does not necessarily make him a devotee of the Cult of the Robe nor does it make him stand at variance with such thinkers as Jerome Frank, who believes that much harm is done by allowing myths to surround jurists,[30] or with Justice Black, who insists that "judges . . . like all the rest of mankind . . . may be affected from time to time by pride and passion, by pettiness and bruised feelings, by improper understanding or by excessive zeal." [31] It is precisely because these things can be true that Justice Frankfurter insists on self-restraint. It is precisely because judges are human that they must limit their power. It is precisely because they are the ultimate judicial voice of the nation that they must be humble in their task. Feeling these propositions so deeply, he apparently believes that anyone who takes on the judging function must become more acutely aware of the responsibilities reposing upon him. In this sense, as he sees it, the robe does change the man. It is not because judges can do no harm that he insists on the robe's transforming qualities; it is because judges can do too much harm that leads him to hope for transformation in its donning.

Perhaps both the strength and weakness of Justice Frankfurter's position lie in the self-consciousness with which he works. He is quite convinced that the Court and its members are only a part, albeit an important part, of our government. On the other hand, he appears as convinced that the Court should try to transmit those values that make that type of government possible. His insistence on law as an inclusive reality not primarily meant to ameliorate the difficulties of a particular litigant is one facet of his solution for the situation when these major themes appear in imminent conflict. It is in working out the total solution that the

---

[29] Public Utilities Commission v. Pollak, 343 U.S. 451, 466 (1952).

[30] See Jerome Frank, *Law and the Modern Mind* (New York: Tudor Publishing Co., 1936).

[31] Green v. United States, 356 U.S. 165, 198 (1958).

agony of judging becomes for him at times almost unbearable.

Deference to the legislature, attempted objectivity, and pronouncement of enduring ideals that cannot be encompassed within any pat formula, are a trio of very difficult propositions with which to work. Justice Frankfurter's opinions discussing the judicial function and the way he, as a representative jurist, conceives of the communication between people and Court often seem to contain "gossamer concepts." The strength of his position is in facing the hardships involved and in trying to put them into words for the edification of the profession; the weakness is his inability successfully to carry the entire burden. If he carries us but part of the way to an understanding of the judicial function, it is a good deal further than most of his brethren have ventured in print, and it is a good deal further than most commentators would be able to go without the insights that he has presented them.

IV

The early, vigorous attacks upon the fiction that judges were not human did not come from the modern, ultrarealist school of jurisprudence but from the group that championed a sociological interpretation of law. Roscoe Pound, Thomas Reed Powell, and to some extent Felix Frankfurter refused to believe that differing social, economic, and political backgrounds did not affect judges or that their variant educations, social affiliations, and environments could be completely discounted in evaluating their work. They were interested in determining how far jurists followed what would be their expected course of actions on the basis of these factors and how far some of them were able to put these factors behind them. In other words, they were interested in judicial motivation. Unlike some determinists who accounted for all behavior in terms of economic interest, they realized that any motivation was much more complex. They were actually talking about the psychology of judges and judging. For those so concerned, looking at their own psychological reactions did not seem remiss.

As a teacher, Frankfurter explicitly mentioned on more than one occasion that psychological factors and a judge's unconscious play an enormous part in understanding the judicial process. How that unconscious was formed and what factors went into any individual's psychological make-up were held important. While individual configurations were basic, sociological jurisprudence also had another element, which shows up to some degree in Justice Frankfurter's opinions. This element was that most individuals who were to become judges had at least some common denominator of background, some common identification with society. Each individual's *Gestalt* was, therefore, formed not only by particular experiences, but also by communal experiences as expressed in mores, customs, and beliefs. When Justice Frankfurter attempts to work with the standards of justice, concepts of ordered liberty, inarticulate major premises, he is in a way trying to limit the range of personal experience and concentrate on the communal. Thus perhaps he is being as consistent as possible with the two major strains of sociological jurisprudence, psychological analysis, and community interpretation. At least these are two of his major concerns in Haley v. Ohio.[32]

Justice Frankfurter's opinion in that case has been called by Professor Herman Pritchett "perhaps the most remarkably frank and courageous analysis of the personal basis of judicial decisions ever included in a Supreme Court opinion." [33] The opinion is one of the most perfect examples of introspective, psychological jurisprudence. Justice Frankfurter's self-consciousness over the need to explore the judicial function in order to avoid bias and approach objectivity is here turned in the direction of self-analysis. While it is one of the most perfect examples of this type of thought, it did not appear on the scene unforeshadowed or totally unexpected. It is in some ways the extreme extension of a judicial philosophy that finds self-restraint basic and in other ways the logical outgrowth of sociological jurisprudence.

In the Haley case, the defendant was a young Negro boy of fifteen. He had been subjected to five hours of continuous ques-

[32] 332 U.S. 596 (1948).
[33] C. Herman Pritchett, *The Roosevelt Court* (New York: The Macmillan Co., 1948), p. 160.

tioning in the middle of the night by police in connection with a burglary and murder. No counsel was present. After the ordeal of oral examination was completed, the lad was not arraigned for several days nor was he allowed to see members of his family. The Court held that even though there was token recognition of constitutional rights in the confession that was signed, the way in which it was obtained and the personal facts surrounding the defendant invalidated a subsequent conviction. Four justices dissented. Justice Frankfurter held the pivotal position and through his concurrence allowed Justice Douglas to announce the judgment of the Court.

Believing that due process is a concept spun from societal values, Justice Frankfurter began by admitting that it was subtle and elusive as a criterion of judgment. Nevertheless, he stated, "we cannot escape the duty of judicial review. . . . The only way to avoid finding in the Constitution the personal bias one has placed on it, is to explore the influences that have shaped one's unanalyzed views in order to lay bare prepossessions." [34] Having established his intention to undertake such a self-analysis, he passed on to the next phase of the opinion.

The jurist in participating in judicial endeavors involving due process not only has to psychoanalyze himself, he has to try in a way to psychoanalyze society. This again is partially the motivation for Justice Frankfurter's concern with the inarticulate major premises of a community or with the conception of ordered liberty that guides a people. To tell whether the confession of a youth of fifteen was coerced or freely given was not a matter of mathematical determination.

> Essentially it invites psychological judgment that reflects deep, even if inarticulate, feelings of our society. Judges must divine that feeling as best they can from all the relevant evidence and light which they can bring to bear for a confident judgment of such an issue, and with every endeavor to detach themselves from their merely private views.[35]

He concluded that these may be unsatisfactory tests because of their inherent vagueness, but such as they were, he thought the

[34] Haley v. Ohio, 332 U.S. 596, 602 (1948).
[35] *Ibid.*, p. 603.

Court must be guided by them and apply them when applicable, as in this case.

It would be difficult to find a more complex approach to the topic of the judicial function, but its very complexity may indicate that Justice Frankfurter has come very close to the core of judicial phenomena. In an extremely able discussion on this whole area of legal thinking, Carl B. Swisher has written that "as in so many aspects of life, deep probing eventually takes us close to the realm of the mystical, to a realm where mere intellectualization and logical phrasing fail us, leaving us to feelings and perceptions that make their appearance from we know not where but which nevertheless have for us compelling weight." [36] Justice Frankfurter's philosophy does have touches of the mystical, but it is a communal mysticism that tries to articulate social feelings and perceptions. Even though the articulation must be done by an individual, the attempt is made, to borrow scientific terms, to have him act as a conductor rather than as a transformer. To be sure, at times there will be short-circuits, but such occurrences are bound to happen in even the simplest electrical system (or, for that matter, in even the simplest thought patterns).

The judicial philosophy of Justice Frankfurter, then, is an amalgam from many sources. Sociological insights that extend into the newer range of psychology as these relate to legal matters become central to his idealization of the judicial function. His fundamental self-conscious effort to remove personal bias, though this can never be done completely, is companion to the thinking of others. Ranyard West has said that

> in most of our lives we shall live on, fighting and striving to adjust ourselves to reality, in total inability to divest ourselves of the many fixed prejudices to which, as normal men, we are heir. It is because of its discovery of the depth and universality of these prejudices formed through unconscious fantasy-identifications, that modern psychology can give confident and insistent support to the maxim . . . that *no man can form an objective and unbiased judgment of a situation in which he is emotionally involved; that no man can safely be admitted a judge in his own cause.*[37]

[36] Swisher, *The Supreme Court in Modern Role*, p. 178.
[37] Ranyard West, *Conscience and Society* (New York: Emerson Books, Inc., 1945), pp. 158–59.

It was a poet long ago who reminded us that "No man is an island, entire of itself; every man is a piece of the continent, a part of the main." [38] Deep and universal prejudices and fantasy-identifications do exist. The jurist in sitting in judgment on others may be psychologically sitting in judgment upon himself; he may in reality be a judge in his own cause. Justice Frankfurter once refused to sit on a case in which he thought himself emotionally involved, saying, "reason cannot control the subconscious influence of feelings of which it is unaware." [39] There are risks involved in turning to the mystical and unconscious for guidance and in trying to transcend personal prejudices and fantasy-identifications in the search for absolute purity from subjective factors, a purity that is unattainable. The risks, however, are no higher, in terms of the judicial function, than are those attendant on other, supposedly simpler, approaches to the problem.

V

As a professor, Frankfurter commented favorably upon the fact that "the pressure upon the Court's time is also giving rise to a tendency to be less patient with arguments. The generous habit of American courts of listening to counsel for the maximum time allowed, is yielding to the necessity of saving time by refusing to hear arguments where the Court feels no doubt about the result." [40] For all his emphasis on conserving the strength of the judiciary, his behavior in questioning counsel or in rapid-fire exchanges with colleagues cannot be traced exclusively, or even primarily, to this source. Here, if anywhere, his personal traits come most clearly to the fore, and it is here that what has been called his irritating inner conviction of his own righteousness seems to become most pronounced.

For the generation in which he has served the Court, his technique has been the Socratic one, a technique that he utilized so

[38] John Donne, *Devotions Upon Emergent Occasions* (1624).
[39] Public Utilities Commission v. Pollak, 343 U.S. 451, 467 (1952).
[40] Frankfurter and Landis, "The Supreme Court at October Term, 1928," *loc. cit.*, p. 36.

successfully in his "formal" teaching. The adjective "formal" is necessary because he thinks that a Supreme Court justice is an educator in many ways, as his philosophy of opinion-writing testifies. This conviction is translated over into his public appearances on the bench. One explanation of his vigorous questioning is that he is anxious to keep members of the bar on their toes. Apparently believing for a long time not only that the students would be better educated in having to formulate answers of their own, but also that the teacher would gain a clearer conception of what his charges were driving at through having them struggle with formulation, Justice Frankfurter has continued to insist on precise explanations from lawyers appearing before him. His manner of doing so has not been above reproach.

From the reports of his law clerks and in view of the admiration, one might almost say adoration, with which they view him, his relationships with those intimately connected with his work may not be as strained as are some of his public clashes. For a variety of reasons, Justice Frankfurter has managed to capture the devotion of the younger men who have worked with him. Indeed, his former law clerks from all over the country gather for a formal dinner in his honor at Washington at least once during the year, usually about the anniversary of his elevation to the Supreme Court. This personal interest in younger people reaches back to his days at Harvard when promising students frequented his home. The Frankfurters are childless, so that in many ways his family position and his interests are reminiscent of another Supreme Court justice who, being without heirs, took into his confidence and comradeship many students and novitiates in the law. The tradition of Oliver Wendell Holmes has more meaning for Felix Frankfurter than can be captured in the law reports.

Granted all the warmth and charm of personal camaraderie, and the educational value to be derived from strict questioning, still and all Justice Frankfurter at times appears to forget himself when participating in such an activity. His garrulousness has been commented upon in many quarters. His interest in so many matters, from the sweep of national affairs to the human side of personal gossip, has also been noted. Being irrepressible in speech, he is often given to outbursts of enthusiasm or outrage. In the heat of an argument, his satirical or biting remarks tend to offend more than he perhaps really means them too. It has been said of him that he has "only half-mastered the old Boston art of being rude graciously." [41] The rapidity with which he throws out questions, the intenseness with which he receives the answers, and his almost total immersion into the subject matter of the law, joined with his wide range of interests, make him a leader in any questioning that the Court may do. It also makes him prone to overstep the line between intense inquiry and invective. For those on the sidelines, his sharp and cutting comments may be interesting and enjoyable. For those to whom they are directed, his excursions into sarcasism can be extremely painful.

Justice Frankfurter's annoyance that concise answers are not always available for the questions that he asks may partially be caused by the fact that the questions are not always fully comprehensible. An extreme example, no doubt, but an example of this possibility, nevertheless, came in questioning of counsel for the Little Rock School Board over the implications of previous Court decisions and the Board's desire to postpone integration. Given below is a question that he asked counsel as it appears on the stenographic record:

> Justice Frankfurter: Mr. Butler, why aren't the two decisions of this court, the first one, which laid down as a Constitutional requirement that this court unanimously felt compelled to agree upon, and the second opinion recognizing that this was a change of what had been supposed to be the provisions of the Constitution, and recognizing that and the kind of life that has been built under the contrary conception said, as equity also has said, you must make appropriate accommodation to the specific circumstances of the situation instead of having a procrustean bed where everybody's legs are cut off or stretched to fit the length of the bed, and who is better to decide that than the local United States Judges, why isn't that a National policy? [42]

No one could deny that this is a mighty one-sentence question. It was an impromptu question that Justice Frankfurter did not

[41] Quoted in *Current Biography* (1941), p. 307.
[42] Quoted by David Lawrence, "National Policy," *St. Louis Globe-Democrat,* September 5, 1958.

have time to revise. But it was the query that counsel was expected to answer. The Justice's irritation at supposed lack of competence on the part of members of the bar might be lessened somewhat if he went back to the stenographic records for a quick survey.

The Court's records and the reports in *United States Law Week* give many examples of the Justice's oral performance. Picking out but recent instances, one can gain the flavor of his remarks. The Justice's tendency to be less than patient with arguments not coming directly to the point or with those that try to make the issues under consideration more complex than necessary was reflected in his questioning of a lawyer at a recent term of the Court. After counsel had been explaining his case for fifteen minutes or so, Justice Frankfurter broke through to ask, "Is that all there is to this case?" The reply was, "No, sir. There's a heap to this case." "As you state it," came the rejoinder, "it's so simple that I'm suspicious. . . . What is the milk in the coconut?" Or again, when the government's legal staff was arguing that the Army's completely arbitrary decision to discharge a serviceman with less than an honorable discharge, because of activities before induction, was not judicially reviewable, the whole Court came to arms. After extended repartee, the Justice, furious at the way things were going, told the government's representative that "You need not take this extreme position." Later, after another assertion of executive discretionary power, he asked angrily, "Are you going to argue that, too? What is there you are not going to argue?" [43] One may surmise that for all his deference to the executive *after* considered judgment, this blatant claim for completely unreviewable, let alone uncontrollable, action was more than he could stomach.

Justice Frankfurter's intonation does not alone inform counsel of his pleasure or displeasure with their performance. He swings to and fro in his chair, looks at the ceiling of the courtroom as if for divine guidance and patience, and, if all else fails, leans back in his chair so that he is hardly visible to persons in the courtroom and suffers a trying martyrdom. John Mason Brown has sug-

[43] These two examples were taken from an article by Anthony Lewis, "High Drama in the High Court," *New York Times,* October 26, 1958.

gested that Frankfurter has the face of an actor.[44] The reference
to acting is not completely out of place because, in his eagerness
to get to the heart of a matter, he can exhibit quizzical, disdainful,
sensitive, or sincerely modest countenances.

This eagerness has not only caused trouble for him in the press
due to the complaints of members of the bar, but it has also
caused some estrangement among the brethren. His passion for
direct statement of position recently led him into an exchange
with Chief Justice Warren. Warren had been questioning an
attorney for some time when Frankfurter began to interrupt, re-
phrasing the Chief Justice's questions. Warren's annoyance
mounted as the interruptions mounted. He finally roared, "Let him
answer my question! I want to hear the answer to my question,"
indicating that only confusion could result from dual interrogation. The response was not long in coming: "Confused by Justice
Frankfurter, I presume!" [45] His apparently irritating habits do not
show up solely in oral questioning; they also make their appearance in the way in which decisions are announced. Members
of the Court have complained that in expounding an opinion on
the requisite Mondays he has not followed the text of the written
version but has inserted or extrapolated materials.

One may only conjecture as to the sources of annoyance among
the justices when they meet for conference. While the Court
carries on the tradition of each member's shaking hands with all
his colleagues before any official function commences, the ritual,
while probably beneficial, cannot alleviate all differences or
animosities. One may be sure that if Justice Frankfurter's lo-
quacity and curiosity show up in his treatment of counsel, thus
causing some discomfort to others, they are no less apparent in
the seclusion of the Conference Room, and, perhaps, with multiplied negative effects. Depending upon the ability of the Chief
Justice to keep his charges in order—Justice Frankfurter has
served under Hughes, Stone, Vinson, and Warren—meetings of
the conference may run late while he pursues some particularly

[44] John Mason Brown, *Through These Men* (New York: Harper & Brothers,
1956), p. 171.
[45] As told by John Osborn, "One Supreme Court," *Life Magazine*, June 16, 1958,
p. 93.

interesting intellectual point or while he lectures on some delicate point of legal history. This tendency to continue as a teacher is probably of value on the bench. In the Conference Room with men who are his equals, it may cause difficulties.

Justice Frankfurter has a tendency to procrastinate in the writing of opinions, often producing most of his work near the end of a term. One reason for this is his desire to seek out all relevant materials, much as he searches in minor form during the conferences, and to take what he considers the necessary time in weighing them. Along with others who have been called ten o'clock scholars, he may be partially responsible for extending the term of the Court a week or two. If so, it fits in the pattern that surrounds the agony of judging that is central to his conception of the judicial function. John P. Frank has said that "the occupational hazard of judging for Justice Frankfurter is making up his mind and getting things done. This is worth comment because is it more than one man's psychological quirk; it is symptomatic of the plight of the intellectual liberal in our time, torn between opposing absolutes." [46] Frank identifies the agony of judging as a hazard and—it is believed mistakenly, at least for Justice Frankfurter—attributes it to a clash of absolutes. Intellectual suffering is not necessarily a negative if it serves to cleanse or purify. Agony can be a very real prelude to triumph over adversity. It is in the attempt to dispose of absolutes that creativity appears, a creativity that has as its source a community mystic and that involves the long and wearisome process of self-examination and attempted transcendence. Although such a process may take a little longer time, expediency can hardly be the main criterion by which to judge judicial performance.

While Justice Frankfurter has had his share of contentions with other members of the Court—contentiousness indeed seeming to be a personal characteristic of many of the justices in the decades of the 1940's and 1950's—his relations on the whole have been satisfactory. On Justice Owen Roberts' retirement, the initial wording of a letter of appreciation was drafted by Stone, but was changed by Justice Black, to whom it was first given.

[46] John P. Frank, "The United States Supreme Court; 1950–51," *University of Chicago Law Review*, XIX (Winter, 1952), 223.

His deletion of all complimentary references so emasculated the draft that Justice Frankfurter with others refused to sign it, thinking that it was far better in these circumstances to follow the maxim that silence is golden rather than to damn by indirection. Of those members with whom he has served, Frankfurter appears to have found most intellectual companionship with Stone and Justice Robert Jackson. At present, he and John Marshall Harlan often find themselves in agreement.

In 1932 Frankfurter had written to Stone, "Why people should resent constant criticism upon their labors—particularly people who have ultimate power—I have never been able to understand. But perhaps the answer is that they have ultimate power." [47] In the legal realm, members of the Supreme Court do hold ultimate power. Since he became a member of that tribunal, Justice Frankfurter has had to stand much criticism, and he has done it graciously, as long as the criticism itself was kept within the bounds of the courteous. While he has received his share of brick-bats, he has also garnered his portion of accolades. On the occasion of his seventy-fifth birthday, many magazines and newspapers around the country noted appreciatively his contributions to public law. More recently, former Senator John W. Bricker, certainly not of the same political or social persuasion as the Justice, contributed his salute. Recognizing that perhaps their difference in political philosophy had made him aware of Frankfurter's profound understanding of the judicial function and remarking on his "honest search for Congressional intent, a decent respect for state legislatures and state judiciaries, and an aversion to the adjudication of issues which are prematurely raised, basically trivial or essentially political in character," [48] Senator Bricker concluded with the hope that the Court would have many more years of service from him. Others would join in this wish.

[47] Frankfurter to Stone, May 10, 1932. Quoted in Mason, *Harlan Fiske Stone,* p. 356.

[48] *New York Times,* January 31, 1958.

XVI

Scholar on the Bench

Felix Frankfurter's judicial career began after the first momentous changes had been made in the direction that constitutional development would take as a result of the replacement of one political and social philosophy by another. It has spanned the decade of New Deal dominance of the Supreme Court, a Court that had to face the perplexing problems growing out of the maelstrom of World War II. He has participated in the disposition of major legal issues stemming from reconversion and the quickly established Cold War. We are now on the threshold, if not inside the door, of the Space Age. Throughout this entire period and for whatever type of problem involved, the feature that seems to stand out above all others is that Justice Frankfurter's tolerance is within the law. By this is meant that when he searches for the elasticity and fluidity necessary to keep a complex, modern society in working order, he does it in terms of legal concepts.

Since law is both the cause and effect of changes within the realm of practical men, any total division between law and practical affairs would be an artificial and unworkable one. As a jurist, however, his major concern is with giving mobility to legal phenomena so that they can meet the demands that society puts upon them. The specific-generic breakdown of the Bill of Rights and his treatment of due process concepts are examples of this drive for elasticity and fluidity. To say that Justice Frankfurter's tolerance is within the law means more than that he is simply interested in keeping the law from becoming static or tied to one set of time-place conditions. It has at least two other implications. It means in the first place that those charged with supervising legal development have a large enough task on their hands, and one delimited by the Constitution and by our historical evolution, to keep them from venturing into political considerations or decisions. Contrariwise, when a matter by right falls under judicial review, courts must be fearless in the exercise of their prerogatives even if it means calling a co-ordinate branch of the government to account.

It means in the second place that the broader concept of law as the ordering force within society and as the articulation in its higher ranges of deep-felt values and desires is not identified with any one legal system. There may be a body of law that is the distillation of American experience, but this is only part of the greater whole. For good or ill, Justice Frankfurter is conscious of world history and from this consciousness has stemmed a rejection of a provincial approach to the law. His citation of English, Australian, or Canadian cases is, in addition to perhaps being an egotistic display of knowledge, a quite logical extension of his denial that any particular legal system is entire in itself.

The fact that any legal system is not entire in itself does not mean that its particular distillation of materials will not be affected by the stresses of its own evolution or by the heritage that it has received. One grounded in sociological and historical jurisprudence could hardly be oblivious to the obvious differences that environment can make. This recognition necessitates inclusion in Justice Frankfurter's thought of an element very akin to natural law with a variable content. He is concerned with ideas set in historical perspective and with ideas as such. This is the point at which he joins with the historical school with its rejection of the proposition that the fiat of a particular situation can determine the content of legal norms for all times. There are also streams from the sociological approach feeding into the mainstream of his philosophy. Awareness of political, economic, and social forces shaping the men who are to articulate the law stands behind his more obvious agreement with sociological jurisprudence's insistence on treating law as the outgrowth of these same factors. In thus envisaging law as having an organic, ongoing nature that must be fitted into the more inclusive organic structure of society, which is itself an amalgam of pluralist elements, Justice Frankfurter takes what is most congenial from both schools of jurisprudence and molds them into his own judicial approach, to which he adds his extension in the form of introspective, or psychological, materials.

Supreme Court justices are primarily lawyers, not theoreticians. Their main concern is the settlement of disputes, not the production of logically self-contained systems of thought, but a judge without a theory or judicial philosophy is somewhat at a loss. Theories are used to settle cases immediately before the Court. They are used in the attempt to account for both continuity and change in constitutional law. Understanding of the meaning of pluralism, with its concomitant dispersal and decentralization of competence and power within branches of the national government, between federal and state governments, and between lesser groups within society, has a real effect upon the way litigation is handled. The differing historical interpretations and theories of Justices Black and Frankfurter cannot be discounted as imminent factors in the way in which arguments will be appraised. Questions of security or social conflict are often answered on the basis of how far up the scale of values national unity is placed by the Supreme Court. Nor can the questions of governmental power over such diverse fields as commerce, taxation, warfare, or immigration be treated unless there is a cohesive approach to the Constitution as an instrument of power. So while it is true that jurists are not primarily theoreticians and that in wielding theoretical concepts they may be dabbling in fields not quite their own, it is also true that because the situation has come to pass and because they are jurists dealing with the practical problems of the law when they deal with cases before them, each jurist's judicial philosophy takes on that much more importance.

Justice Frankfurter combines both continental and Anglo-American approaches to the law. Taking his early formative schooling in Austria and continuing an interest in European publications and ideas, he has absorbed some of the premises of continental education and scholarship, which are apt to be concerned with concepts in their abstract as well as in their practical application and with the development of patterns of logic. From the Continent come studies on legal phenomena that are largely metaphysical, deductive, and abstract in tone. More importantly, his later education in the public schools of the United States and particularly at the Harvard Law School familiarized him with the Anglo-American preference, which is largely empiric, pragmatic, and inductive. The way in which Justice Frankfurter combines such apparently diverse strains is to be empiric, pragmatic, and inductive within and by means of abstract categories that have been arrived at through metaphysical, deductive reasoning. The generic characteristics of certain terms within the Bill of Rights having been established, he can choose pragmatically between alternative choices; the minimum categorizations in the division of power between and within governments having been demonstrated, he can inductively reason to the most feasible and societally approved exercise of power. On the foundation of empiric evidence he attempts to navigate between the abstract, although not absolute, Scylla of protection to the individual at all costs to the community and the Charybdis of sanctioning majority desires at all times to the detriment of minority or nonconformist groups. Through all of this runs his belief that, whether in the Anglo-American world or in other traditions, adherence to procedural requirements is the life-blood of legal-judicial science and his conviction that in the United States, with its peculiarly adequate system of government, judicial power must be tempered by judicial self-restraint.

There are other ways in which Justice Frankfurter makes manifest a combination of different conceptions of law and life. Essentially, Anglo-Saxon or Anglo-American law is a product of juristic practice. The common law of Great Britain, which the Colonies inherited and which the United States has subsequently revised, came into being largely as the outgrowth of judicial pronouncements. It was the common law about which Justice Holmes wrote. It was the common law with which legal education in this country was still primarily concerned at the turn of the century. Those legal systems that are based on the reception of Roman law show the definite imprint of legal education as expounded by the universities. It is in the universities that initial changes are wrought in juristic thought. The Code Civil, on the other hand, is the product of so-called rational legislation. Codes based upon factual investigations are the binding influences upon judges. From these codes they are neither constitutionally nor customarily expected to depart.

Justice Frankfurter's mature interest in comparative law has put him in touch with all these variations. In his own professional training and in his years as a commentator on the work of the Supreme Court he grew to know both the strengths and weaknesses of judicial legislation. On the positive side of the ledger came the advantages that perceptive use of the judicial function could produce in articulating, through personal transcendence, the deep-felt needs of society. Listed as a disadvantage of the common law approach was the infusion of too much individualization, especially individualization of a political caste. His personal acquaintance with the suggestive influence that articles in law school journals could bring to bear on legal development and of the unmeasurable effect of the pronouncements of respected teachers of the law made him aware that the universities play an important, if not central, role in preparing the ground for new ideas. Without stretching a point, a comparison can be made between his deference to legislative and executive wisdom and the like assumption found in countries ruled by statutory codes, that is, an assumption of rational legislation. Justice Frankfurter, as James Bradley Thayer, James Barr Ames, and Justice Holmes before him, believes in rational men as well as rational legislatures. One has but to look at his decisions in the area of administrative law to confirm this suggestion.

A final comparison of the many sources from which Justice

Frankfurter has forged his philosophy may be of service. In civil law countries, or in those greatly influenced by the infusion of the Roman law, both jurists and lawyers are mainly concerned with the solution of conflicting claims and interests. A just balance is sought between the variegated contending forces. It is no accident that one of the first groups advocating a jurisprudence of interests originated in Germany about the time when Roscoe Pound was introducing his sociological concepts into American thought. Persons trained in a common law or constitutionally dominated legal system are more apt to see problems solely as an aspect of the relation between authority and subject, between state and individual, between predominant community and assumedly subordinate persecuted groups. In other words, they tend to see legal problems of power as ones of strictly superordinate-subordinate relations, rather than as ones of adjustment of conflicting interests. Justice Frankfurter, it appears, has caught the essence of the jurisprudence of interests, either in its original form or in the form expounded by Roscoe Pound, and has tried to show in his pre-Court and Court work that an absolute predisposition toward either authority or subject, state or individual, community or group, does not advance legal development. Only through a search for a balance of interests in particular time-place situations can a satisfactory solution be attained, and it is necessary always to keep in mind that the predominant concern of a constitutional court is maintaining the integrity of the system of which it is a part.

Justice Frankfurter may at times appear to be forcing his materials into a schematic arrangement. One can, however, understand the reasoning behind the scheme. At least some predictability for his actions is available. Neither consistency nor predictability should be enshrined as the end-all and be-all for constitutional interpretation. Yet it does seem correct that for those serving on the Supreme Court, the nation's highest tribunal and its ultimate *legal* conscience, some semblance of these traits is desirable. Absolute predictability, in the sense of adherence to an absolute set of personal values irrespective of time-place conditions, does as little for the benefit of the judicial function as does totally erratic behavior that cannot be forecast at all. If it is somewhere near the core of judicial endeavor actually to judge, that is, empirically to weigh the competing demands of various forces as these become evident in time-place relations, then Justice Frankfurter tries to draw near the core by means of his judicial performance, which emphasizes social considerations, competence in other branches of the government, and judicial self-restraint.

When Justice Frankfurter took his place on the Supreme Court, his approach was called by one source a compact eight-fold design that included "scientific realism, evolutism, ethical idealism, sociological integralism, creative activism, experimentalism, personalism, and democratic humanism." [1] Many of these terms are descriptive of certain aspects of Justice Frankfurter's philosophy. But it hardly seems necessary to resort to "isms" to explain his judicial approach. Justice Cardozo at one time suggested that four methods of decision were sufficient to explain judicial behavior for all times and in all places. These were the method of philosophy, in which logical factors predominate; the method of history, in which the jurist looks to communal developments for guidance; the method of custom, in which the present behavior of the group as the culmination of past experience is relied upon; and the method of sociology, in which concepts of social welfare and standards of justice are introduced. Justice Cardozo thought this latter aspect the most significant.

It would be almost impossible to determine which of these elements Justice Frankfurter considers most important, for his judicial theories encompass parts of all of them. Certainly, with his immediate predecessor in the Scholar's Seat, he would not underrate social welfare. Frankfurter's identity with Cardozo reaches beyond this element, however. Felicity of style, sincere desire to search out the central ingredients of the judicial function, and intense interest in all forms of legal phenomena tie the two men together, although their personal characteristics and backgrounds were almost entirely different. One followed the path of the law through state courts and became noted for his retiring, almost ultrasensitive, reactions to the pressures of life

[1] Moses J. Aronson, "The Juristic Thought of Mr. Justice Frankfurter," *Journal of Social Philosophy*, v (January, 1940), 153.

around him; the other devoted his life to the teaching of law and active participation in myriad causes until his elevation to the nation's Highest Tribunal—and even there his teaching functions have not ceased.

Of the many other comparisons between Justice Frankfurter and the men or movements that have influenced him but few words need to be said. Relations with Theodore Roosevelt and Franklin D. Roosevelt undoubtedly infused him with the ideals of liberalism as understood in the early decades of this century and with the transformed version of these ideals in the 1930's. Intimate of men as diverse as Henry L. Stimson, Harold Ickes, Harlan Fiske Stone, Sidney Hillman, Harold Laski, Oliver Wendell Holmes, and Louis D. Brandeis, he could not have helped being familiar with many of the channels flowing into the mainstream of American thought, both legal and extralegal. Behind all the contacts he made in the period after 1920 were the basic ones gained at Harvard Law School as both student and teacher. Thayer and Ames as influences upon a novitiate lawyer, Pound and Powell as interacting, stimulating colleagues, all added their impress upon Felix Frankfurter.

While there are other former members of the Court with whom he can profitably be compared on certain issues, Hughes and Taft to some degree in the realm of economics, Cardozo and Stone to some extent in the area of civil rights, yet, in wide perspective and in broad analysis, the names of Holmes and Brandeis would yet have to predominate. Frankfurter has proudly and publicly acknowledged his intellectual debt to them. Some feel that he has never advanced beyond the positions that they took long ago, positions supposedly no longer valid. Others complain that he wraps himself in their prestige-laden garments and thus protects himself from criticism. If this latter is true, it is true not only for Justice Frankfurter but also for almost every member of the Supreme Court since 1940. In his admirable book on *The Legacy of Holmes and Brandeis,* to which he gives the subtitle, "A Study in the Influences of Ideas," Professor Samuel Konefsky has appraised the still pervasive intellectual force of this outstanding duo. He intimates that a good deal of the confusion and conflict that have characterized constitutional development over the past several decades stems from two facts: one, that claimants to the legacy have been so many and so varied; two, that none of the self-proclaimed heirs wished to share the patrimony.

The heritage of Holmes and Brandeis is a dual one. Though they often came to the same conclusion, they just as often reasoned from basically different premises. Justice Frankfurter in trying to follow simultaneously the lead of both of his former intimates appears occasionally to have an impossible task. He has gone beyond the positions that they formerly took, but he has been able to do so only by alternating in various cases between the premises of Holmes and Brandeis, for their mutual holdings were fortuitous accidents rather than predetermined results based on similar judicial philosophies. From the amalgam of their complementary philosophies came a mutual understanding that new ways of dealing with an evolving society could be reconciled with old principles and that necessary social adjustment need not be confused with a basic attack on society. Legislative experimentation, reasonableness, and judicial self-restraint became the watchwords. They are the watchwords that Justice Frankfurter has echoed.

In alternating between the premises of Holmes and Brandeis, he has had on the one hand a belief in crusading zeal for social and economic betterment, a zeal that is backed by empiric factual materials, a belief that government should actively participate in rearranging the social order. As one of the original workers with Brandeis on the perfection of the techniques employed in the Brandeis brief, he is personally familiar with the considerations that lie behind it. On the other hand, Justice Frankfurter, since the period of his early manhood, has been familiar with the idealized portrait of Olympian disinterestedness that Holmes presented. In talks and in deep study of the Great Dissenter's opinions he gained an understanding of Holmes' abiding interest in most topics, especially those with a philosophic overtone. He has striven mightily to accommodate the premises, as well as the holdings, of Justice Holmes and Brandeis. In the over-all, if one were forced to make a choice between the proportionate influences that the two men wielded, it appears that Justice Holmes' approach has been the more important in the development of

Justice Frankfurter's own unique theoretical structure. Professor Konefsky in his above-mentioned study concludes that "it is Brandeis' extraordinary gifts as a student of American society as well as the strengths of his attachment to the imperatives of the democratic creed which makes him the authentic leader of modern constitutional jurisprudence." [2] If Professor Konefsky's conclusion is valid, it may help to explain the strain that at times becomes evident between Justice Frankfurter and other members of the Supreme Court.

As one intimately knowledgeable of the crusading zeal that forms a fundamental part of the Brandeis approach, Frankfurter may fear the perversions that present-day jurists make of this aspect of Brandeis' philosophy. His own turn toward the more severe and limited judicial ideals of Justice Holmes may in part be accounted for as reaction to excessive zealousness not tempered by Brandeis' understanding that judicial restraint is also necessary under certain circumstances. Because Frankfurter, as one reared in the Holmesian tradition, feels the need for some philosophic underpinning in his opinion, and because he feels that other justices do not do their share in expanding outward the broader implications of constitutional development, he may overcompensate by putting into his writings too much abstract or esoteric material.

His credentials as a scholar were established long before he took his place on the Supreme Court. His scholarship was not limited to lonely researches that resulted in technically competent, but highly limited, works. Professor Frankfurter's interest spanned most legal fields. His ability to teach, to impart knowledge and feelings about the law, was no less important than his writings, which were in themselves broadly educational. In the wider context, a scholar gains real distinction only as his insights become usable by others. Such distinction came to Felix Frankfurter as a teacher and as a publicist. He has continued to follow these paths since becoming a member of the nation's Highest Tribunal. In many ways his influence as teacher and publicist has been enhanced because of the unique position of Supreme Court justices.

[2] Samuel J. Konefsky, *The Legacy of Holmes and Brandeis* (New York: The Macmillan Co., 1956), p. 306.

Aldous Huxley in his outline for *Brave New World* had one of his characters say: "The gods are just. No doubt. But their code of law is dictated in the last resort by the people who organize society; Providence takes its cue from men." [3] Professor Frankfurter before he went on the bench philosophized that "there is no inevitability in history except as men make it." [4] Felix Frankfurter has helped to make history, he has helped to organize society, and, above all, he has tried to articulate a judicial philosophy that would impart better understanding of legal phenomena and of the men whose primary concern is with the judicial function.

[3] Aldous Huxley, *Brave New World* (New York: Harper & Brothers, 1946), p. 283.
[4] Felix Frankfurter, *Mr. Justice Holmes* (Cambridge, Mass.: Harvard University Press, 1938), p. 9.

Index